BOUNDLESS INNOCENCE IN
THOMAS TRAHERNE'S POETIC THEOLOGY

I will wash mine hands in innocency: so will I compass thine altar, O Lord
Psalm 26.6

Boundless Innocence in Thomas Traherne's Poetic Theology

'Were all Men Wise and Innocent ...'

ELIZABETH S. DODD
Sarum College, Salisbury, UK

ASHGATE

© Elizabeth S. Dodd 2015

All rights reserved. No part of this publication may be reproduced, stored in a retrieval system or transmitted in any form or by any means, electronic, mechanical, photocopying, recording or otherwise without the prior permission of the publisher.

Elizabeth S. Dodd has asserted her right under the Copyright, Designs and Patents Act, 1988, to be identified as the author of this work.

Published by
Ashgate Publishing Limited
Wey Court East
Union Road
Farnham
Surrey, GU9 7PT
England

Ashgate Publishing Company
110 Cherry Street
Suite 3-1
Burlington, VT 05401-3818
USA

www.ashgate.com

British Library Cataloguing in Publication Data
A catalogue record for this book is available from the British Library

The Library of Congress has cataloged the printed edition as follows:
Dodd, Elizabeth S.
  Boundless innocence in Thomas Traherne's poetic theology : 'were all men wise and innocent' / by Elizabeth S. Dodd.
     pages cm
   Includes index.
   ISBN 978-1-4724-5397-6 (hardcover) – ISBN 978-1-4724-6803-1 (ebook) –
   ISBN 978-1-4724-6804-8 (epub) 1. Traherne, Thomas, -1674 – Criticism and interpretation. 2. Innocence (Psychology) in literature. 3. Christian poetry, English – Early modern, 1500-1700 – History and criticism. I. Title.
   PR3736.T7Z75 2015
   821'.4–dc23
                                                                                            2015007101

ISBN 9781472453976 (hbk)
ISBN 9781472468031 (ebook – PDF)
ISBN 9781472468048 (ebk – ePUB)

Printed in the United Kingdom by Henry Ling Limited,
at the Dorset Press, Dorchester, DT1 1HD

Contents

Foreword by David F. Ford		*vii*
Acknowledgements		*ix*
Abbreviations		*xi*
Introduction		1
1	Defining Innocence: Issues and Interpretations	25
2	'Perfect innocency by creation': The Estate of Original Innocence	41
3	'No Man is Innocent': The Fall into Misery	71
4	The Trial of Innocence: Innocence in the State of Misery–Grace	93
5	'Innocency of Life': Innocence in the State of Misery–Grace	129
6	'A Light So Endless unto me': The Glory of Innocence	161
7	'Were all men Wise And Innocent …': Innocence in the Optative Mood	193
References		*203*
General Index		*235*
Index of Biblical References		*241*

Foreword

The discovery since the nineteenth century of a series of works by Thomas Traherne has been astonishing and felicitous, important both for literature and theology. I vividly remember the irrepressible delight of Jeremy Maule, usually a very sober scholar, when I happened to sit next to him at lunch just after he had recognised Traherne's handwriting on a substantial manuscript in the Lambeth Palace Library. He then shared some of what he had transcribed from *The Kingdom of God*, and at once it was clear that here was a text to be ranked with the best we already had by Traherne. It combined intelligence, imagination, exuberance, poetic genius and theological profundity, and it seemed to leap across the centuries with its energy and attractiveness undiminished.

Maule's and the other discoveries, along with the works previously available, have set a difficult challenge. It is the task of doing justice to all of the seventeenth-century context: the poetry, the poetic prose, the concepts, the theology, the philosophy, the immense range of reference and allusion, the reception history and Traherne's relevance to current issues. There have been some outstanding contributions focused on Traherne's writings, and he has been influential on a growing number of scholars, thinkers and members of the educated public.

Elizabeth Dodd has succeeded in developing the diverse skills and disciplinary expertise needed to engage with the many dimensions of Traherne. She knows the seventeenth century well and her literary, philosophical and theological knowledge enable her to read Traherne sensitively and with deep understanding of his subject matter. She also covers the whole field of Traherne scholarship, commenting on it perceptively. But beyond all that she is able to do two things that are vital for the full appreciation of Traherne today: she has a dazzling array of concepts that help to redescribe, analyse and explain Traherne's thought and her knowledge of current Christian theology allow him to take his proper place as a one of the wisest Christian thinkers.

As a theologian myself, I am especially impressed by this retrieval of Traherne for twenty-first-century religious thought. In my opinion Traherne is among the greatest Anglican thinkers and writers. Dodd shows herself to be a constructive theologian, and, with innocence as her lens, she not only illuminates the fascinating mind and expression of Traherne but she also recovers for current theology a rich, neglected theme that goes to the heart of living before God and with other people in the midst of the complexities of life.

David F. Ford
University of Cambridge

Acknowledgements

I first encountered Thomas Traherne during my Master of Theology studies under the supervision of Susan Hardman-Moore at Edinburgh University. With the guidance and unstinting support of David Ford at Cambridge University, my initial interest in Traherne and innocence developed into its current form. Along the way I have received encouragement from and enjoyed stimulating engagement with a variety of people. In particular I am grateful for conversations with Denise Inge, Julia Smith, Richard Birt, Ronald Blythe, Kathryn Murphy, Douglas Hedley and Edmund Newey. Fellow travellers with Traherne include Cassandra Gorman, with whom I organised a Traherne symposium in Cambridge and am editing a collection of essays. I am also grateful for the chance to test out ideas on the Ford at Home seminar, the Cambridge University Christian Theology seminar, the American Academy of Religion and Society for the Study of Theology conferences, the Traherne Festival in Credenhill, Herefordshire and the King's College London RIST seminar.

The Bodleian Library, British Library, Lambeth Palace Library, Folger Shakespeare Library and Beinecke Library in Yale have been extremely accommodating in providing access to the manuscripts. I have benefited from the generosity of the Domestic Research Studentship funded by Mark Pigott, along with funds from Cambridge University Divinity Faculty, the AHRC, Hawkshead Grammar School Fund and the Dorothy Mandelstrong Fund of John Ruskin School, Coniston. Finally, this would not have been possible without the unstinting support of my family and friends. I am particularly grateful to my parents, who have supported me in my journey with Traherne, and to my husband George, who has given up a lot for me to spend time with my 'other man'.

Sections of Chapter 2 have appeared in *Literature and Theology* as '"Perfect Innocency By Creation" in the Thought of Thomas Traherne', and material contributing to Chapter 6 appeared in 'The Sacramental Image of the Child in the Thought of Thomas Traherne, and Its Theological Significance', in *Understanding Children's Spirituality*, edited by Kevin E. Lawson.

Abbreviations

ANF	Ante-Nicene Fathers
ATR	*Anglican Theological Review*
ELH	*English Literary History*
ELR	*English Literary Renaissance*
HLQ	*Huntingdon Library Quarterly*
JHI	*Journal of the History of Ideas*
JR	*Journal of Religion*
LCL	Loeb Classical Library
LT	*Literature and Theology*
MLN	*Modern Language Notes*
MP	*Modern Philology*
MT	*Modern Theology*
N&Q	*Notes and Queries*
NPNF[1]	Nicene and Post-Nicene Fathers, series 1
NPNF[2]	Nicene and Post-Nicene Fathers, series 2
ODNB	*Oxford Dictionary of National Biography* (Oxford: Oxford University Press, 2004), <http://www.oxforddnb.com>
OED	*Oxford English Dictionary* (Oxford: Oxford University Press, 2015), <http://www.oed.com>
PBSA	*Papers of the Bibliographical Society of America*
PMLA	*Papers of the Modern Language Association*
PQ	*Philological Quarterly*
SP	*Studies in Philology*
TLS	*Times Literary Supplement*
TT	*Theology Today*
VC	*Vigilae Christianae*

Introduction

Argument of the Book

Innocence is an inchoate term, but it is also a rich and compelling means of expressing human perfection. The rich history of innocence in Christian thought is easily obscured by modern theoretical frameworks, such as Enlightenment ideas of the state of nature, the Romantic ideal of the child or psychological theories of paradisal archetypes. This book traces a path into the multifaceted innocence of Christian thought through the Anglican divine, Thomas Traherne (*c.*1637–74). Traherne has been closely associated with innocence through his meditations and his poetry on childhood. He stands at a crucial point in the history of innocence, since his work looks forward to the Enlightenment praise of nature and the Romantic ideal of the child and backwards to the Church Fathers and the Latin roots of Christian innocence. The current renaissance in Traherne studies, which arose out of the discovery of new manuscripts, has highlighted the need for further work to review this theme and its significance in his thought.[1]

Traherne's language of innocence has often been met with wonder, incredulity and scepticism. It has been viewed as evidence of a nostalgic, sentimental or utopian vision. This book contends that these responses stem from a fundamental misconception of the meaning of innocence for Traherne. The identification of innocence primarily with a state of nature, virgin childhood or the Garden of Eden associates it with inexperience, naïveté or a mythical lost paradise. Traherne's work, by contrast, builds on a tradition of interpretation that identifies innocence as an aspect of holiness, associated with harmlessness, guiltlessness, sinlessness, simplicity and sincerity.

This monograph is based on two premises. The first is that formulations of innocence in contemporary theology would profit from greater sensitivity to historical manifestations of the idea. The second is that Traherne's notion of

---

[1] For details of the manuscripts, see Peter Beal, 'Thomas Traherne', *Catalogue of English Literary Manuscripts*, <http://www.celm-ms.org.uk/introductions/TraherneThomas.html#> (accessed 1 Oct. 2014).

innocence is in urgent need of a reassessment that is attentive to its sources, its intellectual context and its theological orientation. Traherne was a poet as well as a priest, so this book seeks to uncover his poetic theology of innocence by assessing its grammar and poetic voice. This historical, contextual and theological re-reading of Traherne's language of innocence presents a new perspective on its place in his thought, not as a lost paradise but as a stable feature of the spiritual life.

(Re)introducing Thomas Traherne

An understanding of the critical context is key to the significance of this study. The Introduction therefore commences with a survey of the development of Traherne studies from early literary criticism, through the historical turn, to more recent theological interpretations. On this foundation the discussion then turns specifically to interpretations of innocence in his works, before introducing the overall framework and approach of the book.

Early Criticism: Traherne as Romantic Precursor

Traherne's significance for the history of innocence has lain hitherto in his status as a precursor to the Romantic praise of childhood. The association between Traherne and the Romantics goes back to the first publication of his *Poetical Works* by Bertram Dobell in 1903. Dobell likened Traherne's poems of childhood, such as 'Eden', 'Wonder' and 'Innocence', to William Wordsworth's 'Immortality Ode' and William Blake's *Songs of Innocence*.[2] This comparison was consolidated by later literary critics, such as Rose Macaulay, who called Traherne a 'Wordsworthian mystic', and Kenneth Hopkins, who claimed to 'hear the very voice of Wordsworth' in Traherne's 'Eden'.[3] As discussed below, this early Romantic association persisted in later interpretations of the theme of innocence.

---

[2] Thomas Traherne, *The Poetical Works*, ed. Bertram Dobell (London: The Editor, 1903), lxxvii–lxxxi; William Wordsworth, *The Collected Poems*, ed. Antonia Till (Ware, Herts.: Wordsworth Editions, 1994), 701–4; William Blake, *Songs of Innocence and of Experience: Shewing the Two Contrary States of the Human Soul*, ed. Geoffrey Keynes (Oxford: Oxford University Press, 1967).

[3] Rose Macaulay, *Some Religious Elements in English Literature* (London: Hogarth, 1931), 104–5; Kenneth Hopkins, *English Poetry: A Short History* (London: Phoenix House, 1962), 118.

Introduction 3

There are indeed striking ostensible similarities between Traherne's lyric poetry and that of Blake and Wordsworth. Consider the haunting reminiscences between Traherne's 'little Adam in a sphere of joys' and the 'Child of Joy' of Wordsworth's 'Immortality Ode'. In Traherne's newborn declaration 'How Like an Angel Came I down!' one can see Wordsworth's divine child descending to earth 'trailing clouds of glory'. Wordsworth reminds his readers that 'Heaven lies about us in our infancy', while Traherne's rejuvenated child can 'see beneath, as if I were abov the Skies'. Wordsworth describes how, in infancy, everything was 'Apparell'd in celestial light', while Traherne's 'Infant-Ey' sees everything in the 'anchient Light of Eden'. For Wordsworth, this primitive innocence is corrupted by 'dialogues of business, love, or strife', while Traherne laments the education that ties us to the 'outward Bondage of Opinion and Custom'.[4] Such easy comparisons account for the strength of Traherne's Romantic associations, but they must also be read against the background of nineteenth-century revivals of seventeenth-century metaphysical poetry, which most likely coloured early interpretations of Traherne as a 'new' metaphysical poet.[5]

This early association with the Romantics ensured his status within histories of childhood. By the mid-twentieth century, Traherne became an exemplar of a pre-Romantic praise of childhood and a precursor to a Romantic ideal of innocence, alongside Henry Vaughan.[6] He also developed a degree of significance through studies which identified him as a metaphysical poet, alongside George Herbert and John Donne as well as Vaughan.[7] Although not the greatest of these poets, Traherne has nevertheless been seen as an exemplar of this movement, due to his theological concerns. David Reid called him 'the

---

[4]   Thomas Traherne, 'Innocence', *Dobell Folio*, in *The Works of Thomas Traherne*, ed. Jan Ross (Cambridge: D.S. Brewer, 2005–), vol. 6, 10; id., 'Wonder', *Dobell Folio*, 4; id., 'The Approach', *Dobell Folio*, 21; Thomas Traherne, *Centuries of Meditations*, III 4, 8, in *The Works of Thomas Traherne*, vol. 5; Wordsworth, 'Immortality Ode'.

[5]   For a suggestion of a new Romantic revival in the early twentieth century, when Traherne was rediscovered, see Arthur H. Nethercot, 'The Reputation of the "Metaphysical Poets" during the Age of Johnson and the "Romantic Revival" ', *SP* 22 (1925), 131–2.

[6]   See e.g. George Boas, *The Cult of Childhood* (London: Spring Publications, 1990), 45; Alan Richardson, *Literature, Education and Romanticism* (Cambridge: Cambridge University Press, 1994), 9–10.

[7]   See e.g. Jean-Jacques Denonain, *Thèmes et formes de la poésie 'métaphysique'* (Paris: Presses Universitaires de France, 1956), 254–81; James Blair Leishman, *The Metaphysical Poets: Donne, Herbert, Vaughan, Traherne* (Oxford: Clarendon, 1934); Helen Constance White, *The Metaphysical Poets: A Study in Religious Experience* (New York: Macmillan, 1936); Margaret Willy, *Three Metaphysical Poets* (London: Longmans Green, 1961), 31–43.

most metaphysical of Metaphysical poets since only he puts forward a system of theological philosophy.[8] This association ensured Traherne's inclusion in popular anthologies of seventeenth-century metaphysical poetry, albeit in a minor role.[9]

Traherne's Romantic associations also led to critiques of his work. Douglas Bush identified him with naïveté and optimism, arguing that, unlike Blake, he 'never graduated from songs of innocence to songs of experience'.[10] A similar, although more sympathetic, assertion can be found in Dorothy L. Sayers' opinion that, unlike Wordsworth or Dante Alighieri, Traherne was able to hold on to the innocence of his youth.[11] While not a critique in itself, this view is conducive to the accusation that Traherne's poetry of childhood is regressive or elevates a static ideal of childhood innocence.

Post-Romantic critiques of the Romantic ideal of childhood have had an important effect on interpretations of innocence in the works of Thomas Traherne.[12] Literary critics Charles Sommerville and Hugh Cunningham saw a paradox between the nineteenth-century idealisation of childhood and the common reality of abuse and neglect.[13] Judith Plotz identified this with a dangerous nostalgic social conservatism and sentimentalism.[14] Traherne's status as a pre-Romantic tied him to these critiques. Leah Marcus, for example, saw his faith in infant innocence as symptomatic of a wider cultural malaise and nostalgic conservatism within a period of change, similar to that of the eighteenth-century Romantics.[15] Comparisons of Traherne's lyric poetry with Romantic poetry of childhood have implicitly associated his idea of innocence with nostalgia and sentimentality, idealism and utopianism.

---

[8]   David Reid, *The Metaphysical Poets* (Essex: Pearson Education, 2000), 253.

[9]   See e.g. Colin Burrow (ed.), *Metaphysical Poetry* (London: Penguin, 2006), 243–50.

[10]   Douglas Bush, *English Literature in the Earlier Seventeenth Century* (Oxford: Clarendon, 1962), 158.

[11]   Dorothy L. Sayers, 'The Beatrician Vision in Dante and Other Poets', *Nottingham Medieval Studies* 2 (1958), 3–23.

[12]   On the post-Romantic loss of innocence, see Keith D. White, *John Keats and the Loss of Romantic Innocence*, Costerus NS 107 (Amsterdam: Rodopi, 1996).

[13]   Charles John Sommerville, *The Rise and Fall of Childhood* (London: Sage, 1982), 131–2; Hugh Cunningham, *The Children of the Poor: Representatives of Childhood since the Seventeenth Century* (Oxford: Blackwell, 1991), 151–63.

[14]   Judith Plotz, *Romanticism and the Vocation of Childhood* (New York: Palgrave, 2001), xiii–xvi.

[15]   Leah S. Marcus, *Childhood and Cultural Despair: A Theme and Variations in Seventeenth-Century Literature* (Pittsburgh: University of Pittsburgh Press, 1978), 42–93.

Introduction 5

The Historical Turn: Traherne in Biographical and Intellectual Context

The historical turn in Traherne criticism has distanced him from the Romantics, from the label of poet of childhood and felicity and from the idea of innocence altogether. Contextual studies have rooted his work in his biographical and intellectual context. Read in the light of his biography, Traherne is no Blakean nature mystic but a conformist and even cosmopolitan figure.[16] He grew up in royalist Hereford during the turmoil of civil war. Under the Cromwellian protectorate, he attended Brasenose College in Oxford (*c.*1653–56), then under puritan direction. He was appointed to the living of Credenhill, 10 miles outside Hereford, in 1657. Like many young clerics, Traherne quickly conformed to the Restoration of the monarchy, was episcopally ordained in October 1660 and signed the Act of Uniformity soon after its promulgation in 1662.[17] During his career Traherne was not tied to rural Herefordshire. His occasional absences from Credenhill are attested to by his failure to sign the Parish records for the years 1662–63, 1669–71, 1673 and possibly 1666.[18] He continued to visit Oxford, where he attained his BD in 1669. His thesis on the 'Counterfeit Antiquities of the Church of Rome', published as *Roman Forgeries* (1673), mentions a debate with a Catholic on the steps of the Bodleian.[19] Traherne also had links to intellectual circles in London. After 1669, he was appointed chaplain to the former Keeper of the Seals and patron of Cambridge Platonists, Orlando Bridgeman at Teddington, where he died and was buried on 10 October 1674.[20] Traherne shared his work with a circle of acquaintances, some of whose responses appear in marginal annotations in his manuscripts. References to his death by Sir Edward Harley, John Aubrey and George Hickes – in his preface to Traherne's *A Serious and Pathetical*

---

[16]   On Traherne's biography, see esp. Julia J. Smith, 'Traherne, Thomas (*c.*1637–1674)', *ODNB*, 4.

[17]   On the large number of students and Commonwealth clergy who quickly conformed to the Act of Uniformity, see Ian M. Green, *The Re-establishment of the Church of England, 1660–1663* (Oxford: Oxford University Press, 1978), 155–77.

[18]   See Angela Russell, 'The Life of Thomas Traherne', *Review of English Studies* 6/21 (1955), 41; cited in H.M. Margoliouth, 'Introduction', in Thomas Traherne, *Centuries, Poems, and Thanksgivings* (2 vols, Oxford: Oxford University Press, 1958), vol. 1, xxv; corrected in Richard Lynn Sauls, 'Traherne's Hand in the Credenhill Records', *The Library* 24 (1969), 50.

[19]   Thomas Traherne, 'Advertisement to the Reader', in *Roman Forgeries, or a True Account of False Records* (London: S.& B. Griffin for Jonathan Edwin, 1673), B7.

[20]   See Anthony Wood, *Alumni Oxonienses 1500–1714*, ed. Joseph Foster (Oxford: Parker & Co., 1892), vol. 3, 1016.

Contemplation of the Mercies of GOD (1699, also known as the *Thanksgivings*) – attest to the high opinion in which he was held for his character and piety.[21] However, none of the works published around Traherne's lifetime enjoyed notable popularity as none was reprinted, and so a generation after his death Traherne virtually disappeared from view.

From this angle, Traherne appears as a Restoration Anglican priest who was loyal to the national church, albeit with puritan influences from his youth.[22] His career suggests a gentleman priest and eclectic intellectual, who participated in devotional circles such as the Kington group and maintained links to the philosophical school of Cambridge Platonism.[23] His works reveal a theologian engaged in polemical religious debates with the Roman Catholic Church and the radical opinions of Socinians, Quakers, Anabaptists and enthusiasts.[24] The collaborative construction of his manuscripts portrays a figure fully immersed in contemporary devotional culture.[25] Any assessment of Traherne's theology of innocence ought not to be divorced from this context.

The historical turn has distanced Traherne from the image of an innocent rural mystic, but it has also identified the diverse philosophical sources that underlie his language of innocence.[26] Early source criticism, by Carol Marks and others, situated Traherne as philosophically related to Cambridge Platonism.[27] The sources of this school lay in Neoplatonist patristic texts,

---

[21]   See Margoliouth, 'Introduction', in Traherne, *Centuries, Poems, and Thanksgivings*, vol. 1, xxviii–xxix, xxx–xxxi.

[22]   See Julia J. Smith, 'Attitudes towards Conformity and Nonconformity in Thomas Traherne', *Bunyan Studies* 1/1 (1988), 26–35; ead., 'Thomas Traherne and the Restoration', *Seventeenth Century* 3/2 (1988), 203–22; Nabil Matar, 'The Anglican Eschatology of Thomas Traherne', *ATR* 74/3 (1992), 289–303; id., 'The Political Views of Thomas Traherne', *HLQ* 57/3 (1994), 241–53; on radical puritan influences on Restoration spiritual language, see Nigel Smith, *Perfection Proclaimed: Language and Literature in English Radical Religion, 1640–1660* (Oxford: Clarendon, 1989).

[23]   See Malcolm M. Day, *Thomas Traherne* (Boston: Twayne, 1982), 1–4.

[24]   See Denise Inge, 'Thomas Traherne and the Socinian Heresy in *Commentaries of Heaven*', *N&Q* 54 (2007), 412–16; Nabil Matar, 'A Note on Thomas Traherne and the Quakers', *N&Q* 28 (1981), 46–7; for a contrary assertion of Traherne's radical influences, see Christopher Hill, *The English Bible and the Seventeenth-Century Revolution* (London: Penguin, 1993), 202–3.

[25]   See Tomohiko Kohi, 'The Rhetoric of Instruction and Manuscript and Print Culture in the Devotional Works of Thomas Traherne' (PhD thesis: University of Reading, 2004).

[26]   On Traherne as mystic, see e.g. Louise Collier Willcox, 'A Joyous Mystic', *North American Review* 193/667 (1911), 893–904.

[27]   On Traherne and Cambridge Platonism, see Thomas O. Beachcroft, 'Traherne and the Cambridge Platonists', *Dublin Review* 186 (1930), 278–90; Frances L. Colby, 'Thomas

Introduction

Marsilio Ficino's translations of Platonist works and Renaissance Platonists such as Pico della Mirandola and Nicholas of Cusa.[28] Traherne's contemporary influences included the Oxford Platonists Thomas Jackson and Theophilus Gale, Cambridge Platonists such as Henry More and John Everard's translation of Hermes Trismegistus.[29] As will be discussed, Christian Platonist notions of pre-existence, innate ideas, spirit and the divine attributes have important implications for Traherne's depiction of innocence.

Traherne was not a Platonist alone. His loose 'affinities' with contemporary Platonists indicate his philosophical eclecticism, which reflects the eclecticism of seventeenth-century Neoplatonism in general.[30] Later contextual studies have related Traherne to a variety of contemporary intellectual trends. These include Aristotelian metaphysics and ethics, particularly on notions of happiness, value

---

Traherne and the Cambridge Platonists: An Analytical Comparison' (PhD thesis: Johns Hopkins University, 1947); Carol L. Marks, 'Thomas Traherne and Cambridge Platonism', *PMLA* 81/7 (1966), 521–34; for a summary of scholarship on Traherne's Platonism, see George R. Guffey, *Traherne and the Seventeenth-Century English Platonists, 1900–1966*, Elizabethan Bibliographies Supplements 11 (London: Nether Press, 1969).

[28] On the Church Fathers' influence on early modern Platonism, see D.W. Dockrill, 'The Heritage of Patristic Platonism in Seventeenth-Century Philosophical Theology', in G.A.J. Rogers, J.M. Vienne and Y.C. Zarka (eds), *The Cambridge Platonists in Philosophical Context: Politics, Metaphysics and Religion* (Dordrecht: Kluwer Academic, 1997), 55–77; for important surveys of seventeenth-century Platonism, see Ernst Cassirer, *The Platonic Renaissance in England*, trans. James Pettegrove (Edinburgh: Nelson, 1953); Gerald R. Cragg (ed.), *The Cambridge Platonists* (Oxford: Oxford University Press, 1968); Charles A. Patrides (ed.), *The Cambridge Platonists* (London: Arnold, 1969); Daniel Pickering Walker, *The Ancient Theology: Studies in Christian Platonism from the Fifteenth to the Eighteenth Century* (London: Duckworth, 1972), 132–63; Douglas Hedley and Sarah Hutton (eds), *Platonism at the Origins of Modernity: Studies on Platonism and Early Modern Philosophy* (Dordrecht: Springer, 2008).

[29] The general studies cited above do not mention Traherne (cf. Sarah Hutton, 'Platonism in Some Metaphysical Poets: Marvell, Vaughan and Traherne', in Alan Baldwin and Sarah Hutton [eds], *Platonism and the English Imagination* [Cambridge: Cambridge University Press, 1994], 163–77; on Traherne's links with Henry More, see G.R. Sherer, 'More and Traherne', *MLN* 34 (1919), 49–50; Frances L. Colby, 'Thomas Traherne and Henry More', *MLN* 62 (1947), 490–92; on Traherne's hermetic influences, see Carol L. Marks, 'Thomas Traherne and Hermes Trismegistus', *Renaissance News* 19/2 (1966), 118–31; on Oxford Platonism, see Sarah Hutton, 'Thomas Jackson, Oxford Platonist, and William Twisse, Aristotelian', *JHI* 39/4 (1978), 635–52; on Gale's influence, see Dewey D. Wallace, *Shapers of English Calvinism, 1660–1714: Variety, Persistence, and Transformation*, Oxford Studies in Historical Theology (Oxford: Oxford University Press, 2011), 101.

[30] See George Robert Guffey and Carol L. Marks, 'Introduction', in Thomas Traherne, *Christian Ethicks* (New York: Cornell University Press, 1968), xxviii.

and the desire for the good,[31] although such interpretations generally stop short of identifying Traherne as an Aristotelian. Kathryn Murphy, for example, identifies Traherne's deliberate adaptation of Aristotle as evidence of his philosophical eclecticism.[32] Traherne interpreted Aristotle through his Oxford scholastic education and the theology of Thomas Aquinas. Nevertheless, fundamental structures of Aristotelian philosophy, such as the distinction between substance and accident, have a bearing on Traherne's philosophy of innocence. His miscellaneous notions have also been identified with a changing philosophical environment that included the emergence of Baconian experimentalism, atomism, the anti-Hobbesian reaction and the rise of the Royal Society.[33] Under these contemporary influences, Traherne's notions of innocence are very much of their time.

Traherne's compound philosophy defies simple definition, drawing on Florentine and Cambridge Neoplatonism, scholastic Aristotelianism, experimentalism and the New Science. Traherne defined himself as 'a Philosopher a Christian and a Divine'. Since he also thought that 'a Divine includes a Philosopher and a Christian, a Christian includes a Divine and a Philosopher, a Philosopher includes a Christian and a Divine', these three designations were synonymous.[34]

---

[31] James Skeen, 'Discovering Human Happiness: Choice Theory Psychology, Aristotelian Contemplation, and Traherne's Felicity', *Quodlibet Journal* 5/2–3 (2003), <http://www.quodlibet.net/articles/skeen-choice.shtml> (accessed 1 Jan. 2012); David Hawkes, 'Thomas Traherne: A Critique of Political Economy', in *Idols of the Marketplace: Idolatry and Commodity Fetishism in English Literature, 1580–1680* (New York: Palgrave, 2001), 191–212; Paul Cefalu, 'Thomistic Metaphysics and Ethics in the Poetry and Prose of Thomas Traherne', *LT* 16/3 (2002), 248–69.

[32] See Katherine Murphy, '"Aves quaedam macedonicae": Misreading Aristotle in Francis Bacon, Robert Burton, Thomas Browne and Thomas Traherne' (PhD thesis: University of Oxford, 2009), 228.

[33] For an unusual interpretation of Traherne's Dobell poems as using Baconian inductive epistemology, see J.J. Balakier, 'Thomas Traherne's Dobell Series and the Baconian Model of Experience', *English Studies* 70 (1989), 233–47; on Traherne's anti-Hobbesian realism, see Murphy '"Aves quaedam macedonicae"', 244–55; Guffey and Marks, 'Introduction', in Traherne, *Christian Ethicks*, xxiii; on the anti-Hobbesian reaction, see Helen Thornton, *State of Nature or Eden? Thomas Hobbes and His Contemporaries on the Natural Condition of Human Beings* (Rochester, NY: University of Rochester Press, 2005); on Traherne and the scientific revolution, see Marjorie Hope Nicolson, *The Breaking of the Circle: Studies in the Effect of the 'New Science' Upon Seventeenth Century Poetry* (Evanston, Ill.: Northwestern University Press, 1950), 173–9; Robert Ellrodt, 'Scientific Curiosity and Metaphysical Poetry in the Seventeenth Century', *MP* 61/3 (1964), 180–97; on Traherne's atomism, see David Reid, 'Traherne and Lucretius', *N&Q* 45 (1998), 440–41.

[34] Traherne, *Centuries of Meditations*, IV 3; see also Thomas Traherne, 'Philosophie', *Commonplace Book* (Oxford, Bodleian Library, MS.Eng.Poet.c.42), 78r 1–78v 2, citing

Introduction 9

The organising frame of Traherne's philosophy was its theological trajectory.[35] Traherne's sometimes eclectic philosophical compilations were oriented towards a theological end, just as the 'glimmering Light of Nature' of pagan philosophy, he thought, was rightly judged by divine revelation.[36] Just as Ralph Cudworth saw 'Religion [as] the Queen of ... all pure *Naturall knowledge*', Traherne adopted a spiritual philosophy rooted in seventeenth-century devotional culture and congruent with his theological vision.[37]

The framework of Traherne's philosophy is found in ruling ideas such as love, felicity and innocence. Innocence, as will be seen, is expressed through the language of Neoplatonism, anti-Hobbesianism, Aristotelianism, experimentalism and atomism. These voices combine to construct a polyphonic vision of innocence. The consequent philosophical ambivalence or confusion creates a philosophy in motion where the principles and doctrines that loosely structure the works are given life by the very themes that disorganise them. In this sense, Traherne's is a poetic theology, according to Pico della Mirandola's account of Homer, who 'permitteth his fancy to wander a little Wantonly after the maner of a Poet: but most deep and serious things are secretly hidden under his free and luxuriant Language'.[38]

Twenty-First-Century Interpretations: Traherne as Anglican Theologian

A recent revival of interest in Traherne as both theologian and poet has built on the findings of contextual studies but has found a coherent theological poetics underlying his compound philosophical eclecticism. This latest development

---

Theopilus Gale, *The Court of the Gentiles* (4 vols, Oxford and London, 1660–78), vol. 2, 295–6; on Traherne as a 'Christian, Platonist, Mystic', see Gladys Irene Wade, *Thomas Traherne: A Critical Biography. With a Selected Bibliography of Criticism, by Robert Allerton Parker* (Princeton, NJ: Princeton University Press, 1944), 215–38.

[35] On the theological bent of Traherne's Platonism, see John E. Trimpey, 'An Analysis of Traherne's "Thoughts I"', *SP* 68 (1971), 101; Gerald Harvey Cox, 'Thomas Traherne's *Centuries*, a Platonic Devotion of "Divine Philosophy"', *MP* 69/1 (1971), 10–24.

[36] Thomas Traherne, 'Aristotle', *Commentaries of Heaven, Part 2*, in *The Works of Thomas Traherne*, vol. 3, 192; on the discovery of this manuscript, see Elliott Rose, 'A New Traherne Manuscript', *TLS* (19 Mar. 1982), 324; for a similarly theological Platonism, see John Smith, 'Concerning The True Way or method of attaining to Divine Knowledge', in *Select Discourses* (London: J. Flesher, 1660), 1, 17.

[37] Ralph Cudworth, *A Sermon Preached before the Honourable House of Commons at Westminster, March 31, 1647* (Cambridge: Roger Daniel, 1647), v–vii.

[38] Giovanni Pico della Mirandola, *Oration on the Dignity of Man*, trans. A. Robert Caponigri (Chicago: Regnery Gateway, 1956), 55; see Traherne, *Centuries of Meditations*, IV 78.

was galvanised by the discovery of *The Ceremonial Law* and the Lambeth manuscript in 1996–97.[39] The former is an epic poem based on Genesis and Exodus, and the latter contains four theological treatises: *Inducements to Retirednes, A Sober View of Dr Twisses his Considerations, Seeds of Eternity* and *The Kingdom of God*. At the forefront of theological reinterpretations of Traherne is Denise Inge's description of him as 'no naive optimist or rural songster but a serious thinker, debater, theologian and visionary'. For Inge, Traherne's effusive style and sometimes heterodox eclectisim does not diminish the coherence of his theology.[40] Mark McIntosh is noted for his theological interpretation of works that have been hitherto dismissed as merely devotional 'spirituality'. He has highlighted the depth of Traherne's Trinitarian vision of discernment, in which participation in the world as God's gift leads to divine perception.[41] David Ford sees in Traherne's unconventional poetic prose a creative impulse towards *epektasis*, which epitomises the role of praise as 'perfecting perfection'.[42] Ford follows others who have identified the distinctiveness of Traherne's theology in his poetic language.[43] Poetry transcends the boundaries of quotidian language, creating space for Traherne's expansive theological vision. This monograph adopts a similar approach by identifying key features of Traherne's poetic theology of innocence not in his stated doctrinal positions but in the tone, mood, genre and grammar of his work.

As an Anglican divine, Traherne has been interpreted according to commonly identified features of Anglican spirituality, such as the latitudinarian irenicism of

---

[39] See Jeremy Maule, 'Five New Traherne Works: An Overview of London, Lambeth Palace Library MS 1360' (typescript of notes from a talk presented to the Thomas Traherne Conference, Brasenose College, Oxford, 30 July 1997); Julia J. Smith and Laetitia Yeandle, '"Felicity Disguised in Fiery Words": Genesis and Exodus in a Newly Discovered Poem by Thomas Traherne', *TLS* (7 Nov. 1997), 17.

[40] Denise Inge, *Wanting Like a God: Desire and Freedom in the Thought of Thomas Traherne* (London: SCM, 2009), 3–4, 262; for another defence of Traherne's theological vision, see Calum Donald MacFarlane, 'Transfiguration as the Heart of Christian Life: The Theology of Thomas Traherne (1637?–1674) with Special Reference to "The Kingdom of God" and other Recently Discovered Manuscripts' (PhD thesis: University of Southampton, 2005).

[41] Mark Allen McIntosh, *Discernment and Truth: The Spirituality and Theology of Knowledge* (Edinburgh: Alban, 2004), 11–13.

[42] David Ford, *Christian Wisdom: Desiring God and Learning in Love* (Cambridge: Cambridge University Press, 2007), 235–7.

[43] See e.g. L. William Countryman, *The Poetic Imagination: An Anglican Spiritual Tradition* (London: Darton, Longman & Todd, 2000).

an Anglican *via media*.[44] As will be argued in Chapter 2, Traherne's middle way was not a narrow tightrope between the extremes of radicalism and Catholicism but an expansive vision that aimed to encompass all things. Several scholars have interpreted Traherne as part of a cataphatic tradition within Anglicanism and have seen in his spiritual writings a sacramental affirmation of the body.[45] As discussed in Chapter 6, Traherne's approach to the world as a physical sacrament of God's presence has implications for his presentation of spiritual innocence, and his theology of the Fall addressed in Chapter 3 also demonstrates elements of a *via negativa*. Thomas Merton and Donald Allchin identified Traherne's as a 'theology of praise'. Praise is both the substance and the trajectory of Traherne's theology, which is brought to birth, lived and consummated in praise.[46] It is not joy alone, but the preservation of dialogue with God through all the stages of life. This monograph looks at different manifestations of that ongoing dialogue.

A key theme in interpretations of Traherne as an Anglican divine has been the theological role of the affections. Esther de Waal's assertion of Traherne's 'passionate sense of relatedness to the physical world around him' stresses both the affective centre of his theology and its sacramental manifestation.[47] An affective interpretation of Traherne chimes with recent accounts of Anglican spirituality, such as Rowan Williams' defence of Anglicanism's 'passionate patience' and Alan Bartlett's view of the tradition's 'passionate balance'.[48] Traherne's work has the potential to contribute to further exploration of the affective aspect of Anglican spirituality. His theology arguably finds its coherence in the passions of joy, wonder and desire, as they are expressed in the intentional, subjunctive

---

[44]   William J. Wolf, 'The Spirituality of Thomas Traherne', in id. (ed.), *Anglican Spirituality* (Wilton, Conn.: Morehouse, 1982), 49–68.

[45]   See Anne Ridler, 'The Essential Thomas Traherne', in A.M. Allchin, Anne Ridler and Julia Smith (eds), *Profitable Wonders: Aspects of Thomas Traherne* (Oxford: Amate, 1989), 9–21; Gavin Kuchar, '"Organs of thy Praise": The Function and Rhetoric of the Body in Thomas Traherne', in Kathryn Duncan (ed.), *Religion in the Age of Reason: A Transatlantic Study of the Long Eighteenth Century* (New York: AMS, 2009), 59–81; Jonathan Sawday, *The Body Emblazoned: Dissection and the Human Body in Renaissance Culture* (London: Routledge, 1995), 80–83.

[46]   Thomas Merton, *Mystics and Zen Masters* (New York: Farrar, Straus and Giroux, 1967), 133–4; A.M. Allchin, 'The Whole Assembly Sings: Thomas Traherne', in *The Joy of All Creation* (London: Darton, Longman & Todd, 1984), 78–89.

[47]   Esther de Waal, *Lost in Wonder: Rediscovering the Spiritual Art of Attentiveness* (Norwich: Canterbury Press, 2003), 158.

[48]   Rowan Williams, *Anglican Identities* (London: Darton, Longman & Todd, 2004), 8; Alan Bartlett, *A Passionate Balance: The Anglican Tradition* (London: Darton, Longman & Todd, 2007).

12   *Boundless Innocence in Thomas Traherne's Poetic Theology*

and optative moods.[49] By assessing the grammatical moods of Traherne's poetic theology, this book draws out the hidden passions, affections and apprehensions of innocence.

A theological assessment of Traherne's work ought also to take account of his position as a priest during the post-Restoration development of Anglican identity. A commitment to this role is evident in *Church's Year-Book*, a manual of prayers and devotions that promotes the public festivals of the national church.[50] The treatises of the Lambeth manuscript are informed by the language of the King James Bible and the liturgy of the Book of Common Prayer, and the prayers of *A Serious and Pathetical Contemplation of the Mercies of GOD* are indebted to a daily reading of the Psalms. An assessment of Traherne as an Anglican theologian would therefore be thoroughly contextual but may also draw on the insights of current scholarship on the distinctive features of Anglican spirituality.

The Innocence of Thomas Traherne: Aspects of Interpretation

Modern Frameworks

So far, it has been shown that general developments in Traherne criticism have important implications for understanding his vision of innocence and that innocence in his works ought to be interpreted through an approach that is both contextual and theologically and philosophically aware. Looking more closely at assessments of Traherne's idea of innocence, it appears that interpretation has been coloured by several modern intellectual frameworks. Identifying innocence as a natural or psychological state and associating it with naive optimism or solipsism, these approaches distance Traherne from seventeenth-century Anglican devotion.

---

[49]   On the 'affective turn' in scholarship on early modern philosophy, see Brian Cummings and Freya Sierhuis, 'Introduction', in eid. (eds), *Passions and Subjectivity in Early Modern Culture* (Farnham: Ashgate, 2013), 1–9; on desire in Traherne's theology, see Belden C. Lane, 'Thomas Traherne and the Awakening of Want', *ATR* 81/4 (1999), 651–64; Carol Ann Johnston, 'Heavenly Perspectives, Mirrors of Eternity: Thomas Traherne's Yearning Subject', *Criticism* 43/4 (2001), 377–405.

[50]   See A.M. Allchin, 'Sacrifice of Praise and Thanksgiving', in Allchin, Ridler and Smith (eds), *Profitable Wonders*, 22–37; on Traherne as a high-church Anglican, see Barry Spurr, 'Felicity Incarnate: Rediscovering Thomas Traherne', in E.R. Cunnar and J. Johnson (eds), *Discovering and (Re)covering the Seventeenth-Century Religious Lyric* (Pittsburgh, Pa.: Duquesne University Press, 2001), 273–89.

Introduction 13

In some interpretations, Traherne represents a natural innocence that is akin to the Enlightenment or Romantic 'state of nature'. Traherne's praise of nature has long been identified as a central theme in his work and associated with his respect for childhood.[51] These two themes have been united through the idea of a 'natural innocence'.[52] More specifically, Keith Salter associated him with a defence of the natural innocence of childhood, part of a modern secularising shift away from the orthodox Augustinianism of original sin. He defined Traherne's theology of original sin as a forerunner of the 'Romantic heresy' of Pelagianism.[53] As will be discussed in Chapter 2, the imposition of an Enlightenment or Romantic state of natural innocence upon Traherne obscures the theological principles and the traditions of Christian thought which underlie his work. Chapter 3 will address his theology of original sin.

Some mystical and poetic readings of Traherne have inclined towards a psychological interpretation of innocence. Franz Wöhrer's empirical approach to mystical experience imposed psycho-phenomenology upon the seventeenth-century context, tracing the development of Traherne's 'mystical consciousness' from the infant state of innocence.[54] Robert Ellrodt interpreted Traherne's child through Piagetian developmental theory, identifying infant innocence with the pantheistic solipsism of the unformed individual.[55] Similarly, Sharon

---

[51] On Traherne's praise of nature, see Margaret Bottrall, 'Traherne's Praise of the Creation', *Critical Quarterly* 1/2 (1959), 126–33; on Traherne's not as a nature-mysticism but as a 'mysticism through nature', see Henry R. McAdoo, *The Spirit of Anglicanism: A Survey of Anglican Theological Method in the Seventeenth Century* (London: A.&C. Black, 1965), 116–18; Jeannie DeBrun Duffy identifies Traherne's praise of nature with seventeenth-century Protestantism ('Henry Vaughan and Thomas Traherne and the Protestant Tradition of Meditation upon the Book of Creatures' [PhD thesis: Brown University, 1973]); it has also been read through modern ecological issues (see Diane Kelsey McColley, *Poetry and Ecology in the Age of Milton and Marvell* [Aldershot: Ashgate, 2007], 55–6); for the most recent contribution, see Robert N. Watson, *Back to Nature: The Green and the Real in the Late Renaissance* (Philadelphia: University of Pennsylvania Press, 2006), 305.

[52] See e.g. Daniel O'Day, 'Quest for Childhood: A Critical Study of Henry Vaughan and Thomas Traherne' (PhD thesis: Columbia University, 1972), 216.

[53] Keith William Salter, 'Thomas Traherne and a Romantic Heresy', *N&Q* 200 (1955), 153–6; T.E. Hulme, 'Romanticism and Classicism', in Herbert Read (ed.), *Speculations: Essays on Humanism and the Philosophy of Art* (London: K. Paul, Trench, Trubner & Co., 1936), 111–40.

[54] Franz K. Wöhrer, *Thomas Traherne: The Growth of a Mystic's Mind. A Study of the Evolution and the Phenomenology of Traherne's Mystical Consciousness* (Salzburg: Salzburg University, 1982), 99–135.

[55] Robert Ellrodt, *Seven Metaphysical Poets: A Structural Study of the Unchanging Self* (Oxford: Oxford University Press, 2000), 91, 93–4, 97–8; see Jean Piaget, *The Moral*

Seelig's assessment of Traherne's mystical poetry identified his innocence as a 'psychological, rather than a theological state': a form of Adamic or childlike perception rather than the sinlessness of 'essential innocence'.[56] These modern psychological frameworks connect innocence either with a regressive nostalgia for infancy or a utopian yearning for a universal archetype of paradise.[57] While such readings attempt to uncover the psychological impulses behind Traherne's account of innocence, they tie it to modern models of selfhood and obscure the theological background to his thought. Moreover, they have been superseded by theories of cognitive development that portray infants not as models of passive innocence but active learning subjects from the womb.[58]

Readings of Traherne as a Christian humanist have identified his innocence with humanism's attendant qualities of optimism and anthropocentrism.[59] In general, this has been placed within the contextual frame of Renaissance theology, rather than a Burckhardtian narrative of secularisation.[60] John Spencer Hill, for example, sees Traherne's optimism for humanity as based not on ideas of human nature but on an Augustinian theology that emphasises the power of grace and faith. Nevertheless, in this context, the theological connotations of the term 'hope' might be more appropriate than the two-dimensional personality

---

Judgement of the Child, trans. Marjorie Gabain (New York: Free Press, 1965).

[56] Sharon Cadman Seelig, *The Shadow of Eternity: Belief and Structure in Herbert, Vaughan and Traherne* (Lexington: University Press of Kentucky, 1981), 146, 161.

[57] On theories of paradise as a psychological archetype in Carl Jung, Lucien Freud, Mircea Eliade, Norman O. Brown and John Armstrong, see Joseph Ellis Duncan, *Milton's Earthly Paradise: A Historical Study of Eden* (Minneapolis, Minnesota: University of Minnesota Press, 1972), 7–8; Carl J. Jung, 'The Psychology of the Child Archetype', in *Archetypes and the Collective Unconscious*, trans. R.F.C. Hull, Collected Works of C.G. Jung 9/1 (2nd edn, London: Routledge, 1968), 151–81; on utopianism, see Frank E. Manuel and Fritzie P. Manuel (eds), *Utopian Thought in the Western World* (Oxford: Basil Blackwell, 1979); Thomas Molnar, *Utopia: The Perennial Heresy* (London: Tom Stacey, 1972).

[58] S. Ulijaszek, 'Neurological Development', in S.J. Ulijaszek, F.E. Johnston and M.A. Preece (eds), *The Cambridge Encyclopedia of Human Growth and Development* (Cambridge: Cambridge University Press, 1998), 164–5; I. Brundt, 'Cognitive Development', in Ulijaszek, Johnston and Preece (eds), *The Cambridge Encyclopedia of Human Growth and Development*, 245–6.

[59] e.g. S. Sandbank, 'Thomas Traherne on the Place of Man in the Universe', *Scripta Hierosolymitana* 17 (1966), 121, 130; see also Verena Olejniczak Lobsien, 'The Space of the Human and the Place of the Poet: Excursions into English Topographical Poetry', in Andreas Höfele and Stephan Laqué (eds), *Humankinds: The Renaissance and Its Anthropologies* (Berlin: De Gruyter, 2011), 47.

[60] See Jacob Burckhardt, *The Civilization of the Renaissance in Italy* (London: Phaidon, 1990 [1860]); Charles E. Trinkaus, *In Our Image and Likeness: Humanity and Divinity in Italian Humanist Thought* (Notre Dame, Ind.: University of Notre Dame Press, 1995).

trait of 'optimism'. Although Hill distances Traherne from comparisons with Wordsworth, his model for Traherne's optimistic Christian Platonism remains a return to childhood.[61] As will be examined in Chapters 3 to 5, Traherne's apparent optimism does not preclude darker tones, even in his account of innocence. As discussed in Chapter 6, his vision of hope for humanity goes well beyond a return to childhood.

A Childlike Innocence

These three models: the natural innocence of Pelagian heresy, the psychological innocence of the mystic and the anthropocentric innocence of Christian humanism, all find a central model in the child. While none of these interpretations are completely invalid, Traherne's innocence consistently transcends the boundaries of these frameworks. Current criticism has superseded earlier readings of Traherne as poet of childhood and felicity, pantheistic Pelagian, mystic savant or optimistic humanist. The most recent collection of essays on Traherne contains little reference to innocence.[62] Nevertheless, earlier critical assumptions remain embedded within these studies.

Paradoxically, the decline of the significance of innocence in current criticism rests on the very Romantic readings of Traherne which it rejects, because innocence continues to be defined through childlikeness. Denise Inge and Edmund Newey both defend Traherne the theologian against post-Romantic critiques of the Romantic ideal of childhood, by downplaying the centrality of childlike innocence. Inge does not list innocence among Traherne's childlike qualities, while Newey strives to show that his child represents the whole life of the soul and not merely its innocent beginnings.[63] This defence comes out of a reading of Traherne's notion of childlike innocence that is founded upon post-Romantic assumptions. In arguing for the priority of post-lapsarian grace, Inge identifies the prior estate of innocence with the lost estate of childhood: 'His memory of innocence, however bright, is essentially a memory lost'.[64] This echoes the post-Romantic critique of nostalgia and sentimentalism in literature on childhood innocence. Similarly, in

---

[61] John Spencer Hill, *Infinity, Faith and Time: Christian Humanism and Renaissance Literature* (Montreal: McGill-Queens University Press, 1997), 40–66.

[62] Jacob Blevins (ed.), *Re-Reading Thomas Traherne: A Collection of New Critical Essays* (Tempe: Arizona Center for Medieval and Renaissance Studies, 2007).

[63] Inge, *Wanting Like a God*, 63, 100, 150–51, 187–8, 193–4; Edmund Newey, '"God Made Man Greater When He Made Him Less": Traherne's Iconic Child', *LT* 24/3 (2010), 227–41.

[64] Inge, *Wanting Like a God*, 162–3, 183.

his desire to present Traherne's child not as a figure of innocence alone but an 'icon of the whole human condition', Newey reflects post-Romantic anxieties over a two-dimensional idealisation of childhood.[65]

In their attempts to move Traherne criticism away from shallow comparisons with the Romantic poets, Inge and Newey reveal the tenacity of post-Romantic ideas and assumptions surrounding the ideal of innocence. However, Newey also opens up an avenue for new exploration. If, as he suggests, Traherne's child need not be identified with innocence alone, then perhaps innocence can also be interpreted without reference to the child.

New Interpretations

Newey's interpretation of Traherne's child provides the starting point for this monograph. It aims to better understand the various aspects of Traherne's language of innocence, whether or not they conform to the model of a return to childhood. It questions whether the poems of the Dobell and Burney manuscripts ought to be the primary source for interpretations of Traherne's innocence, given that the term only appears nine times in these collections.[66] In the light of the breadth of further manuscript discoveries during the twentieth century, how else does Traherne use the language of innocence? What do Traherne's extensive references to the 'estate of innocence' signify, and do they always mean the same thing? What does it mean when Traherne refers to innocence in an adjectival sense, as in the 'Humble and Innocent Discharge' of duty, 'innocent Mistakes' or 'Innocent Recreations'?[67] Is there any significance to these apparently more commonplace uses of the term, to refer to something that is without malice, without addition or corruption, acting according to its nature or design?[68]

Innocence in Traherne's works is clearly something to be commended, desired and attained, even if it is not a priority for the spiritual life, but are there underlying theological connotations which grant it greater significance? The entry for 'Attainment' in the aspirationally encyclopaedic dictionary of felicity, *Commentaries of Heaven*, lists innocence alongside beauty, learning, riches,

---

[65] Newey, '"God Made Man Greater When He Made Him Less"', 235.

[66] 'Innocence' (6×), 'innocent' (3×) (George Robert Guffey, *A Concordance to the Poetry of Thomas Traherne* [Berkeley: University of California Press, 1974], 224).

[67] Thomas Traherne, *Inducements to Retirednes*, in *The Works of Thomas Traherne*, vol. 1, 20; id., *A Sober View of Dr Twisses his Considerations*, in *The Works of Thomas Traherne*, vol. 1, 91; id., *Centuries of Meditations*, IV 24.

[68] For more mundane usage, see Traherne, 'Adulterie', *Commentaries of Heaven, Part 1*, in *The Works of Thomas Traherne*, vol. 2, 256; id., *Roman Forgeries*, 240, 255, 309.

Introduction 17

preferment, marriage and favour, as among the 'less Principal Attainments' of humanity, the principal attainment being happiness.[69] Elsewhere, the theological subtext makes innocence more than a generally desirable commodity. For example, used in the judicial sense, the term contains either explicit or implicit reference to Christ's crucifixion. This is clear in the definition of 'Action' in *Commentaries of Heaven*, where the phrase 'to kill a Man Innocent' was deleted and replaced with 'to be a Deicide'.[70] The various uses of 'innocence' contain indications of Traherne's theological anthropology, his theology of sin and suffering, his Christology, his moral theology and his eschatology.

The breadth and depth of meaning in Traherne's references to innocence has been hitherto unrecognised in critical study and merits closer analysis. Traherne's is a philosophy played out in several frames, through the interpenetration of ideas organised around his central devotional concerns. Superimposed on this broad foundation, the various modes of innocence raise enticing ambiguities over Traherne's precise understanding of the idea.

The Estates of the Soul and the Frameworks of Christian Innocence

This book uncovers different aspects of innocence in Traherne's theology, using the framework of the four estates of the soul. It illustrates how innocence both belongs to and transcends each estate. Traherne refers to innocence most commonly when talking about the estate of innocence, which precedes the subsequent estates of misery, grace and glory. The trope of the soul's four estates finds its roots in Aristotle and was transmitted through Augustine and the medieval scholastics to early modern philosophy.[71] It was not uncommon in seventeenth-century devotion. William Austin, for example, who influenced Traherne, followed Augustine in styling humanity's four estates as those of natural man, repentance, resurrection and life everlasting.[72]

The progress of the four estates may be interpreted in different ways. A linear interpretation is conducive to a biographical reading of Traherne's works,

---

[69]   Traherne, 'Attainment', *Commentaries of Heaven, Part 2*, 378.

[70]   Traherne, 'Action', *Commentaries of Heaven, Part 1*, 194; see also id., *Centuries of Meditations*, I 59, II 32.

[71]   For a summary of seventeenth-century usage, see Diane Elizabeth Dreher, *The Fourfold Pilgrimage: The Estates of Innocence, Misery, Grace, and Glory in Seventeenth-Century Literature* (Washington DC: University Presses of America, 1982), 1–6; on Traherne, see ibid. 77–98.

[72]   William Austin, *Devotionis Augustinianae flamma* (London, 1635), 254.

in which innocence is the original or first estate of infancy, whether literal, spiritual or metaphorical. A cyclical interpretation of the estates is more akin to the meditative model set out by Joseph Hall in *The Art of Divine Meditation* (1606).[73] In this framework, there is spiritual progress from 'initial innocence' through a fall into misery into a second innocence of grace which culminates in glory.[74] The second innocence is both a recapitulation and an expansion of the first. As this monograph will show, it is the second innocence of the life of faith in the estate of grace with which Traherne is most concerned.

In recent interpretations of Traherne, this cyclical structure of the estates contains echoes of the philosophical theology of Paul Ricoeur and his hermeneutical theory of a 'second naïveté'. Ricoeurian assumptions underlie Richard Chartres' theological assessment of Traherne's innocence in his popular article: 'From the Miserable Gulph to a Second Innocence'.[75] Ricoeur's influence on modern theological interpretations of innocence more generally can be seen in the work of F. Masciandaro, who uses Ricoeur's spiral cycle of recapitulation and progression to distinguish between 'the dream of a future "second innocence" which ignores the irreducible fact of evil, and the recovery of an innocence that is analogous to the innocence of the original myth of Eden'.[76] This manifests a preference for a transcendent recapitulation of innocence over simplistic utopianism.

Elements of Ricoeur's theological hermeneutics of second naïveté may be illuminative for Traherne's language of innocence. This model suggests that the second innocence may be achieved 'in and through criticism', incorporating the insights of experience. It suggests that innocence need not be utopian but may be a theological realism based upon a 'wager' of the possible.[77] However, a Ricoeurian framework is not entirely appropriate for Traherne. Ricoeur's

---

[73] On the dispute between linear and cyclical interpretations of the structure of Traherne's poems, see A. Leigh DeNeef, *Traherne in Dialogue: Heidegger, Lacan, and Derrida* (Durham, NC: Duke University Press, 1988), 138–9.

[74] Barbara Lewalski, *Protestant Poetics and the Seventeenth-Century Religious Lyric* (Princeton, NJ: Princeton University Press, 1979), 357.

[75] Richard Chartres, 'From the Miserable Gulph to a Second Innocence – A Travel Guide', *Church Times* 7727 (21 Apr. 2011), publication of a talk to the Thomas Traherne Conference, St Mary's University College, Twickenham, 12 Mar. 2011.

[76] Franco Masciandaro, *Dante as Dramatist: The Myth of the Earthly Paradise and Tragic Vision in the Divine Comedy* (Philadelphia: University of Pennsylvania Press, 1991), xiv.

[77] Paul Ricoeur, *The Symbolism of Evil*, trans. Emerson Buchanan, Religious Perspectives 17 (New York: Harper & Row, 1967), 350–51; for a summary of interpretations of this theory and an assessment of its strengths and weaknesses, see Mark I. Wallace, *The*

Introduction 19

second naïveté is a response to the deconstructionist 'hermeneutics of suspicion' of Freudian psychoanalysis, whereas Traherne's innocence is presented in terms of spiritual autobiography.[78] The first is a hermeneutic theory, the second a theological narrative. A distinction should be made between the epistemological category of naïveté and the ethical or spiritual concept of innocence. Confusing naïveté and innocence limits innocence to an unknowing of evil, ignoring other connotations such as harmlessness and holiness. Moreover, the implicit association of Ricoeur's hermeneutical arc with Traherne's spiritual life history restricts innocence to a purely cyclical narrative framework.

Although the progress of the estates provides a heuristic tool to illustrate the boundlessness of Traherne's innocence, it is not employed in a straightforward or unambiguous manner. In Traherne's works, the four estates do not only proceed in a linear or cyclical fashion, nor are they always fourfold. Each adaptation of the framework presents a different model of innocence. In *Commentaries of Heaven*, the estates advance like the seasons from the winter and spring of earthly existence to the summer and 'Glorious Autumn' of heaven 'above the Sphere'.[79] This gives the impression of growth and maturation through the estates. In *The Ceremonial Law*, Traherne imposes a binary rather than a fourfold model that distinguishes between historical existence and eternity.[80] Within this framework, Adam's original innocence parallels transcendent glory. Both innocence and glory are viewed within the poem from a fallen perspective, as an absent object of desire: Eden is described as a past paradise and an intimation of the Promised Land represented in the oasis of Elim encountered by the Israelites in the desert, the 'Relick of our Ancient Innocence'.[81] In the former framework innocence is a developmental attribute, in the latter an object of remembrance.

Traherne's epic treatise *The Kingdom of God*, the posthumously published work of moral theology, *Christian Ethicks* (1675), the treatise on election, *A Sober View of Dr Twisses his Considerations*, and *Commentaries of Heaven* contain an alternative binary distinction between two estates of trial and glory.[82]

Second Naiveté: Barth, Ricoeur, and the New Yale Theology, Studies in American Biblical Hermeneutics (Macon, Ga.: Mercer, 1990), 55–6, 112.

[78] Paul Ricoeur, *Freud and Philosophy: An Essay on Interpretation* (New Haven, Conn.: Yale University Press, 1970), 20–58.

[79] Traherne, 'Action', *Commentaries of Heaven, Part 1*, 195.

[80] Thomas Traherne, *The Ceremonial Law*, in *The Works of Thomas Traherne*, vol. 6.

[81] Ibid. 216.

[82] Thomas Traherne, *The Kingdom of God*, 'Cap. XLII. That it was better to be made in a State of Trial, then immediatly placed in the Throne of Glory', in *The Works of Thomas Traherne*, vol. 1, 495–502; id., *Christian Ethicks*, 105; id., 'Article', *Commentaries of Heaven, Part 2*, 234; id., 'Attainment', *Commentaries of Heaven, Part 2*, 383.

A Sober View is an exploration of the statement 'Christ died for the whole World to restore them to a New Estate of Trial.'[83] The first estate of trial is the kingdom of legal righteousness where Adam and Eve are tested by the injunction not to eat from the tree of knowledge. The second is the kingdom of evangelical righteousness wherein humanity overcomes temptation and calamity through faith, hope and love.[84] This framework unites the estates of innocence, misery and grace and distinguishes them from glory. So, in *Christian Ethicks*, the virtues which overlap between the estates of innocence and grace conceal a fundamental binary framework, which distinguishes the current state of trial that began in Eden from the glory to which it tends.[85] In this model, the estate of innocence is the 'Trial of Lov', or of obedience, and is thereby drawn into the drama of history and the activity of existence.[86]

The chapters of this volume follow the model of the four estates in a linear fashion, with, however, an awareness of Traherne's various manifestations of this framework. Indeed, the volume uses this model to demonstrate that, just as all the estates exist in an infinitely intermingled eternity, innocence may be found not only in the estate of innocence but also in different forms in those of misery, grace and glory. In these estates, innocence is marked not only by beauty but also by loss, trial, desire, the limits and joys of material existence and the organic growth of the soul.

Towards a Theological Poetics of Innocence

This book assesses Traherne's theology of innocence through its grammatical tenses and moods, literary conceits and genres.[87] This poetic approach to Traherne's theology is indebted to Ricoeur's and Williams' accounts of the role of the poetic in theological language. It is not the first study to approach Traherne's as a poetic theology, nor is it the first to use the methods of theological

---

[83]   Traherne, *A Sober View*, 48.

[84]   Ibid. 54, 64, 74–5; Smith adopts a similar framework ('Of the Difference between the Legal and the Evangelical Righteousness, the Old and the New Covenant, &c.', in *Select Discourses*, 283–346).

[85]   See Traherne, *Christian Ethicks*, 32, 85, 184.

[86]   See Traherne, 'Spiritual Absence', *Commentaries of Heaven, Part 1*, 44; id., 'Abuse', *Commentaries of Heaven, Part 1*, 69.

[87]   For an alternative 'grammar' of Traherne's works, see Ford on the interrogative, subjunctive and optative 'moods' of Traherne's theology (*Christian Wisdom*, 8, 12, 239–41, 371, 242–4, 245, 248).

Introduction 21

poetics, but it is the first to apply contextual theology to Traherne's poetics of innocence.[88]

This approach is appropriate both for the topic and for the man. Innocence has attracted scholarly attention through its literary and artistic expressions, and Traherne's language is inherently poetic, both in its poetry and its prose. It is poetic because it is irreducible: it cannot be deconstructed since it contains meaning within the mode of discourse.[89] A poetic approach therefore provides the most appropriate assessment of Traherne's symbolic, emblematic and sacramental use of language. As outlined above, the 'logic' of Traherne's theology is not found in adherence to philosophical or doctrinal principles but in the movement of the affections through poetic and rhetorical devices. Secondly, a poetic approach to Traherne's theology pays attention to *poesis* and so finds in the creative use of language a conversation with the creator God.[90] Thirdly, Traherne's language is poetic because it is transgressive or excessive. Kenneth Ames, for example, associated Traherne's 'religious language' with the poetic capacity to transcend boundaries and inculcate 'a unique mode of seeing'.[91] Poetry can say things that are inaccessible to discursive language. It unveils the mystical side of Traherne's theology, his vision of heavenly innocence and his expansive desire to encompass holiness.

Poetic analysis is not a replacement for metaphysics but complements it, so this study does not ignore conceptual questions.[92] The four estates are estates of the soul, and the innocence under discussion is human innocence rather than God's 'innocence' or righteousness in relation to humanity. Within the theological orientation of Traherne's philosophy, the language of human innocence raises questions of theological anthropology. David Kelsey's two-volume theological anthropology, *Eccentric Existence*, classifies these as the 'what', 'who' and 'how' questions of human existence: what are we, who are we and how are we to be in the context of being related-to by God? For Kelsey, 'what' we are is the question of essence, whether that is determined by human

---

[88] See James Charleton, *Non-Dualism in Eckhart, Julian of Norwich and Traherne* (London: Bloomsbury, 2012); Alison Kershaw, 'The Poetic of the Cosmic Christ in Thomas Traherne's *The Kingdom of God*' (PhD thesis: University of Western Australia, 2005).

[89] See Paul Ricoeur, 'Toward a Hermeneutic of the Idea of Revelation', *Harvard Theological Review*, 70/1–2 (1977), 23–4.

[90] See Rowan Williams, 'Poetic and Religious Imagination', *Theology* 80 (May 1977), 179–81.

[91] Kenneth J. Ames, *The Religious Language of Thomas Traherne's* Centuries (New York: Revisionist, 1978), 56; see also John Stewart Allitt, *Thomas Traherne: Il poeta-teologo della meraviglia e della felicità* (Milan: Edizioni Villadiseriane, 2007).

[92] Williams, 'Poetic and Religious Imagination', 182.

origins or actual existence. This is an important question for discussions of the role of Eden and of narratives of original innocence. 'Who' is the question of the 'basic, unsubstitutable personal identity' of a creature in relation to God in whatever estate it finds itself. Answers to this question are found not in abstract principles but in the persons or characters who exemplify innocence. In Traherne's case these are Adam, Christ, Job and David. 'How' is the question not only of action but also of 'our most basic dispositions, attitudes and policies; our defining emotions, passions, and feelings'.[93] It is a question of both the outer and the inner life, of 'how am I to be' in response to God's creative relation to humanity. Chapter 5 addresses the relationship between the innocence of outward actions and inward intentions. Underlying this study is a concern with Traherne's answer to these three questions and what innocence might mean in the context of each.

Summary

To show how innocence features throughout the spiritual life for Traherne, the main chapters proceed through each estate of the soul: from innocence through the Fall, the trials of misery, the recovery of grace and the hope of glory. Each chapter explores the character of innocence in a particular estate and interprets this estate in the light of the Latin Christian tradition, contemporary devotion and modern theoretical frameworks. The discussion looks not only at what innocence means in every estate but how it transcends it. Each chapter indicates what element of Traherne's theological anthropology this aspect of innocence speaks to – whether it be the 'what', 'who' or 'how' of human existence. The chapters conclude with a discussion of the innocence of each estate in relation to Traherne's theological poetics. They draw out the theological implications of each aspect of innocence using a grammatical or literary trope.

Chapter 1 puts Traherne's innocence in context. First, it unravels contemporary theological concerns which shape the interpretation of innocence in historical texts. Then, beginning with its scriptural roots, the chapter introduces the distinctive features of the Latin tradition of innocence represented by the Vulgate and Church Fathers such as Tertullian and Lactantius. It demonstrates how this tradition was translated to the seventeenth-century context through Thomas Wilson's popular *Christian Dictionary*.

---

[93]   David H. Kelsey, *Eccentric Existence: A Theological Anthropology* (2 vols, Louisville, Ky: Westminster John Knox Press, 2009), vol. 1, 1–11.

Introduction 23

Chapter 2 begins with the estate of innocence. It looks at the authority and character of original innocence in Traherne's theology, in particular the significance of Eden and Adam. It explores the interplay between the negative semantics of original *innocens* as the chaos of the primordial void over against the positive order and material beauty of the Garden of Eden. It concludes that innocence subsists in the interplay between the two. It contrasts Traherne's theologically rooted account of 'perfect innocency by creation' with Hobbesian and Enlightenment accounts of the state of nature. Original or essential innocence raises the question of 'what' human beings were or are created to be. Traherne's answer to that question is creaturely. It is bound to an organic and historical process which does not belong to the past narrative of the perfect or the pluperfect but to the ongoing activity of the imperfect tense.

Chapter 3 is not concerned with an estate as such, but with the gap between the estates of innocence and misery–grace. Responding to the affective turn in intellectual history and exploring the harmonies between doctrinal and devotional language in his theology of original sin, it concludes that Traherne's affective poetics defines the Fall as a failure in love. It looks at the nature of the Fall from innocence as, simultaneously, a Platonic decline from infinity to finitude and an Aristotelian loss of a separable accident. It examines the apophatic connotations of an innocence that persists even through the Fall, albeit in fragments, and in the dance between light and shade. Innocence here is present in the negative tense that resonates with the private semantics of *in-nocens*, as an absent ideal invoked by the repeated trope, 'no man is innocent'. The absent presence of apophatic innocence raises questions about nostalgic idealisations of childhood and deconstructionist scepticism towards innocence, entering into the question of 'what' humanity has become.

Chapter 4 moves on to life in this world, the estate of misery or trial, which is the trial of innocence. It begins with the leap from the Fall into the estate of misery–grace. No child is born innocent, but through the sacramental regeneration of baptism they are reborn into a state of graced innocence that is the foundation of the Christian life. This chapter is concerned with 'who' we are or can be in this world, in the face of the world, the flesh and the devil. Temptation is not the end but the test of innocence, and so to be holy in this world is to be innocent in the midst of trial. Innocence in the midst of trial is, almost inevitably, a suffering innocence. Passive suffering is sanctified through the active virtue of suffering in an innocent manner, which is exemplified by the sacrificial lamb. Innocence in trial is modelled by Job and Christ. It is a kenotic innocence that undoes the facile link between innocence and happiness. It is illustrated not by a grammatical but by a literary trope, through Traherne's depiction of the tragic drama of the theatre of miseries.

Chapter 5 continues with the drama of innocence in the estate of misery–grace. Grace suffuses innocence in all the estates but is particularly evident in Traherne's interpretation of what Wilson called 'innocency of life'. This chapter focuses on the plot or action played out on the existential stage, rather than on the tragic elements of drama, as the discussion turns to ethics or 'how' we are to be. This 'how' is explored through the compatibility of innocence with experience and activity through righteous harmlessness; its preservation through sincerity, integrity and purity of heart; and its pursuit through the Christian virtues. Not a sentimental ideal associated with naïveté or inexperience, 'innocency of life' is a clerical vocation followed through chastity and praise, a feature of mature spiritual practice. This is innocence in the imperative, intentional or hortative mood of ethical teaching.

Chapter 6 explores the realm of glory. This is the final estate but also the life of spirit seen through contemplation of the soul, the divine revelation intimated through the sacraments and the light of eternity which unifies the estates. Traherne's vision of the soul as imaging the simplicity of divine innocence is 'who' we are from a heavenly perspective. Nevertheless, glory is not confined to heaven but is glimpsed through various images, emblems or conceits of human perfection. These include conventional metaphors such as the child, dove, garden, pearl and virgin, nakedness and whiteness, but also novel images such as the atom, 'Celestial Stranger' and 'Amazon Queen'. Traherne's sacramental emblematics of innocence situates him within traditions of Christian mysticism but also demonstrates his eclectic imagination. His lyrical images of divine innocence go well beyond paradisal archetypes as they cross the estates of the soul. They do not speak the language of utopianism but of eschatological hope through the subjunctive mood of the possible.

Chapter 7 draws together the arguments of the book by exploring what it means for Traherne to be both wise and innocent. This final conclusion summarises the theological-grammatical theme of Traherne's 'boundless' innocence. It is boundless, firstly, in the sense of transcending the boundaries between the estates of the soul. Secondly, the optative mood of the repeated phrase, 'Were all Men Innocent', expresses a boundless desire for innocence. Understanding innocence in light of the excess or *epektasis* of desire, reveals it not as a simply negative *in-nocens* or absence of harm, sin or guilt. Instead, like the primordial void, the inherently privative nature of innocence is the vacuum which draws the soul towards God, like the lodestone of love to which Traherne often refers.

Chapter 1

Defining Innocence: Issues and Interpretations

Before studying the theme of innocence it is necessary to attempt a definition, although this will be inevitably cursory and contestable. Firstly, the history of innocence has been sorely neglected in academic scholarship. While there are surveys of childhood and interpretations of Eden, there has been no comprehensive study of the history of innocence.[1] A lack of knowledge of earlier traditions is apparent in modern theological dictionary and encyclopaedia definitions, which neglect earlier connotations of the term. Secondly, innocence is a problematic theological term. Aside from doctrinal disputes and uncertainties (or perhaps underlying them) there is a problem of semantics. Innocence has a Latin root and therefore stands at least one remove from the original scriptural languages of Hebrew and Greek. This makes it difficult to assess theological treatments of innocence, which are rooted in scriptural sources. In addition, the semantic range of innocence makes it almost impossible to establish a precise concept. The first problem is what this chapter in a small way seeks to address. The second problem is more an opportunity, since it opens up the rich semantic field of innocence to interpretation.

Issues and Associations in Modern Theology

Shifting cultural contexts have shaped the changing status of innocence in modern theology. Definitions in encyclopaedias of Christian ethics over the last century reveal a dramatic shift in interpretation. At the close of the long nineteenth century, Robert Ottley in the *Encyclopaedia of Christian Ethics*

---

[1] See e.g. Philippe Ariès, *Centuries of Childhood*, trans. Robert Baldick (London: Jonathan Cape, 1962); Jean Delumeau, *History of Paradise: The Garden of Eden in Myth and Tradition* (New York: Continuum, 1995); Gerard P. Luttikhuizen, (ed.), *Paradise Interpreted: Representations of Biblical Paradise in Judaism and Christianity* (Leiden: Brill, 1999); Michael E. Stone, *A History of the Literature of Adam and Eve* (Atlanta, Ga.: Scholars Press, 1992).

identified innocence as a peculiarly Christian quality, a 'characteristic grace of Christians'. This was essentially innocence as the grace of a pure heart, which was 'practically equivalent to that simplicity or singleness of mind which springs from whole-hearted and entire devotion to God'. Ottley traced this definition through a broadly consistent Latin tradition, illustrated by the work of Tertullian, Augustine of Hippo, Lactantius and a putative sermon of Bernard of Clairvaux's. He also drew heavily on contemporary devotion to describe innocence as an aspect of mature Christian living, notably the sermons of John Henry Newman, John Illingworth and Richard Rainy. [23]

By the 1960s, innocence as an idyllic feature of the Christian life had all but disappeared. Ian Henderson's influential entry in the *New Dictionary of Christian Ethics* provided the model for later encyclopaedia definitions of innocence.[4] Henderson drew a line under the past. He stated that 'older theology tended to identify innocence and perfection, to see in Aristotle the ruins of an Adam', whereas modern theology, exemplified by F.R. Tennant's *Concept of Sin* (1912), recognised the stages of moral development and humanity's ongoing vulnerability to temptation.[5] Henderson thought that innocence had been transformed from an absolute and static perfection to a limited and mutable sinlessness, following Tennant's definition of sinlessness as 'always relative to the capacity of the growing and expanding subject'.[6]

Henderson's assertion that there was a dramatic departure from tradition in modern theologies of innocence rests not just on Tennant but also on the existentialist theology of Søren Kierkegaard. Kierkegaard did not abandon the traditional narrative of Edenic innocence but interpreted it so that the Fall was necessary for existence and the exercise of freedom. Interestingly, while Tennant wrote about the limits of innocence, he stopped short of identifying

---

[2]   Robert L. Ottley, 'Innocence', in *The Encyclopaedia of Religion and Ethics*, ed. James Hastings et al. (Edinburgh: T.&T. Clark, 1914), vol. 7, 329a–330a.

[3]   John Henry Newman, 'The State of Innocence', in *Parochial and Plain Sermons* (London: Rivintons, 1868), vol. 5, no. 8; id., 'Ignorance of Evil', in *Parochial and Plain Sermons*, vol. 8, no. 18; John R. Illingworth, *University and Catholic Sermons* (London: Macmillan, 1893), no. 7; Richard Rainy, 'The Child Element in Christianity', in *Sojourning with God and Other Sermons* (London: Hodder & Stoughton, 1902), no. 9.

[4]   Cf. D.P. Kingdon, 'Innocence', in David J. Atkinson and David H. Field (eds), *New Dictionary of Christian Ethics and Pastoral Theology* (Leicester: Inter-Varsity Press, 1995), 490a–491a; John Deigh, 'Innocence', in Lawrence C. Becker and Charlotte B. Becker (eds), *Encyclopaedia of Ethics* (2nd edn, New York: Routledge, 2001), vol. 2, 856b–858b.

[5]   Ian Henderson, 'Innocence', in James F. Childress and John Macquarrie (eds), *The New Dictionary of Christian Ethics*, (London: SCM, 1986), 302b–303a.

[6]   F.R. Tennant, *The Concept of Sin* (Cambridge: Cambridge University Press, 1912), 38.

Defining Innocence 27

innocence with ignorance and distinguished limited perfection from the child's blameless ignorance.[7] Kierkegaard, by contrast, did equate innocence with ignorance through a psychological retelling of the story of Eden. His innocence was a 'state of anxiety' where the vertiginous idea of the possibility of freedom compelled humanity to fall towards finitude. Henderson saw Kierkegaard's work as a 'positive' alternative to traditional theology, because it highlighted that innocence is always already past and gone and so can only be expressed in abstract terms or in the pluperfect tense, as irrelevant to human experience.[8]

The representative status of Henderson's definition is evident in other works of modern theology. Kelsey's *Eccentric Existence* defines perfection in a manner that echoes Henderson's dual definition of innocence. Kelsey associates pre-modern notions of perfection with the Edenic 'state of innocence', in which Adam and Eve as historically actual beings existed in a state of perfect freedom lacking nothing. Modern 'romanticist, existentialist, and psychological theories of the self' turn this perfection into a state of 'inexperience', or Paul Tillich's 'dreaming innocence', an echo of Kierkegaard's state of anxiety. This origin is 'hardly "being" at all': it is an amoral state that precedes the fall into experience and the process towards fully actualised perfection.[9] In this account of two opposing theologies, of original perfection and original inexperience, the traditional story of original perfection is associated with an oppressive Augustinian ideal of lost and unattainable innocence. In the old theology, humanity will always and inevitably fall short of innocence through sin. In place of this, Kelsey argues that perfection is found in quotidian existence. He abandons Genesis and draws a model for 'finite human perfection' from the book of Job.[10] Kelsey's redefinition of perfection, a term often synonymous with innocence, illustrates the dramatic impact of the apparent shift in interpretation of innocence for modern theology. However, it will be argued that the modern interpretations summarised by Henderson rest on an overly simplistic reading of the 'old theology'.

Ottley's definition was not only rooted in the Latin tradition but was also a product of its immediate intellectual context, illustrating a Romantic interpretation of Christian innocence. His innocence is easily associated with a nineteenth-century glorification of childhood, being defined through Christ's exhortation to childlikeness in Matthew 18.3, Mark 10.15 and Luke 18.7, as 'the childlikeness, the simplicity, which our Lord requires in the citizens of His Kingdom'.[11] In light

---

[7] Ibid. 30–31.

[8] Henderson, 'Innocence', 303a.

[9] Kelsey, *Eccentric Existence*, 205–7.

[10] Ibid. 300–301.

[11] Ottley, 'Innocence', 329.

of the growing scepticism of the Romantic ideal of the child discussed in the Introduction, this innocence became associated with idealism, sentimentalism and anti-intellectualism. An examination of Ottley's sources shows that such charges are not entirely baseless. For example, although Illingworth stated that innocence was 'obviously a relative term', his tone presented it as an ideal holiness: 'the grace of those who have loved God at first sight, and have never fallen away from that first love'. He veered close to anti-intellectualism by describing innocence as an imaginative intuition that is opposed to the secular sin of curiosity.[12] Illingworth gestured towards sentimentalism when describing 'the peculiar effluence which radiates from innocent souls ... their flesh a sacrament, their voice a sermon, their glance a revelation of the spiritual world'.[13] Similarly, Newman defined Christian innocence as a recapitulation of the lost innocence of Eden in childhood, which is like Adam in being 'simple, inartificial, inexperienced in evil, unreasoning, uncalculating, ignorant of the future, or (as men now speak) unintellectual'. He wrote eloquently about the irrevocable loss of Eden and drew a 'mysterious real connexion between the garden of Eden and our childhood'.[14] In modern theology, the child as a model of Christian innocence has continued to be influential in Roman Catholic theologies of childhood, inspired by the childlike figures and works of Saint Thérèse of Lisieux, G.K. Chesterton, Charles Péguy and Georges Bernanos.[15]

Tenannt, writing two years before Ottley, was essentially disenchanted with this vision of innocence. Instead, he adopted a limited innocence that drew on the theories of developmental psychology and was triggered by the Freudian challenge to the myth of childhood sexual innocence.[16] However, Tennant's limited innocence was not an inferior perfection. The passage which Henderson cites is part of a broader discussion of the sinlessness of Christ which is both

---

[12]   Illingworth, *University and Catholic Sermons*, 107–8.

[13]   Ibid. 112, 113.

[14]   Newman, 'State of Innocence', 102–3.

[15]   See Karl Rahner, 'Ideas for a Theology of Childhood', *Theological Investigations* (London: Darton, Longman & Todd, 1971), vol. 8, 33–50; Mary Ann Hinsdale, '"Infinite Openness to the Infinite": Karl Rahner's Contribution to Modern Catholic Thought on the Child', in Marcia J. Bunge (ed.), *The Child in Christian Thought* (Grand Rapids, Mich.: Eerdmans, 2001), 406–45; Hans Urs von Balthasar, 'Jesus as Child and His Praise of the Child', trans. Adrian Walker, *Communio* 22/4 (1995), 625–34; John Saward, *The Way of the Lamb: The Spirit of Childhood and the End of the Age* (Edinburgh: T.&T. Clark, 1999); for a Protestant example, see Jürgen Moltmann, 'Child and Childhood as Metaphors of Hope', *TT* 56/4 (2000), 592–603.

[16]   Sigmund Freud, *On Sexuality: Three Essays on the Theory of Sexuality and Other Works*, ed. Angela Richards (London: Penguin, 1977).

human and divine, developmental and perfect.[17] Developmental innocence may be limited but, as D.P. Kingdon states, it also denotes the potential for growth and so is an expansive concept.[18] In place of the ideal of childhood innocence, which was now seen as a regressive delusion, a new theological definition of innocence emerged that identified innocence not with absolute perfection but with moral limitation.

While not necessarily dismissed altogether, innocence has been increasingly circumscribed by deconstructionist critiques and has become a despised and neglected theological concept.[19] These transformations can be linked to Freudian critiques and to a Nietzschean 'hermeneutics of suspicion' towards claims to innocence. Nietzsche considered declarations of innocence to be the result of a denial of responsibility and ignorance of oneself.[20] His hermeneutics of suspicion has been appropriated by political theologies that critique claims to innocence on the grounds that they are invariably false, that they adopt a feigned ignorance or helplessness to deny responsibility or that they are attempts to preserve power and assuage feelings of guilt by externalising evil.[21] In feminist theologies, innocence has been identified with an oppressive idealisation of femininity. Women's acceptance of an ideal of passive feminine innocence automatically confers guilt, because it involves an abdication of responsibility.[22]

---

[17] See Tennant, *The Concept of Sin*, 1–2, 7–9, 13, 17, 37–8.

[18] Kingdon, 'Innocence', 490b.

[19] See e.g. Rollo May, *Power and Innocence: A Search for the Sources of Violence* (New York: Norton, 1972); Peter Johnson, *Politics, Innocence, and the Limits of Goodness* (London: Routledge, 1988); Marc H. Ellis, *Beyond Innocence and Redemption: Confronting the Holocaust and Israeli Power: Creating a Moral Future for the Jewish People* (San Francisco: Harper & Row, 1990).

[20] Friedrich Nietzsche, *On the Genealogy of Morals: A Polemic*, I §11, III §19, trans. D. Smith (Oxford: Oxford University Press, 1996).

[21] See Andrew Shanks, *Against Innocence: Gillian Rose's Reception and Gift of Faith* (London: SCM, 2008), ix–xii, 12, 178 n. 7; Rowan Williams, *The Truce of God* (London: Collins, 1983), 110–13; Allan Aubrey Boesak, *Farewell to Innocence: A Socio-Ethical Study on Black Theology and Black Power* (Maryknoll, NY: Orbis, 1974), 1–8.

[22] See Angela West, *Deadly Innocence: Feminism and the Mythology of Sin* (London: Mowbray, 1995), xiii–xviii; Alistair I. McFadyen, *Bound to Sin: Abuse, Holocaust, and the Christian Doctrine of Sin* (Cambridge: Cambridge University Press, 2000), 137–44; Rita Nakashima Brock, 'Losing Your Innocence but not Your Hope', in Maryanne Stevens (ed.), *Reconstructing the Christ Symbol: Essays in Feminist Christology* (New York: Paulist Press, 1993), 30–53; for a summary of the critical debate on an influential model of feminine innocence, virginity in Victorian literature, see F. Elizabeth Gray, *Christian and Lyric Tradition in Victorian Women's Poetry* (Abingdon: Routledge, 2010), 91.

Hence, the modern transformation of innocence is in these areas a diminution of its status and significance.

Reclaiming Innocence: Ways Forward

Beyond these transformations in modern understandings of innocence, there are emerging attempts to reclaim the term for theologies of childhood and literary criticism. Despite the ongoing supremacy of developmental theories in theologies of childhood, there are calls for the rehabilitation of a positive notion of childlike innocence. Marcia Bunge and John Wall, for example, have attempted to complexify the contradictory myth of the child as either an innocent angel or a demonic reprobate.[23] Through a more nuanced description of childhood, they hope to give innocence its proper place.[24] David Hadley Jensen's use of the phrase 'graced vulnerability' to describe childhood demonstrates a veiled movement towards a theology of childlike innocence without recourse to the term.[25] This phrase avoids the suggestion that children are born innocent but also defines children primarily in terms of their openness to harm, thereby implicitly associating 'graced vulnerability', or innocence, with suffering. Much more explicit is Robert A. Davis' recent argument for the re-examination and restoration of the idea of the innocence of childhood. Davis argues for the diversity and complexity of 'lost histories of innocence', which include the 'Renaissance poetic theologies' of Traherne and Vaughan. This book contributes to Davis' project to unearth part of the 'wider and more ancient

---

[23] See Marina Warner, *Managing Monsters: Six Myths of Our Time* (London: Vintage, 1994), xv.

[24] Marcia Bunge, 'The Child, Religion, and the Academy: Developing Robust Theological and Religious Understandings of Children and Childhood', *JR* 86/4 (2006), 549–79; John Wall, 'Fallen Angels: A Contemporary Christian Ethical Ontology of Childhood', *International Journal of Practical Theology* 8/2 (2004), 160–84; on the difficulty of defining childhood, see Michael O'Loughlin, 'The Curious Subject of the Child', in Michael O'Loughlin and Richard T. Johnson (eds), *Imagining Children Otherwise: Theoretical and Critical Perspectives on Childhood Subjectivity* (New York: Peter Lang, 2010), 209.

[25] David Hadley Jensen, *Graced Vulnerability: A Theology of Childhood* (Cleveland, O.: Pilgrim Press, 2005); on broader developments in the theology of childhood, see Jerome Berryman, 'Children and Christian Theology: A New/Old Genre', *Religious Studies Review* 33/2 (2007), 103–11.

historical grammar of innocence'.[26] However, it is not confined to the child, but listens to the polyphonic voices of innocence in Traherne's works.

There is a growing historical awareness of the theme of innocence in literary studies. Carl E. Findley III charts a brief history of innocence in the introduction to his dissertation on innocence in the modern novel. His survey of innocence from Hebraic texts to Aquinas provides a useful introduction to the broader history of Christian innocence but glosses over its early association with Eden and childhood, which he identifies with late medieval scholasticism.[27] In the absence of current scholarship on the history of innocence, Findley is forced to turn back to Ottley's 1914 definition to find an account of earlier Christian tradition. He sidesteps post-Romantic scepticism by unearthing a 'little known counter-narrative' of innocence, which views it not as an Edenic, childlike or virginal state of perfection prior to the acquisition of knowledge but rather as an exceptional virtue.[28] Findley's assessment comes from Lactantius, who cites patience and innocence as the 'greatest virtues'.[29]

This book explores a similar counter-narrative of innocence, which is not tied to ignorance and naïveté but is a mature state of the soul to be sought for and preserved. However, the innocence of Thomas Traherne is not precisely a virtue. It might be better described as the condition of virtue, its apprehension, affection, intention and its goal. Following Jensen one might call Traherne's a 'graced innocence' that is constituted by God's merciful relating to humanity. While Eden and childhood remain important in Traherne's works, this project explores how alternative discourses of innocence are integrated with more conventionally recognised themes.

Translating the Scriptural Sources: תָּמִים, ἀκέραιος and *Innocentia*

The meaning of innocence rests on uncertain ground. This is partly due to ambiguous etymologies which have coloured its interpretation. The popular association of innocence with ignorance or naïveté might be linked to a false etymology that defines innocence as *in-gnocens* (unknowing), as opposed

---

[26]   Robert A. Davis, 'Brilliance of a Fire: Innocence, Experience and the Theory of Childhood', *Journal of Philosophy of Education* 45/2 (2011), 379–97.

[27]   Carl E. Findley III, 'Perfecting Adam: The Perils of Innocence in the Modern Novel' (PhD thesis: University of Chicago, 2011), 9–55.

[28]   Ibid. 2.

[29]   Lactantius, *The Divine Institutes*, VI 18, trans. William Fletcher, ANF 7 (Buffalo, NY: T.&T. Clark, 1886).

32   *Boundless Innocence in Thomas Traherne's Poetic Theology*

to the proper etymology of *in-nocens* (harmless).[30] The etymological waters are muddied further when one considers translations from Greek into Latin. According to the nineteenth-century biblical scholar Robert Trench, the Latin etymology of innocence as harmlessness may itself rest on a false etymology of the Greek ἀκέραιος (*akeraios*). Biblical translators rendered this term 'harmless' based on an etymology that defined it as ἀ-κέρας (*a-keras*) or 'without a horn'. The proper meaning of ἀκέραιος is something that has an 'absence of foreign admixture', giving it connotations of integrity, purity and simplicity rather than harmlessness.[31]

There is a large semantic range within the scriptural sources of Christian innocence which span the Hebrew Bible, Septuagint and Greek New Testament. In the Hebrew Bible alone, וְיִקָּיֹן (*niqqayon*) encompasses senses of freedom, exemption from guilt, acquittal, purity, cleanness and whiteness, as in Genesis 20:5: 'in the integrity of my heart and innocency of my hands have I done this'. The term קְיִדַצ (*tsaddiq*), signifies righteousness and justice, as in Job 22:19, which through the classic parallelism of Hebrew poetry associates innocence with righteousness: 'The *righteous* see it, and are glad: and the *innocent* laugh them to scorn'. In the same book, the term םֹתּ (*tam*) denotes integrity, soundness, wholeness, blamelessness and perfection, as in Job 1:8: 'there is none like him in the earth, a *perfect* and an upright man'. Finally, רָשָׁי (*yashar*) carries connotations of uprightness, as in Proverbs 16.17: 'the highway of the *upright* is to depart from evil'.[32] The Greek New Testament terms translated as 'innocent' include words that mean pure, as in without stain or like refined gold, unravaged, unharmed, intact, incorruptible and blameless but also guileless, simple, harmless and, in the Septuagint, even ignorant.[33]

Findley's summary of the history of innocence makes a distinction between the Hebraic religio-moral sense of the term, the juridical concerns of classical literature and the meekness and guilelessness of Christian innocence.[34] Current biblical scholarship resists such distinctions, noting rather the common judicial,

---

[30]   For a comprehensive etymology, see C.T. Onions et al. (eds), *The Oxford Dictionary of English Etymology* (rev. edn, Oxford: Oxford University Press, 1969), s.v. 'Innocent', 476.

[31]   Robert C. Trench, *Synonyms of the New Testament: The Two Parts in One* (rev. edn, London and Cambridge: Macmillan, 1865), 197.

[32]   Willem A. VanGemeren (ed.), *New International Dictionary of Old Testament Theology and Exegesis* (5 vols, Carlisle: Paternoster, 1996), vol. 3, #5927, #7405; vol. 4, #9462; vol. 2, #3837.

[33]   G. Kittel and G. Friedrich (eds.), *Theological Dictionary of the New Testament*, trans G.W. Bromily (10 vols, Grand Rapids, Mich.: Eerdmans, 1964–71), vol. 1, 209–10, 115–6, 356–7; vol. 3, 482.

[34]   Findley, 'Perfecting Adam', 1.

ethical and cultic senses which draw the traditions together. Nevertheless, the eschatological connotations of innocence apparently belong only to the New Testament letters, and the notion of innocence as righteousness belongs to Gospel descriptions of Christ.[35] The peculiar Septuagint connotation of ignorance is striking, as it suggests the possible influence of classical thought upon the Greek texts. The righteous and upright innocence of the Hebrew scriptures also provides a helpful contrast to modern associations of innocence with weakness and vulnerability. Placing these different terms alongside each other highlights the paradoxical significations of innocence that are held together in the scriptural sources of Christian thought. In these texts, innocence might be both a privative freedom from guilt or punishment and a positive righteousness or justice. It might denote a purity that has cultic ritual connotations and a guileless, simple or harmless quality of the regenerate Christian.

In English, the Latinate term 'innocence' is rooted in the Christian tradition. Translations from the Vulgate Bible contain among the earliest recorded uses of the term in modern English.[36] The New Testament of the King James Bible, Traherne's main scriptural source, broadly follows the Latin text in its uses of 'innocence' in line with earlier English translations of the Vulgate. Both the KJV and the Vulgate translate ἀβλάβεια (*ablabeia*) (following Cicero and Augustine), ἀθῷος, ἄκακος (*athoos, akakos*) and ἀκέραιος as 'innocent' or *innocens*. These terms cover connotations of blamelessness, purity, righteousness and simplicity.[37] There are three places in the New Testament where the Vulgate's *innocens* is rendered differently in the KJV. In Hebrews 7.26, the term is rendered 'harmless' in the English, in Matthew 12.7 it is rendered 'guiltless' and in Romans 16.19 is translated as 'simple'. To do justice to the influence of this tradition on seventeenth-century devotion, these connotations of harmlessness, guiltlessness and simplicity should all be taken into account. Further divergences between the Vulgate and the KJV appear in the Hebrew Bible translation, where *innocentia* in the Vulgate is commonly rendered in the KJV as 'integrity' and sometimes as

---

[35]   Abraham Smith, 'Innocence', in Katherine Doob Sakenfeld (ed.), *The New Interpreter's Dictionary of the Bible* (5 vols, Nashville: Abingdon, 2009), vol. 3, 46a.

[36]   See e.g. Richard Rolle, *The Psalter or Psalms of David, and Certain Canticles*, ed. and trans. H.R. Bramley (Oxford: Clarendon, 1884), Ps. 17.28, cited in *OED*, s.v. 'Innocent'; *The Earlier Version of the Wycliffite Bible*, ed. Conrad Lindberg (Stockholm: Almquist and Wiksell, 1959–97), Ps. 23(24).4; 1 Sam. 26.9; Prov. 22.3; Matt. 12.7; Rom 16.18; Heb. 7.26, cited in *OED*, s.v. 'Innocent'.

[37]   Robert Young, *An Analytical Concordance to the Holy Bible* (8th edn, London: Lutterworth, 1961), 517; Theodore A. Bergren and Alfred Schmoller, *A Latin–Greek Index of the Vulgate New Testament: Based on Alfred Schmoller's Handkonkordanz Zum Griechishen Neuen Testament*, Resources for Biblical Study 26 (Atlanta, Ga.: Scholars Press, 1991), 82.

34   *Boundless Innocence in Thomas Traherne's Poetic Theology*

'uprightness' or 'perfection'.[38] The English translation seems to adopt a difference in tone between Hebrew Bible and New Testament innocence, with the former implying an upright moral status and the latter suggesting a Christlike quality. The scriptural sources alone thus provide a variety of rich connotations for innocence.

From all this it is clear that it is impossible to clearly define innocence. Psalm 37.37 (Vulgate/Douay-Rheims, 36.37), 'Mark the perfect man', provides a further example of the fluidity of the term. The original term here is תָּם (*tam*). The Vulgate translates it as *simplicitatem*, the Douay-Rheims rendering of the Vulgate into English translates it as 'innocent', whereas the KJV adopts the term 'perfect'. From another perspective, while the single Latin term *innocentia* is translated in various ways, English also translates several Latin terms as 'innocence'. Ottley's encyclopaedia definition lists three Latin terms as equivalent to the English 'innocent': *simplex, sine dolo* and *innocens*, carrying connotations of simplicity and harmlessness.[39]

The various meanings of innocence carry important theological implications. Used in a compound noun, the common Vulgate phrase *sanguinem innocentem* (from דָּם יָקִי [*dam naqi*]) or 'innocent blood' appears 17 times in the Hebrew Bible (or Old Testament) and cements a strong link between innocence, suffering and persecution.[40] Innocence cannot therefore be simplistically equated with optimism or happiness. This phrase's one appearance in the New Testament (Matthew 27.24) refers to Christ, who is thereby associated with the sacrifices of the Hebrew Bible.[41] Curiously, the Latin translation of this verse distinguishes between earthly innocence and Christ's divine righteousness by describing his blood as *sanguinem justum* instead. The English re-establishes the link between Christ and other sacrificial innocents in translating this verse as 'innocent blood'.

The most common use of the term *innocens* (plural *innocentes*) in the Vulgate denotes a status of freedom from responsibility, guilt or shame before

---

[38]   The Vulgate term *innocentia/innocentiam* is translated as 'integrity' in the KJV in Job 2.3; 27.5; Ps. 8.9; 25.1; 25.11; 41.12; 77.2. In Ps. 84.11 it is translated as 'them that walk uprightly' and in Ps. 101.2 as 'I will walk within my house with a perfect heart'.

[39]   Ottley, 'Innocence', 329a.

[40]   In the Vulgate, variations on the phrase *sanguinem innocentem* appear in Deut. 21.8; 27.25; 2 Kings 2.31; 24.4; Ps. 93.21; 105.38; Isa. 59.7; Jer. 2.34; 7.6; 19.4; 22.3; 22.17; 26.15; Joel 3.19; Jon. 1.14; 1 Macc. 1.8; 2 Macc. 1.39. Consider also the reference to *lacrimus innocentum* in Eccles. 4.1, which the KJV translates as 'the tears of [such as were] oppressed'.

[41]   VanGemeren, *New International Dictionary of Old Testament Theology and Exegesis*, vol. 3, #5927.

society and God.[42] This innocence is a title that is conferred in community and through relationship. This is not a natural but a relational innocence, and it is the first recorded English usage of the word.[43] The Vulgate tradition of Christian innocence thus includes an association of innocence with suffering and an understanding of innocence in relational terms, which subverts some of the optimistic and solipsistic associations of innocence in Traherne's work.

Tied to the Latin heritage of Christian thought, innocence is perhaps a peculiarly Western problem. It is also a perennial and persistent theme within devotional literature, which makes it a problem worth solving. Rather than a single conceptual definition, innocence operates through what Kelsey calls 'functional equivalents' of the term.[44] Although the primary meaning of innocence in the Latin sense is harmlessness, it also carries connotations from the Hebrew and Greek traditions of righteousness, blamelessness, simplicity and guilelessness. Innocence belongs equally to a variety of contexts: the cultic ritual of the temple, especially the purifying water and the sacrificial altar; the declarations of the law court; the private voice of conscience and the heart lifted in worship and devotion. It carries both positive and privative connotations of action and suffering, righteousness and freedom from sin. Due to the semantic complexity of the term, its meaning is best determined through its usage in context and through its grammar, tone, tense and genre.

Foundations of Seventeenth-Century Innocence: The Latin Tradition

The Latin tradition of Christian innocence, on which seventeenth-century ideas were based, presents Christian innocence not only as humanity's original state but as an ongoing part of the life of faith. Deeper than moral rectitude but less abstract than ideal perfection, this is the Christian innocence which Tertullian asserted in order to defend Christians against persecution. By *nos ergo soli innocentes* (therefore we alone are innocent), Tertullian meant not only that Christians were guiltless of offences that they were commonly accused of but also

---

[42] Compare the Vulgate version of Jer. 46.28, *nec quasi innocenti parcam tibi*, with the KJV, 'yet will I not leave thee wholly unpunished'. Innocence as a status appears in Gen. 20:5; Ps. 19.20; Job 33.9; Jer. 2.35; Matt. 27.24. For innocence as a title given to the 'innocent', see Vulgate, Deut. 21.9; Prov. 13.6; Ps. 14.5; 17.26; 24.21; 25.6; 72.13; Job 9.23; Eccles. 4.1; Jer. 25.29; Dan. 13.53; 2 Macc. 4.47; Matt. 12.7.

[43] See *OED*, s.v. 'Innocent' (B.*n*.1.a), citing *Vices and Virtues* (*c*.1200), 79.

[44] Kelsey, *Eccentric Existence*, 987.

that they possessed a revealed knowledge of goodness and a divine righteousness through which they sought to live in perfect innocence.[45]

The Latin discourse of Christian innocence was born out of persecution, but it found its home in praise. Lactantius' *Divine Institutes* spoke of innocence primarily with respect to the true worship and proper sacrifice of an upright spirit and pure heart, 'For that sacred and surpassing majesty requires from man nothing more than innocence alone'.[46] According to Lactantius, the innocence of the just is not feigned or self-justifying. Instead, he encourages humility and penitence, 'lest any one should chance to place confidence in his integrity and innocence'.[47] Innocence in Lactantius' theology marries the two harmonious voices of praise and penitence as holy conversation with God.

Lactantius also refers to innocence with respect to the ethical life. In this context, it is the harmlessness which refuses to injure others, even in vengeance.[48] This activity is not only just but wise, since to harm others is sinful and 'the wise man abstains from sin'.[49] There is therefore a connection between wisdom and innocence in this theology. Lactantius presents an innocence that is at once weak and powerful, since the good suffer harm without impunity, but are invulnerable to the purgative flame.[50] Innocence is elusive because it is rare, but it is also fundamental since humanity was created for innocence.[51]

Innocence in this view is both a condition for, and a goal of, human flourishing. As Lactantius says, if people were innocent they would be happy and the law of God would rule in the realm of perfect innocence.[52] This paradoxical Latin tradition simultaneously locates innocence at the heart of Christian living and expresses wonder at its impenetrable glory. The richness of the Latin tradition is seen in Traherne's poetic theology of innocence, which also plays the notes of suffering and felicity, praise and penitence, strength and weakness, wisdom and simplicity, calling others to enact an innocence that is true to humanity's origin, essence and vocation.

---

[45] Tertullian, *Apology* 44 §§1–2, in *Apology and De Spectaculis; with Octavius*, trans. T.R. Glover, LCL (Cambridge, Mass.: Harvard University Press, 1931).

[46] Lactantius, 'Of the Worship of the True God, and of Innocency, and of the Worship of False Gods', *Divine Institutes*, VI 1.

[47] Ibid. VI 25.

[48] Ibid. VI 18.

[49] Ibid.

[50] Ibid. III 17, VII 21.

[51] Ibid. V 7, VI 19.

[52] Ibid. V 8.

Defining Innocence 37

Thomas Wilson's *Complete Christian Dictionary* and Seventeenth-Century Devotion

The Latin tradition endured in seventeenth-century devotion. Dictionary definitions followed the Latin in identifying innocence primarily as harmlessness. Francis Gouldman, for example, defined *innocens* as 'Harmless, having no harm or evil in it: that hurteth not'.[53] However, innocence was much more than harmlessness. Vavasor Powell, for example, adopted a threefold definition of the 'innocent' as harmless, guiltless and righteous: as 'One that doth no harm', 'free from a particular *guilt*', '[A] righteous person' and 'Innocent'.[54]

Wilson's *A Complete Christian Dictionary* provides a useful encapsulation of themes in contemporary theologies of innocence. Wilson's was the first dictionary of the Bible in English. It drew on the broader Christian tradition, being explicitly derivative of the 'most approved Authours, both Ancient and Modern', especially the sixteenth-century Catholic work by Petrus Ravanellus, *Bibliotheca sacra*.[55] The dictionary can be considered relatively representative for its period, being first published in 1612 but expanded by other hands, revised and reprinted 11 times in the seventeenth century alone. Given the patchwork construction of this work, Wilson's Reformed theology need not be considered overly determinative, although it should not be ignored.[56] This work had a comparable aim to *Commentaries of Heaven*'s project of heavenly redefinition, as Edmund Calamy described it as a 'Divine Dictionary, *teaching us the* language *of the* holy Ghost *in our own* native tongue'.[57]

---

[53]   Francis Gouldman, *A Copious Dictionary in Three Parts* (London: John Field, 1664), 818.

[54]   Vavasor Powell, 'Innocent', in *A New and Useful Concordance to the Holy Bible* (London, 1671).

[55]   Thomas Wilson, *A Complete Christian Dictionary*, ed. J. Bagwell and A. Simson (7th edn, London: E. Cotes, 1661), title page.

[56]   On Wilson and the dictionary, see Ian M. Green, *The Christian's ABC: Catechisms and Catechizing in England, c.1530–1740* (Oxford: Oxford University Press, 1996), 746–7; Stephen Wright, 'Wilson, Thomas (1562/3–1622)', *ODNB*; Kathleen Curtin, 'Jacobean Congregations and Controversies in Thomas Wilson's *Christian Dictionary* (1612)', *Seventeenth Century* 25/2 (2010), 197–214; Leif Dixon, 'Calvinist Theology and Pastoral Reality in the Reign of King James I: The Perspective of Thomas Wilson', *Seventeenth Century* 23/2 (2008), 175.

[57]   Edmund Calamy, 'An Epistle to the Reader', in Wilson, *A Complete Christian Dictionary*, A4.

The expanded 1661 edition, the most contemporaneous with Traherne's active period of writing, has not one but three definitions of 'Innocency'.[58] None of these mentions childhood as its particular model, and all are rooted in scriptural sources (Genesis 1.26–7; 2; Psalm 26.6, 11; Psalm 7.8; Daniel 6.22). The primary definition of innocence is a 'meer voydnesse of fault, and freedome from all sin. In this estate *Adam* was created. This is perfect innocency by creation.'[59] This primary and perfect 'innocency by creation' is the original innocence of Eden. The second definition of innocence is a 'certain measure of this [first] estate in all regenerate persons, who indevour to serve God in innocency of life, having also Christs innocency imputed to them. Psalm 26.6, 11. *I will wash my hands in innocency.* This is innocency of a person restored.'[60] Innocence is not therefore confined to humanity's original estate but is an element of Christian living. Innocency of life is only a 'certain measure', a partial manifestation of an innocence that in its origin is imagined as perfect and whole. It is seen in the light of primal perfection but is characterised by the finitude of fallen humanity in a state of grace. This second innocence is twofold: the moral 'innocency of life' which the believer offers to God through holy living and the gift of grace through baptism and faith. The use of the language of imputation connects innocence with the imputed righteousness of Christ. This provides evidence of Wilson's Reformed theological leanings but more interestingly draws a link between innocence and righteousness and illustrates the centrality of Christ to theological discussions of innocence: innocence of life combines the activity of *imitatio Christi* and the passive reception of the innocence of Christ. It is both an 'indeavour' and the free gift of grace to the elect.

Wilson's third definition of innocence is 'Uprightnesse in some speciall or particular cause'. This is the innocence of 'the innocent', those who may be unjustly accused, persecuted or afflicted but who are vindicated in the sight of God and honoured in heaven. It is similar to Andrew Symson's definition of the 'innocent' as 'one that hath deserved no punishment'.[61] It is therefore a limited innocence, similar to the modern psychological and judicial readings outlined above. However, uprightness in a cause suggests more than an absence

---

[58] Note Findley uses the 1612 edition of Wilson, *A Complete Christian Dictionary* ('Perfecting Adam').

[59] Wilson, *A Complete Christian Dictionary*, 336.

[60] Ibid. 336b.

[61] 'Innocent', in Andrew Symson, *Lexicon Anglo-Graeco-Latinum Novi Testamenti, or, A Complete Alphabetical Concordance of All the Words Contained in the New Testament* (London: W. Godbid, 1658).

of particular guilt, implying also an intention towards the good. Wilson's more casuistical entry for the adjective, 'innocent', describes 'one innocency of the Act, another of the Affect'. The innocence of the affections is the desire or will for purity, the inner innocence of the spirit. Innocence of act is public but is perfected through spiritual exercise. Together they make up innocence of life. It is this latter innocence which, it will be argued, is the main concern of Traherne's poetic theology.

Wilson does not only outline the meanings of innocence in different spheres of Christian life, he also sets a standard for Christian innocence. By his definition, the 'innocent' may have Christian qualities, being 'simple and upright, without guile or malice'. They may be, in a more limited sense, 'free from some one particular fault' or, in an even more limited sense, 'free from punishment'. They may manifest righteous actions as a 'just and righteous person which liveth uprightly', or they may present a Christian meekness before persecution, being 'Harmlesse, with relation unto such as would or doe wrong them'. Of the three causes of innocence, only one is 'virtuous and acceptable to God'. The first, 'Ignorance or want of skill to doe ill', is the dovelike incapacity for sin of Matthew 10.16. 'Impotency, or want of power and meanes to perform ill' is related to the proverb, 'temperance in old age is not temperance but impotence'.[62] Only the third definition, 'Unwillingness or want of will to doe ill', is true innocence. In line with Augustine's rejection of the supposed innocence of infants, Wilson asserts that true Christian innocence is not that of ignorance or incapacity but an innocence of the will.[63]

Wilson's threefold definition draws attention to the various ways in which Traherne employs the language of innocence and the ways in which they echo the context of seventeenth-century devotion. The ensuing discussions expand on the characteristics of Wilson's Christian innocence: regeneration and recovered grace; incompleteness, limit and finitude; the combination of act and affection, activity and passivity, harmlessness and heroism. A focus on Wilson's second and third definitions forms a picture of 'graced' or regenerate innocence that complements, but is not identical with, the original innocence of Adam and Eve.[64]

---

[62] *Temperantia in senectute non est temperantia sed impotentia* (Wilson, *A Complete Christian Dictionary*, my trans.).

[63] Augustine, *Confessions*, I.7.xi, trans. Henry Chadwick (Oxford: Oxford University Press, 1991); see Martha E. Stortz, '"Where or When Was Your Servant Innocent?" Augustine on Childhood', in Bunge (ed.), *Child in Christian Thought*, 78–102.

[64] For a comparison of regenerate faith and Adam's continuance 'in the way of Legall obedience', see William Whately, *Prototypes, or, The Primarie Precedent Presidents out of the Booke of Genesis* (London, 1640), 8–9, 49–50.

Chapter 2

'Perfect innocency by creation': The Estate of Original Innocence[1]

'For the first things are the most perfect, and the Rule of them that follow': Order and Unity

Traherne's structure of the four estates of innocence, misery, grace and glory gives particular prominence to the estate of innocence. The purpose of *Commentaries of Heaven* is, for each entry, to 'see the Whole Historie of it, in its Original Nature, Object, Extent and End, in its Measures and Degrees, in its Effects and Several Estates'.[2] Within these definitions, innocence takes a foundational role. It is the measure against which misery is defined and is that which is recovered in grace and glory. Seventeen entries in *Commentaries of Heaven* contain a section on the several estates of the subject. The estate of innocence is often treated more extensively, and the subsequent estates are described primarily in comparison to it. In the entry for 'Appetite', for example, the section on 'Innocency' is over three times as long as that on 'Grace' and ten times as long as that on 'Glory'.[3] The definition for 'The Second Adam' opens with the statement: 'Tho the Estate of Man in Eden compared to that of Glory differeth as much as Infancy from perfect Manhood, yet is that Estate the Patern of our Life on Earth'.[4] The original innocence of the estate of innocence has a normative status within Traherne's account of human existence.

Within this framework, the authority of origins lends a narrative order to history that from a poetic perspective is reminiscent of the order and unity of an Aristotelian epic. Aristotle's *Poetics* defined epic as 'a single piece of action, whole and complete in itself, with a beginning, middle and end, so that like a

---

[1] An earlier version of this chapter was published as Elizabeth S. Dodd, '"Perfect Innocency By Creation" in the Writings of Thomas Traherne', *LT* 29/2 (2015): 216–36 (reprinted with permission of Oxford University Press).

[2] Traherne, 'Abhorrence', *Commentaries of Heaven, Part 1*, 11.

[3] Traherne, 'Appetite', *Commentaries of Heaven, Part 2*, 152–6.

[4] Traherne, 'The Second Adam', *Commentaries of Heaven, Part 1*, 227.

single living organism it may produce its own peculiar form of pleasure'.[5] In the modern theological aesthetics of Ben Quash and Francesca Aran Murphy, this singular narrative or epic voice is associated with the indicative mood and the authoritative tone suited to the systematic exposition of theoretical concepts.[6]

Authority, unity and order are terms that seem inappropriate to Traherne's theological style. The organisation of Traherne's texts has been described as 'polyphonic' by Slawomir Wacior, Stanley Stewart has heard a double voice of subjectivity and objectivity in Traherne's poetry of the child and the adult, and several scholars have noted the ambiguous structure of the poems of the Dobell manuscript and the collection of meditations on the world, soul and God, *Centuries of Meditations*.[7] Tanya Zhelezcheva has gone so far as to interpret Traherne's serial failure to finish a work as a distinctive 'non-finito genre'.[8] The ambiguous, sometimes confused, often reworked and even abandoned structures of Traherne's works seem anathema to the order of an epic or narrative theology.

Nevertheless, just as in Aristotelian poetics 'beauty consists in magnitude and ordered arrangement', so does Traherne manifest a concern with order and right relation.[9] An inclination towards ordered unity is evident in a repetitive, recapitulatory and digressive style that reflects the comprehensiveness of the

---

[5] Aristotle, *The Poetics*, 1459b (XXIV 6–7), trans. W. Hamilton Fyfe, LCL (revd edn, Cambridge, Mass.: Harvard University Press, 1982); Kelsey adopts a more systematic approach to epic comprehensiveness in the triple-helix narrative structure of *Eccentric Existence* (see 10–11).

[6] Ben Quash, *Theology and the Drama of History*, Cambridge Studies in Christian Doctrine (Cambridge: Cambridge University Press, 2005), 41–2; Francesca Aran Murphy, '"Whence Comes this Love as Strong as Death?": Rosenzweig's "Philosophy as Narrative" in Hans Urs von Balthasar's Theo-Drama', *LT* 7/3 (1993), 236; cf. Aristotle, *Poetics*, 1459a (XXIII 1).

[7] Slawomir Wacior, *Strategies of Literary Communication in the Poetry of Thomas Traherne* (Lublin: Redakcja Wydawnictw Kul, 1990), 58–61, 204–5; Stanley Stewart, *The Expanded Voice: The Art of Thomas Traherne* (San Marino, Calif.: Huntingdon Library, 1970), 212; for different assessments of the Dobell poems' structure, see Dobell, 'Introduction', in Traherne, *Poetical Works*, lxx; Denonain, *Thèmes et formes de la poésie 'métaphysique'*, 255–7; John Malcolm Wallace, 'Thomas Traherne and the Structure of Meditation', *ELH* 25/2 (1958), 80–81; Arthur L. Clements, *The Mystical Poetry of Thomas Traherne* (Cambridge, Mass.: Harvard University Press, 1969), 61.

[8] Tanya Zhelezcheva, 'The Poetics of the Incomplete in the Works of Thomas Traherne (ca. 1638–1674)' (PhD thesis: Northeastern University, 2011).

[9] Aristotle, *Poetics*, 1451a (VII 8–9).

Renaissance epic.[10] It is apparent in a totalising tendency that is found in the projects of universal synthesis: *The Kingdom of God*, *Commentaries of Heaven*, *Centuries of Meditations* and *The Ceremonial Law*. All of these works present a vision of the whole in the light of infinity, albeit only in aspiration, as all remained unfinished, being most likely curtailed by the finitude of death.

The numerous cross-references in *Commentaries of Heaven* and *Commonplace Book* betray a desire to draw everything into one by exhibiting the interconnectedness of 'Al Things'.[11] For example, *Commentaries of Heaven*'s entry for 'Atheist' cross-references, and thereby unites, 'Bounty, Blessedness, Goodness, Wisdom, Reason, Providence, Glory, Liberty, Soul, Comprehension, Gods Works, Ways, Laws, Counsels, &c. ... Lov Harmony. &c'.[12] Cross-references such as these intimate the surprising conjunctions that occur within infinite unity. They form links between 'the furthest of all Words', such as 'Abilitie, Abomination, Act, Abundance, Accident ... Generation, Eternity, Bounty, GOD ... Trinity, the World, Zeal'.[13] This particular passage runs from A to Z, and groups together terms that might be considered positive such as 'Bounty', with others that might be considered negative such as 'Abomination'. Traherne's harmonious order is not therefore logical or straightforward but reflects the vibrancy of a creation that combines infinite variety into one.

Traherne's inclination towards an organic epic harmony is most evident, and most successfully implemented, in universal themes such as felicity, love, desire, infinity and innocence.[14] He frequently describes the soul, for example,

---

[10] For a summary of seventeenth-century epic as 'comprehensive', 'transcendental' and 'diffuse', see Joan M. Webber, *Milton and His Epic Tradition* (Seattle: University of Washington Press, 1979), 3–9; on the Augustinian function of Traherne's repetitive style in approaching and reaffirming divine truth, see Louis L. Martz, *The Paradise Within: Studies in Vaughan, Traherne, and Milton* (New Haven, Conn.: Yale University Press, 1964), 43–54.

[11] See Jan Ross, 'Introduction', in *The Works of Thomas Traherne*, vol. 2, xxxii; for a catalogue of the cross-references, see ibid. 523–8. *Commonplace Book* is a thematically arranged collection of quotations and notes, bound up in the Dobell manuscript, which contains parallel entries to *Commentaries of Heaven*.

[12] See Traherne, 'Atheist', *Commentaries of Heaven, Part 2*, 329.

[13] Traherne, 'Of Acceptance in God', *Commentaries of Heaven, Part 1*, 92.

[14] Felicity has been a central theme in Traherne studies. Verena Olejniczak Lobsien reads it as an adaptation of a Plotinian *Eudaimonia* and enjoyment (*Transparency and Dissimulation: Configurations of Neoplatonism in Early Modern English Literature* [Berlin: De Gruyter, 2010], 167–74); on felicity see also Thomas O. Beachcroft, 'Traherne and the Doctrine of Felicity', *Criterion* 9 (1930), 291–307; Renée Grandvoinet, 'Thomas Traherne and the Doctrine of Felicity', *Études de lettres* 13 (1939), 164–77; M.V. Seetaraman, 'The Way of Felicity in Thomas Traherne's "Centuries" and "The Poems"', in V.S. Seturaman (ed.), *Critical Essays on English Literature: Presented to M.S. Duraiswami on the Occasion of his*

according to the Neoplatonist commonplace (which at the time was attributed to Hermes Trismegistus) of a circle whose centre is everywhere and circumference nowhere: 'an Infinit Sphere in a Centre'. Traherne uses this imagery repetitively in a variety of contexts, including in reference to the 'sphere of felicitie': the circle of belovedness, love and glory that is communion with God.[15] His repeated reference to the infinite circle provides an example of a theme and its variations which suffuses his works with a sense of and desire for infinite unity.

Themes such as these provide the centre towards which Traherne's works are magnetically drawn and the cords that bind them together. It is not fixed philosophical structures but the motive force of major themes which shape his theology. As a ruling idea, innocence expands beyond its conventional sphere, the estate of innocence, to encompass the regenerate life of faith brought to birth in baptism. Thus, while the estate of innocence may be normative, as will be seen in Chapter 4, the regenerate innocence 'of a person restored' is just as effectively essential as the original innocence of Eden.[16]

Sixty-First Birthday (Bombay: Orient Longmans, 1965), 81–104; J.J. Balakier, 'Felicitous Perceptions as the Organizing Form in Thomas Traherne's Dobell Poems and *Centuries*', *Bulletin de la Société d'études Anglo-Américaines des XVIIe et XVIIIe siècles* 26 (1988), 53–68; on love, see Brian W. Connolly, 'Knowledge and Love: Steps Toward Felicity in Thomas Traherne' (PhD thesis: University of Pittsburgh, 1966); Itrat Husain, *The Mystical Element in the Metaphysical Poets of the Seventeenth Century* (Edinburgh: Oliver & Boyd, 1948), 294–5; Paul Cefalu, *English Renaissance Literature and Contemporary Theory: Sublime Objects of Theology* (New York: Palgrave Macmillan, 2007), 141–206; on desire, see Lane, 'Thomas Traherne and the Awakening of Want'; Johnston, 'Heavenly Perspectives, Mirrors of Eternity'; on infinity, see Traherne, *Centuries of Meditations*, V 1–5; Rosalie L. Colie, 'Thomas Traherne and the Infinite: The Ethical Compromise', *HLQ* 21/1 (1957), 69–82; Marie-Dominique Garnier, 'The Mythematics of Infinity in the *Poems* and *Centuries* of T. Traherne: A Study of its Thematic Archetypes', *Cahiers Élisabéthains* 28 (1985), 61–71; on the spiritual implications of modern ideas of infinity, see Alexander Koyré, *From a Closed World to the Infinite Universe* (Baltimore, Mass.: Johns Hopkins University Press, 1957).

[15] See Traherne, *Kingdom of God*, 279; id., *Centuries of Meditations*, II 80; id., 'My Spirit', *Dobell Folio*, 27; id., 'Fullnesse', *Dobell Folio*, 31; id., 'Thoughts III', *Dobell Folio*, 70; id., 'Thoughts IV', *Dobell Folio*, 73. Marks notes the doubtful origin of the trope's attribution to Hermes Trismegistus ('Thomas Traherne and Hermes Trismegistus', 128 n. 25); for a summary of seventeenth-century usage, see Robin Small, 'Nietzsche and a Platonist Tradition of the Cosmos: Center Everywhere and Circumference Nowhere', *JHI* 44/1 (1983), 93; see also Ralph Cudworth, *The True Intellectual System of the Universe. Wherein all the Reason and Philosophy of Atheism is Confuted and its Impossibility Demonstrated* (London: for Richard Royston, 1678), 549, 569, 591; Henry More, *Philosophical Poems* (Cambridge, 1647), 193, 207, 409; Nicholas of Cusa, *On Learned Ignorance*, I.23.lxx–lxxiii, trans. Jasper Hopkins (Minneapolis, Minn.: Arthur J. Banning, 1981).

[16] Wilson, *A Complete Christian Dictionary*, 336b.

'A meer voydnesse of fault': Innocence and Primordial Chaos

Traherne clearly identifies innocence with origins, but it is not straightforward to locate this original innocence within the Christian creation narratives. The location of original innocence has obvious implications for its character and qualities. Read in the light of Genesis 1, Wilson's definition of innocence as 'meer voydnesse of fault' can be associated with original chaos and the doctrine of *creatio ex nihilo*. The reference to the void alludes to the primordial והב (*bohu*) of Genesis 1.2. This association with emptiness sees innocence in inherently privative terms. It draws attention to the apophatic Latin semantics of *innocentia* or 'harm-less-ness', a term which is defined etymologically by what it lacks. The emptiness of original innocence suggests a precariousness goodness that is never far from the vacuity of original chaos.

For Traherne, by contrast, influenced by the Hermetic translations of John Everard and by Florentine Neoplatonism, the emptiness of the void is entirely negative. He describes humanity's origin *ex nihilo* in unfavorable terms. As he states in 'The Circulation':

> Whatever's empty is accurst:
> And this doth shew that we must some Estate
> Possess, or never can communicate.[17]

Traherne does not identify the estate of innocence with the void but with the creation of the world and the acquisition of existence. Innocence is distinguished from original chaos by the attribute of communication. Communication is a feature of all created things which give and receive in constant motion. It is also indicative of the communicative nature of humanity's relationship to God, through the grace which is returned in praise.

This distinction of the estate of innocence from creation's origin in nothing is most clearly set out in Traherne's definition of the atom, where he delineates the eras of creation history as follows:

> Eternity being thus divided into Parts, the first Period from Everlasting to the Creation exhibiteth Nothing but GOD in himself. The second Period from the Creation to the Fall exhibiteth Nothing but Beauty and Innocence, the Third

---

[17]   Traherne, 'The Circulation', *Dobell Folio*, 46; cf. id., 'Empty', *Commonplace Book*, 40r 1, *Hermes Mercurious Trismegistus, His Divine Pymander, In Seventeen Books*, trans. John Everard (London, 1657), 140–44.

Period, from the Fall of Man to the Day of Judgement, is full of Mixture. The fourth and last is of Glory and Perfection.[18]

Innocence is found not in absolute origins but the second estate of creation before the Fall.

Although Traherne adopts several different models for the progress of the soul, according to this framework it would be broadly incorrect to identify his estate of innocence with a pre-existent spiritual state of the soul before a 'fall' into the body. Traherne criticism has been hitherto divided on this issue. Terry Givens, among others, has identified Traherne with a seventeenth-century revival of the perennial Platonic heresy of the spiritual pre-existence of the soul.[19] Givens identified pre-existence in Traherne's works as compatible with a notion of original and essential innocence.[20] Malcolm Day also strongly asserted Traherne's doctrine of pre-existence on the basis of his Platonic influences.[21] Other studies have been more circumspect: Harold Ridlon identifies 'at least a provocative ambivalence' in his descriptions of pre-existence.[22] Other studies deny Traherne's belief in pre-existence altogether, citing his Platonic imagery as mere poetic licence.[23] In light of the general structure of the estates, the weight of evidence seems to be toward the latter interpretation.

---

[18]   Traherne, 'Atom', *Commentaries of Heaven, Part 2*, 338.

[19]   For an example of seventeenth-century debate on the subject, see the critiques of Henry More in Edward Warren, *No Præexistence; Or, A Brief Dissertation against the Hypothesis of Humane Souls* (London: T.R., 1667); Samuel Parker, *A Free And Impartial Censure of the Platonick Philosophie* (Oxford: W. Hall, 1666).

[20]   Terry L. Givens, *When Souls Had Wings: Pre-Mortal Existence in Western Thought* (Oxford: Oxford University Press, 2010), 173–6; see also Martz, *The Paradise Within*, 30.

[21]   Malcom M. Day, 'Traherne and the Doctrine of Pre-Existence', *SP* 65 (1968), 81–97; see also Ernst Christ, *Studien zu Thomas Traherne* (Tübingen: Eugen Göbel, 1932), 24; Ernst Lehrs, *Der Rosenkreuzerische Impuls im Leben und Werk von Joachim Jundius und Thomas Traherne* (Stuttgart: Freies Geistesleben, 1962), 36–7; Stewart, *The Expanded Voice*, 172; Trimpey, 'An Analysis of Traherne's "Thoughts I"', 95; Joan Webber, *The Eloquent 'I': Style and Self in Seventeenth Century Prose* (Madison: University of Wisconsin Press, 1968), 239.

[22]   Harold Ridlon, 'The Function of the "Infant-Ey" in Traherne's Poetry', *SP* 61 (1964), 630.

[23]   See Thomas Richard Sluberski, *A Mind in Frame: The Theological Thought of Thomas Traherne, a Seventeenth Century Poet and Theologian* (Cleveland, O.: Lincoln Library Press, 2008), 86–7; Colby, 'Thomas Traherne and the Cambridge Platonists', 30; W.L. Doughty, *Studies in Religious Poetry of the Seventeenth Century* (London: Epworth Press, 1946), 152; Marcus, *Childhood and Cultural Despair*, 182; Gladys E. Willett, *Traherne (An Essay)* (Cambridge: W. Heffer & Sons, 1919), 22.

'Perfect innocency by creation'

Pre-existence presents a dualistic framework for innocence, making it a purely spiritual state separate from the body.[24] Although in some of his poems, such as 'The Salutation', Traherne implies the possibility of a pre-existent state before bodily existence, this is carefully distinguished from the estate of innocence. Pre-existence is an era before communication:

When silent I,
So many thousand thousand yeers,
Beneath the Dust did in a Chaos lie.[25]

Similarly, in *Ceremonial Law* he sees the chaos of eternity in a purely negative light:

Lets sojourn in the Desert Wilderness
Of long and uncreated nothing

.   .   .   .   .   .

The Silence Darkness and Deformitie
In which we nothing plainly nothing see

.   .   .   .   .   .

Twill clearly make us find our Heaven here.[26]

It is the impulse to 'find our Heaven here' which means that Traherne's original innocence is a created innocence. It is associated less with the emptiness of the void than with the physical delights of material creation.

Having said all this, there are affinities between Traherne's characterisation of original innocence and that of Wilson's void. While the estate of innocence is attached to material creation, it is distinct from it and precedes it: 'the Seed of Heaven being Sowen in Innocency, and budding forth in Eden'.[27] This model appears to fit a twofold Augustinian account of creation. Jackson, a major influence upon Traherne, translated Augustine in these terms: '*terrae filius, nihili nepos*; Man is the son of the earth, and the grandchilde of nothing'.[28] Similarly, Traherne describes the creation of Adam:

---

[24]   See Plato, *Pheadrus*, 246c–d, 248c, trans. A. Nehemas and Woodruff in *Complete Works*, ed. John M. Cooper (Indianapolis: Hackett, 1997).

[25]   Traherne, 'The Salutation', *Dobell Folio*, 3.

[26]   Traherne, *Ceremonial Law*, 224.

[27]   Traherne, 'Adam', vol. 2, 214.

[28]   Thomas Jackson, *A Treatise of the Divine Essence and Attributes*, Part I (London, 1628), 89.

Amazing Sight! A Pile of Dust appeard,
A Beautious Angel, out of Nothing reard![29]

In this double creation the estate of innocence may be viewed in Adam's dust-formed body and angelic spirit, but the reference to 'Nothing' hints at its privative origins. The primordial void is not forgotten, it casts a shadow on the glory of innocence. The beauty of innocence is drawn into the abundant goodness of paradise, but it remains caught between emptiness and Eden.

'A World of Innocence as then was mine, In which the Joys of Paradice did shine':[30] Innocence in the Paradisal Garden

The complex innocence of this double creation is seen in Traherne's descriptions of Eden. As will be explored further in Chapter 3, his Eden has been much discussed in relation to the theology of original sin. However, through their concern with the causes of sin these important discussions rarely fully address the character of innocence in itself. Traherne himself asserts that it is 'som thing Difficult' to determine precisely the nature of Adam's innocent state, but through imagination he attempts it nevertheless.[31]

The creaturely character of perfect innocence in Eden can be illustrated by a brief return to Wilson's definition of 'perfect innocency by creation', which contains a rich ambiguity that is absent from Henderson's account of the absolute perfection of pre-modern Edenic innocence. In two senses his phrase, 'meer voydness of fault, and freedome from all sin' suggests a conjunction of finitude and perfection in original innocence. Firstly, the term 'meer' in this period signified not only limited scope but also something that was pure, perfect or absolute.[32] This double meaning evokes a sense both of littleness and of infinite capacity. Secondly, the combination of faultlessness and freedom in innocence implies both a static state of sinlessness and the activity made possible by freedom. Traherne presents a similar mixed innocence through the figures of Adam, the atom and the garden. Theirs is a finite, material and organic perfection, a creaturely innocence.

Traherne's Adam is an apparently ambiguous combination of Irenaean and Augustinian influences. There are important Ireneaean features in Adam's

---

[29]   Traherne, 'Adam', *Commentaries of Heaven, Part 1*, 225.

[30]   Traherne, 'Silence', *Dobell Folio*, 25.

[31]   Traherne, 'Adam', *Commentaries of Heaven, Part 1*, 218.

[32]   See *OED*, s.v. 'Mere, adj.2'.

estate, such as the 'Dimness of his Understanding' by which he is 'a little further removed from God'.[33] However, despite comparisons of the infant self to Adam in poems such as 'Innocence', Traherne's Adam is not the child of Irenaean theology; he is a man with 'Duty', 'Employment', 'Obligations and Rewards'.[34] Similarly, Eden contains the physical and spiritual perfections that Augustine described in Chapter 11 of the *City of God*.[35] Traherne eloquently expounds its natural fertility and its 'Divine and Great and Heavenly, Durable Beautifull Bright and Necessary, Usefull and Servieable many and Precious' riches. Eden is characterised not only by innocence, but also by the benefits of 'Ease, Safety, Innocency; Joy and Security; Peace and Dominion; Subjection and Government, Joys and Praises'.[36] However, as explained in the *Church's Year-Book*, Eden's 'Spiritual, Celestial and Divine' benefits are fragile, being dependent on innocence and lost along with it, as that 'from which by Sin only we fell'.[37]

Traherne resolves these contrasting influences through a typically Anglican *via media*, with Augustinian and Hermetic resonances. In *Commentaries of Heaven*, Adam does not possess supernatural perfection but an innocence sufficient to his finite estate, which is 'Imperfect if we respect the Glory in which it must End, tho perfect if we respect the Things that (for that Season) were needful for him: or the Sin into which he fell'. Through recollection, or anamnesis, Traherne sees an Adam who is both humble and glorious, who 'In a lowly Simplicity of Innocent Nature ... sate upon the Ground, and could fall no lower. yet there beheld an infinit Depth out of which he was raised'. This middle state of limited perfection results from Adam's unification of spirit and body, which is described in terms echoing the Chalcedonian definition of Christ's unity of divinity and humanity: 'Adams weak Estate had all the Marks of perfection in it. ... He had two Natures in one Person, which made Him more perfect then the Angels.'[38] It is also described in hermetic terms: 'That union was the Golden Tie of all Visible and Invisible Things.' This combination of perfection and imperfection in Adam's estate will be explored further in the conclusion to this chapter.

---

[33] Traherne, 'Adam', *Commentaries of Heaven, Part 1*, 220; for the seminal argument for Traherne's Irenaean theology, see Patrick Grant, *The Transformation of Sin: Studies in Donne, Herbert, Vaughan, and Traherne* (Amherst: University of Massachusetts Press, 1974), 170–97.

[34] Traherne, 'Innocence', *Dobell Folio*, 10; id., 'Adam', *Commentaries of Heaven, Part 1*, 216–18.

[35] Augustine, *The City of God against the Pagans*, trans. R.W. Dyson (Cambridge: Cambridge University Press, 1998).

[36] Traherne, 'Adam', *Commentaries of Heaven, Part 1*, 214–15, 218.

[37] Thomas Traherne, *Church's Year-Book*, in *The Works of Thomas Traherne*, vol. 4, 129.

[38] See also Traherne, *Kingdom of God*, 483, 484.

50   *Boundless Innocence in Thomas Traherne's Poetic Theology*

Adam's is a paradoxically mixed estate, both 'Happy, and Mutable, Pious and Weak, Free and Imperfect'.[39] His innocence is similarly qualified, not in substance but in syntax. Despite asserting the independence of good from evil, Traherne finds it difficult to describe perfect innocence without comparing it to its opposites. This evokes a linguistic interplay between positive and negative in Traherne's descriptions of innocence. *A Sober View* declares that the estate of innocence was independent of evil but is unable to describe it without reference to it: 'in Innocency without Sin there might have been Perfect Happiness ... Perfection without a foil, Beauty without a Blemish, and perfect Glory without Deformity.'[40] Similarly, *Commentaries of Heaven* defines the state of innocence by what it is free from: 'all contagious Habits, depraved Dispositions, Distracting Objects, Seducing Allurements, Prepossessing Engagements'.[41] The picture of innocence, when described in relation to its opposites, is muddied and qualified, as blemish and deformity arise in the mind as the shadow of innocence.

Adam's is a limited but also a living innocence, following a holy 'Rule of Life'. It is not only a state but also a relational status, as 'Heir of Eternal Glory. Infinitly Beloved of the Eternal King'.[42] The estate of innocence is also an estate of trial for Adam's glory.[43] This suggests that the dynamics of relationship and the power of freedom are at work, as Adam is, in a sense, on trial before God. The picture of God talking and walking with Adam is a repeated trope in Traherne's poetry and prose. *Commentaries of Heaven* declares: 'In the Estate of Innocency Man was in the Heart of GODs Kingdom, God appeared to him, and walked with him.'[44] For God to walk and talk with Adam implies that original innocence is not a primal state of unity with the divine mind such as that outlined by Plotinus.[45] Rather, it is a relationship that involves separation between humanity and God. For Adam to walk with God evokes, not a static state, but a journey in 'the Way / Of God.'[46] This is the preview of Augustine's 'blameless way', which both 'begins

---

[39]   Traherne, 'Adam', *Commentaries of Heaven, Part 1*, 218, 215, 222, 218.

[40]   Traherne, *A Sober View*, 74.

[41]   Traherne, 'Adam', *Commentaries of Heaven, Part 1*, 218.

[42]   Ibid. 214, 224.

[43]   Ibid. 217.

[44]   Traherne, 'Ambassadors', *Commentaries of Heaven, Part 2*, 20; see also id., *Ceremonial Law*, 198; id., *Centuries of Meditations*, II 17.

[45]   Plotinus, *The Enneads*, I.1.ix–xii, trans. S. MacKenna (rev. edn, London: Faber & Faber, 1969).

[46]   Traherne, 'Adam's Fall', *Poems of Felicity*, in *The Works of Thomas Traherne*, vol. 6, 107. This collection was edited by Traherne's brother Philip, so the Dobell manuscript is used where the same poem appears in both.

and ends in innocence'.[47] The innocence of Adam is thus not a static 'fixed state of reciprocal love', as Edmund Newey has described it, but is defined through active relationship to God.[48]

The atom is the first matter of the universe, an element of the dust in which Adam sits and out of which he was formed. As such it represents the glory of material existence created *prope nihil* (from almost nothing).[49] Like More, Traherne uses the atom as a symbol of the soul, and its attributes echo the virtues of innocence.[50] The atom's glory is its smallness and simplicity. It is the smallest creature, even 'infinitly small, being immediatly next to Nothing'.[51] As such it has affinities with humanity at creation, born out of nothing to the glory of God. The atom embodies humanity's humble nature, but 'Its very Smalness is securitie / Against all Force and Power that can be.'[52] The smallness in which the atom finds protection is the result of its simplicity, which is a form of purity:

> But simple Atoms, tho in various Shapes,
> Tho subject unto forcible Assaults, and Rapes
>
> .   .   .   .
>
> are found so pure
> That they will ever, ever more endure.[53]

Pure simplicity makes the atom immutable and protects it from penetration, 'Even as Holy Men retain their Nature, tho they assist the World in the Way to Happiness.'[54] Thus the tiny atom is an image of the strength and divine power of innocence: 'for Atoms shew / An Incorruption even here below.'[55] The atom

---

[47]   *Quae est via immaculata? Audi sequentia: Deambulabam in innocentia cordis mei, in medio domus meae. Haec via immaculata ab innocentia coepit, in ipsa etiam pervenitur* [What is the blameless way? Hear what follows: I will walk in the innocence of my heart, in the midst of my house. This is the blameless way which both begins and ends in innocence] (Augustine, *Expositions on the Book of Psalms*, Ps. 101.2, ¶iv [6 vols, Oxford: J.H. Parker, 1847–57], my translation).

[48]   Edmund Newey, *Children of God: The Child as Source of Theological Anthropology* (Farnham: Ashgate, 2012), 35.

[49]   Augustine, *Confessions*, XII.8.

[50]   See Stephen Clucas, 'Poetic Atomism in Seventeenth-Century England: Henry More, Thomas Traherne and "Scientific Imagination"', *Renaissance Studies* 5 (1991), 327–40.

[51]   Traherne, 'Atom', *Commentaries of Heaven, Part 2*, 343.

[52]   Ibid. 359–60.

[53]   Ibid. 362.

[54]   Traherne, *Kingdom of God*, 344.

[55]   Traherne, 'Atom', *Commentaries of Heaven, Part 2*, 358.

52 *Boundless Innocence in Thomas Traherne's Poetic Theology*

exemplifies material innocence, which is found in a smallness that denotes creation's humble origins and a simplicity that images holiness.

The atom's pure simplicity is a little, impenetrable world, an enclosed garden separated from sin. It is an easy form of holiness, the lost 'Paradice of Ease' that Traherne laments in *Christian Ethicks*:

> Were all men Wise, Divine, and Innocent,
> Just, Holy, Peaceful, and Content,
> Kind, Loving, True, and alwaies Good,
> As in the Golden-Age they stood;
> 'Twere easie then to live
> In all Delight and Glory, full of Love,
> Blest as the Angels are above.[56]

However, Traherne's descriptions of the garden expand this protective shell beyond the original estate. Just as Traherne's account of origins draws spirit into matter, so the garden image diffuses Edenic virtues into the life of grace. 'Simplicitie / Was my Protection when I first was born', Traherne insists in 'Eden', but the walled garden is also recapitulated in the Resurrection life.[57] In *Church's Year-Book*, an ever-expanding commentary on Christ as gardener expounds a typology of Eden and the Resurrection. Edenic imagery is applied to the life of faith in the estate of grace through the statement that Christ 'rose in a Garden, becaus our Fall was in a Garden'. Hence, Christ is not only the 'Ancient Gardener of the fairest Garden that ever was, for He planted Paradice', he also waters the garden of our souls like the Edenic mist 'with the Dew of Heaven, His Heavenly Grace'.[58] The garden here is a type not only of protection but also of nourishment and growth. Through the garden-image, innocence moves beyond an original state of protection from sin to take on connotations of the blessing of grace for God's people.[59]

Traherne's Eden is more than an enclosed state of easy innocence because its virtues are organically diffused into the other estates. Milton scholarship has debated whether Milton's Eden represents the 'blank innocence and effortlessness' of static holiness leaning back to the void or whether it is a living

---

56 Traherne, *Christian Ethicks*, 196.
57 Traherne, 'Eden', *Dobell Folio*, 8.
58 Traherne, *Church's Year-Book*, 17, 19; see Jer. 31.11, Gen. 2.6.
59 For a modern theology of creation along these lines, see Claus Westermann, *Blessing in the Bible and the Life of the Church*, trans. K. Crim (Philadelphia, Pa.: Fortress, 1978), 4–8.

'Wild Garden'.[60] As described above, Traherne's Eden is not the untamed garden of *Paradise Lost* but does incline towards the 'active, growing and conditional perfection' of a living garden in the way it seeps through the porous boundaries between the estates.[61] *Christian Ethicks* explains that the virtues granted by nature in the estate of innocence 'must be exercised in the state of Grace and will abide for ever in the State of Glory'.[62] This organic development appears also in *Centuries of Meditations*' description of the world as a pomegranate containing 'the Seeds of Grace and the Seeds of Glory'.[63] *Kingdom of God* charts the final stage of this process, as God's kingdom contains 'the flowers of paradise, and the fruits of Eden'.[64] There are echoes here of Dante's *Purgatorio*, in which the elevated Eden 'impregnates air with seeding force', through the seeds of grace which descend to be sown on earth.[65]

This organic materiality is balanced by the estates' permanent place in the perspective of infinity. In this model the estates intermingle in eternity and 'One Estate is fed by another' through the perichoresis of the breath of life.[66] So, 'however distant they are in Time, in Eternity they are all together, immutably freely and stably Beautifying and adorning each other with perfect Harmony in their proper Places'.[67] Whether Traherne accesses innocence through the Hermetic ubiquity of the soul or through Augustinian recollection, there is in his works a living unity that draws innocence into the life of grace, which means that 'the flaming Sword is not able to hinder its Access into Paradice'.[68] The organic interplay of the estates reflects the diffusion of created innocence within the life of faith.

Eden is drawn into existence because its echoes resonate in the life of faith. Traherne's Eden does not belong to Adam alone. It is also an Origenist 'paradise within', a spiritual state of bliss that may be recaptured by the one whose soul is

---

[60] Basil Willey, *The Seventeenth Century Background* (New York: Columbia University Press, 1967), 255; John R. Knott, 'Milton's Wild Garden', *SP* 102 (2005), 66–82.

[61] J. Martin Evans, *Paradise Lost and the Genesis Tradition* (Oxford: Clarendon, 1968), 269.

[62] Traherne, *Christian Ethicks*, 31.

[63] Traherne, *Centuries of Meditations*, II 96.

[64] Traherne, *Kingdom of God*, 267.

[65] Dante Alighieri, *Purgatorio*, 28:110, in *The Divine Comedy*, trans. Allen Mandelbaum (Berkeley: University of California Press, 1980).

[66] Traherne, *Inducements to Retirednes*, 20.

[67] Traherne, 'Atom', *Commentaries of Heaven, Part 2*, 338.

[68] See Augustine, *Confessions*, X.18; Traherne, 'Accesse', *Commentaries of Heaven, Part 1*, 104.

54   *Boundless Innocence in Thomas Traherne's Poetic Theology*

> Transparent, full of Heavenly Light
> And like the GODHEAD fair and infinit
>
> .   .   .   .   .   .
>
> Already in his Eden safe He is;
> Being Himself a Paradice of Bliss.[69]

Several critics identify this interiorised paradise with the impending decline of the historical Eden and with secularizing movements towards the supremacy of the individual. For them Traherne, alongside Milton, represents the beginning of the end of Eden.[70] Joanna Picciotto's recent daring survey of seventeenth-century experimentalism similarly interprets the poetic and Platonic inner paradise as a modernising abandonment of the material Eden for current 'paradized' perceptions. However by 'verbing' paradise, she also evokes the vitality and present activity of Eden.[71] The living perfection of innocence is seen in Traherne's material and spiritual Eden. It is not a nostalgic glance backwards, but that '[to which here beneath we ought to aspire,] to which all Wisdom directs, and felicity allures'.[72] Original innocence is present as an object of hope, a sketch of God's eternal 'Innocent and Holy Kingdom'.[73]

Eden embodies a creaturely perfection, finite, material and organic. It is a status in relationship to God which is not static but dynamic and growing. It is not only the security of simplicity but also the nurturing of grace within the life of faith. It is not enclosed but diffused into existence. As such, Eden is much more than the silver lining to the dark cloud of the Fall. It is a model of 'perfect innocency by creation'.

---

[69]   Traherne, 'The Delights of Ages', *Commentaries of Heaven, Part 1*, 352; on paradise within, see Arnold Stein, 'The Paradise Within and the Paradise Without', *Milton Quarterly* 26 (1965), 586–600.

[70]   See Peter Harrison, *The Bible, Protestantism, and the Rise of Natural Science* (Cambridge: Cambridge University Press, 1998), 148–9, 211; Beverley Sherry, 'A "Paradise Within" Can Never Be "Happier Farr": Reconsidering the Archangel Michael's Consolation in *Paradise Lost*', *Milton Quarterly* 37 (2003), 85.

[71]   See Elizabeth S. Dodd, 'Joanna Picciotto, *Labors of Innocence in Early Modern England* (Cambridge, Mass.: Harvard University Press, 2010)', *Seventeenth Century* 27/2 (2012), 235–7; Joanna Picciotto, *Labors of Innocence in Early Modern England* (Cambridge, Mass.: Harvard University Press, 2010), 133–47, 129.

[72]   Traherne, 'Second Adam', *Commentaries of Heaven, Part 1*, 227, [] indicates insertion.

[73]   Traherne, *Kingdom of God*, 290.

Recapitulating Innocence: The Typology of Adam and Christ

Creaturely perfection is diffused into the other estates of the soul, but it is also recapitulated through an Irenaean Adam–Christ typology.[74] Scriptural typologies are an important device in Traherne's poetic theology, which draw the reader into the gospel narrative of salvation. Typology is particularly evident in *Ceremonial Law* and in the characters of Adam, David and Job. Traherne's treatment of Adam comes out of a tradition of Adamic self-fashioning through which 'Adams Duties Employments, Riches and Pleasures are mine. Who am my self an Adam were I alone in the World and Head of all Mankind.'[75] According to Douglas Jordan, this typology of Adam and Christ creates an analogy between the macrocosm of salvation history and the microcosm of individual life.[76] This can be seen in the Adamic persona of poems such as 'Fullnesse', whose narrator shares Adam's duties and is, like him, 'An Univers enclosd in Skin'.[77] For Barbara Lewalski, Traherne's recapitulation of Adam is more than imitation. It is a character that is 'actually repeated' in the individual.[78] This interpretation is justified by *The Ceremonial Law*, which asserts that through Christ, types from the Hebrew Bible are drawn into the real drama of life: 'That we no fiction make, but see the Thing, / Which from the Type most realy doth Spring.'[79]

Adam is often treated alone, but in *Commentaries of Heaven* the paired sections, 'Adam' and 'The Second Adam' are explicitly situated within an Adam–Christ typology.[80] Here, Adam is less a particular historical individual than the archetypal human being of which Christ is the perfect example. For Traherne, 'evry Son of Man is another Adam', which links humanity as a whole with the Christological title of the 'Son of Man'.[81] The *telos* of this typology is in the second Adam who is the ultimate model of Christian innocence: his 'full Perfection is the Measure of the Stature of the New Man after which we ought to

---

[74] Grant, *The Transformation of Sin*, 184–5.

[75] Traherne, 'Adam', *Commentaries of Heaven, Part 1*, 223.

[76] Richard Douglas Jordan, *The Temple of Eternity: Thomas Traherne's Philosophy of Time* (New York: Kennikat, 1972), 61–3; followed by Barbara Lewalski, 'Typological Symbolism and the "Progress of the Soul" in Seventeenth-Century Literature', in Earl Miner (ed.), *Literary Uses of Typology: From the Late Middle Ages to the Present* (Princeton, NJ: Princeton University Press, 1977), 79–114.

[77] Traherne, 'Fullnesse', *Dobell Folio*, 30.

[78] Lewalski, *Protestant Poetics and the Seventeenth-Century Religious Lyric*, 143.

[79] Traherne, *Ceremonial Law*, 218.

[80] Traherne, 'Adam', *Commentaries of Heaven, Part 1*, 214–26; id., 'Second Adam', *Commentaries of Heaven, Part 1*, 227–35.

[81] Traherne, *Inducements to Retirednes*, 31.

56   *Boundless Innocence in Thomas Traherne's Poetic Theology*

Aspire'.[82] While Picciotto has identified a supersession of the medieval *imitatio Christi* by the *imitatio Adami* in seventeenth-century Protestant literature, this passage in Traherne's works demonstrates the primacy of Christ over Adam as the model of human perfection.[83]

Adam's recapitulation and perfection in Christ illustrates the Irenaean features of Traherne's doctrine of salvation.[84] Unlike Grant, Inge and Kershaw see in Traherne's recapitulatory soteriology not a problematic return to childlike innocence but a progression to a new or higher innocence.[85] Recapitulation through the second Adam is not a return to origins but the inauguration of the earthly material paradise described above.[86] Traherne employs these chiliastic resonances in the pursuit of a present paradise that is unified with its typological parallels, so that 'at this day the Heavens and the earth are Not onely like Adams Eden but the Stage and Theatre of my Saviours passion'.[87]

The details of *Commentaries of Heaven*'s Adam–Christ typology illustrate Adam's subordinate role, as a type who is defined in relation to Christ. Adam

---

[82]   Traherne, 'Second Adam', *Commentaries of Heaven, Part 1*, 229; see: 'Finally, through the Word he seeks to relearn and can recover the innocent words of the second Adam' (Ira Clark, *Christ Revealed: The History of the Neotypological Lyric in the English Renaissance* [Gainesville: University Presses of Florida, 1982], 153).

[83]   See Picciotto, *Labors of Innocence in Early Modern England*, 8, 75–87. Picciotto cites, but in fact reverses the position of, Deborah Kuller Shuger (*The Renaissance Bible: Scholarship, Sacrifice, and Subjectivity* [Berkeley: University of California Press, 1994], 89).

[84]   On important recent work on Irenaeus of Lyons and recapitulation, see Matthew Craig Steenberg, *Irenaeus on Creation: The Cosmic Christ and the Saga of Redemption* (Leiden: Brill, 2008), 51–60.

[85]   Patrick Grant, 'Original Sin and the Fall of Man in Thomas Traherne', *ELH* 38/1 (Mar. 1971), 49, 51; Denise Inge, *Happiness and Holiness: Thomas Traherne and His Writings* (Norwich: Canterbury Press, 2008), 148–9; Kershaw, 'The Poetic of the Cosmic Christ', 184–6; on seventeenth-century atonement theories, see Charles A. Patrides, 'Milton and the Protestant Theory of the Atonement', *PMLA* 74/1 (1959), 7; on the soteriological import of recapitulation in Irenaeus, see J. Fantino, 'Le Passage du premier Adam au second Adam comme expression du salut chez Irénée de Lyon', *VC* 52 (1998), 418–29.

[86]   On the derivation of Irenaeus' chiliastic eschatology from his doctrine of creation, see Christopher R. Smith, 'Chiliasm and Recapitulation in the Theology of Irenaeus', *VC* 48 (1994), 315–18; on the bi-directional and reciprocal quality of Irenaean recapitulation which unifies protology and eschatology and is associated with Origenism and chiliasm, see Steenberg, *Irenaeus on Creation*, 60, 115, 98–100.

[87]   Thomas Traherne, *Select Meditations*, II 7, in *The Works of Thomas Traherne*, vol. 5; Steenberg identifies recapitulation not only with atonement theory, but with a Christological theological anthropology and an anthropogenic soteriology whose promised end is the 'perfection of humanity' (*Irenaeus on Creation*, 99, 58).

is a comprehensive figure because he encapsulates all four estates: he was born in innocence, fell and was redeemed. In this Traherne saw Adam as being 'like unto our Savior filling all things'.[88] However, the comprehensiveness of Christ far surpasses that of Adam, since his perfection encompasses everything: 'we are all made Perfect in one, becaus one is the Comprehensor of all'.[89] Adam participates in the cosmic Christ's act of creation: his first thought being 'a Mixture of Reverence Admiration Gratitude and Joy attending the World he conceived in his Mind'.[90] That act of intellectual conception was the divine spark of creative power in the human being, but it cannot equal the creativity of the Logos.

Within the salvation narrative, Adam is Christ's counterpart and opposite, as summed up in the Irenaean claim: 'To that we are restored by the Second Adam which we lost in the first.'[91] So, Adam's authority is an ironic imitation of Christ who holds the keys of heaven and hell, since where Adam failed Christ succeeded. In his choice about the apple Adam was 'the Lord over Fate, the Arbiter of Life and Death, that held the Gate of Destinie, and by one Act was able to let in, or keep sin out of the World'.[92] Christ bore the consequences of Adam's failure. This is alluded to in the passage on 'Adam's Fall' in *The Ceremonial Law*, which describes the very first sacrifice in the animal that was killed to clothe Adam and Eve: 'One Sind, another died: A Beast was slain; / An Innocent was kild, a Foe doth reign.'[93] *Commentaries of Heaven* elaborates on this theme through a conflation and adaptation of 1 Corinthians 15.22 and Romans 5.12–21:

> As in Adam all died so in Him are all made alive. As in Adam all sinned so in Him are all justified. As Adam was the fountain of our Life so is He of our Happiness. As Adam was our Example in Innocency, so is He in our misery and especialy our Patern in the State of Grace.[94]

---

[88] Traherne, 'Adam', *Commentaries of Heaven, Part 1*, 223.

[89] Traherne, 'Second Adam', *Commentaries of Heaven, Part 1*, 234.

[90] Traherne, 'Adam', *Commentaries of Heaven, Part 1*, 217.

[91] Traherne, 'Second Adam', *Commentaries of Heaven, Part 1*, 229; Irenaeus of Lyons, *Against the Heresies*, III.18.i, in *The Apostolic Fathers with Justin Martyr and Irenaeus*, ed. and trans. Alexander Roberts and James Donaldson, Ante-Nicene Christian Library 1 (Edinburgh: T.&T. Clark, 1869).

[92] Traherne, 'Adam', *Commentaries of Heaven, Part 1*, 222; see Rev. 1.18.

[93] Traherne, *Ceremonial Law*, 198.

[94] Traherne, 'Second Adam', *Commentaries of Heaven, Part 1*, 229.

58   *Boundless Innocence in Thomas Traherne's Poetic Theology*

While Adamic self-fashioning is an important feature of Traherne's poetic theology, it is combined with and superseded by the *imitatio Christi* which pursues a perfection that surpasses original innocence.[95]

Traherne's Irenaean Adam–Christ typology intimates the subordinate relationship of Adamic original innocence to Christological perfection. According to *A Sober View*, Christ supersedes Adam because Adam is in potential what Christ is in act: 'Adams Power of Continuing Innocent was never reduced into Act' but has been perfected in Christ and may be manifest in us.[96] Christ exceeds Adam, because Adam is in ease what Christ is in difficulty. Adam's 'Accurat and Perfect Righteousness' is less than Christ's, 'in that amid the Poverties and Riches of this World, the Contrary Opinions and Practices of men, the Sins and Curses that oppress the Earth all which make it difficult to be innocent [Christ] remained Blessed'.[97] Finally, Adam is in a limited manner what Christ is consummately: his limited perfection, outlined above, cannot match the absolute perfection of Christ.

Adam's limited excellence is less than the fullness of Christ's perfection but is incorporated into it and is thereby expanded. Adam's paradoxically mixed estate of happiness and mutability, piety and weakness, freedom and imperfection is consummated in Christ in whom 'All Wisdom and Happiness were couched together all Holiness and Glory embraced each other all Innocency and Perfection Beautified the same'.[98] Through redemption, Christ restores the originally intended blamelessness by which humanity is made to be 'Holy and unblameable before [God] in Love, which we lost in the first but recover in the second Adam'.[99] What Christ achieves is not an inanimate crown of victory but a renewal of right relation, a vocation to holiness and the hope of inheriting glory.[100] Christological perfection recovers Eden but moves beyond it. Adam's little estate of 'Ease, Safety, Innocency' turns into Christ's grand 'Innocent Humble Pious Safe Easy Life free from all Contention and

---

[95]   This matches the two significations of recapitulation in Irenaeus: 'correspondence' and 'summing up' (Smith, 'Chiliasm and Recapitulation in the Theology of Irenaeus', 322–6).

[96]   Traherne, *A Sober View*, 141.

[97]   Traherne, 'Adam', *Commentaries of Heaven, Part 1*, 219; id., 'Second Adam', *Commentaries of Heaven, Part 1*, 229.

[98]   Traherne, 'Adam', *Commentaries of Heaven, Part 1*, 218; id. 'Second Adam', *Commentaries of Heaven, Part 1*, 228.

[99]   Traherne, *A Sober View*, 116.

[100]   On recapitulatory salvation as a recovery of original vocation or inheritance, see Steenberg, *Irenaeus on Creation*, 56.

strife'.[101] Christ's absolute innocence, 'Spotless as the Day, as Pure as the Sun', replaces the original innocence of Adam as the model of innocent life.[102]

Christ is the exemplar of a higher innocence which is the image of God, the perfection of Adam and the model of humanity.[103] Christ's innocence is not inaccessible but may be imitated, since he, 'being a man Subject to passions as we are, and compassed with Infirmities hath taught us ... notwithstanding the Temptations wherwith we are surrounded, to live the Life of Adam still, to which we are again restored'.[104] It is through the *imitatio Christi* therefore that Adamic self-fashioning is possible, and through grace that innocence is restored.

'A Native Health and Innocence Within my Bones did grow':[105] Innocence and Nature

This interpretation of Traherne's original innocence as 'perfect innocency by creation' informs aspects of his concept of 'Native' innocence, suggesting that it may be better understood through the doctrine of creation than through eighteenth-century primitivism. This is not to deny the value that Traherne places upon nature but to disinvest it of anachronistic associations with Enlightenment glorifications of nature, which are tied to previously popular readings of Traherne as a form of nature mystic. The notion of created innocence has implications for his apparently primitivist approach to 'natural man', who is innocent only insofar as he images original innocence. It highlights the poetic nuances of human nature, which in its nakedness is not bare innocence but a layered construct. It reveals in the light of nature not only reason and purity but also grace. It underscores the important role played by the notion that the law of nature is the law of love, love being the condition of relationship. Traherne's natural innocence participates in a diverse intellectual context surrounding early modern concepts of 'nature'. This discussion is framed according to the Cambridge Platonist Nathaniel Culverwel's distinction between [human] nature, the light of nature and the

---

[101] Traherne, 'Adam', *Commentaries of Heaven, Part 1*, 218; id., 'Second Adam', *Commentaries of Heaven, Part 1*, 230.

[102] Traherne, 'Second Adam', *Commentaries of Heaven, Part 1*, 230.

[103] On recapitulation as fulfilling the vocation of a dynamic image of God, see Steenberg, *Irenaeus on Creation*, 56–7.

[104] Traherne, 'Second Adam', *Commentaries of Heaven, Part 1*, 229.

[105] Traherne, 'Wonder', *Dobell Folio*, 5.

law of nature, but focuses on how aspects of 'perfect innocency by creation' inform Traherne's account of natural innocence.[106]

Traherne's treatment of human nature has been identified with a primitivist impulse, in which natural innocence is a 'pre- or supramoral innocence' that is 'morally positive but intellectually negative', an ignorant state of nature abstracted from the world of experience.[107] This model draws Traherne into a 'long eighteenth century' that saw Adam's original righteousness replaced with the primitive innocence of Rousseau's *Émile*.[108] The primitivist elements in Traherne's account of nature are best understood not through Enlightenment utopianism but through Pierre Charron, whose influence is most evident in *Christian Ethicks*. Charron was the main conduit through which Montaigne's sceptical philosophy was conveyed to seventeenth-century England.[109] For him, innocence is displayed in the natural world: in the moderation, peace, liberty, lack of ceremony, and simplicity belonging to beasts, barbarians, children and rural life. By undoing humanity's alienation from nature, innocence is recovered. By following the animals' example man 'frameth himselfe to innocencie, simplicitie, libertie, and that naturall sweetnesse which shineth in beasts'.[110]

Traherne's appeal to the innocence of primitive nature may appear straightforward, but it is not unambiguous. The passage most commonly cited as evidence of Traherne's primitivism is in *Centuries of Meditations*, where he argues that 'Rude and Barbarous Indians that go Naked and Drink Water and liv upon Roots are like Adam, or Angels in Comparison of us'. This has

---

[106] Nathaniel Culverwel, *An Elegant and Learned Discourse of the Light of Nature* (London, 1652). 13.

[107] William Poole, 'Frail Originals: Theories of the Fall in the Age of Milton' (PhD thesis; University of Oxford, 2000), 286–8.

[108] For interpretations of Traherne's natural innocence which rely on Enlightenment notions of nature, see Anne Davidson, 'Innocence Regained: Seventeenth Century Reinterpretations of the Fall of Man' (PhD thesis: Columbia University, 1956), vi–vii; Husain, *The Mystical Element in the Metaphysical Poets*, 290, 292; White, *The Metaphysical Poets*, 334; on the secularization of the Eden narrative in the eighteenth century, see Duncan, *Milton's Earthly Paradise*, 270–71; cf. Ana M. Acosta, who challenges this secularization thesis, arguing for the continuing authority of the Genesis narrative in early modern and Enlightenment utopianism (*Reading Genesis in the Long Eighteenth-Century: From Milton to Mary Shelley* [Aldershot: Ashgate, 2006], 2–3).

[109] Ellrodt defines Traherne's 'apology of primitive life' as looking back to Montaigne and forward to Rousseau (*Seven Metaphysical Poets*, 288).

[110] Pierre Charron, *Of Wisdom Three Bookes* (London: William Hole, 1608), 104–5, 168, 204, 207, 112.

'Perfect innocency by creation' 61

been interpreted as an assertion of the primitive innocence of natural man.[111] However, Traherne's purpose here is not to declare the innocence of savages but to demonstrate the 'absurdly Barbarous' character of supposedly civilised Christendom.[112] In a similar passage in *Christian Ethicks*, Traherne adopts primitivist conceits to combat Hobbes' view that 'the condition of Man ... is a condition of Warre of every one against every one'.[113] Drawing on Bernard of Clairvaux, Traherne attacks the 'Atheistical fool', who thinks that '[to] love another more than ones self is absurd and impossible'.[114] While Traherne accepts that 'In Nature [as it is now] it is so', he uses diverse examples of self-sacrifice, from bears to brides, to show that love of others is not against nature but stems from the principle of self-preservation by which we desire to be beloved.[115] Samuel Mintz interprets this as an argument that love of others takes priority over self-love.[116] Taken in context, this passage is not arguing for natural innocence but rather defends the love of God as natural, since '[it] is natural to all them that love themselves, to love their Benefactors'. Interestingly, the heathen in the 'state of nature' are ignorant of this fact. The principle behind Traherne's apparently primitivist argument in this case is not humanity's natural innocence but the imperative to love God.

Fundamental to Traherne's account of human nature is the fourfold structure of the estates, which *ordo salutis* distinguishes between 'our Nature falne, and our Nature Innocent'.[117] Humanity's excellence is most evident in innocence: 'all Nature is a Lover of Pleasure, but Innocent nature loves that pleasure which is Sincere and Pure'.[118] Natural humanity after the Fall is 'born into the World as the Prophet speaketh like a Wilde Asses Colt ... alienated from the Life of God through the Ignorance that is in them ... Strangers to themselvs'.[119] In being defined by alienation from God and oneself, this natural state is the antithesis

---

[111] e.g. Keith William Salter, *Thomas Traherne. Mystic and Poet* (London: Edward Arnold, 1964), 133; Marks, 'Thomas Traherne and Cambridge Platonism', 527.

[112] Traherne, *Centuries of Meditations*, III 12.

[113] Thomas Hobbes, *Leviathan*, pt I, ch. 14, ¶4, ed. Richard Tuck (rev. edn, Cambridge: Cambridge University Press, 2008).

[114] See Nabil I. Matar, 'Thomas Traherne and St Bernard of Clairvaux', *N&Q* 32 (1985), 182–4.

[115] Traherne, *Christian Ethicks*, 261.

[116] Samuel I. Mintz, *The Hunting of Leviathan: Seventeenth-Century Reactions to the Materialism and Moral Philosophy of Thomas* (Cambridge: Cambridge University Press, 1962), 144–5.

[117] Traherne, *A Sober View*, 133.

[118] Thomas Traherne, *Seeds of Eternity*, in *The Works of Thomas Traherne*, vol. 1, 233–4.

[119] Traherne, 'Delights of Ages', *Commentaries of Heaven, Part 1*, 343.

of innocence. While it is not quite Francis Bacon's world 'full of savage and unreclaimed desires, of profit, of lust, of revenge', nor is it Rousseau's sanguine presentation of a peaceful and ignorant state where self-love is moderated by natural compassion.[120]

Traherne praises 'Natures purity' in his 'Virgin Youth' not according to the state of nature but the estate of innocence. The allusions to the duties and activities of Adam in Eden are clear in the following passage from 'Nature':

> I was by Nature prone and apt to love
> All Light and Beauty, both in Heaven above,
> And Earth beneath, prone even to Admire,
> Adore and Prais as well as to Desire.[121]

Here, poetic licence conflates youth and natural innocence. Traherne's prose makes it clear that humanity is not innocent in its fallen primitive nature but only in its pre-lapsarian state. *Centuries of Meditations*, when stating that we are by nature sons of God, takes care to clarify that by this is meant only 'the Principles of Upright Nature ... before they were Muddied and Blended and Confounded. for now they are lost and buried in Ruines. Nothing appearing but fragments, that are worthless shreds and Parcels of them.'[122] In this, Traherne takes to heart Calvin's warning against philosophers who, ignoring the Fall, conflate pre- and post-lapsarian human nature and look 'for a complete building in a ruin, and fit arrangement in disorder'.[123]

The rich allusions surrounding natural innocence make it both a compelling and a complex notion to unravel. This is evident in Traherne's use of the symbol of nakedness. The nakedness associated with so-called savages does not necessarily connote their innocence. As described in *Commentaries of Heaven*, the Picts' nakedness is not evidence of moral innocence, but is merely an example of the physical possibility of survival without clothes.[124] However, the poem 'The

---

[120] Francis Bacon, *The Advancement of Learning*, I.7.ii, ed. Arthur Johnston (Oxford: Clarendon, 1974 [1605]); Jean-Jacques Rousseau, *Discourse on the Origins of Inequality (Second Discourse); Polemics; and, Political Economy*, ed. Roger D. Masters and Christopher Kelly, trans. Judith R. Bush (Hanover, NH: University Press of New England, 1992), part I.

[121] Traherne, 'Nature', *Dobell Folio*, 32.

[122] Traherne, *Centuries of Meditations*, IV 54; see Plato, *Phaedo* 110d–e.

[123] John Calvin, *Institutes of the Christian Religion*, I. 15. vii, trans. Henry Beveridge (London, 1953).

[124] Traherne, 'Apparel', *Commentaries of Heaven, Part 2*, 133.

'Perfect innocency by creation' 63

Person' shows how, even after the Fall, nakedness expresses the glory of bare matter without added adornment:

> The Naked Things
> Are most Sublime, and Brightest shew,
> When they alone are seen.[125]

Nakedness in *Ceremonial Law*'s 'The Paschal Lamb' expresses the vulnerability and solitude of innocent suffering, as the lamb is 'Exposed Naked unto Shame & pain'. It also denotes Israel's dependence upon God:

> Who are this Naked people? What this rude,
> Weak, strange, & unexperienc'd Multitude?
>
> .   .   .   .
>
> A Simple flock of unexperienced sheep
>
> .   .   .   .
>
> That simply place their Hope alone in GOD,
> And hav no Weapon with them but His Rod
>
> .   .   .   .
>
> And by some Miracle of Providence
> Are still preservd. This is the hidden sence
> That lurks beneath their Nakedness.[126]

Nakedness here signifies a vulnerability expressed in dependence upon divine aid, an openness to God and a direct relation without intermediary. Like the atom that rises 'Naked to the Skies', nakedness is a fragile, creaturely beauty which finds through proximity to God a glory that is reflected in the human form.[127] These connotations colour the nakedness of natural innocence, so that it connotes not only primitive nature and shamelessness but also unmediated relationship, glory and vulnerability.

Traherne's account of the light of nature is similarly nuanced. Francis Bacon's twofold description of *synderesis* in *The Advancement of Learning* is instructive here, since he acknowledges both the light of reason 'according to the laws of heaven and earth' and the 'inward instinct, according to the law of conscience, which is a sparkle of the purity of his first estate'.[128] Traherne's treatment of the

---

[125] Traherne, 'The Person', *Dobell Folio*, 39.
[126] Traherne, *Ceremonial Law*, 211.
[127] Traherne, 'Atom', *Commentaries of Heaven, Part 2*, 354.
[128] Bacon, *The Advancement of Learning*, II.25.iii.

light of nature similarly extends beyond a purely rationalist reification of right reason, to encompass the purity indicative of innocent creation. These two strands do not sit in tension, being united through a Christian Platonist marriage of knowledge and love: as Jackson styled it, 'knowledge of things amiable being come unto maturitie is alwayes laden with love, as with its naturall fruit'.[129] While the 'candle of the Lord' of Proverbs 20.27 is for Traherne the light of reason, it is also the 'Innate and Essential Light' of inherent righteousness.[130] It is the 'simple Light from all Contagion free' of the 'Infant-Ey' whose sight is pure knowledge, but also the moral purity of Eden: 'as all would have been instructed by the Light of Nature, so had all been Innocent, and Just, and Regular'.[131]

The light of nature is also the light of conscience, which indicates the continuing presence of grace in fallen nature.[132] The grace of the light of innocence conforms to Traherne's view of the inherence of grace in human nature: 'Grace and Nature are Distinct Things. Grace may be without Nature, and Nature without Grace, tho Grace cannot be in a Man without Nature, and tho Grace and Nature are both within.'[133] Traherne writes of innate goodness as divinely infused into the empty soul by grace and the 'Intrinsick Goodness' of creation being actively 'innated' in it.[134] The boundaries of nature and grace are so blurred and natural dispositions such as ambition are so 'interwoven in the Essence of a man' that Traherne describes them as 'a Grace innate'.[135]

The blurring of boundaries between nature and grace uncovers a mismatch between Platonic and Aristotelian principles in Traherne's account of nature. On the one hand, there are Platonic notions of innate ideas and the purity of 'Natural Affections [which] are always innate and one, being permanent and immutable'.[136] On the other, there is the Aristotelian *tabula rasa* of the empty and unblemished soul, which may either put on perfection or become blemished by sin, as described in *Centuries of Meditations* I 1. These contradictions are not

---

[129] Thomas Jackson, *A Treatise containing the Originall of Unbeliefe* (London: John Clarke, 1625), 445.

[130] Traherne, *A Sober View*, 143.

[131] Traherne, 'An Infant-Ey', *Poems of Felicity*, 96; id., *Christian Ethicks*, 33.

[132] See Robert A. Greene, who, in identifying Traherne's *synderesis* with the inspiration of the Holy Spirit, similarly connects the light of nature (in reason) with the workings of grace ('Whichcote, the Candle of the Lord, and Synderesis', *JHI* 52/4 [1991], 637 n. 60).

[133] Traherne, 'Assistance', *Commentaries of Heaven, Part 2*, 268; see Aquinas, 'Whether Man was Created in Grace?', *Summa Theologica*, IA.96.i, trans. Thomas Gilby (Cambridge: Blackfriars, 1964–81).

[134] Traherne, 'Delights of Ages', *Commentaries of Heaven, Part 1*, 337.

[135] Traherne, 'Ambition', *Commentaries of Heaven, Part 2*, 44, 40.

[136] Traherne, 'Affection', *Commentaries of Heaven, Part 1*, 275.

explicitly resolved, unless it be that bare nature is blank and empty, but the light of grace is so deeply implanted in creation as to be practically essential to it. Either way, these tensions are subsumed under the language of grace. One cannot therefore talk about Traherne's natural innocence without taking into account the workings of grace.[137]

Traherne's interpretation of natural law is equally informative for his concept of natural innocence. *Kingdom of God*'s exposition of natural law is explicitly based upon 'The judicious Hooker' who, it says, delved into the origin and essence of things. Like many of his contemporaries, Traherne saw in Richard Hooker a bastion of Anglican orthodoxy, a 'Glorious Beam of the English Church'. In the context of this relatively philosophical treatise, he uses Hooker to display the Anglican credentials of what is an essentially Thomist account of natural law. *Kingdom of God* is structured according to the four causes, and natural law is identified with the first and final causes. The fountain of natural law is the 'first and Eternal Law', the 'Being of God' who 'is a Kind of Law to his Working; for that Perfection which God is, giveth Perfection to that he doth'. The natural perfection proceeding from God is the cause of all love of good and hatred of evil. Divine perfection is the teleology of creation, as illustrated by the aphorism, 'the Works of Nature do always aim at that which cannot be bettered'.[138] Natural innocence therefore has its first and final cause in God.

Since natural law is founded in God, it must have God's loving nature. As Traherne puts it in *Ceremonial Law*,

> Love gave the Law, Love made the World, and Love
> The very Substance of the Law doth prove.[139]

Traherne thus expounds a Lutheran or Thomist argument that the law of nature is the law of love, the law of grace.[140] This is set out more clearly in *Commentaries of Heaven*, where Traherne states that 'the Laws of Love are the Laws of Nature, the truest and the Highest'. It follows that innocent nature is a loving nature, since 'Nature without Love is a bare and barren nature, as base as it is drie, and

---

[137] On the centrality of a grace that makes everything 'sheer gift' to Traherne, see McIntosh, *Discernment and Truth*, 245.

[138] Traherne, *Kingdom of God*, 369; Richard Hooker, *Of the Lawes of Ecclesiasticall Politie Eight Bookes* (London, 1604), 47, 55.

[139] Traherne, *Ceremonial Law*, 237.

[140] See R.S. White, *Natural Law in English Renaissance Literature* (Cambridge: Cambridge University Press, 1996), 37.

as drie as Worthless'.[141] The principle of the law of nature as the law of love conforms to the relational model of innocence outlined above.

The Cambridge Platonists have been credited with uniting the scholastic metaphysics of nature with experimentalist theories on the laws governing inanimate objects, and Traherne conforms to this trend.[142] *Kingdom of God* paraphrases Ralph Cudworth, describing love as the 'inward self moving principle, living and abiding in the heart'.[143] This language of motion connects Traherne's discourse on love and nature with his description of the atom and with the material character of created innocence. Just as More posited the 'self-activity' of spirit 'guiding [the physical monads] in such Motions as answer the end of the spiritual Agent', so Traherne suggested that atoms moved in a manner 'As if their Actions did proceed from Lov'.[144]

This theme of love as life in motion also draws on other important influences upon Traherne. Firstly, there is the notion of circulation in Renaissance Neoplatonism.[145] This is the cycle of gift and receipt which constitutes creation. Secondly, there is the gravitational pull of Augustine's *pondus animae* by which the soul is drawn to God, as 'Things unknown ... like the Centre of the Earth unseen, violently Attract it'.[146] The eclectic combination of these various influences is ordered by a focus on divine love, which is apparent in Traherne's account of natural law and runs throughout his work. The Law of Nature is the Law of Love and the principle of life, so natural innocence for Traherne is not the 'Dead and quiet Principles' of a bare physical nature.[147] It is the living and loving motion which proceeds out of God and returns to God through desire.

Traherne's natural innocence is modelled less on ideas of nature than on the estate of innocence. It is a complex innocence whose nakedness signifies purity, vulnerability, dependence and relationship. It is not the brute innocence of

---

[141] Traherne, 'Affinity', *Commentaries of Heaven, Part 1*, 300.

[142] See J.-M. Vienne, 'Introduction', in Rogers, Vienne and Zarka (eds), *The Cambridge Platonists in Philosophical Context*, xii; Knud Haakonssen, 'Divine/Natural Law Theories in Ethics', in Daniel Garber and Michael Ayers (eds), *Cambridge History of Seventeenth-Century Philosophy* (Cambridge: Cambridge University Press, 1998), 1317–20.

[143] Traherne, *Kingdom of God*, 305, paraphrasing Cudworth, *A Sermon Preached before the Honourable House of Commons*, 73–9.

[144] Henry More, *Divine Dialogues, Containing sundry Disquisitions & Instructions Concerning the Attributes and Providence of GOD* (London, 1668), 128; Traherne, 'Atom', *Commentaries of Heaven, Part 2*, 356.

[145] See Inge, *Wanting Like a God*, 201–7.

[146] Traherne, *Centuries of Meditations*, I 2.

[147] Traherne, *A Sober View*, 89.

natural man, but conformity to natural law rooted in creation's origin in and relationship with God.

'O make me Excellent and bright within. Illustrious Glorious Stable Void of Sin':[148] Perfect Innocency

'Perfect innocency by creation', as described by Wilson and Traherne, is more than simple perfection or original innocence. It is a complex and sometimes contradictory notion which combines both privative and positive associations, which may be understood both as a static estate and a dynamic process. It is not an absolute perfection but a creaturely innocence tied to the finitude of material existence and dependent upon God's creative act. Created innocence maintains the significance of Eden without necessarily being tied to a historical interpretation of it, since it is not confined to cosmogony but takes on an important role in the inner life of faith.

To approach Traherne's theme of original and natural innocence through the doctrine of creation uncovers the theological principles which underlie it. These include *creatio ex nihilo*, the finitude of human perfection, God as the principle of love at the heart of creation, humanity's dependence upon God and the all-pervasiveness of grace. Traherne's depiction of natural innocence is better understood through Christian accounts of creation than Enlightenment ideas of nature. In acknowledging the relevance of these theological principles to Traherne's account of nature, his natural innocence is shown to be not a bare, blank or static innocence but a creaturely and created innocence stirred by love and infused with grace, the offspring of divine creation.

Perfect or Imperfect? Original Innocence

The original innocence of Eden raises an aetiological question of the 'what' of human existence. A humanity that is created innocent may also be innocent essentially, in which case innocence may, at least theoretically, be preserved or recovered. In the Christian Neoplatonism of Traherne's mystical way, original or essential innocence can be identified with pure being. The French Platonist mystic and philosopher Simone Weil described innocence thus: 'If we consider what we are at a definite moment – the present moment, cut off from the past

---

[148] Traherne, 'Ascension', *Commentaries of Heaven, Part 2*, 248.

and the future – we are innocent. We cannot at that instant be anything but what we are.'[149] G.W.F. Hegel was more dismissive about this state of perfect being, seeing the innocence of the unity of subject and object as 'merely non-action, like the mere being of a stone, not even that of a child'.[150] If innocence as a state of pure being is mere inactivity, then it is irrelevant to existence. By contrast, in existentialist philosophy, innocence is precisely not-being, belonging to an estate prior to the leap into existence. Innocence, for Kierkegaard, is something which 'when it is annulled, and as a result of being annulled ... for the first time comes into existence'.[151]

The theological status of original innocence is indicated by the grammatical tense in which it is described. Weil and Hegel's notions of innocence as pure being turn the grammatical perfect past tense of human origins into the present tense of an eternal reality that is disconnected from the narrative of experience. Kierkegaard's state of innocence has always already been annulled and so exists only in the abstract world of the pluperfect tense. In both of these accounts: innocence as pure being and innocence as the negative from which being is drawn, innocence is abstracted from the world of experience.

The previous chapter discussed an apparent theological shift from a pre-modern Augustinian emphasis on a lost 'perfect' or 'absolute' original Edenic innocence to a modern existentialist focus on an 'imperfect', 'limited' or developmental human innocence. Traherne's Edenic innocence is not absolute but a creaturely perfection that is subordinate to the absolute human perfection modelled by Christ. Adam's innocence is perfect within its own sphere but limited by the ease and safety of his estate. Traherne's Adamic or original innocence is therefore both perfect and limited. It belongs both to the perfect past tense of human origins and to the imperfect tense of ongoing creaturely existence.

In a grammatical sense, Traherne's estate of innocence is both a perfect, imperfect and present reality. The poems of Edenic innocence, 'Wonder', 'Eden' and 'Innocence', are all in the perfect past tense, indicating a perfect past world.

---

[149] Simone Weil, *Gravity and Grace* (London: Routledge, 1952), 32.

[150] George William Friedrich Hegel, *Phenomenology of Spirit*, trans. A.V. Miller (Oxford: Oxford University Press, 1977), 282.

[151] Søren Kierkegaard, *The Concept of Anxiety*, trans. R. Thomte and A. Anderson (Princeton, NJ: Princeton University Press, 1980), 26, 36, 41–3, 48; for an exposition of Kierkegaard's anti-Hegelian distinction between immediacy and innocence, which identifies innocence with origin rather than essence, see Peter Koslowski, 'Baader: The Centrality of Original Sin and the Difference of Immediacy and Innocence', in Jon Stewart (ed.), *Kierkegaard and His German Contemporaries*, vol. 1: *Philosophy* (Aldershot: Ashgate, 2007), 5.

However, the ordered linear narrative of the perfect past tense is disrupted by the ways in which Eden bleeds into the present and the future. The conclusion of 'Innocence' binds together future hope, past experience and a present imperative, ending thus:

> An Antepast of Heaven sure!
> I on the Earth did reign.
> Within, without me, all was pure.
> I must becom a Child again.[152]

In these four lines, heaven's glory is paralleled with Adam's kingship, and the purity of innocence is paralleled with a childlike spirituality. The past, present and future are bound together through the anamnesis of memory, as the poem recounts personal experience using the first person. Similarly, in 'Adam', Traherne does not use the imperfect tense but does use a confusing mixture of past and present tenses:

> How faire and Comly doth it shine, how Bright,
> How full of Vigor and Celestial Light!
> The Sun admird to see a Thing so fair
> Beneath it self shining more Bright.[153]

This tensile ambiguity encourages the reader to see both Adam and the soul in this description. Whether through memory or the hermetic ubiquity of the soul, the innocence of Eden is both a perfect past glory and a present reality.

Although the imperfect tense does not feature prominently in Traherne's descriptions of Eden, it is an appropriate category to designate the peculiar mixture of past and present through which Traherne indicates the organic finitude of creaturely perfection. Just as the imperfective aspect embeds a present participle within a description of the past, as in 'was being', so through the creative impulse original innocence is drawn into existence. Traherne's Eden describes a process through which non-being is drawn into being, in response to the attraction of the beauty of innocence. Thus, both in a grammatical and a theological sense, Traherne's original innocence is both perfect and imperfect.

---

[152] Traherne, 'Innocence', *Dobell Folio*, 10.
[153] Traherne, 'Adam', *Commentaries of Heaven, Part 1*, 225.

Chapter 3
'No Man is Innocent': The Fall into Misery

Mending the Fall: The Unity of Doctrine, Reason and Experience

The Genesis literature of Traherne's time has often been situated within literary-critical grand narratives of secularisation. In these accounts, the seventeenth and eighteenth centuries saw a transition from an Augustinian theology of original sin to a Pelagian or humanist celebration of humanity's potential for goodness. Traherne has been located at the tipping point of this transformation: looking both back to the patristic and scholastic roots of seventeenth-century theology and forward to the development of the modern individual.

Current interpretations of Traherne's theology of original sin incline to a disjunction between the 'orthodox' pre-modern boundaries of Traherne's overtly doctrinal statements and the optimistic humanism of his modern mystical experience, which appears to negate the effects of the Fall. A reading of *A Sober View of Dr Twisses his Considerations* in the light of the affective turn in intellectual history and through the lens of love, reveals that there is no genuine contradiction between doctrine and experience in Traherne's theological poetics of the Fall. Affection reintegrates the varying trajectories of human existence by finding in the abyss of love the source of the reunification of the soul.

Critical interpretation of Traherne's doctrine of the Fall has centred on his relative orthodoxy or heterodoxy. In this endeavour he has been interpreted through Pelagian, Anglican, Augustinian and Irenaean frameworks.[1] In a recent significant contribution to critical debate, William Poole agrees with Patrick Grant's influential thesis that Traherne's theology of the Fall follows Irenaeus more than Augustine.[2] In Irenaean theology, Adam and Eve in Eden are like ignorant children. Out of misunderstanding they eat the apple and so lose

---

[1] See William H. Marshall, 'Thomas Traherne and the Doctrine of Original Sin', *MLN* 73 (1958), 161–5; George Robert Guffey, 'Thomas Traherne on Original Sin', *N&Q* 14 (1967), 98–100; Franz K. Wöhrer, 'The Doctrine of Original Sin and the Idea of Man's Perinatal Intimations of the Divine in the Work of Thomas Traherne', *Wiener Beiträge zur Englischen Philologie* 79 (1984), 89–106.

[2] Poole, 'Frail Originals', 277–8; Grant, *The Transformation of Sin*, 170–97.

paradise, but their Fall is a mere childish mistake.[3] Their original imperfection is perfected through a process of redemption which is allied to maturation. Following John Hick's controversial critique of Augustine through Irenaeus, Grant set this gentler narrative against the dominant Augustinian tradition in which the glory of Eden's original innocence magnifies the horror of the first couple's transgression.[4]

In likening Traherne to Irenaeus rather than Pelagius, Grant drew Traherne within the fold of orthodoxy. However, he continued to identify Traherne with a broader post-Miltonian movement from Augustine to Pelagius, Classicism to Romanticism and conviction of human fallenness to belief in inherent innocence.[5] Poole sustains this thesis of a general doctrinal shift but detects in Traherne a mixture of both old and new. In so doing, he distinguishes between Traherne's public and private voices, between his 'maximal' Augustinian public pronouncements about the serious significance of the Fall and his 'minimal' poetic expressions which minimise its effects and extol the possibility of innocence. Poole's dualistic terminology creates its own linguistic fall by dividing doctrine from spiritual experience and one aspect of religious identity from another. This duality evokes a consciousness that within the spirit there is something other and yet interior to itself. In this divided framework there would be no possibility of a redemptive recovery of innocence, since doctrine remains unintegrated with the experience of faith.

Poole's dualistic interpretation is not consonant with the holistic inclinations of Traherne's theology as a whole. The integration of his 'public' and 'private' voices is evident both in the construction of the manuscripts and their content. His works were inherently public because of their collaborative construction and dissemination. The manuscript of *A Sober View*, for example, includes marginal comments in another hand, and there is evidence that it was prepared for publication or at least circulation.[6] There is an apparent harmony between personal spiritual experience and Traherne's public priestly role. In the early devotional work, *Select Meditations*, Traherne prays, 'O make me Comprehensiv of all thy Gloryes'. This mystical aspiration

---

[3] Irenaeus, *Against the Heresies*, IV.38.i, see also id., *Apostolic Preaching*, 12; cf. Russell M. Brown's definition of Traherne and Milton's fall as the acquisition of false knowledge ('Knowledge and the Fall of Man in Traherne's *Centuries* and Milton's *Paradise Lost*', *Lakehead University Review* 4/1 [1971], 41–9).

[4] John Hick, *Evil and the God of Love* (London: Macmillan, 1966).

[5] See Salter, 'Thomas Traherne and a Romantic Heresy'; Michael Ponsford, 'Traherne's Apostasy', *Durham University Journal* 76 (1984), 177–85.

[6] Ross, 'Introduction', in *The Works of Thomas Traherne*, vol. 1, xxii.

to glory is, more specifically, a desire both to 'See to the Peace and Quiet of thy people, and at the Same Time regard the Purity of an Inward Life'.[7] From this it seems clear that Traherne considered the consummation of glory to emerge out of the fusion of private devotion with public vocation.

Poole's dual interpretation of Traherne's Fall is further challenged by a consideration of love and the affections as a unifying category in *A Sober View*. Possibly written in the early 1660s, near the beginning of his career, it is ostensibly a relatively orthodox text. Its style is less idiosyncratic than some of Traherne's later writings, such as *Commentaries of Heaven* and *Centuries of Meditations*.[8] It adopts a conventional format for theological disputation, as a direct response to contemporary tracts, and addresses the commonly contested doctrine of election. Its own doctrine of election is based explicitly on orthodox patristic sources, both Augustine and Irenaeus, in opposition to Pelagius and the Gnostics.[9] It is also based on major pillars of the contemporary national church: Augustine's *On the Predestination of the Saints*, the Thirty-Nine Articles of Religion, the Book of Common Prayer's catechism and orders for Holy Communion and Baptism, alongside other authorised prayers and standard scriptural proof-texts on election.[10]

Traherne treads what he presents as an Anglican *via media* between the horror of the Reformed doctrine of double predestination, in which the reprobate are chosen by God for eternal damnation, and the pride of an Arminian theology that finds salvation in the individual's will to choose the good. The central argument is found in the title epigraph:

> Christ died for the whole World to restore them to a New Estate of Trial: for the Elect only to bring them absolutly and Effectualy into Glory. They that are restored to a State of Trial may conditionaly, the Elect shall irresistibly, be saved. all if they repent and believ; only the Elect out of the Depth of their Rebellion.[11]

---

[7] Traherne, *Select Meditations*, I 87.

[8] On the difficulty of dating *A Sober View*, see Ross 'Introduction', in *The Works of Thomas Traherne*, vol. 1, xx–xxi.

[9] Traherne, *A Sober View*, 53, 58, 137.

[10] See Traherne, *A Sober View*, Section II, which discusses Augustine, and Section VI, 78, in which the argument turns to the doctrine of the Church of England expressed in the 39 Articles, the creeds, catechism and prayers of the Book of Common Prayer; see also ibid., Section VIII, 87, Section IX, 93 on the parable of the talents and the vineyard.

[11] Traherne, *A Sober View*, 48.

74 *Boundless Innocence in Thomas Traherne's Poetic Theology*

God desires salvation for all and provides all with the means of grace. None can respond to this offer and so some are elected to salvation despite their sin, in order that they might declare salvation to the rest. None are reprobated or hated by God unless they first hate and reject God.

Love is the unifying theme in this discourse. Just as Milton sought to 'justify the ways of God to men', so a defence of the love of God was a key concern for the contemporary theologies of election and reprobation that Traherne responds to.[12] This is evident in their titles alone: William Twisse's *The Riches of Gods Love unto the Vessells of Mercy, consistent with His Absolute Hatred or Reprobation of the Vessells of Wrath* (1653), Samuel Hoard's, *Gods Love to Mankind. Manifested, By Dis-prooving his Absolute Decree for their Damnation* (1633) and Henry Hammond's Χάρις καὶ Εἰρήνη (Charity and Peace, 1660).

Love is a central concern throughout Traherne's treatise. It is addressed from the beginning, as in Section III's assertion of love as a free and voluntary act. This critiques a Pelagian interpretation of Ephesians 1.4–5, which would identify the salvation of the elect with God's foresight that they would become 'Holy and unblameable before him in Love' through Christ. Traherne rejects such supra-lapsarianism, asserting instead that the elect become unblameable only once they have chosen to love: 'We are Elected in Christ *that we should* be Holy and unblaemeable before him in Love.'[13] In the course of this discussion, Traherne expands upon the love which is the fruit of election through quotations from the Song of Songs. Love is also a primary concern of the final five sections of the treatise, which defend the original, primordial and infinite love of God for all humanity through an extended treatment of Romans 9.13: 'Jacob have I loved, Esau have I hated.' Traherne marshals all the resources of contemporary biblical interpretation to prove that Esau was originally loved by God and not hated until he had rejected God. Traherne thus elevates humanity's will to love God and defends God's love for humanity.

Love is a pervasive presence that infuses all good works, 'for unless they Spring from Love which is the only Fountain of Good Works, they are despoyled of all their Glory'.[14] This notion is founded on the axiom of love as the first and final cause. It follows a Platonic idea of love as the principle of life and motion and an Aristotelian ethics of the universal desire for the good, as

---

[12] John Milton, *Paradise Lost*, I.26, in *The Major Works*, ed. Stephen Orgel and Jonathan Goldberg (Oxford: Oxford University Press, 1991).

[13] Traherne, *A Sober View*, 53, 54 (italics added).

[14] Ibid. 55.

Traherne states, 'it is an Easy matter to prove that Love is the Cause and the End of Things. For nothing but Love could move God to give a Beginning and Being to Creatures, since Hatred cannot frame an object from which it naturally flies'.[15]

The ubiquitous theme of love unites doctrine and experience in Traherne's theological poetics of the Fall. Echoing Ephesians 3.17, a key passage for the treatise, he concludes in Section XXVIII that 'all Religion is rooted and founded in Divine Love'.[16] He does not see a disjunction between the doctrine of divine election and the experience of free will to love or hate. On the basis of the unity of doctrine, experience and reason, he criticises those that do draw such a distinction: 'he that denieth the Article of Election, loppeth away one great Branch from the Doctrine of the Ch. Of England: as he that denieth the Gift of Liberty doth violat a great part of Experience and Reason'.[17]

The harmonisation of Traherne's public and private voices through love is most clearly seen in his appropriation of the Book of Common Prayer. Prayer is a repeated theme within the treatise, as humanity's path back to its pre-lapsarian state.[18] Prayer is the bridge from the island of misery to that of glory, 'the Key of Heaven by which we unlock the Heavenly Treasurie. ... It is the Jacobs Ladder by which we Ascend.'[19] Traherne finds support for his affective theology in the official prayers of the national church, believing that 'It is easy to see that Gods Love unto all Mankind is the Hypothesis or foundation of all our Publick Performances and Prayers'.[20] This interpretation is evident in his adaptation of the Book of Common Prayer's prayer for Ash Wednesday in Section VI, which emphasises God's love using italics: 'Everlasting God *Who hatest Nothing that thou has Made*'.[21] This reveals an editorial intention to inculcate a sense of God's love for humanity through nationally authorised prayers. This use of these prayers encompasses the account of the Fall within a tone of praise that emphasises the possibility of redemption. Thus the unity of priest and poet, of maximal and minimal theologies of the Fall, is most evident in Traherne's voice of prayer and praise.

---

[15]   Ibid. 59.
[16]   Ibid. 193.
[17]   Ibid. 83.
[18]   Ibid. 184.
[19]   Ibid. 81; see also 180.
[20]   Ibid. 80.
[21]   Ibid.

'God did not love them enough': The Fall as a Failure in Love

As love infuses Traherne's treatise on election, so it provides the cause of the Fall. Its direct cause is an Irenaean 'misapprehension' which is more than an ignorant mistake, the death of love. As Traherne explains at the end of the treatise:

> The first thing the Devil persuaded our first Parents in Paradice was that God did not love them Enough. ... He cannot endure that we should believ that *God is Love*. He would fain have us believ he loveth us not. And when we believ that, he knoweth what follows Naturaly.[22]

What follows is 'Alienation and Enmity' against God. It is interesting to note that in the entire treatise Traherne only refers to the Fall narrative explicitly twice. In both cases it is not the apple or the serpent which is the subject, but Adam's withdrawal from God out of fear, hiding amongst the trees of the garden.[23] Adam's misapprehension of God's hatred is a form of mistrust and as such is a failure both of faith and love. This alienation from God is a kind of death, 'For Death implies Want of Power and want of sence. Being fallen into Sin, before we were redeemed we had no power to love God.'[24] The Fall in this treatise is alienation, the death of love and the seed of hatred.

Misapprehension is both the cause and the character of the Fall, being a reorientation of the will that blinds humanity to the heavenly kingdom which surrounds it. As Traherne explains elsewhere in the poem 'Misapprehension':

> Men are not wise in their Tru Interest,
> Nor in the Worth of what they long possesst:
> They know no more what is their Own
> Than they the Valu of't have known.[25]

Misapprehension is, essentially, a failure to see or to know the works of God in the world, and humanity's interest in them. Misapprehension is allied to 'inconsideration', being a distortion both of reason and of the affections: 'First there was all the reason in the World that Adam should stand ... yet he fell ... because he was inconsiderat, and by that Omission ... deserted Reason

---

[22] Ibid. 194–5.

[23] Ibid. 117, 144.

[24] Ibid. 117.

[25] Traherne, 'Misapprehension', *Poems of Felicity*, 135.

... his Posterity becoming Apostates unto Reason ever since'.[26] Through inconsiderateness or indifference, Adam and Eve lost the affection of love for God: 'our Parents Carelessness at first obliterated the Love which ought to allure us'.[27] Traherne asserts the seriousness of this Fall against Hammond's overly charitable interpretation of human nature, declaring that the 'Inconsideration' which let sin into the world 'separates the Soul from the most Glorious Objects. ... Inconsiderateness being the very Path that leadeth unto Hell.'[28]

The depth of this Fall is expressed in *Centuries of Meditations*, where the inconsiderate are those who 'Neglect to see the Beauty of all Kingdoms, and Despise the Resentments of evry Soul'.[29] The words 'neglect' and 'despise' allude to Isaiah 53.3, associating inconsiderateness with the rejection of Christ, the ultimate apostasy. The guilt of misapprehension and inconsiderateness reflects a Pauline theology of sin as ignorance of righteousness, 'No Obstacle being like the Blindness of the Mind'. The link between reason and the affections is reinforced here, as, in the same interpretation of Ephesians 4.18–19, Traherne emphasises the verse, 'Being blinded in their Heart they are past feeling'.[30] The Irenaean and Pauline echoes in this theology of the Fall as an affective misapprehension do not present a 'minimal' mistake but a 'maximal' catastrophe of the human affections. Through inconsideration, the mouth of praise is silenced and the circulation of love, praise, honour, glory and delight between humanity and God ceases, negating humanity's primary purpose, to worship.[31]

This immediate cause of the Fall is founded upon a primary cause, which is love. Traherne follows the Hobbesian principle that self-love is the foundation of natural law: 'Man Naturaly loves him self, and loving him self, naturaly desires his own Preservation, and loves all those things that be good for him, and hates all those that be hurtfull.' Self-love includes the desire to be beloved, which is the root of the love of virtue and of love for a loving God: 'to be Beloved is the chiefest Good, and to be Hated the Chiefest Evil, especially of God ... The loss of that Love is Hell: The Sight and Possession of that Love is Heaven.' So, in Eden 'it was natural to hate Evil, and Love Good ... When Man was faln into Sin, ... It was natural to him then to hate God, becaus Nature told him he was hated of him.'[32] The estrangement and hostility caused by the primordial misapprehension

---

[26]   Traherne, *A Sober View*, 88.
[27]   Ibid. 144.
[28]   Ibid. 91–2.
[29]   Traherne, *Centuries of Meditations*, I 85.
[30]   Traherne, *A Sober View*, 148.
[31]   On the divine cycle of love, praise, honour, glory and delight, see ibid. 60.
[32]   Ibid. 132–3.

comes from a dividing of the will, wherein the natural principle of self-love is separated from the natural instinct or duty to love a loving God. In becoming convinced that God does not love them, Adam and Eve believe that obedience is not in their interest. So, love of God turns into hatred, and the natural principle of self-love turns into anxious self preservation and the pursuit of advancement.

'The least Sin is of infinite Demerit': The Decline from Infinity to Finitude

The love which is the principle of life is an infinite love, so its loss is an infinite Fall. *A Sober View*'s concluding paragraph reads: 'For *God is Love*: and Love is infinit in Goodness and Bounty'.[33] The infinite Fall from this state is encapsulated in the oxymoronic phrase, 'infinit Guilt', which appears across Traherne's works and indicates the absurdity of an infinite decline into the finitude of sin.[34] 'Infinit guilt' carries several significations. Firstly, it suggests that a single transgression can overturn the whole law: 'As a little Poyson turnes the best Meat from Nourishment into Poyson so doth one Vice cherished and allowed corrupt and viciate all the Vertues in the whole World'.[35] Secondly, it defines sin as a 'long Parenthesis in the fruition of our Joys'.[36] As a decline from infinity to finitude, this parenthesis is not merely a temporary digression but an awful gap between experience and eternal bliss.[37] This is supported by *Kingdom of God*, which persuasively links the boundless gulf between infinity and finitude with the enmity between God's goodness and fallen humanity's sin: '[God's] Goodness is so Infinit, that he hateth the least obliquity, the least defect, the least Shadow of Sin or Miserie.'[38] Thirdly, infinite guilt is irreducible and therefore eternal: 'a Sin once committed, can never be undone; it will appear in its place

---

[33]   Ibid. 195.

[34]   Ibid. 141; Traherne, *Select Meditations*, III 56, III 31.vi; id., 'Angell', *Commentaries of Heaven, Part 2*, 65; id., 'Article', *Commentaries of Heaven, Part 2*, 225; id., 'Abuse', *Commentaries of Heaven, Part 1*, 72 ('a Guilt which endureth Eternaly').

[35]   Traherne, *Christian Ethicks*, 156.

[36]   Traherne, *Centuries of Meditations*, III 51.

[37]   Cf. Francis King, who uses this passage to define sin as 'only a blurring of the eye' ('Thomas Traherne: Intellect and Felicity', in H. Love [ed.], *Restoration Literature: Critical Approaches* [London: Methuen, 1972], 141–2).

[38]   Traherne, *Kingdom of God*, 288; see also the insertion: 'And I think it is the Glory of God, that his Essence is infinitly distant from the least Imperfection; that the Enmitie between his Nature, and Defect is immeasurable, and that no Alloy can agree with his Divinity' (ibid. 273).

throughout all Eternity'.[39] The Fall, therefore, which is a mere gap between the estates of innocence and misery, has an eternal place in the tapestry of infinity. However, this need not be a cause of despair, because sin persists in eternity only as transformed into good, as in 'Ascension', where 'the places of our shame shall Know us again in our Triumph and Glory'.[40]

In this framework, the Fall is not a narrative but a diptych. On one side is the scene of innocence wherein humanity is united with God in love. On the other side is the scene of wisdom, wherein God works to repair that original kingdom. These two scenes are juxtaposed and, in their parallels, transposed atop one other, as the bliss, order and power of innocence is compared to the deformity and difficulty of trial after the Fall.[41] This Fall is less an Irenaean or Augustinian narrative of ascent or descent, more the hinge between these two pictures, an abyss of the absence of love or the infinite ocean that divides humanity from God.

Bridging the Gap: Infinite Love

Humanity's love for God may be lost in the Fall, but the principle of love is a constant that draws lines of continuity between pre- and post-lapsarian states and reunites finitude with infinity. Based on an Augustinian theology of the Holy Spirit as the bond of love between the Father and the Son, Traherne explains that the 'Desire of Happiness and the Love of Goodness is so implanted in the Soul that it can never be rooted out'. It is such a deeply rooted 'Inclination' that it has become natural and essential to human existence, so that 'in all Estates it is incorruptible'. This is the love of goodness which is the 'Spark of [God's] Immutablity', that draws humanity to the good. [42] Love is the constant which traverses the abyss of hatred that divides the soul.

Love is also the agent of conversion, as Traherne describes in his narrative of the mending of the Fall. He recounts a parable of a people exiled to an 'Iland of Misery', whose king provides a bridge for them to return to the heavenly kingdom. This story emphasises the infinite distance between humanity and God: 'The Sea being the Distance between God and him, ocassiond by the Fall'. The bridge must therefore be an infinite bridge, 'evry Arch as wide as the Skie, and the Length infinit becaus the Distance, is infinit between sin and Glory'.

---

[39] Traherne, *Christian Ethicks*, 186.
[40] Traherne, 'Ascension', *Commentaries of Heaven, Part 2*, 238.
[41] Traherne, *A Sober View*, 74–5.
[42] Ibid. 134.

The first two arches of the bridge are love. The first is 'Love in the Bosom of God, infinit and Eternal Love towards the Sinner'. The second arch 'is an Effect of this Love, and that is the giving his Son to be our Savior'.[43] Love in this account takes an active role in undoing the effects of the Fall.

Traherne's descriptions of conversion evoke the enticement of the soul to return to the love of God. In so doing they attempt to excite the same passions in the reader. The discovery of the love of God through Christ's crucifixion awakens the soul:

> But when GOD was pleased above all Imagination to reveal a New Abyss and Mine of Love unhoped, unexpected, in giving a Savior, the Winter was past, the Night of Darkness was gone, the very self same Principle of self Preservation made it natural again for man to love, and rejoyce in God.[44]

This description of love as an abyss creates a parallel with the abyss of sin into which humanity has fallen. However, love is not a chasm but a mine out of which treasure emerges, a model of the kenotic love of Christ. Love removes the impediments to desire that misapprehension places upon the soul:

> But an infinit change was wrought when Gods redeeming Love was discovered. For therby we were quickned and made able to love him ye more then before ... the Desire that in us was baffled with Despair, exerts it self naturaly, like a Spring when the impediment is removed, and our Love of Happiness naturaly carries us to it when it is proposed before us. Gods Love enflaming us with Love.[45]

Here, love is the restoration of life, the motion of desire. Traherne draws on the passionate language of medieval meditations on the Song of Songs and the theatrical language of drama to express this restoration of love as a 'scene wherin Sin itself enflamed unto Love'.[46] This emotive language is intended to excite and allure the reader to be themselves enflamed by love. The effect of love is the reunification of division, as, in learning to love God's law, 'we are Cemented together, all being united into one Body, and evry one made the Possessor of all'.[47] Love permeates Traherne's account of the Fall. It is that which is lost and

---

[43] Ibid. 178–80.
[44] Ibid. 133.
[45] Ibid. 117.
[46] Ibid. 75.
[47] Ibid. 61.

the means of its recovery, the fountain of creation and the affection by which soul recovers innocence.

Alluring the Soul: An Affective Theological Poetics

The act of love which repairs the Fall is instigated by the affections. Traherne's privileging of the affections follows the Cambridge Platonist philosophers who drew an Augustinian link between knowledge and love or reason and the affections.[48] Following a Thomist theology of virtue as the desire for the good, Traherne believed that 'Goodness is not the Power, but affection, of doing Good'.[49] Although conventional distinctions were often drawn between virtuous affections and sinful passions, in Traherne's usage even passions such as ambition are primordially positive affections. Several times, he refers to covetousness and ambition as natural affections which, in innocence, are desires for true treasure and heavenly glory.[50] These and other such 'Natural Dispositions Concreated with the Soul' incline humanity to love as an act of the will.[51] Nevertheless, the Fall has 'blotted out those Sweet and Innocent Apprehensions he had of GOD', through sinful lust.[52] God's infinite love is an active love that 'hath been doing all things to awaken and allure us to Good Works'.[53] By grace, God prepares the affections, softening and quickening them to receive the apprehension of love.[54] Traherne's theology of the Fall is thus a theology of the corruption and restoration of the affections and is rooted in the internal life of the spirit.

In light of this theology, the priestly duty is to allure the affections to love God, which is Traherne's intention in *A Sober View*. His primary aim, to teach and train the affections, is evident from the dearth of polemical material on this highly contentious subject. It is also found in his interpretation of election, in which the elect are redeemed so that they can convince others of salvation: 'for we are to persuade that and all other Creatures that God loves them. Which is the only Motive we can use to persuade them to love him.'[55]

---

[48] On this wider context, see Susan James, *Passion and Action: The Emotions in Seventeenth-Century Philosophy* (Oxford: Oxford University Press, 1999), ch. 10.

[49] Traherne, *A Sober View*, 158.

[50] Ibid. 61, 151.

[51] Ibid. 105.

[52] Ibid. 106.

[53] Ibid. 59.

[54] Ibid. 105.

[55] Ibid. 194.

82   *Boundless Innocence in Thomas Traherne's Poetic Theology*

The attempt to persuade the reader to love is a key feature of Traherne's theology and his poetics. He persuades not only through argument, scriptural scholarship and appeal to authoritative sources but also uses the rhetorical tool of the language of praise and worship. Traherne has often been styled a naive optimist, due to the positive tone of his lyrical poetics.[56] His theology of the Fall demonstrates that this is not a spontaneous effusion of emotion but a rhetorical device to convince the reader of God's love and to excite an imagination of the possibility of right relation. His lyric poem on 'Love' evokes the moment of conversion when, as explained in *A Sober View*, 'the Desire that in us was baffled with Despair, exerts it self naturaly, like a Spring when the impediment is removed'. 'Love' exclaims at that moment:

> Did my Ambition ever Dream
> Of such a Lord, of such a Love![57]

Similarly, the *Commentaries of Heaven* poem, 'Allurement', is both a description of God's manifold expressions of love in creation and a linguistic act of allurement. By addressing himself in the second person, the narrator implicitly incorporates the reader into the meditation:

> Awake my Soul, and soar upon the Wing
> Of Sacred Contemplation; for the King
> Of Glory wooes; he's pleased to allure
> Poor feeble Dust![58]

After recounting, in cumulative unpunctuated lists, the glories of creation and expressing through exclamation marks the wonder of that vision: O Glory! O Delight beyond compare! / O Ravishments of Joy!' Traherne ends with a final call to the reader: 'His Soul, thy Soul, and all his Friends say Come: / GOD is alone thy Glory and thy Home.'[59]

Although *A Sober View* is written in prose, it has a similar purpose to 'Allurement', enticing the soul to love. The final section has a stinging critique

---

[56] See e.g. Francis Towers, 'Thomas Traherne: His Outlook on Life', *Nineteenth Century* 87 (1920), 1024–30; Ronald E. McFarland, 'Thomas Traherne's *Thanksgivings* and the Theology of Optimism', *Enlightenment Essays* 4/1 (1973), 3–14.

[57] Traherne, 'Love', *Dobell Folio*, 61.

[58] Traherne, 'Allurement', *Commentaries of Heaven, Part 1*, 367–8.

[59] Ibid. 368, 370.

of Reformed theologies of double predestination, based mainly upon their emotional impact. In interpreting Romans 8.19, Traherne declares:

> It is my Wonder therefore how it should be possible for men to pinch so hard upon one Text, and to squeeze Blood and Desperation and Terror out of it, and Odiousnesse and Injustice and Tyranny with whatsoever else is evil, while there is no Expression in the Bible like it.[60]

However one interprets the phrase 'Jacob have I loved and Esau have I hated', he implores, 'be sure I say to believ firmly that Esau was once an Object of God's Love, and that every man Primitively and Originaly is so'. The final sentence expresses concern for those who believe a doctrine of hate because 'through fear and Dread, they first think basely of themselvs and dislike GOD, and then are presently or finally estranged from him'.[61] For Traherne, a Reformed theology of election only repeats and reinforces the Fall of alienation from God. His theology of election attempts both to protect the affections from the hatred which Adam learnt and to excite them to love and so to mend the Fall. In this there is a perfect harmony between doctrine and spiritual experience.

Entering the Abyss: The Trajectory of the Fall

The trajectory of the Fall helps to account for the place of innocence within it. It has been suggested that there is no artificial disjunction between Traherne's doctrine and experience of the Fall and that for him redemption is a reharmonisation of the soul with its primordial affections, through the love of God. Nevertheless, the Fall remains a fault line across human existence. *A Sober View* does not adopt a narrative structure for the Fall. As discussed above, it is presented through the juxtaposed tableaux of the estates of innocence and misery, between which it appears as a gap or parenthesis. There is no linear trajectory within this account, either of descent into misery or ascent into heaven. Rather, the Fall of *A Sober View* is an infinite abyss in human experience which is transcended, bridged and infilled by the equally infinite abyss of love.

In conversion, infinite guilt and infinite love are brought together within the double, or divided, fallen self: 'For in Order of Time those Things may be

---

[60] Traherne, *A Sober View*, 194.

[61] Ibid., 195.

together, that in order of Nature are asunder'.[62] This surprising conjunction is the catalyst for the spark of redemption: 'For God bringeth Light out of Darkneness, Good out of Evil, Order out of Confusion. which is far more then to Creat Good out of Nothing'.[63] Here, the abyss of the Fall becomes a mine or fertile void out of which a new and more glorious creation emerges.

This Fall has a double trajectory of both descent and ascent. In 'Amendment' this is described as the expansive trajectory of divergent poles: 'Loss adding Nothing made our Gain far more / Our Fall hath raisd us higher then before.'[64] This picture is consonant with Traherne's expansive mysticism of the soul's movement into infinity through *theosis*. However, the juxtaposition of infinite guilt and infinite love also gives a sense of contraction, through the unification of their infinite disunity in the sinner who is *simul justus et peccator*. This theological poetics thus encompasses the heights and depths of human existence within the Fall event, all subsumed by 'the breadth and length and height and depth' of the love of God (Ephesians 3.18).

A 'Separable Accident': The Loss of Innocence

The cause and character of the Fall has been discussed so far but not the manner of the loss of innocence. Traherne defines the process of the soul's decline from infinity to finitude through the classical terminology of substance and accidents, through which innocence is lost as a 'separable accident'.[65] Origen stated that 'in the Trinity alone ... does goodness exist in virtue of essential being; while others possess it as an accidental and perishable quality'.[66] *Commentaries of Heaven* extends this metaphysical principle by classifying innocence as a separable accident of the soul. Unlike inseparable accidents, which are the essential attributes of human being, separable accidents 'can be taken away from their Subjects; but so that themselvs are Destroyed therby, though their Subjects

---

[62] Ibid. 69–70.

[63] Ibid. 148.

[64] Traherne, 'Amendment', *Commentaries of Heaven, Part 2*, 54; see also id., *Kingdom of God*, 498, which explains how 'lowness it self [is] the Rise of our Exaltation'.

[65] Cf. Murphy, who links Traherne's 'Accidents and Occasions' to 'the loss of innocent simplicity', as 'necessary complications of fallen, corrupted intellect' ('"Aves quaedam macedonicae"', 226–7).

[66] Origen, *De Principiis*, I.6.ii, trans. Frederick Crombie, ANF 4 (Edinburgh: T.&T. Clark, 1867–73).

remain. As Heat from Iron, Beauty from the face, Innocence from the Soul.'[67] If innocence is non-essential to the soul, then the power of continuing innocent will 'Depend upon the Liberty of Free Agents', although it comes 'from [God] also Mediately; becaus He gav the Power of Producing them'.[68] Original innocence is not, therefore, simple nature but a fragile accident of human essence maintained by infused grace and the will of the subject.

The language of accidents intimates a paradoxical innocence that is characterised by vulnerability and baseness, ironically combined with glorious potential: 'What is more Weak then an Accident? That cannot stand by it self. ... What is more Contemptible? It hath no Being of its own ... and yet all the Glory of Heaven and Earth is Derived therfrom.'[69] Murphy interprets Traherne's reification of accidents as an anti-Aristotelian realism of thoughts over things, but it also reflects a genuine delight in paradox.[70] It is the subversion of expectations which makes the glory of accidents wonderful:

> to the Honor of Accidents it may be said, that All Created Goodness is Accidental, and the more Wonderfull for being so. For that Goodness should lie in such a fading Weak Invisible Thing, and yet be so Strong and Real; is Exceeding Strange: and another Goodness in Goodness it self.[71]

Accidents such as holiness, glory, truth, blessedness, wisdom, righteousness, joy, dominion, greatness, power, life and majesty, as well as innocence, are the beauty of the soul to be contemplated and enjoyed 'Till we can feel their Existence Spiritualy, and Taste their Sweetness, and be Ravished with their Beauty, we can never be Satisfied'.[72] Perfected accidents behave as if they were essential attributes: 'Acquired Accidents infused into the Soul, tho they are not Attributes, yet they are as like to Attributes, when Perfect and Glorious, as Nature will bear, or the

---

[67] Traherne, 'Accident', *Commentaries of Heaven, Part 1*, 110; on original righteousness as an inseparable accident of the image of God, see: 'Original Justice had more Essential dependence upon the image of God in Man, then Rotunditie hath with a Sphere' (Thomas Jackson, 'Of the Primæval estate of the First Man', *An Exact Collection of the Works of Doctor Jackson* [London, 1654], 3006).

[68] Traherne, 'Accident', *Commentaries of Heaven, Part 1*, 110.

[69] Ibid. 111.

[70] Murphy, '"Aves quaedam macedonicae"', 221–3, 246; on Traherne and paradox, see Rosalie L. Colie, *Paradoxia Epidemica: The Renaissance Tradition of Paradox* (Princeton, NJ: Princeton University Press, 1966), 145–68.

[71] Traherne, 'Accident', *Commentaries of Heaven, Part 1*, 112.

[72] Ibid. 114.

86   *Boundless Innocence in Thomas Traherne's Poetic Theology*

Soul can desire'.[73] Innocence as a separable accident is thereby paradoxically glorified as a beauty which, when perfected, appears as the soul's very nature.

'Lights and Shades': Innocence and Guilt

The juxtaposition of divergent trajectories within Traherne's account of the Fall is echoed in his language of innocence. As, in a finite world, opposites are pushed together, so after the Fall, innocence becomes semantically tied to guilt.[74] The root of this unlikely pairing lies in the fact that the Fall provides the motivation to speak of innocence or to speak at all. Michael Suarez considers Traherne's dialectic between misery and felicity, sin and grace, as the 'animating tension that lies at the heart of his poetry and prose'.[75] Similarly, Kershaw states that sin is 'the impetus behind all of his encouragements towards a recovery of Innocence, the recognition of Grace and the attainment of Glory'.[76] Sin may be a motivation for speech, but a more fundamental cause of the juxtaposition of innocence and guilt is beauty. *Centuries of Meditations* declares that 'as Pictures are made Curious by Lights and Shades ... so is Felicitie composed of Wants and Supplies, without which Mixture there could be no Felicity'.[77] In the same way, sin is a marring of the light of innocence which, after the Fall, can no longer be viewed without its shadow.

Although there is objectively no conversation between good and evil, within the 'intermixd' state of subjective experience a dialogue exists between innocence and guilt.[78] This notion finds a source in the parable of the wheat and tares of Matthew 13.24–30, which was echoed in Milton's defence of free speech, *Areopagitica*: 'Good and evil, we know in the field of this world grow up together almost inseparably.'[79] For Traherne, in the various states of the soul, innocence and guilt interact as light and shade, reality and dream. In the state of innocence, the virtue of abhorrence of sin is a work of 'Shaping Imaginary Objects', since sin is only a 'possibilitie' which threatens Edenic bliss.[80] In misery,

---

[73]   Ibid. 121.

[74]   Traherne generally uses the terms 'guilt' and 'sin' interchangeably.

[75]   Michael F. Suarez, 'Against Satan, Sin, and Death: Thomas Traherne and the "Inward Work" of Conversion', in J.C. Hawley (ed.), *Reform and Counterreform: Dialectics of the Word in Western Christianity since Luther* (Berlin: Mouton de Gruyter, 1994), 93–4.

[76]   Kershaw, 'The Poetic of the Cosmic Christ', 204.

[77]   Traherne, *Centuries of Meditations*, I 41.

[78]   Traherne, *Ceremonial Law*, 233.

[79]   John Milton, *Areopagitica*, in *The Major Works*, 247.

[80]   Traherne, 'Abhorrence', *Commentaries of Heaven, Part 1*, 7; id., *Kingdom of God*, 288.

the opposite occurs, and innocence appears to the sinful only as 'a Beautifull Chimera, a Dream, a Shadow, not a real Existence'.[81] The dialogue between innocence and guilt is therefore one between reality and imagination or dreams. Both subsist in dialogue within the regenerate who 'retain a Zeal between / Sleeping and Waking', who are, in a Lutheran sense, *simul justus et peccator*.[82] Sluberski has interpreted this trope in Traherne's works as simply 'see[ing] the sin and the sinner connected for the purpose of judgement but separated for the purpose of salvation', but this does not fully account for the intertwining of innocence and sin.[83]

'Acceptance' and 'Abhorrence' in *Commentaries of Heaven* further illustrate the ambiguous conjunction of innocence and guilt after the Fall. These companionate positive and privative faculties epitomise the unity of light and shade, as they are both in God: 'of which two [Acceptance] is the Light, [Abhorrence] is the Shadow'.[84] Abhorrence of evil is 'the Necessary Concomitant of Delight in Good, and as naturaly follows it as a Shadow the Light that Shineth upon a Body. We could not lov Good did we not abhor Evil.'[85] Although in temporal experience abhorrence and acceptance are partners, as perfected in God they are one: 'Abhorrence of Evil is the Lov of Good.'[86] This theme intimates the ultimate unity of privative and positive goodness in innocence and the necessity of the privative or negative aspects of righteousness.

More ambivalently, abhorrence unites virtue and vice by engendering both innocent and guilty acts. Abhorrence is fundamentally 'the Effect of Self-love, arising upon a Sence of evil. It floweth from the Principle of Self-Preservation, which is Engraven in all our Natures.'[87] It is therefore a virtue only when it is turned against evil and a vice when turned against God.[88] In this world, abhorrence is itself a composition of good and evil mixed 'with Mutability', creating joy but 'with more Imperfection.'[89] It participates in the ambiguity of existence, forced to 'abhor the most Lovly Object in the Whole World ... where there is a Mixture

---

[81]   Traherne, *Kingdom of God*, 292.

[82]   Traherne, *Christian Ethicks*, 166.

[83]   Sluberski, *A Mind in Frame*, 119. Traherne adopts this trope in *A Sober View*, 124; *Centuries of Meditations*, II 30.

[84]   Traherne, 'Acceptance', *Commentaries of Heaven, Part 1*, 77, 79–80.

[85]   Traherne, 'Abhorrence', *Commentaries of Heaven, Part 1*, 6.

[86]   Ibid. 13.

[87]   Ibid. 5.

[88]   Ibid. 10–11.

[89]   Ibid. 9; on mixed human existence, see also: 'in the Estate of Grace Virtu and Vice seem to meet together and to inhabit in it' (Traherne, 'Ambition', *Commentaries of Heaven, Part 2*, 34).

of Good Alluring us unto Evil'.[90] Even as a virtue, abhorrence is a parenthesis in joy because it 'seizeth a Man' with physical revulsion and horror.[91] It is a suffering as result of sin, albeit in reaction against it rather than submission to it.

In the drama of existence, innocence and guilt coexist within a soul at war. The regenerate Christian is mixed of opposites: 'an humble and pious Soul, a Penitent and Grateful Person, sensible (at once) of his infinite Guilt and Grandure'.[92] The paradoxical conjunction of innocence and guilt is a line drawn between the estates of innocence and misery–grace that runs throughout Traherne's depiction of the spiritual life. This is not to deny the triumphal progression of Traherne's theology overall, but it does highlight his engagement with the ambiguity of existence, the complexities of experience and the consequences of the Fall in the process.

'No Man is Innocent': The Negation of Innocence

The character of the loss of innocence and its conjunction with guilt after the Fall have been examined. But can innocence persist even within the abyss? Traherne's spirituality has been frequently described as cataphatic, or 'affirmative', which is a reference to the sacramentalism of his theology, the verbiage of his style and his cheerful temperament. The apophatic aspect of his 'shadow side' is apparent in his insistent repetition of the phrase from Romans 3.10: 'there was none righteous no not one'.[93] This is the negation of innocence, which is how it appears in the chasm of the Fall.

A Sober View contains a recurrent lament of the impossibility of present innocence, explicitly following Romans 3.10 and Psalm 14, and also echoing Ecclesiastes 7.20.[94] This theme was found elsewhere in contemporary devotion. Edward Stillingfleet saw innocence slipping through humanity's fingers, since 'we are compounded of such disagreeing and contrary principles, that we are not able to preserve divine, pure and inspotted Innocency'.[95] Lancelot Andrewes lamented the state of the world in which, '*in thy* all-seeing *sight, shall no man*

---

[90] Traherne, 'Abhorrence', *Commentaries of Heaven, Part 1*, 12–13.

[91] Ibid. 6–7.

[92] Traherne, *Christian Ethicks*, 61.

[93] Traherne, *A Sober View*, 89.

[94] See ibid. 91.

[95] Edward Stillingfleet, *Origines Sacræ, or a Rational Account of the Grounds of Christian Faith* (London: R.W., 1662), 511.

living in this vale of misery, *be justified*, or found innocent'.[96] Similarly, *Kingdom of God* expresses anxiety and frustration that as a consequence of the Fall: 'Nothing is Holy, nothing pure in its Essence: but all is Arbitrary and uncertain.'[97] The philosophical principle behind this lament is the distinction between substance and accidents, or essential and conditional nature, found in Benjamin Needler's assertion that 'There is no created good *per essentiam*, but *per participationem* ... holinesse is a quality in man, and not his essence'.[98] Beyond this theoretical distinction, however, the comprehensiveness of 'nothing' and 'no man' lends a note of despair to the thought that no one is innocent. Traherne does not share Jackson's shallow optimism that 'though there be none that doth good, no not one, yet some there be doe lesse evill than others'.[99] His use of the phrase evokes the tragedy of the loss of innocence.

The mere evocation of innocence draws attention to it, even in declarations of its absence. 'No man is innocent in this world', the litany declares, but in the spaces between the words hangs the implication that humanity was created innocent and that the calling to innocence remains. In the section of *Kingdom of God* cited above, the absence of innocence does not preclude the possibility of righteousness, but is the basis of the 'Grand Law of Nature' by which it is necessary to both love good and hate evil.[100] This is similar to Origen, for whom the fact that nothing is essentially holy apart from God is an incitement to righteousness, since it signifies 'that it lies within ourselves and in our own actions to possess either happiness or holiness' (Origen, *De Principiis*, I.5.v). In *Select Meditations* this is a priestly calling. The phrase here is less lament than recognition of the honour and difficulty of the clergy's task: 'Innocent no man is in this world. much Less a Congregation.' Therefore it is difficult to remain innocent amongst one's flock, but a glorious calling to serve them, as 'wheather Innocent or miserable it is a weighty thing to be conversant a mong them and not to Erre'.[101] This is both challenge and exhortation,

---

[96]   Lancelot Andrewes, *Holy Devotions with Directions to Pray* (5th edn, London, 1663), 262 (Ps. 143.2).

[97]   Traherne, *Kingdom of God*, 327.

[98]   Benjamin Needler, *Expository Notes, with Practical Observations; Towards The opening of the Five First chapters of the First Book of Moses called Genesis* (London: T.R. & E.M., 1644), 72.

[99]   Jackson, *A Treatise of the Divine Essence and Attributes*, 185.

[100]   Traherne, *Kingdom of God*, 327; .

[101]   Traherne, *Select Meditations*, IV 52. Ross has corrected the original manuscript which has 'wheather Innocence or miserable' (Beinecke Rare Book and Manuscript Library, Yale University, New Haven, Conn., James Marshall and Marie-Louise Osborn Collection, Osborn b308).

as he who succeeds in this weighty calling is 'more beautifull then if he had never Sinned'.[102]

The negation of innocence evokes the hope of redemption through repentance. Francis Quarles adopted this trope to stress that the apostles' zeal and faith lay not in their essential innocence but their status as redeemed sinners: 'the best of men have sins; None lives secure, / In Nature nothing's Perfect, nothing Pure.'[103] Similarly, 'Apostle' describes them as sinful men 'made Heroical and Divine by their zeal for GODs Glory and their Lov to Mankind'.[104] The absence of innocence leads to an encomium on redemption and a call to repentance:

> Integrity is a most sure Defence
> And purer souls find Rest in Innocence.
> But Innocence is to Sublime a Thing
> For Man. A Sinner too may sit and sing
> And when surrounded find a sure defence
> Against all Ills in lowly Penitence.[105]

The call to innocence through its negation indicates the apophatic character of the language of innocence in light of the Fall. This ephemeral paradox of present absence is illustrated by Heinrich Bullinger's use of contradictory aphorisms in his scripturally based definition of innocence: 'Every man ought to defend hys Innocency, and to clear hym selfe of false suspections' and 'Noman is innocent in the syghte of God'.[106] Traherne defines innocence in similarly contradictory ways, in reference to sin and through what it excludes as much as what it includes. So in God's kingdom 'there is no Spot nor Blemish in it, no Sin, no Sickness, no offence, no Distaste, no Death, no Miserie all is pure without any Mixture; Sincerity, Beauty and Delight, Holiness, Wisdom Goodness without Enormitie or Defect'.[107]

The negation of innocence is not only a lament, expressing loss and frustration but also evokes the imagination of innocence, which is the root of

---

[102] Ibid.

[103] Francis Quarles, *Job Militant: With Meditations Divine and Morall* (London: Felix Kyngston, 1624), meditation 6.

[104] Traherne, 'Apostle', *Commentaries of Heaven, Part 2*, 128.

[105] Traherne, 'Affliction', *Commentaries of Heaven, Part 1*, 308.

[106] Heinrich Bullinger, 'Innocence', in *A Brief and Compendiouse Table, in a Maner of a Concordaunce* (London: S. Mierdman, 1550).

[107] Traherne, *Kingdom of God*, 429–30.

desire and hope. The function of the negation of innocence is not primarily to draw attention to its lack. Rather, it points away from human essence and origins to the grace of repentance and to redemption. The phrase therefore has an apostolic function. To declare 'no man is innocent' is not to focus on human innocence; rather, after the manner of Leonardo da Vinci's *St John the Baptist* (*c*.1513–16), it points away from humanity to the innocence of Christ and the grace of God.[108]

---

[108] See Mark 1.7; Gal. 2.20. Da Vinci's painting is in the Louvre, Paris.

Chapter 4

The Trial of Innocence: Innocence in the State of Misery–Grace

Misery and Grace

While separated in the structure of this book, Traherne's estates of misery and grace both concern earthly existence. Misery is a post-baptismal state of apostasy, trial and suffering. However, grace is already present in misery, as the apostate youth of *Centuries of Meditations* still desires God amid his dreams of worldly trinkets.[1] This chapter is not concerned with misery alone but with trial, which spans the estates. The conventions of the genre of tragic drama provide a hermeneutical key to the themes of tension, conflict, dialogue and action that characterise innocence on trial in a sinful and suffering world.

In *Theological Dramatic Theory*, Quash argues that the dramatic mode is most appropriate for a theological aesthetics concerned with worldly existence. Just as in the seventeenth century John Dryden defended the naturalism of English dramatic poetry as an imitation of true speech, so Quash believes that drama provides 'categories for giving voice to the truth of creaturely life before God'.[2] In a 'really dramatic drama', humanity is the players on the stage who do not know the ending, reflecting life's uncertainty and indeterminacy.[3] Quash's characterisation of drama is allied to a Ricoeurian theological poetics that prefers a 'sometimes ragged, discursive and open-ended mediation' to an abstract totalising grand narrative.[4] Following Mikhail Bakhtin, it asserts the

---

[1]   Traherne, *Centuries of Meditations*, III 14–15.

[2]   Quash, *Theology and the Drama of History*, 25; John Dryden, 'Of Dramatic Poesy: An Essay (1668)', in *Of Dramatic Poesy and other Critical Essays*, ed. George Watson (London: Dent, 1962), vol. 1, 78–9; see also Thomas Sprat, *Observations on M. De Sorbier's Voyage into England* (London, 1665), 251; Aristotle, *Poetics*, 1449a (IV 18–19).

[3]   Quash, *Theology and the Drama of History*, 167, 26, 35.

[4]   Ibid. 5 n. 4, referring to Paul Ricoeur, *Time and Narrative*, trans. Kathleen McLaughlin and David Pellauer (Chicago: University of Chicago Press, 1984–8), vol. 3, 256.

'unfinalizability' of existence.[5] It is imbued with Donald MacKinnon's emphasis on the modern theologian's duty to 'reckon continually with what is historically particular and contingent' and 'to do justice to the intractable difficulties of human historical experience – to the tragic realities of human moral failure and suffering'.[6]

Traherne is known more for the lyricism of his poetry and his epic projects of universal synthesis than for the dramatic features of his theology. However, Traherne uses theatrical language which betrays a familiarity with Aristotle's *Poetics* and a consideration of the theological implications of drama.[7] His theology does not fit Quash's model of tragic drama, but dramatic categories facilitate investigation into the tragic elements in his work.[8] These include his engagement in the war with sin and his acknowledgement of existential vulnerability and finitude. Like Quash's 'real' dramas, Traherne writes from the middle of the action without full knowledge of the end. *Kingdom of God* acknowledges the uncertainty of existence by extolling the virtue of the person who is able

> To Act on obligations yet unshewn,
> To Act upon Rewards, as yet unknown,
> To Keep Commands whose Beauty is unseen.[9]

This chapter explores the dramatic elements of Traherne's theology of innocence, looking at innocence in trial, suffering innocence and the character of innocence in a sinful and suffering world.

Graced Innocence: Sacramental Regeneration

Before this chapter can move on to the estates of misery and grace, however, it must address the leap from the Fall to regenerate existence. This occurs

---

[5]   Quash, *Theology and the Drama of History*, 107; Mikhail Bakhtin, *Problems of Dostoyevsky's Poetics*, trans. R.W. Rotsel (Ann Arbor, Mich.: Ardis, 1973), 47, 55–6, 229.

[6]   Donald M. MacKinnon, *Themes in Theology: The Three-Fold Cord: Essays in Philosophy, Politics and Theology* (Edinburgh: T.&T. Clark, 1987), 234; Quash, *Theology and the Drama of History*, 10.

[7]   On seventeenth-century reception of Aristotle, see Marvin Theodore Herrick, *The Poetics of Aristotle in England* (New Haven, Conn.: Yale University Press, 1930), 35–79.

[8]   On the 'tragic element in Christianity', see Donald M. MacKinnon, *The Problem of Metaphysics* (Cambridge: Cambridge University Press, 1974), 130.

[9]   Traherne, 'For Man to Act', *Kingdom of God*, 502; the poem also appears in id., *Christian Ethicks*, 165–6.

through baptism, on which is built the sacramental model of graced innocence found in *Church's Year-Book, A Sober View of Dr Twisses his Considerations* and *Commentaries of Heaven*.

A baptismal model of innocence implies the non-innocence of infants. This was a contested issue in early modern devotion, although Dreher and Marcus have noted the baptismal prerequisite for infant innocence in much seventeenth-century theology and its medieval antecedents.[10] The Book of Common Prayer's 'Ministration of Publick Baptism to Infants' illustrates their ambiguous status in contemporary Anglican devotion. The exhortation following the gospel could be read as an assertion of natural innocence, reminding the congregation of Christ's injunction to become like children and to 'follow their innocency'.[11] However, grace provides the context for this prayer, which emphasises God's goodwill towards infants and concludes with their need for grace: 'Give thy Holy Spirit to this Infant, that he may be born again, and be made an heir of everlasting salvation.' Traherne rehearses the need for infant regeneration in the *Church's Year-Book*'s devotions to John the Baptist. He laments the impurity of procreation, claiming that that 'No Child is so Contemptible and polluted in the Dungeons of the Womb, As I was then'. Justification and purification come through Christ, and he wonders at the miracle that John the Baptist was regenerated by Christ even in the womb, 'who Cleansing him from Original Sin, Justified him with his grace'.[12] Infant innocence therefore appears to be a graced innocence.

Whether infants are born innocent or guilty, through baptism they receive a graced innocence. Luther described baptism as an inauguration into an innocent life: 'It is as if the sponsors, when they lift the child up out of baptism, were to say, "Lo, your sins are now drowned, and we receive you in God's name into an eternal life of innocence."'[13] Andrewes shared this sentiment, styling innocence alongside peace, sincerity and patience as one of the '*virtues Baptismales*, the very virtues of our Baptisme'.[14] The centrality of baptism to regenerate innocence may account for the uncommonly polemical tone in Traherne's defence of

---

[10]   Dreher, *Fourfold Pilgrimage*, 20; Marcus, *Childhood and Cultural Despair*, 70–71.

[11]   Cf. Jeremy Taylor's assertion of the natural innocence of children (*Unum Necessarium, or, The Doctrine and Practice of Repentance* [London: James Flesher, 1655], 400).

[12]   Traherne, *Church's Year-Book*, 163.

[13]   Martin Luther, 'The Holy and Blessed Sacrament of Baptism, 1519', in *Luther's Works*, ed. E. Theodore Bachmann and Helmut T. Lehmann (Philadelphia. Pa.: Muhlenberg Press, 1960), vol. 35, 31; cf. Calvin, 'Of Baptism', *Institutes*, IV 15.

[14]   Lancelot Andrewes, *XCVI Sermons by the Right Honourable and Reverend Father in God, Lancelot Andrewes, Late Lord Bishop of Winchester* (London: George Miller, 1629), 681.

96 *Boundless Innocence in Thomas Traherne's Poetic Theology*

paedobaptism.[15] In *Commentaries of Heaven*, this was directed against the Anabaptist John Tombes, 'great Ringleader of that Sect' in nearby Leominster and author of a three-part treatise against paedobaptism.[16] Traherne would have encountered him early in his career, as Tombes was assistant to the Herefordshire commission on 29 September 1657 (Traherne was admitted on 30 December that year) and remained in Leominster until his ejection in 1662.[17]

The central theme of Traherne's baptismal theology in *Commentaries of Heaven* and *A Sober View* is a defence of sacramental regeneration: 'so is evry one Regenerated, that is Baptized, in a Sacramental Maner'.[18] His position on its effectiveness was not uncontroversial. *A Sober View*'s marginal commentator found his view 'most Congruous to Truth ... yet you will find thos much Opposed'.[19] Traherne defends sacramental regeneration using the Book of Common Prayer's 'Thanksgiving appointed after Public Baptism', which identifies it with spiritual adoption and incorporation into the church.[20] Traherne's definition of the baptised as 'Consigned over to the Grace of God, declared to be his Child, and incorporated into his Holy Church' demonstrates a confidence in sacramental regeneration that surpasses Cranmer's view of the sacraments as signs only of the spiritual work of grace which they signify.[21] Baptismal promises must be fulfilled for salvation, but baptism remains the conduit of regeneration.[22]

Baptismal regeneration is the model of graced innocence. The graced, rather than natural innocence of the baptised child provides a foundation for Christian living. Regenerate innocence is no mere natural 'Ignorance or want of skill to doe ill', accompanied only by the certainty of future moral decay.[23]

---

[15] This is evidence against A.B. Chambers' assertion that Traherne was committed only to internal rites of spiritual regeneration over outward sacramental acts (*Transfigured Rites in Seventeenth-Century English Poetry* [Columbia: University of Missouri Press, 1992], 48–58).

[16] Traherne, 'Baptism', *Commentaries of Heaven, Part 2*, 452; John Tombes, *Anti-Pædobaptism* (3 vols, London, 1652–57).

[17] Julia J. Smith, 'Tombes, John (1602–1676)', *ODNB*.

[18] Traherne, 'Baptism', *Commentaries of Heaven*, 450.

[19] Traherne, *A Sober View*, 81.

[20] Ibid. 80.

[21] Ibid. 81; Thomas Cranmer, 'On the Sacrament of the Lord's Supper', in *The Works of Thomas Cranmer*, ed. John Edmund Cox (Cambridge: Cambridge University Press, 1846), vol. 1, 124–5; see Brian D. Spinks, *Reformation and Modern Rituals and Theologies of Baptism: From Luther to Contemporary Practices* (Aldershot: Ashgate, 2006), 66–73.

[22] Traherne, *A Sober View*, 81.

[23] Wilson, *A Complete Christian Dictionary*, 336b; See also Irenaeus, *Against the Heresies*, IV 38.

It is a source of 'Confidence' and hope but also of obligation.[24] The sins of the regenerate are worse than those of nature because they are apostate: as Traherne states in *Commentaries of Heaven*, 'a Heathen cannot, but an Infant Baptized may become an Apostate'.[25] Baptism has an imperative tone, laying a duty on the infant not to betray their calling:

> In Baptism vow I will
>
> .   .   .   .   .
>
> Do all that GOD doth by his Law require:
> I surely then must set the World on fire
>
> .   .   .   .   .
>
> But then I must, if to triumph I mean
> Keep Soul and body, washt in Baptism, clean.[26]

Baptismal innocence is the imputation of Christ's righteousness, the model and measure of Christian innocence. It is expressed through the imperative of duty and the optative of hope for the covenant promise. Nevertheless, this is a certain promise, looked forward to as already fulfilled in the consummation of glory. It is the model of graced innocence, which covers the entire life of faith.

Innocence in Trial

The 'furniture of Stages and Theatres':[27] *The World, the Flesh and the Devil*

Traherne's theology of baptismal regeneration would be incomplete without the struggle with that renounced at baptism: the world, the flesh and the devil.[28] Early Traherne criticism assumed that, in Anne Davidson's words, 'Traherne never really struggled with the world, the flesh and the devil; temptations to him were mere tinsel'.[29] James Osborn's discovery of *Select Meditations* in 1964

---

[24]   Traherne, *A Sober View*, 82.

[25]   Traherne, 'Baptism', *Commentaries of Heaven, Part 2*, 453; see id., 'Apostasie', *Commentaries of Heaven, Part 2*, 124–7.

[26]   Traherne, 'Baptism', *Commentaries of Heaven, Part 2*, 454–5.

[27]   Traherne, 'Adam', *Commentaries of Heaven, Part 1*, 214.

[28]   See: 'Grant that he may have power and strength to have victory, and to triumph, against the devil, the world, and the flesh' (Book of Common Prayer, 'Publick Baptism').

[29]   Davidson, 'Innocence Regained', 272; see e.g. Husain, *The Mystical Element in the Metaphysical Poets of the Seventeenth Century*, 292; Bush, *English Literature in the Earlier*

changed this landscape by uncovering numerous personal prayers of lamentation and repentance.[30] Since then, Traherne's battle with sin has been increasingly acknowledged.[31] Rosalie Colie thought that, 'Gentle as he was, Traherne was adamant against the sins of men', while Elizabeth Jennings claimed that he 'demonstrates too the weakness and fallibility of man and he finds that the only answer to man's needs and miseries is the infinite compassion of God'.[32]

In general, Traherne's works are oriented towards a consideration of goodness and away from evil. This is founded on an intention, expounded in *Centuries of Meditations, Christian Ethicks* and *Commentaries of Heaven*, to address only what conduces to felicity. *Centuries of Meditations* is filled with '*Enriching Truths*' to 'lead you into Paths Plain and Familiar. Where all Envy, Rapine, Bloodshed, Complaint, and Malice shall be far removed; and nothing appear but Contentment and Thanksgiving.'[33] This resolute contemplation of the good is manifest in cumulative raptures which resonate with the exhortation in Philippians 4.8: 'whatsoever things are true, whatsoever things are honest, whatsoever things are just, whatsoever things are pure, whatsoever things are lovely, whatsoever things are of good report ... think on these things.'[34]

Traherne's focus on felicity follows the Plotinian principle that 'that which is Straight is the measure of it self, and of what is crooked'.[35] Good has priority over evil because both are defined by good. Traherne thus defends his *Christian Ethicks*, which focuses on the virtues and neglects the vices, by arguing that virtue is 'so full and perfect in it self, that it needeth not the aid of those additional Arts, which labour to set off the dignity of imperfect things by borrowed Commendations'.[36] Traherne's attentiveness to the good stems not from shallow optimism, but from a firm philosophical principle.

Seventeenth Century, 158; A.S.P. Woodhouse, *The Poet and his Faith: Religion and Poetry in England from Spenser to Eliot to Auden* (Chicago: University of Chicago Press, 1965), 85–6.

[30] James M. Osborn, 'A New Traherne Manuscript', *TLS* (8 Oct. 1964), 928.

[31] Webber, *The Eloquent 'I'*, 225; Sharon Cadman Seelig, 'Origins of Ecstasy, *Select Meditations*', *ELR* 9 (1979), 419–31 (421); Julia J. Smith, 'Introduction', in Thomas Traherne, *Select Meditations* (Manchester: Carcanet, 1997), xv, xx–xxi.

[32] Colie, 'Thomas Traherne and the Infinite', 76–7; Elizabeth Jennings, 'The Accessible Art: A Study of Thomas Traherne's *Centuries of Meditations*', *Twentieth Century* 167 (1960), 151.

[33] Traherne, *Centuries of Meditations*, I 1, 4.

[34] On the rhapsodic effect of Traherne's lists of felicities, see Carl M. Selkin, 'The Language of Vision: Traherne's Cataloguing Style', *ELR* 6 (1976), 92–104.

[35] Traherne, 'Apprehension', *Commentaries of Heaven, Part 2*, 169; Plotinus, *Enneads*, I.8.ix.

[36] Traherne, *Christian Ethicks*, 207.

The Trial of Innocence   99

Traherne does not ignore evil but incorporates it into the theatre of virtue. In *Commentaries of Heaven*, the problem of evil closely shadows the substance of felicity. Within this project to discover 'ALL THINGS ... to be Objects of Happiness', he makes a point of demonstrating how the worst aspects of misery conduce to the good.[37] For example, in 'Accusation' he declares:

> That all things in Heaven and Earth are Treasures to the Soul ... we may see by Accusation. for it is an Object as uncapable of Fruition as can be prepared: Evil in its Nature, Invisible to the Ey, Transeunt in its Duration. And yet all Accusations ... may be made our Joy, and be turned into Glory.[38]

The same exercise is undertaken for each entry that addresses an apparent evil. Despite appearances, 'Abhorrence' is 'one of the Joys of Heaven'.[39] 'Spiritual Absence' cannot be redeemed but Traherne thinks 'it not inexpedient to Detect this Evil ... that we might Escape so great and injurious a Banishment, and return again into GODs Kingdom, which is that of Glory'.[40] 'Abuse' originates in the 'Power to Abuse' which is granted by God as 'a Jewell. without which Man could not be an Illustrious Creature'.[41] 'Affliction' is the occasion of submission to the 'Heavenly Physician'.[42] 'Amendment', echoing Socrates, is 'so desirable, as if it were alone the Thing which GOD endeavored in all his Servants'.[43] To act 'Amisse' is looked upon kindly, since 'We aim at Felicity in all our Deeds, but when we endeavor it by Evil Deeds we miss of our purpose'.[44] Anger 'may be a 'troublesom vexatious passion' but was originally implanted as 'a Consequent in the Soul attending upon Love'.[45] 'Avarice' may be virtuous, since 'in the Court of Heaven an insatiable Desire is an infinit Virtue'.[46] As 'all Things are Objects of Miserie to the Wicked, and of Bliss to the Virtuous', so 'Babel' is 'a Woe to the one, and a Joy to the Other'.[47] Finally, 'Baseness' has an exalted origin and end: 'The end why God made some Things Baser then other[s], was the Ornament

---

[37] Traherne, *Commentaries of Heaven, Part 1*, 3 (title page).
[38] Traherne, 'Accusation', *Commentaries of Heaven, Part 1*, 139.
[39] Traherne, 'Abhorrence', *Commentaries of Heaven, Part 1*, 13.
[40] Traherne, 'Spiritual Absence', *Commentaries of Heaven, Part 1*, 39.
[41] Traherne, 'Abuse', *Commentaries of Heaven, Part 1*, 64–5.
[42] Traherne, 'Affliction', *Commentaries of Heaven, Part 1*, 304.
[43] Traherne, 'Amendment', *Commentaries of Heaven, Part 2*, 47.
[44] Traherne, 'Amisse', *Commentaries of Heaven, Part 2*, 55.
[45] Traherne, 'Anger', *Commentaries of Heaven, Part 2*, 82.
[46] Traherne, 'Avarice', *Commentaries of Heaven, Part 2*, 407.
[47] Traherne, 'Babel', *Commentaries of Heaven, Part 2*, 440.

100   *Boundless Innocence in Thomas Traherne's Poetic Theology*

and Beauty of the whole Creation' and 'There is nothing left *Base*, because evry Thing is Directed by the Goodness of GOD to most *Excellent* Ends'.[48]

At points, Traherne's attempt to draw evil into the victory of felicity only serves to emphasise misery. Some evils are only made good through their undoing. 'Adulterie' only leads to felicity as a 'Caution' against temptation.[49] 'Apostasie' only incites prayers to avoid it, that 'I never will in Heart Tongue Hand apostatize'.[50] The 'Atheist' must be cured and brought to felicity.[51] 'Backsliding' must be reversed by repentance.[52] The 'Bastard' has hope of salvation if he repents.[53] At the darkest end, 'Antichrist' is one of the few express enemies of felicity, as its 'Great Enrager'.[54] Close to this, 'Barrenness' in the baptised is 'inconsistent with their Duty Beauty and Felicitie'.[55] The trouble taken to incorporate evils into a consideration of the good reflects a sincere grappling with the world, the flesh and the devil matched only by an equally strong determination to see all things in the light of glory.

The Dialectic of Innocence: The Double World

The flesh and the devil provide the furniture of the divine drama, but the world is the stage for the war with sin and also for the innocent life. Existence is a theatre of combat between two worlds. *Kingdom of God* describes the dialectic of the two cities of God and the devil, but Traherne's clearest exposition of this division appears in *Centuries of Meditations*.[56] In this passage Augustine's two cities are presented as two worlds:

> Truly there are two Worlds. One was made by God, the other by Men. That made by GOD, was Great and Beautifull. Before the Fall, It was Adams Joy, and the Temple of his Glory. That made by men is a Babel of Confusions: Invented Riches, Pomps and Vanities, brought in by Sin.[57]

The second world of man is that whose vain pomp and glory is renounced at baptism. It is the 'Horrid howling Wilderness' of exile in which the church

---

48 Traherne, 'Baseness', *Commentaries of Heaven, Part 2*, 463–4.
49 Traherne, 'Adulterie', *Commentaries of Heaven, Part 1*, 258–9.
50 Traherne, 'Apostasie', *Commentaries of Heaven, Part 2*, 127.
51 Traherne, 'Atheist', *Commentaries of Heaven, Part 2*, 327–9.
52 Traherne, 'Backsliding', *Commentaries of Heaven, Part 2*, 445.
53 Traherne, 'Bastard', *Commentaries of Heaven, Part 2*, 467.
54 Traherne, 'Antichrist', *Commentaries of Heaven, Part 2*, 113.
55 Traherne, 'Barrenness', *Commentaries of Heaven, Part 2*, 456.
56 Traherne, *Kingdom of God*, 264.
57 Traherne, *Centuries of Meditations*, I 7; Augustine, *The City of God*, IX.

languishes in *The Ceremonial Law*.[58] It is the godless world of *Select Meditations* that descends back into the void, a 'silent Chaos, a Dull and Empty wilderness'.[59] It is the world without the angelic influence of virtue in *Church's Year-Book*'s meditations on St Michael, 'a Den of Dragons and a Chaos of Confusion'.[60] The second world of man is the frustration of false treasure, the yearning of wilderness exile and the emptiness and horror of evil.

The double world of Eden and Babel plays out the internal dialectic of fallen existence between finitude and infinity. It is the individual's 'Double selfe, according as He is in God, or the world. In the world He is confined, and walketh up and Down in Little Roome: but in God He is evry where'.[61] This internal conflict is the soul's misery which is resolved through a dialectical process of supersession: 'Giv all (saith Thomas a Kempis) for all. Leav the one that you may enjoy the other'.[62] For Thomas, this was God's call to humanity to 'Forsake thyself ... [and] stand purely and undoubtingly in me'.[63] Traherne reinterprets it as abandoning Babel for Eden. What for Thomas was an act of self-immolation, for Traherne was a transfer of riches. The dialectic of misery and grace is resolved not through victory but translation from one state to another. *Christian Ethicks* describes this as a journey where virtue 'teacheth us through many Difficulties in this Tempestuous World to Sail Smoothly, and attain the Haven'.[64]

'A Condition wherein we are to Toyl, and Sweat, and travail hard': The Theatre of Trial

Life in the double world is characterised by trial:

> For this purpose we are to remember, that our present Estate ... is an Estate of Trial, not of Fruition: A Condition wherein we are to Toyl, and Sweat, and travail hard, for the promised Wages; an Appointed Seed Time, for a future Harvest; a real Warfare, in order to a Glorious Victory: In which we must expect some Blows, and delight in the Hazzards and Encounters we meet with.[65]

---

58 Traherne, *Ceremonial Law*, 227.
59 Traherne, *Select Meditations*, II 42, see also II 14, IV 7.
60 Traherne, *The Church's Year-Book*, 218.
61 Traherne, *Select Meditations*, II 92.
62 Traherne, *Centuries of Meditations*, I 7.
63 Thomas à Kempis, 'Of Pure Resignation of a Man's Self', *Imitation of Christ*, 3.37, trans. Aloyisus Croft and Harold Bolton (Nashville, Tenn.: Thomas Nelson, 1999).
64 Traherne, *Christian Ethicks*, 17.
65 Ibid. 19.

Inge, Kershaw and Jordan categorise trial within the framework of the four estates, as either the conflation of misery and grace or as the estate of misery. These interpretations identify Traherne with an Augustinian view of life as tribulation.[66] Traherne's ubiquitous and potent references to trial, however, do not denote a particular estate. Trial is a general feature of existence: of working, yearning, fighting and suffering for promised glory. The Platonist mystic Jacob Boehme similarly saw trial throughout the history of salvation; in the '*forty dayes Adam* was tryed in his Innocency', Moses' forty days on the mountain, Israel's forty years in the desert and Christ's forty days in the wilderness and forty hours in the grave.[67] The whole human state from innocence to grace can be characterised as an 'estate of trial'.

The continuity of trial from innocence through misery and grace suggests not a single *felix culpa*, or 'fortunate fall', but a continuous *felix probatio*, or 'fortunate trial'. Within trial, apostasy remains a present danger, but there is also a growing opportunity for evil to transform into good. As *Christian Ethicks* explains, the trials of Adam in Eden were lesser, being 'just as many as were needful for the trial of his Obedience, Gratitude, [and] Fidelity'.[68] The second estate has more difficulty and more reward, being created 'for [humanity's] greater Trial and more perfect Glory'.[69] As *Select Meditations* avers, glory is achieved through trial: 'By how much the Greater the Difficultie is by So much the more Glorious the Soul is that over comes it.'[70]

Trial is essential to human existence, because it is a condition of freedom and finitude. Kershaw recognises this, stating that 'Traherne sees the great drama or "spectacle" inherent in the estate of Trial – in the journey of an independent soul at perfect liberty, and also completely vulnerable'.[71] 'Voluntary acts' are a free response to trial, but this freedom is married to mutability. As Traherne explains in his definition of an Angel, 'It was impossible but that Creatures made som thing out of Nothing must be Changeable'. Without activity, creation returns to nothing, so trial is 'absolutely necessary to the Perfection of their Glory'.[72] Trial

---

[66]   Inge, *Happiness and Holiness*, 151; Kershaw, 'The Poetic of the Cosmic Christ', 204; Jordan, *The Temple of Eternity*, 64, 68; see Augustine, *Expositions on the Book of Psalms*, Ps. 77.4, ¶iv.

[67]   Jacob Boehme, *Mysterium Magnum, or An Exposition of the First Book of Moses called Genesis* (London: Lodowick Lloyd, 1656 [1623]), 81.

[68]   Traherne, *Christian Ethicks*, 167; this expands on Calvin, who describes the injunction not to eat from the tree as a 'trial of obedience' (*Institutes*, II.1.iii).

[69]   Traherne, *Christian Ethicks*, 168.

[70]   Traherne, *Select Meditations*, III 3.

[71]   Kershaw, 'The Poetic of the Cosmic Christ', 210.

[72]   Traherne, 'Angell', *Commentaries of Heaven, Part 2*, 68.

as a constant feature of human existence binds creaturely vulnerability into a cosmic process of perfection.

Trial is the stage on which difficulty and activity bring forth beauty. *Kingdom of God*'s final chapter contains an impassioned argument 'That it was better to be made in a State of Trial, then immediatly placed in the Throne of Glory'.[73] Without trial, heroic acts are impossible and virtue is dead. Earlier in *Kingdom of God*, Traherne complains that 'Virtu is Insensible of its own Existence without Some Kind of Exercise. [It rusts without Employment.]'[74] This parallels the argument of Milton's *Areopagitica*, which presents trial as the perfecter of innocence:

> Assuredly we bring not innocence into the world, we bring impurity much rather: that which purifies us is trial, and trial is by what is contrary. That vertue therefore which is but a youngling in the contemplation of evill, and knows not the utmost that vice promises to her followers, and rejects it, is but a blank virtue, not a pure; her whitenesse is but an excrementall whitenesse.[75]

Traherne's extolment of 'Heroick Actions' similarly presents the glorious lustre of virtue won through trial against the 'excrementall whitenesse' of stale passivity. Active and courageous virtue is a model of innocence in trial.

The beauty of virtue in trial is how it moves its spectators.[76] Like the audience of a drama, those who witness virtuous acts have their affections incited towards the good: 'Virtuous, and Heroick Actions ... awaken the Concern, and desire of the Soul'. An easy path 'affordeth litle Delight to the *Spectator*', whereas trial 'commend[s] the *Actor* to a more high Esteem, infusing Life, and Beauty into the *Scene*'.[77] Trial is real-life drama, performing virtue on the stage of the existential quotidian, as Traherne states in *Commentaries of Heaven*:

> The Cruelties and Straights. Severities and Distresses, Violences and Pains and Agonies and Dangers and Self Denials of a person being Actualy seen, are not Chimera's but real Things, moving Resentments of Pitty and Tenderness, Esteem and Gratitude in the Soul of the Lover answerable to the Nature and Qualitie of them.[78]

---

[73] Traherne, *Kingdom of God*, 495; see also id., *Centuries of Meditations*, IV 89; id., *Christian Ethicks*, 164.

[74] Traherne, *Kingdom of God*, 299, [] indicates insertion; see also id., *Centuries of Meditations*, IV 97.

[75] Milton, *Areopagitica*, 248.

[76] See Kershaw, who thinks that trial has 'the makings, according to Traherne, of a great dramatic spectacle' ('The Poetic of the Cosmic Christ', 208).

[77] Traherne, *Kingdom of God*, 498 (italics added).

[78] Traherne, 'Appetite', *Commentaries of Heaven, Part 2*, 147.

These passages subvert the Aristotelian tragic conventions that Milton followed in his description of the power of tragedy: 'by raising pity and fear, or terror, to purge the mind of those and such-like passions, that is to temper and reduce them to just measure with a kind of delight, stirred up by reading or seeing those passions well imitated'.[79] For Traherne, the authentic drama of experience incites the affections but not in a cathartic sense tending towards their annihilation. In the spectacle of virtue, conventional tragic affections of pity and tenderness are joined by 'esteem and Gratitude'.[80] These latter affections have no need of temperance, as they lead to thanksgiving. Not daunted by horror, the soul is instead inclined to praise and even imitate the suffering of the blessed. Trial is the theatre of glory wherein, through encounter with difficulty, affections are not pacified but are transformed into activity.

'The smallest Trial weaker spirits blinds':[81] Temptation as the End of Innocence

The *telos* of trial is the soul's perfection, but it also contains genuine danger. Kershaw sees Traherne's estate of trial as merely the 'complication' within the drama that makes the plot more thrilling but does not alter the ending.[82] This assessment is appropriate for Traherne's more eschatologically oriented *Kingdom of God*. However, *A Sober View*'s doctrine of election necessitates the possibility of failure, as 'they that are restored to a State of Trial may conditionaly, the Elect shall irresistibly, be saved'.[83] Trial may defeat the weak or degenerate, and the reprobate is one 'chosen to the Means [of grace], and upon his Trial, Corrupt'.[84]

Temptation illustrates the dangers of trial. It is problematic for a theology that asserts the possibility of innocence, since capacity to be tempted can be interpreted as evidence of guilt. For Thomas à Kempis, it belongs to fallen existence, as temptations 'come from within us – in sin we were born'.[85] Traherne denies this in his discussion of 'Appetite', although he is unable to explain precisely

---

[79]   John Milton, 'Of That Sort of Dramatic Poem which is Called Tragedy', in *The Major Works*, 671; Aristotle, *Poetics*, 1449b (VI 2–3).

[80]   Both Donne and Sidney add 'admiration' to the passions of pity and fear incited by drama, see Dryden, 'Of Dramatic Poesy', 46 n. 3.

[81]   Traherne, *Ceremonial Law*, 221 ('Trial' misquoted by Ross as 'Trail', see id., *The Ceremonial Law* [Folger Shakespeare Library, MS.V.a.70], 16r).

[82]   Kershaw, 'The Poetic of the Cosmic Christ', 209; Aristotle, *Poetics*, 1455b (XVIII 1).

[83]   Traherne, *A Sober View*, 48 (title page).

[84]   Ibid. 122.

[85]   Thomas à Kempis, *Imitation of Christ*, 1.13.2; for contemporary examples of this view, see Stanley Fish, *Surprised by Sin: The Reader in Paradise Lost* (London: Macmillan,

The Trial of Innocence   105

'how Adam in his Innocency could [without Sin] be tempted to Sin'.[86] John Owen's treatise *Of Temptation* also noted the difficulty of explaining Adam's temptation. He responded that Adam 'had nothing *in him* to entice or *seduce* him', temptation being not the 'seduction to sinne' but only the more neutral 'matter' used to seduce.[87] Traherne addresses this question through the appetites, which are originally innocent: 'The first Impression of Desire is a Natural Effect inevitable, upon the Presence of the Object; and as innocent as Natural.'[88] Therefore Adam could have desired the fruit without sin if his will had overruled his sense to prevent his eating it: 'For then all his Faculties had discharged their Duty, in evry part of his Soul it had been innocent, and he himself justified before GOD'.[89] After Adam, temptation represents the risk of apostasy.[90] To remain innocent against temptation is not impossible but never easy: 'no man can safely come within the Reach of Temptations and Allurements. Howbeit ... the Wise man, of which Ulysses the Poet is made the Pattern, by tying him self fast to the Centre of his felicity may secure his Constancy.'[91] The firm mast which preserves innocence is the Cross of Christ. Notably, it is the poet who clings to it.

Temptation, like trial, is an opportunity for improvement through labour. Thomas à Kempis stated that 'temptations, though troublesome and severe, are often useful to a man, for in them he is humbled, purified, and instructed'.[92] Similarly for Traherne, 'To be Good where there is no Occasion or Temptation of being otherwise is cheap and familiar, and a thing almost of no Observation, but to be vigorous and faithfull in retaining Goodness, in the midst of Assaults Allurements and Temptations, is to be Good indeed'.[93] Temptation is therefore an aspect of trial; the test rather than the limit of innocence, ordained to 'make us like the King of Sufferings *pure* and *perfect*'.[94]

1967), 41, citing the *Garden of Spirituall Flowers* (1638), 285; T. Watson, *Christian Soldier* (1669), 52; J. Corbet, *Self-Imployment* (1681), 41–2.

86   Traherne, 'Appetite', *Commentaries of Heaven*, vol. 3, 150–51, [] indicates insertion.

87   John Owen, *Of Temptation* (Oxford, 1658), 16, 38–9.

88   Traherne, 'Appetite', *Commentaries of Heaven, Part 2*, 150 ['without sin' inserted].

89   Ibid. 151.

90   See Traherne, 'Backsliding', *Commentaries of Heaven, Part 2*, 444–6.

91   Traherne, 'Allurement', *Commentaries of Heaven, Part 1*, 364.

92   See Thomas à Kempis, *Imitation of Christ*, 1.13.2.

93   Traherne, 'Appetite', *Commentaries of Heaven, Part 2*, 146–7.

94   Traherne, *Christian Ethicks*, 190–91, referring to Ps. 11.4–5; Dan. 11.35; Zech. 13.9.

Suffering Innocence

The Problem of Innocent Suffering

Suffering is an aspect of misery with significant implications for innocence, not only the problem of innocent suffering but also the virtue of suffering innocently and the glory of innocent sacrifice.[95] Suffering is an important theme for Traherne, who writes eloquently of the spiritual suffering that stems from sin. *Ceremonial Law* paints a vivid portrait of Israel's wilderness trials as a type of spiritual affliction. In 'Manna', theirs is the disappointment of illusory temporal pleasures, which

> Pleas Allure and Promise fair being viewd
> Far off: but nearer hand they us delude:
> And make us perish of a Double Death,
> While Want and Anger robs us of our Breath.[96]

Israel knows the anguish of unrequitable desire in exile:

> But here we may not Sojourn long, we must
> Away again, and travail through the Soultry Dust
> One Drop of Ease doth but increas the fire:
> A Tasted Joy thats lost we more Desire.[97]

As in his descriptions of sin, suffering is generally evoked with felicity in view:

> The Way for Men to see how Excellent
> Their Blessings are, the Way to be Content
> Is first to dive into the Loss of Things.[98]

In misery–grace, innocence and suffering are connected through the interrogative of why the innocent suffer. In modern theological tragic theory, suffering's irreducible particularity is betrayed by attempts to explain it. For

---

[95] For modern theological responses to the problem of innocent suffering, see Elizabeth W. Moberly, *Suffering, Innocent and Guilty* (London: SPCK, 1978); John E. Thiel, *God, Evil, and Innocent Suffering: A Theological Reflection* (New York: Crossroad, 2002).

[96] Traherne, *Ceremonial Law*, 215.

[97] Ibid.

[98] Ibid. 225.

The Trial of Innocence 107

Williams, accounting for suffering is 'an attempt to forget it *as* suffering'.[99] By contrast, seventeenth-century providentialist theologies required an explanation for suffering. Donne concluded that affliction makes one 'fit for God', while after spending four 'Affliction' poems wrangling with God, Herbert decided in 'Affliction V' that 'We are the trees, whom shaking fastens more'.[100] For Peter Sterry, Protestant persecution was an essential stage in the divine drama, the crisis point of the plot resolved by redemption.[101] Sceptical philosophy provided a minor counterpoint to these providentialist conclusions. Charron described unjust punishment of innocents as meaningless, unredemptive and reflective of 'humane imbecilitie'.[102] He alluded to Augustine's judgement of unjust torture in his castigation of the miserable state of human society.[103]

For Traherne, as for Sterry, suffering is the crisis point in a providential drama of faith 'that like the sun breaking thorow a Cloud he shall shine more Brightly after the shade is over'.[104] His account of suffering also draws on earlier works of Christian theodicy. *Commentaries of Heaven*, after the manner of Origen, presents it as a painful cure administered by the divine physician;[105] *Ceremonial Law* echoes Gregory the Great's *Morals on the Book of Job*.[106] Israel's passage through the Red Sea is a type of spiritual affliction, which is redemptive because

---

[99] Rowan Williams, 'Trinity and Ontology', in K. Surin (ed.), *Christ, Ethics and Tragedy: Essays in Honour of Donald MacKinnon* (Cambridge: Cambridge University Press, 1989), 78; on Ricoeur, see also Larry Bouchard, *Tragic Method and Tragic Theology: Evil in Contemporary Drama and Religious Thought* (University Park: Pennsylvania State University Press, 1989), 41.

[100] John Donne, *Devotions Upon Emergent Occasions* (Ann Arbor: University of Michigan Press, 1959), meditation 17; George Herbert, 'Affliction' I–V, *The English Poems of George Herbert*, ed. Helen Cox (Cambridge: Cambridge University Press, 2007), 162–3, 224, 265–6, 328, 350.

[101] Nabil I. Matar, 'Aristotelian Tragedy in the Theology of Peter Sterry', *LT* 6/4 (1992), 315; see Aristotle, *Poetics*, 1455b (XVIII 1); on the pedagogical role of tragedy in seventeenth-century thought, see David Houston Wood, *Time, Narrative and Emotion in Early Modern England*, Literary and Scientific Cultures of Modernity (Farnham: Ashgate, 2009).

[102] Charron, *Of Wisdom*, 128–30, 133–4, 183, 422.

[103] Augustine, *City of God*, XIX 6.

[104] Traherne, 'Accusation', *Commentaries of Heaven, Part 1*, 247.

[105] Traherne, 'Affliction', *Commentaries of Heaven, Part 1*, 305–6; Frances Young, 'Suffering', in Adrian Hastings, Alistair Mason and Hugh Pyper (eds), *The Oxford Companion to Christian Thought: Intellectual, Spiritual, and Moral Horizons of Christianity* (Oxford: Oxford University Press, 2000), 688a.

[106] See Gregory the Great, *Morals on the Book of Job*, I.I, preface, trans. C. Marriot, Library of the Fathers of the Holy Catholic Church (Oxford, 1844–47); see also Thomas Aquinas, *Literal Exposition on Job: A Scriptural Commentary Concerning Providence*, trans. Anthony Damico (Atlanta, Ga.: Scholars, 1989), prologue, 67–9.

it turns believers away from evil who 'seeming to be drownd, escape their Foe'. Affliction leads to consolation, since 'Discomforts Comfort bring', and it can prevent sin: 'A Freezing Smart Affliction doth som times / Save from a Worser Deluge; that of Crimes.'[107] These explanations are comparable to Gregory's, for whom the 'scourges' of God include those for spiritual correction, 'the prevention of future [misdeeds]', the demonstration of 'the power of the Deliverer' and the increase of glory through patience.[108]

Nevertheless, innocent suffering remains a problem to be solved. 'Affliction' lists three kinds of affliction overall: 'Persecutions for virtue, or Chastisements for sin, or els casual Accidents in general Providence'.[109] Persecution has value, 'For a Good cause infuseth its Goodness into the Calamity suffered for it'. Purgative suffering is the most common, since even those with apparently innocent intent are not without sin: 'Afflictions are nothing but the Counterpanes of our Guilt.'[110] Innocent suffering comes not under persecution but under 'Casual Emergents' which are 'hard to be born' because they have no legitimate cause and therefore no meaning except as they are submitted to God.[111] Thus, Traherne does acknowledge the problem of innocent suffering, although only as a minor counterpoint within a broader providentialist framework.

'Suffer in a Wise and Vertuous manner': Suffering Innocently

Despite employing conventional providentialist arguments, Traherne's theology of innocent suffering is not primarily a theodicy but has a didactic concern with how to suffer innocently. The *Elizabethan Homilies*, the template for Church of England preachers, distinguished between innocent suffering and suffering innocently. The sermon 'Of the Passion for Good Friday' refers to those who suffer 'undeservedly' in a description of the beatitudes, but its main concern is that the persecuted should 'endure innocently and guiltles', with a 'Perfect patience' that 'studieth to suffer innocent, and without deserving'.[112] Innocent suffering is unmerited punishment, while to 'suffer innocent' is to suffer virtuously. *Christian Ethicks* makes a similar distinction. Alone, 'meer

---

[107] Traherne, *Ceremonial Law*, 212.

[108] Gregory the Great, *Morals on the Book of Job*, I.I, preface, xii.

[109] Traherne, 'Affliction', *Commentaries of Heaven, Part 1*, 310.

[110] Ibid.

[111] Ibid. 312.

[112] *Certaine Sermons or Homilies Appointed to be Read in Churches in the Time of Queen Elizabeth I*, ed. Mary Ellen Rickey and Thomas B. Stroup (Gainesville, Fla.: Scholars' Facsimiles & Reprints, 1968), vol. 2, 13, 178.

Sufferings have no Vertue': to suffer innocently is to suffer with love, as 'It is a vain and insipid thing to Suffer without loving *GOD* or Man'. To suffer with love is to suffer vicariously. According to Traherne, 'the chief Elixir of its Nature is founded in the Excellency of a Spirit, that Suffers for anothers sake'.[113] Therefore, suffering innocently is suffering vicariously.

Christ models the activity of suffering innocently, uniting passive victimhood with active sacrifice through love.[114] A deleted section of *Centuries of Meditations* describes Christ as both passive suffering servant and active man of justice, who saves '[in suffering, as well as doing'].[115] Nevertheless, the glory of vicarious suffering belongs not to Christ alone, but to all, as in *Christian Ethicks*: 'When we suffer any thing for *GOD*'s sake, or for our Neighbours good, we suffer in a Wise and Vertuous manner.'[116] This combination of wisdom and virtue emphasises the maturity and righteousness of suffering innocently over the vulnerability and passivity of the innocent sufferer. The virtue of suffering innocently, rather than the misfortune of innocent suffering, perfects the soul, as in the following declaration: *'We are made perfect through Sufferings* [Heb. 2.10]: though the Way be mysterious, and the Manner almost incomprehensible.'[117]

This standard for suffering innocently may help to account for *Commentaries of Heaven*'s seemingly harsh assertion that only those 'of an Inferior Caytiff Disposition', who are 'Strangers to GOD', truly suffer under unjust punishment, since they lack the knowledge, courage and patience of the holy.[118] While unpalatable to modern theological accounts of the irreducibility of suffering, this theology is founded on the redemptive holiness of patience, the potency of love and the value of vicarious suffering.

Ricoeur has identified the virtue of suffering innocently with wisdom: 'Wisdom does not teach us how to avoid suffering. ... It places suffering into a meaningful context by producing the active quality of suffering.' This 'active quality' is the active voice of suffering innocently, as opposed to the passive voice of innocent suffering. It bestows meaning on affliction, without justifying it, by negating passivity and helplessness and identifying suffering with active

---

[113] Traherne, *Christian Ethicks*, 187, 189.

[114] On passivity and agency in innocent suffering, see Tiina Allik, 'Narrative Approaches to Human Personhood: Agency, Grace, and Innocent Suffering' *Philosophy and Theology* 1/1 (1987), 305–33.

[115] Traherne, *Centuries of Meditations*, II 36, [] indicates deletion; see *The Works of Thomas Traherne*, vol. 5, 215.

[116] Traherne, *Christian Ethicks*, 189.

[117] Ibid. 188.

[118] Traherne, 'Accusation', *Commentaries of Heaven, Part 1*, 145.

110   *Boundless Innocence in Thomas Traherne's Poetic Theology*

righteousness rather than existential accidents.[119] Traherne similarly describes the innocent in the active voice as, 'ever Blessed, either by suffering unjustly, or escaping Gloriously'.[120] Attached to the activity rather than the passivity of suffering, the privative aspects of innocence as an absence of guilt become less significant, and its positive capacities for righteousness and holiness can take centre stage.

'Abov the reach of malice': Innocence and Impassibility

The notion of suffering innocently raises important theological issues. If to suffer is to be affected by an external object then it entails, if not passivity, then passibility. On the one hand, Traherne's description of suffering patiently appears to negate suffering by mirroring divine *im*passibility, echoing the Plotinian notion of spirit.[121] On the other, his account of suffering arises out of a context identified as the cradle of modern ideas of divine passibility. Jennifer Herdt argues that nineteenth-century theologies of the passible God are rooted in Cudworth's seventeenth-century concept of sympathy, and J.K. Mozley and Jürgen Moltmann identify the foundations of the kenotic theology of the suffering God in sixteenth-century Lutheranism.[122] Against this background, Traherne's account of suffering innocently combines elements of impassibility and passion.

Commentaries of Heaven describes a righteous response to persecution in terms analogous to divine impassibility: 'He that is removed into the Kingdom of GOD is secure from Accusations becaus his Interests and concernments are Eternal. His Enjoyments ... Immovable' and 'abov the reach of malice' and 'especialy becaus the Original of his Security is Divine, and Glorious'.[123] The term 'security' evokes the Reformed assurance of the elect who are 'not to be seated in a fickle Estate, but

---

[119]   Ricoeur, 'Toward a Hermeneutic of the Idea of Revelation', 12.

[120]   Traherne, 'Accusation', *Commentaries of Heaven, Part 1*, 144.

[121]   See Plotinus, *Enneads*, III.6; for a modern defence of the classic doctrine of the impassibility of God, see David Bentley Hart, 'Impassibility as Transcendence: On the Infinite Innocence of God', in James J. Keating and Thomas Joseph White (eds), *Divine Impassibility and the Mystery of Human Suffering* (Grand Rapids, Mich.: Eerdmans, 2009), 1–26, 299–323.

[122]   Jennifer Herdt, 'The Rise of Sympathy and the Question of Divine Suffering', *Journal of Religious Ethics* 29/3 (2001), 367–99; J.K. Mozley, *The Impassibility of God: A Survey of Christian Thought* (Cambridge: Cambridge University Press, 1926), 121–2; Jürgen Moltmann, *The Crucified God*, trans. R.A. Wilson and J. Bowden (2nd edn, New York: Harper & Row, 1974), 233–4.

[123]   Traherne, 'Accusation', *Commentaries of Heaven, Part 1*, 146.

always Secure'.[124] In *Select Meditations*, the patient soul lives in God's kingdom: 'enjoying Eternity and the Omnipresence of God in which it is Seated. which while it is doing External Accidents are so far beneath it, So Inconsiderable weak and little, that How troublesome Soever they Seeme unto others, they Cannot annoy it'.[125] The infinite perspective of right reason is not troubled by suffering because it sees its glorious end: 'for he Seeth all Accidents clearly, in their Consequences and causes; and How all Calamities are to a Triumphant Soul Sublime Advantages: And Cannot therefore be afflicted at them'.[126]

Patience may mirror impassibility, but suffering innocently is not passionless. As explained above, Traherne's account of the drama of trial does not purge the passions but consummates them. Similarly, affliction 'quickens and excites us to Action' by jolting the soul out of the lethargy of false ease, which is not true peace but 'a Defect contracted by the Fall ... which Weakness of our Souls is relieved by Exercise'.[127] Affliction excites the affections towards God because 'By any Calamitie, our Love, our fear, our Sorrow, our Hope, our Joy, our Desire, our Trust our Devotion is awakened, and our soul it self brought neer unto God'.[128]

Both the impassibility of patience and the passion of suffering innocently are found in Traherne's Christological poetics. In *The Ceremonial Law*, Noah's rainbow reflects the faithful Christian conquering suffering through the act of a God made vulnerable for humanity's security:

> It is a Bow whose Back is next the Skies
> His Anger turnd away it Typifies.
> The Arrow upwards towards Heaven doth flie,
> As if it meant to Wound the Dietie.[129]

Humanity's impassible patience is made possible through Christ's gracious affliction. At the same time, Traherne defends Christ's divine impassibility, as his body alone is destroyed while his divinity is unharmed:

> A Body taken from the Earth we lend,
> A Dietie from Heaven GOD doth send.

---

[124] Ibid. 148.

[125] Traherne, *Select Meditations*, II 95.

[126] Ibid. II 96.

[127] Traherne, 'Affliction', *Commentaries of Heaven, Part 1*, 309–10.

[128] Ibid. 310.

[129] Traherne, *Ceremonial Law*, 202.

The One is Kild, the other in His Bliss
Resplendent Glorious and Eternal is.[130]

In general, Traherne emphasises Christ's physical and spiritual affliction over his divine impassibility, as *Christian Ethicks* states: 'THE Corporeal Sufferings of our Saviour are not comparable to the Afflictions of his Spirit.'[131] In *Commentaries of Heaven*, Christ models a divine vulnerability of openness to humanity; through him, God is 'Abused in evry Man ... . Not metaphoricaly as the maner of Divines ... but Realy, most Deeply, and infinitly.'[132] Through Christ's passionate sacrifice, humanity receives the impassibility of patience and the grace of suffering innocently.

'An Innocent, that from all Blemish free': Innocent Sacrifice

The epitome of suffering innocently is innocent sacrifice, exemplified by Christ, the Lamb of God. Innocent sacrifice inspires a devotion that arises out of wonder at innocent suffering. In the Restoration national church this was manifest in the festival of the Holy Innocents: the infants massacred by Herod (Matthew 2.16–18).[133] 'Innocents' Day' remained an important festival in the Book of Common Prayer, and Edward Sparke defended them as models of innocence: a 'Circle of such *harmless simplicity*, and self-shielding *Innocence*'.[134] By contrast, Traherne's devotion to 'All Saints' does not privilege the Holy Innocents, whom he saw as inferior saints because they died before they faced trial. They are 'a Sort in thine Eternal Kingdom that never passed the Test of any Trial', who 'Emulat our Virtues Battails Encouragements Advantages Victories and Triumphs, with which we com Laden into Heaven!'[135] Traherne finds a model of innocent suffering not in the holy infants but in the sacrificial Lamb.

---

[130] Ibid. 200.

[131] Traherne, *Christian Ethicks*, 185.

[132] Traherne, 'Abuse', *Commentaries of Heaven, Part 1*, 67–8.

[133] See Rev. 14.1–5; on early devotion to the Holy Innocents, see A. Hayward, 'Suffering and Innocence in Latin Sermons for the Feast of the Holy Innocents, *c.* 400–800', in David Wood (ed.), *The Church and Childhood* (Oxford: Oxford University Press, 1994), 67–80; M.R. Dudley, '*Natalis Innocentum*, the Holy Innocents in Liturgy and Drama', in Wood (ed.), *The Church and Childhood*, 233–42. This devotion contributed to later narratives of the children's crusade and holy infant death, see Gary Dickson, *The Children's Crusade: Medieval History, Modern Mythistory* (Basingstoke: Palgrave Macmillan, 2008), 137–9.

[134] Edward Sparke, *Scintilla Altaris* (London: W.G. and R.W.), 107.

[135] Traherne, *Church's Year-Book*, 253.

The white and spotless lamb is a conventional symbol of the purity and vulnerability of Christian innocence. According to Sterry, it represented 'the sincerity, truth, simplicity of an innocent, gentle, meek spirit'.[136] In Traherne's works, it appears through the biblical types of the beast slain to clothe Adam and Eve, 'Abels Lamb', 'The Paschal Lamb', the sacrificial 'Lamb of God' instituted 'From the beginning of the World' and the victorious lamb of revelation.[137] These are all types of Christ, the Lamb of God who 'Offered up himself a Sacrifice without Spot ... [which] alone is the Meritorious Atonement'.[138] The lamb is the only emblem which explicitly associates innocence with sacrificial suffering. Traherne does not exploit the sacrificial connotations of the dove nor virginity's common association with martyrdom.

For Traherne, sacrificial innocence embodies abundance and strength. *Ceremonial Law* presents the innocent lamb as an appropriate sacrifice: an 'Innocent, that from all Blemish free, / Owning no Sin, might aptly Die for me.'[139] As Inge has noted from a soteriological perspective, Traherne makes it clear that only innocent sacrifice is redemptive, since God's 'Altar wils no Guilty Sacrifice'.[140] The lamb's innocence is therefore bound up with its sacrificial role, but it does not inevitably entail vulnerability and passivity. In 'Abels Lamb' and 'The Paschal Lamb', Traherne does not refer to the verses on which the image of the vulnerable and passive sacrificial lamb is founded, such as Isaiah 53.7 or Acts 8.32. Rather, he emphasises the positive qualities that make the lamb an acceptable sacrifice, such as its usefulness as a source of food and clothing, 'How Apposite; How plain, how full!'[141] The lamb-like martyr-saints of *Church's Year-Book* similarly marry innocence and strength: 'Those Lion-like Lambs. that Resemble in one the Lamb and Lion of the Hous of Judah'.[142] The sacrificial lamb emblematises the power of innocence over its worldly vulnerability and the effectiveness of innocent sacrifice over the injustice of spilling innocent blood.

---

[136] Peter Sterry, *Free Grace Exalted, and Thence Deduced Evangelical Rules for Evangelical Sufferings* (London, 1670), 5.

[137] See Traherne, *Ceremonial Law*, 198–9, 199–200, 210–13; id., *Church's Year-Book*, 37–8, 121, 158, 167, 250, 252–3; id., *A Serious and Pathetical Contemplation of the Mercies of GOD*, 353, 391; id., *Centuries of Meditations*, I 100; id., 'Application', *Commentaries of Heaven, Part 2*, 165.

[138] Traherne, 'Atonement', *Commentaries of Heaven, Part 2*, 366; see also id., 'Assumption', *Commentaries of Heaven, Part 2*, 287.

[139] Traherne, *Ceremonial Law*, 199.

[140] Inge, *Happiness and Holiness*, 147; Traherne, *Ceremonial Law*, 200.

[141] Traherne, *Ceremonial Law*, 199.

[142] Traherne, *Church's Year-Book*, 252.

Innocent sacrifice is not confined to misery but holds a key role throughout the estates. Sacrificial love is a fundamental principle of creation whereby, through the death of one, another is given life. *Kingdom of God* explains the universal sacrificial impulse as one of the 'Generous principles of Nature', it describes praise as a priestly sacrifice of the soul to God and considers the sacrificial character of 'perfect Love'.[143] Sacrificial innocence, unlike innocent suffering, is not a problem to be justified but is integral to the drama of love.

On first reading, Traherne's theology of suffering can appear indifferent to the particularity of pain, presenting a facile providentialist response to the problem of innocent suffering. However, understood as a theology of suffering innocently, it expresses the boundless energy of kenotic love that bears transforming fruit within the heat of affliction, just as sap leaks from wood in the flames:

> Thy Church, she was a Bramble void of fruit
>
> . . . .
>
> But now she shines tho Barren, and she Bears
> Even in the midst of fire. What fruit? Her Tears.[144]

The Character(s) of Innocence

Conceptual discourse on the nature of sin and suffering may not be the best way to assess the particular, personal, relational and irreducible drama of misery.[145] 'Who' we are in trial is a question of identity and relationship. Therefore, 'who' can live an innocent life in a sinful and suffering world is perhaps best addressed through an assessment of character, which is revealed in conflict with the world, in relationship to others and in dialogue with God.

Traherne's use of biblical characters as literary personae has been commented upon in relation to seventeenth-century Protestant literary style and changing notions of selfhood. Lewalski identified Traherne's appropriation of David's voice with a Protestant biblical poetic.[146] Conversely, Joan Webber thought his use of biblical personae reflected a medieval anthropology in which the

---

[143] Traherne, *Kingdom of God*, 293, 276, 278.

[144] Traherne, *Ceremonial Law*, 203.

[145] On the historical, sociological and psychological 'proximate contexts' of human identity and on the relationality of human identity in relation to God, see Kelsey, *Eccentric Existence* 3, 5, 8.

[146] Lewalski, *Protestant Poetics*, 352–3.

individual is a microcosm of salvation history.[147] Differently again, Ira Clark identified him with a novel framework of type, antitype and neotype, which describes a literary and psychological progression from the first Adam to the second (Christ) and third (the self).[148] While these analyses were mainly concerned with literary constructions of selfhood, this section is more interested in Traherne's construction of character through the appropriation of conventional biblical tropes. The *Church's Year-Book* prays to be as meek as Moses, courageous as Joshua, chaste as Joseph, patient as Job, zealous as the apostles, wise as Solomon, sincere as David and pure as the angels.[149] Traherne's adaptation of such conventional analogies indicates his interpretation of the character of innocence.

The characters of innocence are dramatic characters. *A Serious and Pathetical Contemplation of the Mercies of GOD* describes saints as actors in the divine drama: 'Those Jewels in thy Cabinet, those Persons on thy Stage, that fill the World with wonderful Actions'.[150] Following the Aristotelian stipulation that characters be 'good' men, saints function as exemplars through which the art of poetic imitation reflects back from text to life.[151] Some characters in particular are recurrent in Traherne's work: Job and Christ, who are discussed here; Adam, who was discussed in Chapter 2; and David, who will be discussed in Chapter 5. According to Aristotle, characters are not agents as such, but 'that which determines the quality of the agents'.[152] In the same way, these characters portray different qualities of innocence. Job illustrates the relational aspect of injured innocence in dialogue with God, while Christ is the exemplar of perfect innocence, of whom the others are merely types. Chapter 2 saw Christ as the model of an innocent life; this chapter sees his innocence enmeshed in a theatre of sin and suffering.

---

[147] Webber, *The Eloquent 'I'*, 237.

[148] Clark, *Christ Revealed*, 28, 133–59.

[149] Traherne, *Church's Year-Book*, 144–5; on Abel exemplifying innocence, Enoch pure action, Noah enduring through hope, Abraham obedience, Isaac chastity, Jacob patience, Joseph returning good for evil, Moses meekness, Joshua assurance in trial and Job patience, see Gregory the Great, *Morals on the Book of Job*, I.I, preface, xiii.

[150] Traherne, *A Serious and Pathetical Contemplation of the Mercies of GOD*, 421.

[151] Aristotle, *Poetics*, 1454a (XV 1–3); cf. Hegel's 'world-historical individuals' defined by their acts, and von Balthasar's saints modelling 'heroic effort' (Quash, *Theology and the Drama of History*, 67, 78–9).

[152] Aristotle, *Poetics*, 1450a1 (VI 8).

'He will laugh at the trial of the innocent': Job

Job is a dramatic character, being considered in seventeenth-century literary theory the original model of tragic drama.[153] He appears as hero or anti-hero in several contemporary epic poems and may have provided a source for Milton's *Paradise Lost* and *Paradise Regained*.[154] In Traherne's works, Job is rarely the object of attention for more than a paragraph, but he is an exemplar of innocent suffering and suffering innocently in Traherne's accounts of 'Accusation', 'Affliction' and 'Patience'.[155] Job's experience provides a model that was both 'permitted and Written, that we may see in this Instance, what we otherwise would scarcely believ'.[156] He is also the source of aphorisms for a pure and perfect life, such as 'Behold God will not cast away a perfect man' (Job 8.20) and 'as Job saith, no Man can bring a clean thing out of an unclean' (Job 14.4).[157] The latter maxim lies behind Traherne's suggestion that illegitimate children are unsuitable for baptism, since it is hard to believe 'how Sin should give a Being to the Divine Image'.[158]

Alongside these various connotations, Job presents the character of innocence in trial. Called 'perfect and upright, and one that feared God, and eschewed evil' in Job 1.1, his perfection is a relational status intimated by the fact that it is God who declares it. Conventional reception of this verse by the seventeenth century defined him as innocent in perfection or simplicity; the KJV translates תָּם

---

[153] See David J.A. Clines, *Job 1–20*, Word Biblical Commentary 17 (Dallas: Thomas Nelson, 1989), lxiv, lxix–lxx.

[154] Quarles, *Job Militant*; John Duport, *Thenothriambos, sive, Libert Job Graeco carmine redditus* (Cambridge: Thomas Buck and Roger Daniel, 1637); Henry Oxinden, *Jobus Triumphans* (London, 1651); on Job as model for *Paradise Lost* and *Paradise Regained*, see Harold Fisch, 'Creation in Reverse: The Book of Job and *Paradise Lost*', in J.H. Sims and L. Ryken (eds), *Milton and Scriptural Tradition: The Bible into Poetry* (London: Routledge and Keegan Paul, 1984), 104–16; Barbara Lewalski, *Milton's Brief Epic* (London: Methuen, 1966), 10–36, 102–29.

[155] On Job as model of patience, see Traherne's references to James 5.11 (*A Serious and Pathetical Contemplation of the Mercies of GOD*, 395; *Church's Year-Book*, 59; *Christian Ethicks*, 188); on Job as model of pagan wisdom, see 'Article', *Commentaries of Heaven, Part 2*, 230.

[156] Traherne, 'Accusation', *Commentaries of Heaven, Part 1*, 141; 'Affliction', *Commentaries of Heaven, Part 1*, 305; see Gregory the Great, *Morals on the Book of Job*, I.I, preface, v–vi; Aquinas, *Literal Exposition on Job*, 83 (Job 1.12a).

[157] Traherne, *A Sober View*, 122; id., *Kingdom of God*, 292. The latter alludes to the Douay-Rheims translation or the Vulgate.

[158] Traherne, 'Bastard', *Commentaries of Heaven, Part 2*, 466.

The Trial of Innocence   117

(*tam*) as 'perfect' while the Vulgate renders it *simplex*.[159] Aquinas followed the Vulgate in designating Job's innocence as a sincere simplicity, 'properly opposed to deceit'.[160] For Gregory the Great, this passage intimated a dual goodness of outward obedience and inward innocence, wherein 'the ornament of obedience is always connected with innocent minds'.[161]

The extent of Job's innocence was a long-contested issue. Gregory defended it because Job's guilt would make God a liar, nevertheless accepting that Job could not be wholly without blame.[162] Aquinas similarly defended God's providence, asserting that 'Sometimes ... it happens that just men are pressed by adversities for some special reason', but believed Job guilty by divine standards.[163] Quarles thought that Job was guilty in the end for thinking God unjust, although he may have been innocent of the sins of which he was accused.[164] This ambivalence is apparent in Traherne's interpretation of Job 1.1, which he renders as: 'Holy Job. Who was a Sinner, but yet perfect and Upright, one that feared GOD and Eschued Evil'.[165] Traherne's prefatory addendum to the citation, 'a Sinner, but yet', defends Job's innocence in terms compatible with Protestant orthodoxy by intimating the doctrine of *simul justus et peccator*. This Lutheran theme evokes the conflicted and finite character of innocence in history. This is not a limited innocence measured by human standards alone.[166] It is the paradoxical ambiguity of an existential innocence that coexists with guilt.

In *Christian Ethicks*, Job exemplifies the trial of innocence, embodying the principle that 'Man is magnified by his Trials'. Traherne explicitly quotes Job 7.17–18: 'What is man, that thou shouldest magnify him? And that thou shouldest set thine heart upon him? And that thou shouldest visit him every morning, and try him every moment?' However, this passage is also imbued with the language of the Psalms and therefore implicity echoes Psalm 8.4's more hopeful exclamation of God's love and care: 'What is man ... ?' Merging Job's voice with the spirit of the Psalms, Traherne pulls lament into praise by

---

[159]   The Septuagint renders Job 1.1 as ἀληθινός ἄμεμπτος (true and blameless).

[160]   Aquinas on Job 1.1, *Literal Exposition on Job*, 72.

[161]   Gregory the Great, *Morals on the Book of Job*, III.VI.35.xxxii.

[162]   Ibid. ix–x.

[163]   Aquinas *Literal Exposition on Job*, 72 (Job 1.1); see Eleonore Stump, 'Aquinas on the Suffering of Job', in ead. (ed.), *Reasoned Faith* (Ithaca, NY: Cornell University Press, 1993), 340.

[164]   Quarles, *Job Militant*, 17–18, 27, 36, 42, 46, 48.

[165]   Traherne, 'Accusation', *Commentaries of Heaven*, 140. The adjective, 'Holy', comes from the added term in the LXX which designates Job as δίκαιος.

[166]   Clines attributes this worldly definition of innocence to Eliphaz (*Job 1–20*, xli); see also Gregory the Great, *Morals on the Book of Job*, III.VI.35.ix.

rooting humanity's glory in existential struggle. Hence, he explains that '*GOD* hath placed our Trial in sharp and bitter Atchievments, because the Love that is exprest in Agonies and Conflicts, acquires other kind of Beauties, that produce more violent and strong Effects in the Mind of the Spectator'.[167] This depiction of the lyric beauty of suffering incites the affections through the existential drama of innocent Job.

Job's dialogue with God intimates the relational character of innocence: a loving rather than juridical relationship. As discussed above, trial is the state of the actualisation and perfection of virtue. Therefore, Traherne does not exploit the judicial connotations of Job as placing God on trial or of being on trial before God. In the *Christian Ethicks* passage cited above, God relates to humanity as advocate not as judge, while Satan is the accuser who wills humanity's destruction. Traherne harmonises Job's complaints against God into a relational framework by adapting Job 9.23, which states that God 'will laugh at the trial of the innocent'. Traherne was not alone in finding this verse difficult. Sterry addressed the problem of God's seeming insensitivity by claiming that God is not indifferent to the sufferings of wicked or innocent, but 'the Eye of God is fixed upon his own Divine Loveliness and Glory alike in both'.[168] *Commentaries of Heaven* defends God's providential care for the righteous by identifying 'him that laugheth at the Trial of the Innocent' not as God, but earthly despisers who mock the righteous sufferer. By contrast, 'God infinitly loves an Innocent, and tenders his Welfare as the Apple of his Ey'.[169] The divine–human drama is therefore not conflictual but neither is it straightforward. Innocence is being-in-relation-with-God, exemplified by Job as a man whose prayers God will hear.[170] This is a loving but perilous relationship, viewed through Satan's accusation as well as God's acceptance.

In *Christian Ethicks*, Job 9.23 undergoes a more intriguing alteration. Traherne finds an innocent response to trial in joy, because the virtuous can 'laugh at the Trial of his own Innocence and make a Game of Difficulties and Terrors'.[171] This is the joy of victory arising out of virtue's courage and confidence. Joy also links Job with the Psalms of David and the restoration of felicity through

---

[167] Traherne, *Christian Ethicks*, 191.

[168] Peter Sterry, *A Discourse of the Freedom of the Will* (London, 1675), 145.

[169] Traherne, 'Affliction', *Commentaries of Heaven, Part 1*, 312.

[170] Traherne, 'Acceptance', *Commentaries of Heaven, Part 1*, 83.

[171] Traherne, *Christian Ethicks*, 161; see also ibid. 282 where the righteous man 'gladly yields some Trials of his Obedience' in light of Christ's sacrifice.

praise.[172] A joyful response to trial models redemptive praise in its determination to 'worship God for nothing' (Job 1.9), betraying an innocence of heart which seeks no reward for virtue.[173] Augustine's commentary on Psalm 57 highlights this attribute of Job, claiming that the devil's temptations did not prevent him from praising God.[174] This virtuous endeavour expresses how lyrical dialogue with God can defeat trial: as Ricoeur put it, 'the knowledge of how to suffer is surpassed by the lyricism of supplication in the same way that narration is surpassed by the lyricism of praise'.[175]

In Job, the divine–human dialogue progresses from accusation and complaint to prayer and praise. This is seen in *Church's Year-Book*'s 'Acts of Adoration and Thanksgiving' for Rogation week, which is modelled on Job 12, 28 and 36. This passage draws the whole world into dialogue with God, joining Job in asking all creatures to teach him to praise, 'for they shall Declare; that in all these Things thy Hand O Lord is seen'. It also transforms and directs earthly conversation towards God, turning Job's admonition to his friends in Job 12.7–10 into a prayer. Finally, it draws wisdom into divine dialogue, turning the aphorisms of Job 12 and 28 into a second-person prayer of praise.[176] Although the book of Job begins with lament, its *telos* is an act of praise which is dialogue with God.

Traherne's Job is more than a representation of the state of misery.[177] He intimates the character of innocence in trial, which is bounded by paradoxical ambiguity but oriented towards glory, formed in the context of loving relationship and marked by redemptive joy. This characterisation goes some way to accounting for the ambiguous, dialogical and relational innocence manifest in what Quash calls Job's 'existential register'. Not just a figure of patient suffering, Job portrays innocence in a sinful and suffering world or 'how to exercise freedom with obedience in the midst of unique, uncontrolled and unforeseen challenges, and how integrity and growth are possible in such a world'.[178]

---

[172] On the link between David and Job in Calvin's theology of suffering, see Susan E. Schreiner, *Where Shall Wisdom be Found? Calvin's Exegesis of Job from Medieval and Modern Perspectives* (Chicago: University of Chicago Press, 1994), 96–105.

[173] On this notion, see Gregory the Great, *Morals on the Book of Job*, I.I, preface, vii; Augustine, *Expositions on the Book of Psalms*, Ps. 56.13, ¶¶xix–xx.

[174] Augustine, *Expositions on the Book of Psalms*, Ps. 57.8, ¶xvii.

[175] Ricoeur, 'Toward a Hermeneutic of the Idea of Revelation', 14.

[176] Traherne, *Church's Year-Book*, 67–9.

[177] Cf. Dreher, *The Fourfold Pilgrimage*, 32.

[178] Quash, *Theology and the Drama of History*, 150–52.

The 'Historically Achieved' Innocence of Christ

Christ has already been mentioned as an exemplar of human innocence and examined as a model of sacrifice. The full implications of Christ as a model of human innocence are illuminated by an assessment of Traherne's treatment of the crucifixion in the light of modern theological debates. For MacKinnon, historical existence inevitably entails causing harm. As Williams has pointed out, this makes it difficult to talk about Christ's innocence without separating it from his humanity, but such a move would run counter to Nicene orthodoxy. Instead, insofar as Christ's innocence is located in his human nature, 'It must be something compatible with the experience of what we would have to call "moral limit"'. MacKinnon addresses this problem through a notion of 'historically achieved innocence', which is not ontologically absolute but is the relational sinlessness of a life judged to retain a capacity for good in spite of participating in the causes of suffering.[179] Thus, Christ's human innocence is circumscribed by existential constraints. As inseparable from harm, it cannot be ignorant of evil. As 'achieved' through difficulty, it responds to conflict through both action and suffering. As a title bestowed by an external judge, it is constructed in a relational context. This finite and indefinite model of Christological innocence, enacted in the turmoil of history but viewed through relation to the divine, is the innocence of the estate of misery.

While earlier critics failed to spot a strong Christology in Traherne's work, it is no longer considered a minor theme. Peter Maitland's thesis of Traherne's 'missing Christ' has been comprehensively challenged by Kershaw and Inge.[180] Kershaw's argument centres on the notion of an all-pervasive cosmic Christ in Traherne's theological poetics. As this cosmic Christ is often implicit, she therefore still sees the Cross as a 'comparatively minor concern'.[181] Inge identifies what Kershaw has missed in the kenotic theme of Christ as sacrifice and substitute in Traherne's later works.[182] In *Ceremonial Law*, Christ is the reality to which all types point, the thing which is the object of all thoughts: 'The Vail is don away in Christ, the Skreen / Removd, the Cloud disperst,

---

[179] Williams, 'Trinity and Ontology', 80–81.

[180] Peter Maitland, 'Thomas Traherne's Path to Felicity: The Missing Christ' (MA thesis: Carleton University, Canada, 1994).

[181] Kershaw, 'The Poetic of the Cosmic Christ', 12, 4, 181, 199; previous interpretations of an indirect or implicit Christ include Martz, *The Paradise Within*, 59; Clements, *The Mystical Poetry of Thomas Traherne*, 184–5; Alison J. Sherrington, *Mystical Symbolism in the Poetry of Thomas Traherne* (St Lucia: University of Queensland Press, 1970), 98.

[182] Inge, *Happiness and Holiness*, 147–8.

when he is seen.'[183] Christ is the ultimate dramatic character in Traherne's poetic theology, actively participating in and transforming the existential world of guilt and miseries.[184]

Across Traherne's works, Christ is the model of innocency of life in spite of a hostile world. Beyond what Stillingfleet called 'the *unspotted innocency of his life*', Traherne's Christ exhibits 'how in the midst of Evil Customs and Corruptions to live a Life of Happiness and Glory'.[185] Christ's passion portrays a murdered innocence, embroiled in sin and suffering.[186] Although there is no conversation between innocence and guilt, the two are conjoined and guilt is redeemed in Christ's sacrifice, in whom one sees 'all Kingdoms Adoring a Malefactor: An Innocent Malefactor, yet the Greatest in the World'.[187] Christ as the paradoxical innocent malefactor is the exemplar of human innocence, the perfect divine abstract of the upright and justified sinner: he 'that was made Sin, yet not by Sin defiled'.[188]

Christ also exemplifies innocent suffering and suffering innocently, evoking in *Church's Year-Book* the wonder that one who 'never offended' must suffer, for others' sake.[189] Patrick Pinsent assumed that Traherne's passion meditations in *Centuries of Meditations* were artificial or forced, because as a nature mystic he was not concerned with Christ's suffering.[190] On the contrary, Christ's affliction is graphically described in meditations echoing the tone of medieval devotion:

> Pale, Withered! Extended! Tortured! Soyld with Blood and Sweat and Dust! Dried! Parched! O Sad! O Dismal Spectacle! All His Joynts are dissolved, all His

---

[183]   Traherne, *Ceremonial Law*, 241.

[184]   See Traherne, 'An Advocate', *Commentaries of Heaven, Part 1*, 261–6; id., 'Atonement', *Commentaries of Heaven, Part 2*, 364–75; id., *Centuries of Meditations*, I 55–100; for a similar view of Christ as dramatic character in Barth's Christology, see Quash, *Theology and the Drama of History*, 16.

[185]   Stillingfleet, *Origines Sacræ*, 288; Traherne, 'Second Adam', *Commentaries of Heaven, Part 1*, 227.

[186]   See Traherne, 'Atonement', *Commentaries of Heaven, Part 2*, 372; id., *Church's Year-Book*, 10.

[187]   Traherne, *Centuries of Meditations*, I 59.

[188]   Traherne, *Ceremonial Law*, 228.

[189]   Traherne, *Church's Year-Book*, 27.

[190]   Patrick Pinsent, 'The Image of Christ in the Writings of Two Seventeenth-Century English Country Parsons: George Herbert and Thomas Traherne', in Stanley E. Porter, David Tombs and Michael A. Chaplain Hayes (eds), *Images of Christ: Ancient and Modern* (Sheffield: Sheffield Academic Press, 1997), 233; cf. Justin Miller, 'Thomas Traherne: Love and Pain in the Poet of Felicity', *Historical Magazine of the Protestant Episcopal Church* 49 (1980), 209–20.

Blood is Shed: to the last Drop! All his Moysture is consumed! What is here but a Heap of Desolations! a Deformed Carcais! a Disfigured Countenance! A Mass of Miseries; and silent Footsteps of Innumerable Sufferings![191]

In *Commentaries of Heaven*, Christ epitomises the problem of innocent suffering, raising the question of how God could 'slayeth so Glorious a Person being Innocent'.[192] In *Christian Ethicks*, meditation on Christ's death turns affliction to joy, as 'the height of our Extasie is in the Reality of his Passion'.[193] The Cross is the culmination of the Old Testament symbolism of innocent blood, manifest as a mysterious object of adoration: 'Perhaps we cannot tell how an Innocent should justly be punished for a Guilty Person ... nor yet perhaps how Blood should purge'.[194] However, his suffering innocence is not only an object of wonder but a pattern for living, as stated in *Centuries of Meditations*: 'Whoever suffereth innocently and justly in anothers steed, must becom a Surety by His voluntary Act.'[195] The Cross is a conjunction of paradoxes: guilt and innocence, suffering and felicity, which evoke the interrogative mood of wonder. Christ's innocence is often the object of this wonder, which directs meditation on the passion to a vision of perfection and incites the affections to action.

'A Centre that doth Spread Over all Worlds': Kenotic Innocence

Christ's sacrifice is rooted in history, but its model of kenotic innocence transcends the boundaries of the estates. The passion appears typologically throughout the history of Israel: in the sacrificial lamb, the rainbow after the flood, the Red Sea and the wood that heals the waters at Elim:

> From Earth we offer up a Sacrifice,
> And GOD sends down Salvation from the skies.
> Upon the Altar He appears in fire,
> The Rainbow Him in splendor doth Attire.
> In Abels Lamb He's picturd here with Blood
>
> .   .   .   .

---

[191] Traherne, *Centuries of Meditations*, I 89.

[192] Traherne, 'Assumption', *Commentaries of Heaven, Part 2*, 287.

[193] Traherne, *Christian Ethicks*, 189.

[194] Traherne, 'Atonement', *Commentaries of Heaven, Part 2*, 371.

[195] Traherne, *Centuries of Meditations*, II 32.

The Type from Heaven always doth remain
The Sacrifice on Earth is by us slain.[196]

The Cross is present throughout the progress of the soul: in *Kingdom of God* it is already a 'Trophie' of victory in the estate of glory.[197] This is a type which transcends time and eternity, appearing in *Centuries of Meditations* through the scriptural conceits of Jacob's ladder and the bronze serpent, pointing from earth to heaven and from trial to glory.[198]

The Cross is not only a feature of each estate. In *Centuries of Meditations* it is the centre of history through which 'we may see the most Distant Things in Eternity united'. It links Eden with heaven and innocence with glory, as 'the Abyss of Wonders, the Centre of Desires, the Schole of Virtues, the Hous of Wisdom, the Throne of Lov, the Theatre of Joys and the Place of Sorrows' and also 'the Root of Happiness, and the Gate of Heaven'. The Cross as the centre of history has a magnetic pull that draws all things to itself, just 'as on evry side of the Earth all Heavy things tend to the Centre'.[199] On the other hand, in *Commentaries of Heaven*, it is an ever-expanding sphere; Christ's 'Death is like a Centre that doth Spread / Over all Worlds'.[200] The Cross as both gravitational centre and infinite sphere is an attractive and expansive object which encompasses all things.

Significantly, in *Centuries of Meditations*, the Cross is present in the estate of innocence as '*that Tree of Life* in the midst of the Paradice of GOD!'[201] It is not only contained within Eden but stands at its centre and gives it life, as a reminder of the loss of innocence and the price of its recovery. Thus the passion is contained in the memory of original innocence, and the innocent eye sees felicity through the crown of thorns: 'the only Mirror, wherin all things appear in their proper Colors. that is sprinkled in the Blood of our Lord and Savior'.[202] As sight is purified through blood, the return to innocence is undertaken through contemplation of Christ who makes it possible.

---

[196] Traherne, *Ceremonial Law*, 200, see also 199–200, 207, 209, 212, 215.

[197] Traherne, *Kingdom of God*, 266.

[198] Traherne, *Centuries of Meditations*, I 57, 60.

[199] Ibid. 56–8.

[200] Traherne, 'Atonement', *Commentaries of Heaven, Part 2*, 374; see also id., *A Serious and Pathetical Contemplation of the Mercies of GOD*, 395.

[201] Traherne, *Centuries of Meditations*, I 55; cf. Kershaw, who views Traherne's Cross as an Irenaean tree of knowledge, not tree of life, based on Olivier Clément, *The Roots of Christian Mysticism* (London: New City, 1993), 48–9 (Kershaw, 'The Poetic of the Cosmic Christ', 197).

[202] Traherne, *Centuries of Meditations*, I 59.

The drama of the Cross is imprinted on every soul: 'I Admire to see thy Crosse in evry Understanding, thy Passion in evry Memory, thy Crown of Thornes in evry Ey, and thy Bleeding, Naked Wounded Body in evry Soul.'[203] Through sensory imagery, personal lyrical meditation is drawn into the drama of living, as to be 'Washt in Tears' is to be made pure and white through grief and to smell the 'Pure / And Sweet' smell of Christ's death is to sense paradise in the midst of suffering. The imitation of Christ enacts the drama of this trial in the believer:

> Only thou must be pure, and weep, and tear
> Thy vices off, Couragious be, and bear
> His Cross, and be like Him, a serious Lover.[204]

To imitate Christ is to grow into innocence, to 'Crucify / My Loathsom flesh' and to transform the soul to its original whiteness. Like Christ, the soul in pursuit of innocence is to pass through death and resurrection to 'Suffer Exterior Ignominy that my Soul may Shine with Interior Light'.[205]

The perspective of infinity is incorporated into the drama of the passion. Christ in suffering retains the beatific vision: 'To this poor Bleeding Naked Man did all the Corn and wine and Oyl, and Gold and Silver in the World minister in an Invisible Maner, even as he was exposed Lying and Dying upon the Cross.'[206] Such benefits may appear as 'fragments' to the human eye. Nevertheless they are the essence of the event, just as Christ's physical wounds are 'Shady Impressions' of his divinity, and the 'Bloody Characters' of the Cross are a 'Dim' light through which one reads the 'Lustre and Perfection' of the Godhead.[207] So, in the Cross, 'the Hights of all Goodness Justice and Mercy are united together, all the Depths of Misery and Love and Blessedness, all the Riches of Eternal Wisdom in our Saviors Cross are Glorified for us'.[208] In the same way, the fragments of goodness and innocence glimpsed through the drama of the Christian life reveal hints of an uncompounded unity underlying the estate of misery.

---

[203] Ibid. 86.

[204] Traherne, 'An Advocate', *Commentaries of Heaven, Part 1*, 266.

[205] Traherne, 'Adulterie', *Commentaries of Heaven, Part 2*, 259; id., *Church's Year-Book*, 12; see also id., *Centuries of Meditations*, I 89.

[206] Traherne, *Centuries of Meditations*, I 60; see also id., 'Second Adam', *Commentaries of Heaven, Part 1*, 230–31.

[207] Traherne, *Centuries of Meditations*, I 64.

[208] Traherne, 'Assumption', *Commentaries of Heaven, Part 2*, 287.

'In the midst of a crooked and perverse nation': Innocence in the Dramatic Mode

The dramatic features of Traherne's estate of misery may be interpreted through Aristotle or through modern theodramatics. Read in the light of Aristotelian conventions, innocence in the dramatic mode is a virtuous art. *Centuries of Meditations* calls wisdom the 'Diviner Art ... of Extracting Good out of evil'. This is not the sublimation but the transformation of evil, turning guilt and misery into felicity. For the wise man, 'the very Miseries and sins and offences that are in [the world], are the Materials of his Joy and Triumph and Glory'.[209] Traherne's struggle with sin is a process of assimilation into infinite goodness. In *Commentaries of Heaven*, for the man at the centre of God's kingdom

> the very Calamities Afflictions and Persecutions of the World are turned into felicities, and all Accusations, like a Drop of Water falling into a Tun of Wine, being Ascribed into a New famely, by the prevailing Ingredient are bereaved of their Nature, and turn into the more Noble. They lose their Bitterness and are turned into Joys.[210]

The art of wisdom is the art of innocence, purifying all things and transforming them into light.

The art of finding innocence in trial is akin to the sentiment of Philippians 2.15: 'that ye may be blameless and harmless, the sons of God, without rebuke, in the midst of a crooked and perverse nation'.[211] Traherne does not cite Philippians directly, but *Church's Year-Book* refers to related passages in its description of James: 'O my God giv me Grace to Serv Thee in the midst of a perverse Generation as thy H. Apostle S. James did.'[212] The determination to fulfil this prayer is evident in *Ceremonial Law*, which aims 'to shew How here, even in the Wilderness, / We might full Draughts of Heavenly Joy possess.'[213] Success is seen in the 'friend' of *Centuries of Meditations*, who teaches him 'to be Happy in the midst of a Generation of Vipers', and in Noah's family, who in *A Sober View* are able through extraordinary providence to 'continue Heavenly in a world of

---

[209] Traherne, *Centuries of Meditations*, IV 21; see Rom. 8.28.

[210] Traherne, 'Accusation', *Commentaries of Heaven, Part 1*, 148.

[211] See Matt. 10.16; 17.17; Luke 9.41; 10.3.

[212] Traherne, *Church's Year-Book*, 56; see Deut. 32.5; Matt. 17.17; Luke 9.41; James 1.27.

[213] Traherne, *Ceremonial Law*, 208.

126   *Boundless Innocence in Thomas Traherne's Poetic Theology*

Wickedness'.[214] These examples echo Gregory's description of Job's innocence, as 'a lily among thorns ... *simple and upright*'.[215] In this context, Traherne's is very much an innocence *in* trial, rather than *on* trial.

The pursuit of innocence in trial fulfils God's purpose to 'continu a Righteous Kingdom, notwithstanding the Fall and Ineptitude of Men'.[216] Innocence is blamelessness and harmlessness in conflict with a hostile world, where 'on evry side we are environed with Wrongs, beseiged with offences, receiving evil for Good, being disturbed by fools, and invaded with Malice. This is the true Estate of this World.'[217] Its value is related to the horror it overcomes: 'by how much the more Desolate the world is left by Revolting Sinners, by how much the Greater the Number is of owls and Dragons that Defile it with their manners, by How much the more is an inestimable man in the Midst of Dragons; that being wise and Holy walketh with God in the Enjoyments of His works'.[218]

Read in the light of modern theodramatics, innocence in the dramatic mode is bounded by existential particularities and characterised by conflict and relationality. The world as a theatre of trial evokes the dramatic tension inherent in the human estate: in its dual hope of glory and fear of falling, its battle between love for God and love of world, its disjunction between humanity's origin in nothing and end in glory. Trial expresses human freedom and finitude and the dynamic and dangerous character of Christian life. The authorial perspective here is not a dispassionate narrator on a metaphysical plane, but a spectator in the midst of the drama, constructing its own stage of experience. Just as Bacon believed that 'in this theatre of man's life it is reserved only for God and angels to be lookers on', so Traherne draws the reader into the drama of his poetry.[219] In 'Elim' and 'Manna' in *Ceremonial Law*, for example, he uses 'we' to refer alternately to Israel and to the reader. This dual use of the first-person plural applies the history of Israel typologically to the present life of faith.[220]

From this perspective, Traherne's presentation of the innocent life in the face of a hostile world is fully immersed in the miseries of suffering and sin. While avoiding the depths of existential dread, Traherne enters into the quotidian encounter with evil. The dramatic elements in Traherne's thought reveal a creative tension at the heart of his work in the midst of which humanity sits

---

[214] Traherne, *Centuries of Meditations*, IV 20; id., *A Sober View*, 48v.

[215] Gregory the Great, *Morals on the Book of Job*, I.I.1.i, drawing on Song 2.2.

[216] Traherne, *A Sober View*, 50.

[217] Traherne, *Centuries of Meditations*, IV 20.

[218] Traherne, *Select Meditations*, II 14.

[219] Bacon, *The Advancement of Learning*, II.22.viii,

[220] Traherne, *Ceremonial Law*, 213–7, 221–7.

as *hymenaeus* uniting earth and heaven. Humanity's is a historical innocence situated between the finitude of existence and God's infinite kingdom. However, its sacrificial model is not partial or limited by finitude, but demonstrates the infinite kenotic power of suffering innocence.

Chapter 5

'Innocency of Life': Innocence in the State of Misery–Grace

'Drama in the form of "living holiness"':[1] **Experimental Innocence**

Post-Blakean readings of Traherne set innocence and experience in a dialectical relationship. They highlight the corrupting power of experience, imparted through education, on the pure intuitions of innocence.[2] The autobiographical sections of the *Centuries of Meditations* chart a clear decline through childhood education: 'The first Light which shined in my Infancy in its Primitive and Innocent Clarity was totaly Ecclypsed ... by the Customs and maners of Men.'[3] At the same time, Traherne celebrates the original intuited knowledge 'Collected again by the Highest Reason', which includes the study of divinity and humanity.[4] This use of the scholastic terms, 'high' or 'right reason', places the recovery of innocence through learning within a holistic epistemological framework that combines natural philosophy with theology.

For Traherne, innocence is not in direct opposition to education or experience but to corrupted customs. Innocent intuitions are recovered through reason and, as discussed in the last chapter, the experience of trial reveals the 'Secret Strength' of the soul, which is not 'discerned but by Exercise'.[5] In addition, he places great philosophical value upon personal experience, as shown by his strong reliance upon first-person accounts in the poems, *Select Meditations* and *Centuries of Meditations*.[6] The autobiographical Century III begins with the premise that pure apprehensions 'are unattainable by Books, and therfore I will

---

[1]   Quash, *Theology and the Drama of History*, 64.

[2]   See e.g. Ben Drake, 'Thomas Traherne's Songs of Innocence', *Modern Language Quarterly* 31 (1970), 492–503.

[3]   Traherne, *Centuries of Meditations*, III 7.

[4]   Ibid. 2.

[5]   Traherne, *Centuries of Meditations*, IV 97.

[6]   Traherne's personal philosophy is most cogently and influentially expressed by T.S. Eliot ('Mystic and Politician as Poet: Vaughan, Traherne, Marvell, Milton', *Listener* 3 [2 Apr. 1930], 590–91).

teach them by Experience'.[7] Therefore, experience is not automatically the enemy of innocence.

The amity of innocence and experience stems from a holistic medieval epistemology, but it is further clarified by Traherne's appropriation of modern experimentalism. According to Picciotto, the Royal Society recovered Eden through Adamic ingenuity, the objective perception of the innocent eye through the microscope and the primal virtue of curiosity through coffee-house culture.[8] This was the 'Ironizing [of] the Golden Age', a new experimentalist paradise of labour which 'scrambled the concepts of "advancement" and return'.[9] Seventeenth-century experimentalists pursued innocence through experience and greater knowledge and understanding of the world.

Traherne's attraction to the New Science and Baconian experimentalism has been well documented. Charron compared the sciences unfavourably to natural knowledge, as they invent 'whatsoever is an enemie to innocencie', while natural intuition 'willinglie lodgeth with simplicitie and ignorance'.[10] Traherne does not appear to have shared these concerns. His short unfinished treatise on the soul, *Seeds of Eternity*, draws on 'Chimists and Physicians' to praise the body's glorious symmetry.[11] The work is framed by experimentalist principles, which defend the study of humanity as 'the most certain of all Sciences, becaus we *feel* the Things it declares, and may by Experience, prove all it revealeth'.[12] In this citation, the authority of experience rests on the testimony of the affections, which is defined as a form of experimentalism.

Traherne expounds a kind of double experimentalism, whereby knowledge of the world is transmitted to the soul through the physical senses, and knowledge of the divine is communicated to the body through the spiritual senses. Drawing on Neoplatonic emanationism, Traherne explains how the light of the soul shines upon the passions and affections, which mediate and diffuse the innate knowledge of self to the body.[13] The self-knowledge which is the subject of the humanities is therefore the epitome of spiritual experimentalism.[14] This

---

[7]   Traherne, *Centuries of Meditations*, III 1.

[8]   For a fuller account, see Dodd, 'Joanna Picciotto, *Labors of Innocence in Early Modern England*'.

[9]   Picciotto, *Labors of Innocence in Early Modern England*, 133–47, 129, 255–9.

[10]   Charron, *Of Wisdom*, 468.

[11]   Traherne, *Seeds of Eternity*, 240.

[12]   Ibid. 233.

[13]   Ibid. 241–2.

[14]   Traherne looks to Tully, Plotinus and Plato to elevate the Delphic injunction to 'know thyself' (ibid. 237, 239).

'Innocency of Life' 131

knowledge is not the *ratio* of intellection but a contemplation which participates in divine mystery.

The combination of experience and experiment, found in *Seeds of Eternity*, illustrates the relationship between innocence and experience. In *Kingdom of God*, the encounter with evil through experience inclines humanity to forget the love of God: 'we are accustomed so much to Malevolence, and Mishap, that our Experience makes us Blind.' However, infinite love is evident through observation of the world (experiment): 'It whispers in evry Gale of Wind. and Speaks aloud in Thunder. It is trampled on the Earth and Crowns us in the Heavens.'[15] Knowledge of God is revealed through experimental knowledge of the created world.[16] If therefore, as Inge suggests, Traherne sought a 'higher innocence wrought by experience', then this was found in experimental knowledge of self and world.[17] Unlike Blake's *Songs of Innocence and of Experience*, innocence and experience are not for Traherne 'contrary states of the soul', but experimental innocence is achieved through affective experience. The compatibility of innocence with experience forms the basis of Traherne's ethical notion of 'innocency of life', which is the drama of innocence, explored below through its activities, virtues and vocations.[18]

'Innocency of the Act'

'Innocency of life' includes Wilson's under-developed concept of 'innocency of the Act', which allies inner affections with outward actions.[19] This 'how' of human existence is, as in Kelsey's theological anthropology, not merely concerned with visible behaviour but with basic orientations, affections and dispositions.[20] Act is an important philosophical category for Traherne, and his treatment of it has clear implications for the innocent activity of Christian life.[21] *Commentaries of Heaven* includes three entries related to act: 'Act',

---

[15]   Traherne, *Kingdom of God*, 313.

[16]   Although knowledge of redemption is only possible through revelation (see Traherne, *Christian Ethicks*, 119).

[17]   Inge, *Happiness and Holiness*, 148; see also Kershaw, 'The Poetic of the Cosmic Christ', 184–5.

[18]   Wilson, *A Complete Christian Dictionary*, 336b.

[19]   Ibid.

[20]   Kelsey, *Eccentric Existence*, 2.

[21]   On Traherne's spiritual progress as an imitation of God-as-act, built on Neoplatonic and Aristotelian foundations, see Benjamin J. Barber, 'Syncretism and Idiosyncrasy: The Notion of Act in Thomas Traherne's Contemplative Practice', *LT* 28/1 (2014), 16–28.

'Action' and 'Activity'.[22] These concepts are fundamental to existence, being defined as life's substance, motion and inclination. From the perspective of moral theology, act, action and activity combined express not only the outward moral rectitude of innocent actions but a full righteousness that is born in the heart and brought into being through motion.

Wilson distinguished the affections and actions of innocence, stating without explanation that 'there is also one innocency of the Act, another of the Affect'.[23] By contrast, Traherne unites innocent affections and actions through activity.[24] Traherne's key affections of desire, sight and love are defined as 'Immanent Actions' that are necessary to relationship between humanity and God.[25] Inward activity has a reciprocal relationship with its public manifestation in action: 'by the inward Conceptions and Thoughts of the Mind, are all the outward Actions of the Life occasioned Cherished and perfected, and by the outward Actions the Life is Beautified, and the Person Glorified'.[26]

This dynamic interaction between inner affection and outward action intimates a virtue ethics that mediates between the *habitus* of infused dispositions and the behavioural concerns of 'practical morality'.[27] In relation to innocence, it suggests that Traherne's moral theology was conducive to a double definition of innocence as both inward and outward, passive and active. Inward activity and outward action together express the full 'indeavour' of the innocent life.[28]

Traherne's holistic philosophy of act intimates the character of the drama of innocence.[29] Firstly, the fundamental status of act accounts for *Christian Ethicks'*

---

[22]   Traherne, *Commentaries of Heaven, Part 1*, 170–207.

[23]   Wilson, *A Complete Christian Dictionary*, 336b.

[24]   Cf.: 'it is probable our hearts are right with God, and our intentions innocent and pious, if we set upon actions of religion or civil life with an *affection proportioned* to the quality of the work' (Jeremy Taylor *The Rule and Exercises of Holy Living* [London, 1650], 22).

[25]   Traherne, 'Action', *Commentaries of Heaven, Part 1*, 189–90.

[26]   Ibid. 193.

[27]   On post-Reformation tension between these two models of virtue, see Paul Cefalu, *Moral Identity in Early Modern English Literature* (Cambridge: Cambridge University Press, 2004), 3, 16, 192.

[28]   Wilson, *A Complete Christian Dictionary*, 336b. Note the Arminian connotations of 'endeavour' sit uncomfortably with Wilson's puritan tendencies, and may reflect the dictionary's Catholic sources.

[29]   For theodramatic studies which define drama in terms of act or performance, rather than tragedy or dialectical tension, see Sam Wells, *Improvisation: The Drama of Christian Ethics* (London: SPCK, 2004); Trevor A. Hart and Steven R. Guthrie (eds), *Faithful Performances: Enacting Christian Tradition* (Aldershot: Ashgate, 2007).

concern with the characters' actions over the drama's metaphysical stage: 'Be the Theatre never so magnificent, the Actions and the Actors are more Delightful to the Spectators than the Gildings, and Dead Engravings.'[30] The importance of act to the drama of innocence reflects the centrality of the plot in Aristotelian drama.[31] As Traherne further explains in *A Serious and Pathetical Contemplation of the Mercies of GOD*, a theatre without action is a void:

> Empty Cases,
> Cabinets spoiled are dum shews.
> The *Jewels*, O Lord, and *Scenes* and *Actions*;
> These are the Treasures which most we prize.[32]

The drama of innocence is an inward drama of the soul, with 'My Bosom the Stage of those Calamities'. However, it also intimates the riches contained within outward actions: 'What infinite Depths may lie concealed, In the rude appearance of the smallest Actions.'[33] The manifestation of the inner activity of innocence in outward acts is an essential feature of the drama of innocence in Christian life.

Harmlessness and the War with Sin

The activity of innocence is expressed through a martial language that denounces the dreamy innocence or, as *Kingdom of God* puts it, 'defectiv goodness' whose 'Interests are Dim, and its Concernes dull, its Enjoyments flat, and its Intentions Dreaming ... [which] Springs from its Incapacitie, Lukewarmness, Indifference and stupiditie'.[34] In *Commentaries of Heaven*'s definition of 'Armour', active innocence is participation in dramatic conflict with the world: 'A Christians Life being rightly stiled a Spiritual Warfare, since Satan the World and the flesh

---

30   Traherne, *Christian Ethicks*, 59.

31   See Aristotle, *Poetics*, 1450a–b (VI 19–21); Ricoeur, *Time and Narrative*, vol. 1, 34.

32   Traherne, *A Serious and Pathetical Contemplation of the Mercies of GOD*, 420–21.

33   Ibid. 421, 395; for a discussion of the spiritual epic of the soul in this period, see David Loewenstein, 'The Seventeenth-Century Protestant English Epic', in Catherine Bates (ed.), *Cambridge Companion to the Epic* (Cambridge: Cambridge University Press, 2010), 146–66.

34   Traherne, *Kingdom of God*, 299–300; cf.: 'many cease from sin out of fear alone, not out of innocence or love of vertue, and they (as yet) are not to be called innocent, but timerous' (Taylor, *The Rule and Exercises of Holy Living*, 27).

134 *Boundless Innocence in Thomas Traherne's Poetic Theology*

are his Enemies.'[35] This combat is enacted on what John Smith called the 'inner Stage of mens Souls' and is testament to the 'inward life and power, vigour and activity' of the virtuous.[36]

For Traherne, proof of virtue is found in courageous activity, as in *Kingdom of God*: 'How often is Courage buried in an Hermits Cell? How frequently Does Valor languish in desert Solitudes!'[37] *Commentaries of Heaven* describes how the active affections were created for this combat: hope, 'that no Difficulties might discourage it, nor any Opposition extinguish its Endeavors'; anger, 'that it might by rage and fury surmount all Opposition'; and self-love, so the soul 'might Triumph over Enemies and Assaults after Victorie, and enjoy the Travail of its Sweat and Labors.'[38] *Christian Ethicks* describes courage as essential to the Christian life. It is 'stiled *Manhood* among the English ... As if the Essence of a man was founded in Courage, because his Vigor is emasculated, and his Dignity lost, that is Effeminate and Timerous; for he is scarce a Man that is a Coward.'[39] Traherne revels in the masculine connotations of the Latin etymology of *virtu*, and thereby contrasts active virtue to feminine passivity, as 'Love is more effeminate in a condition of Repose.'[40] This masculine model of virtue and active innocence provides an interesting counterpoint to post-Romantic critiques of feminine ideals of innocence.

This martial imagery of virtue ostensibly sits uncomfortably with the primary etymological definition of innocence as harmlessness. According to Findley, Augustine replaced the 'classical' innocence of mundane harmlessness with the 'Christian' innocence of virtuous action.[41] However, harmlessness clearly remained integral to seventeenth-century definitions of innocence. Traherne's language of virtuous innocence combines harmlessness with might. His *Commonplace Book* cites a meditation of Hermes Trismegistus which did not tie innocent harmlessness to weakness and limitation but to power: the light of good is greater than the sun, 'more swift and sharp to pierce, and innocent or

---

[35] Traherne, 'Armour', *Commentaries of Heaven, Part 2*, 212, drawing on Eph. 6.11–17; also quoted in id., *Kingdom of God*, 262–3; on spiritual warfare, see id., *Ceremonial Law*, 202; id., *A Sober View*, 146; id., *Christian Ethicks*, 193, 220–23, 232; id., *Church's Year-Book*, 33; id., *Centuries of Meditations*, III 7–14.

[36] J. Smith, *Select Discourses*, X 4.

[37] Traherne, *Kingdom of God*, 299.

[38] Traherne, 'Affection', *Commentaries of Heaven, Part 1*, 284.

[39] Traherne, *Christian Ethicks*, 162; see also id., *Select Meditations*, IV 58.

[40] Traherne, *Christian Ethicks*, 192.

[41] Findley, 'Perfecting Adam', 2–3.

'Innocency of Life' 135

harmlesse withall'.[42] This image of glorious harmlessness might be incorporated into *Commentaries of Heaven*'s description of the beasts of Eden: 'Terrible in their Harmlessness, and Pleasant in their Terribleness'.[43] The terrible glory of harmless innocence is the awesomeness of withheld might.

The harmlessness of innocence means not to *cause* harm but also not to *receive* harm. Wilson identifies harmless innocence in 'one which doth no hurt nor harm unto any others', but harmlessness also carries a veiled signification of invulnerability.[44] Traherne's 'Adam' combines harmlessness with impervious integrity. Through divine assistance, 'nothing was able (keeping himself Innocent) to destroy, or to harm him'.[45] Adam's invulnerability relies upon relationship to God, as only Christ is absolutely and essentially harmless: *Kingdom of God* explains that his 'Essence too, is too Compleat, / To be so Injurd!'[46] So, in *Christian Ethicks* it is through sight of God's glory that the righteous

> wonder to behold our selves so nigh
> To so much Sin and Misery,
> And yet to see our selves so safe from harm![47]

The virtue of humility unites the two aspects of harmlessness. The humble do not harm their enemies but are not thereby made vulnerable. In *Select Meditations*, the harmless beasts of Eden are replicated in the humble person who 'can be as Low as His Enemies would have Him ... [who] may be as bold as a Lion, becaus He is uncap[a]ble of being Hurt or Injured'.[48] The harmlessness of innocent humility is akin to courage, as both are a bulwark against guilt and misery. The combination of harmlessness and activity in innocence is both the

---

[42] Traherne, 'Beatifick', *Commonplace Book*, 20v 2; citing *Hermes Mercurious Trismegistus, His Divine Pymander, In Seventeen Books*, IV 14, 51, trans. John, Everard (London, 1657).

[43] Traherne, 'Adam', *Commentaries of Heaven, Part 1*, 218–19.

[44] Wilson, *A Complete Christian Dictionary*, 336b; cf Charron's Machiavellian version of this theme: 'By offending no man, a man taketh a course to be offended by none' (*Of Wisdom*, 408).

[45] Traherne, 'Assistance', *Commentaries of Heaven, Part 2*, 269.

[46] Traherne, *Kingdom of God*, 303.

[47] Traherne, *Christian Ethicks*, 202; see also: the enemy 'must first break thorow the Wrath of GOD ... before he can either dare or be able to hurt us' (id., 'Anger', *Commentaries of Heaven, Part 2*, 89).

[48] Ibid. *Select Meditations*, IV 68; MacKinnon explores this idea in his discussion of the 'paradox of the vulnerability of the invulnerable, of the invulnerability of the vulnerable' (*Themes in Theology*, 235).

not-causing and not-receiving of hurt. In this double movement, innocence is both a privative and positive quality of the Christian life, ostensibly weak but actually glorious.

'Innocency joyned with swelling': Hypocrisy as False Innocence

The war against sin includes a battle with the false innocence of hypocrisy. Hypocrisy in seventeenth-century devotion was often identified with pride: William Whately's *Prototypes* defined it as an 'innocency joyned with swelling, lifting up our selves and despising others'.[49] For Wilson and Traherne, hypocrisy is not only a proud but also a mixed or insincere innocence, which unsettles the harmony of the inner and outer life. Wilson identifies hypocrisy with 'mixture', as opposed to the purity of sincere faith.[50] Traherne's concern with hypocrisy begins in his earliest works. His *Early Notebook*, begun during his student days in Oxford, contains a section on hypocrites that draws on Bacon's exposition of hypocrisy as pride. It is, however, most critical of those who cultivate only the outward appearance of righteousness and 'make the applause of others the foundation of their vertues'.[51]

Traherne's concern with hypocrisy is allied to anti-Catholic and anti-Semitic polemic, but has deeper philosophical roots. *Roman Forgeries* begins with citations from 1 Timothy 4.2 and from Bernard on the medieval church, 'varnished over with *Hypocrisie* in the *Noon* of her prosperity'.[52] The *Commonplace Book* cites Jackson on the Jewish and Roman authorities' 'secret instinct or working of hypocrisie' which 'sought to stuffe their fancies with imaginations of their holinesse ... they dreamed the substance of that holinesse to be rooted in their hearts, whose shadowe or representation floated in their braines'.[53] The language of dreams and imagination in this latter quotation provides a source for Traherne's concern with hypocrisy that is not purely polemical but expresses a more fundamental tension between appearance and reality.

---

[49] Whately, *Prototypes*, 56.

[50] See Wilson, *A Complete Christian Dictionary*, q.v. 'Sincere faith', 589b.

[51] Thomas Traherne, 'Of Hypocrites', *Early Notebook* (Oxford, Bodl.MS.Lat.misc.f.45), 85; see Bacon, 'Of Vain-Glory', *Essays, Civil and Moral*, Harvard Classics 3/1 (New York: P.F. Collier and Son, 1909–14), #54; see also Carol L. Marks, 'Thomas Traherne's Early Studies', *PBSA* 62 (1968), 536.

[52] Traherne, *Roman Forgeries*, frontispiece; Traherne, 'An Advertisement to the Reader', *Roman Forgeries*, 19–24, citing Bernard, *The Song of Songs: Selections from the Sermons of S. Bernard*, #33, ed. B. Blaxland (London: Methuen, 1901).

[53] See 'Hypocrisie', *Commonplace Book*, 54v 1–2, citing Jackson, *A Treatise containing the Originall of Unbeliefe*, 307–8.

The Ceremonial Law's description of the illusory oasis of Marah outlines the connection between hypocrisy and the appearance of false treasure or false virtue:

> The Place
> Did Type Hypocrisie. for in the face
> Distilling Nectars did to us appear,
> And Liquid Pearls; but none indeed were there.[54]

Hypocrisy is a shadow that conceals reality. *Commentaries of Heaven* calls it a mundane 'shew of piety made in falshood. as 2. Cor. 5.12. Which glory in Appearance, but not in heart'.[55] The falsity of hypocritical innocence is no superficial insincerity but a fundamental failure to image God. Its dreamy translucence cannot sincerely reflect the 'Solid Integritie' of God's works, whose 'very Essence and Nature is Truth, he truly is what, or more then, he appearath'.[56] The innocent life combats hypocrisy by harmonising the activity of the affections with outward actions, both being itself and exceeding itself in the image of God.

'For the Preservation of our Innocence': The Activities of Sincerity, Integrity and Purity of Heart

The inward activities of the affections were of great concern in the seventeenth-century works of moral theology with which Traherne interacted, such as Richard Allestree's popular *The Practice of Christian Graces or The Whole Duty of Man* (1658).[57] Allestree distinguished the externals of innocent actions from the pure heart: 'if there were the perfectest innocence in our tongue, and hands, yet if there be not this purity of heart, it will never serve to acquit us before

---

54 Traherne, *Ceremonial Law*, 214; see Exod. 15.22–7.

55 Traherne, 'Appearance', *Commentaries of Heaven, Part 2*, 137.

56 Ibid. 137, 138.

57 For Traherne's rejection of Allestree and Charron's 'ordinary' exposition of virtue as duty, prudence and earthly honour, see Traherne, 'To the Reader', *Christian Ethicks*, 3; on Traherne's cautious reception of Allestree and a comparison of *Christian Ethicks* and *The Practice of Christian Graces*, see Kevin Laam, 'Thomas Traherne, Richard Allestree, and the Ethics of Appropriation', in Blevins (ed.), *Re-Reading Thomas Traherne*, 37–64; on the puritan focus on the inner innocence of intent, see Perry Miller, *The New England Mind: The Seventeenth Century* (New York: Macmillan, 1939), 52.

138   *Boundless Innocence in Thomas Traherne's Poetic Theology*

[God]'.[58] The inner innocence of the pure heart was largely something to be preserved rather than pursued, identified as an inner state of passive ease. So William Birchley prayed, 'Lord, how secure and quiet they live, whom thy grace preservs in innocence!'[59] In Traherne's works the 'Preservation of our Innocence' through sincerity, integrity and purity of heart is an inward activity united to outward action.[60]

The Preservation of Sincerity: The Innocent Affection of the Pure Heart

Sincerity applies to both the mundane ethics of public behaviour and the inner spiritual affections. John Tillotson's treatise on the subject defined the scriptural characters Nathaniel and Jacob as sincere because each was a 'downright honest Man, without fraud, and guile, without any arts of hypocrisie and deceit', possessing 'a simplicity of Mind and Manners'. Sincerity was thus the outward expression of an honest life, but also an essential quality of religion imitating Christ's sinless perfection, 'who did no Sin, neither was Guil found in his mouth'. Sincerity's guileless innocence was the unity of the self before God, where 'the outward expressions of our Piety and Obedience to him, are the genuine issue of our inward apprehensions of him, and affections towards him'.[61] Traherne's sincerity is also both a quality of public virtue and an inner disposition towards it. Righteous actions may be performed in a sincere manner, but sincerity is also the affective activity of innocency of life. So, as a gloss on 2 Corinthians 9.7, 'Almes' states that God 'loveth a Sincere ... giver', adding that 'Sincerity is shut up in Cheerfulness'.[62] Sincerity thus applies to both the actions and the affections.

Scholarly criticism on the development of sincerity has highlighted its changing meaning during this period, from a medieval notion of purity to the self-knowledge and transparency of the modern individual. John Jeffries

---

[58]   Richard Allestree, *The Practice of Christian Graces, or, The Whole Duty of Man* (London, 1658), 262.

[59]   William Birchley, *Devotions in the Ancient Way of Offices* (London, 1668), 165.

[60]   Traherne, *Christian Ethicks*, 18.

[61]   John Tillotson, *Of Sincerity and Constancy in the Faith and Profession of the True Religion* (London, 1695), 3, 27–8; on the 'sincerity of an honest, and ingenuous, and a fearless person', see Jeremy Taylor, 'Of Christian Simplicity', in *The Whole Works of the Right Rev. Jeremy Taylor*, ed. Reginald Heber (London: Ogle, Duncan and Co., 1822), vol. 6, 141; 'sincere *Intention* is Evangelical Perfection' (Benjamin Whichcote, *Moral and Religious Aphorisms*, ed. W.R. Inge [London: E. Mathews & Marot, 1930], #815).

[62]   Traherne, 'Almes', *Commentaries of Heaven, Part 1*, 371. Traherne perhaps planned an entry for sincerity in *Commentaries of Heaven*, see *The Works of Thomas Traherne*, vol. 2, 525.

Martin argues for the 'invention of sincerity' in Renaissance literature, relating a transition from a medieval *concordia* or harmony with the image of God to a Reformation psychological sincerity of an emerging modern anthropology of the affections.[63] Broader hypotheses chart a rise in utopian sincerity from 1660 to 1800, rooted in early modern values of purity and honesty but developed through puritanism from the pursuit of pure religion to an inner sincerity of heart, in line with the modern rise of the individual.[64]

Modern sincerity is a literary as well as a moral virtue, previously identified with the Romantic principle of simple language and with Traherne's simple style.[65] Against this, Herbert Read has argued that however simple the language of Traherne's poetry of childhood, the artifice of literature cannot express the pure experience of an unreflective infant subject. He therefore returned to a moral definition of sincerity as the truthfulness of the individual to itself. He identified it as a core modern concept since, following Buber's 'principle of individuation', 'To ask "What is sincerity?" is in effect to ask "What is man".[66]

In seventeenth-century thought, sincerity continued to be defined through its traditional etymology as 'That which is pure, and without mixture'.[67] The emerging modern ideal of sincerity was an unfeigned unity of inner affection and outward action. The transitional stage between these two significations is embodied in the combination of purity with individual conscience, in More's definition of sincerity as: 'a Vertue of the Soul, by which Will is intirly and sincerely carried on to that which the mind judgeth to be absolutely and simply the best'.[68]

For Traherne, sincerity similarly combines purity and honesty, the medieval and the modern idea. 'Acknowledgement' defines sincerity as honest innocence in its assertion of 'the Singular Innocency of Acknowledging a Crime before

---

[63] John Jeffries Martin, 'Inventing Sincerity, Refashioning Prudence: The Discovery of the Individual in the Renaissance', *American Historical Review* 102/5 (1997), 1327–32.

[64] Leon Guilhamet, *The Sincere Ideal: Studies on Sincerity in Eighteenth-Century English Literature* (Montreal: McGill-Queen's University Press, 1974), 6, 280–81; Lionel Trilling, *Sincerity and Authority* (Cambridge, Mass.: Harvard University Press, 1971), 2–3, 12–13.

[65] See Henri Peyre, *Literature and Sincerity* (New Haven, Conn.: Yale University Press, 1963); David Perkins, *Wordsworth and the Poetry of Sincerity* (Cambridge, Mass.: Harvard University Press, 1964), 1–60; Malcom Day, '"Naked Truth" and the Language of Thomas Traherne', *SP* 68 (1971), 305–25.

[66] Herbert Read, *The Cult of Sincerity* (London: Faber & Faber, 1968), 13–37.

[67] See Wilson, *A Complete Christian Dictionary*, q.v. 'Sincere', 589a.

[68] Henry More, *An Account of Virtue: Or Dr. Henry More's Abridgement of Morals, Put into English* (London, 1690), vol. 2, 104–5.

140   *Boundless Innocence in Thomas Traherne's Poetic Theology*

a Judge the Candor and Sincerity of Preferring Truth before ones Life, the Integrity of a Soule Detesting a Sin even to the Death'.[69] In *Kingdom of God*, sincerity is an offshoot of free will, from which develops a 'desire to be Sincere in our Judgments, and true in our Apprehensions'. The sincerity desired is that of love towards God, which is purity of heart: 'It is opposit and Destructiv to the Nature of Love, to be feigned, or Constraind: If we must Love him with all our Heart, and with all our Soul, we must of Necessity Approve him, and Delight in him throughly'.[70] The connection between sincerity and purity of heart highlights sincerity as a key component in the preservation of innocence. Traherne expresses the importance of this task in *Centuries of Meditations*, in a citation of Proverbs 4.23: 'In all thy Keeping Keep thy Heart, for out of it are the Issues of Life and Death'.[71]

The Pursuit of Integrity

Keeping innocence entails preserving the integrity of the soul, which Wilson defined as a Christian quality of 'Innocency, honesty, uprightness, soundness. A note of the godly'.[72] In devotional literature the Edenic state of innocence was also designated a state of integrity.[73] Integrity as a state is an object to protect or recover, not an activity to pursue. However, critical discussion on integrity in seventeenth-century literature has presented alternative perspectives on this issue. Richard Horwich defines Shakespearean integrity not as the singleness of Edenic unity but as 'an integrated personality', a model suited to the compound essence of the fallen soul.[74] Larry Bouchard redefines early modern integrity in relational and performative terms as a self-emptying 'kenotic integrity' exemplified by Christ, not Adam.[75] This kenotic model of integrity is apparent

---

[69]   Traherne, 'Acknowledgement', *Commentaries of Heaven, Part 1*, 155.

[70]   Traherne, *Kingdom of God*, 274.

[71]   Traherne, *Centuries of Meditations*, IV 41.

[72]   Wilson, *A Complete Christian Dictionary*, q.v. 'Integrity', 337b.

[73]   See Jackson, *A Treatise of the Divine Essence and Attributes*, Part I, 105; William Ames, *The Marrow of Sacred Divinity* (London: Edward Griffin, 1642), 219; Culverwel, *An Elegant and Learned Discourse of the Light of Nature*, 126; Thomas Boston, *Human Nature in its Fourfold State: Of Primitive Integrity, Entire Depravity, Begun Recovery and Consummate Happiness or Misery* (Edinburgh, 1720).

[74]   Richard Horwich, 'Integrity in Macbeth: The Search for the "Single State of Man"', *Shakespeare Quarterly* 29/3 (1978), 371–2.

[75]   Larry D. Bouchard, *Theater and Integrity: Emptying Selves in Drama, Ethics, and Religion* (Evanston, Ill.: Northwestern University Press, 2011), xi–xiii, 3–26, 241–53.

in *Centuries of Meditations*, wherein 'it is an Happy Loss to lose one self in Admiration at ones own Felicity: and to find GOD in exchange for oneself'.[76]

Against this background, Trahernian integrity may entail the preservation of wholeness, but it is also a compound and complex quality that combines passive protection with active pursuit. This is evident in Traherne's use of mirror imagery. In *Commentaries of Heaven* the integrity of the soul's pure apprehension must be preserved, 'As it is the Mirror receiving all ideas, and their Objects by them I ought to keep it Clear, fair, and Resplendent'.[77] Contrastingly, *Kingdom of God* describes minds as 'lively Mirrors', not only active but alive.[78] Integrity's pure mirror is not only a passive reflection of the good but a dynamic reception and reproduction of it which participates in the creative act.

Integrity is not only a state but a path to be followed. Traherne's treatise on spiritual retirement, *Inducements to Retirednes*, cites Psalm 26.11 where to 'walk in mine Integrity' is to follow righteousness.[79] Andrewes uses this language in his priestly prayer that 'I may walk before thee, in my vocation, without offence, *as in the day*, clean, unspotted, and unblamable'.[80] The adjective, 'unblameable', connotes a more complex innocence than its synonym, 'blameless'. The prefix denotes the negation of a capacity to be blamed, while the suffix evokes ability and activity rather than a mere absence of blame. Traherne's repeated use of this term in *A Sober View* is significant in evoking the dynamic and impervious integrity of unblameable innocence.[81] It is therefore appropriate to speak of the pursuit of integrity as part of the preservation of innocence.

The link between preserving integrity and pursuing righteousness is apparent in *Christian Ethicks*' discussion of prudence, which cites 1 Peter 3.10–13:

> He that will love Life and see good Days, let him refrain his Tongue from Evil, and his Lips that they speak no Guile: let him eschew Evil, and do Good, let him seek Peace and ensue it, for the Eyes of the Lord are over the Righteous: And who is he that will harm you, if ye be followers of that which is Good?[82]

---

[76]   Traherne, *Centuries of Meditations*, I 18.

[77]   Traherne, 'Apprehension', *Commentaries of Heaven, Part 2*, 175.

[78]   Traherne, *Kingdom of God*, 287.

[79]   Traherne, *Inducements to Retirednes*, 8.

[80]   Andrewes, *Holy Devotions*, 113.

[81]   Jeremy Taylor uses this term in an active sense: 'it is a great ... ingagement to do unblameably' (*The Rule and Exercises of Holy Living*, I.3.xxxiii).

[82]   Traherne, *Christian Ethicks*, 157. Traherne omits the more forbidding verse 12b: 'but the Face of the Lord is against them that do evil'.

142 *Boundless Innocence in Thomas Traherne's Poetic Theology*

Guileless innocence here is not privative ignorance but a voluntary retention of speech and an active pursuit of righteousness which protects the innocent from harm. Andrewes expresses a similar sentiment when, following the Douay-Rheims translation of Psalm 37.37 as an injunction to 'Keep innocence, and behold justice', he describes God's dual commandment as '1. To keep innocency, and to do that which is right (Psal. 37.38). 2. And to do no evil (Eclus 7.10)'.[83] This translation unites preserving innocence with pursuing righteousness and distinguishes both from a negative abstention from evil. In this sense innocence is a positive as well as privative ethical term.

The Sincerity and Integrity of Innocent Hands

Seventeenth-century exegesis of the scriptural imagery of innocent hands expressed the unity of an inner sincerity of affective activity with outward righteous actions and of the passive preservation of integrity with the dynamic pursuit of unblameableness. For Wilson, 'Innocent hands' designate active righteousness and freedom from evil: they 'signifie a righteous life, or actions rightly framed, free from wrong, deceit, blood and violence'.[84] The KJV translation of Genesis 20.5 conjoins integrity and innocence, affection and action, through the parallelism of 'the integrity of my heart and innocency of my hands'.[85] These largely interchangeable terms, defined in Henry Ainsworth's annotations on the passage as '*perfection*] or, '*integrity, simplic*[it]*y, sincerity*', '*truth*' or '*a pure heart*', are united in opposition to hypocrisy, a complete innocence where even the hidden palms are clean.[86]

The Virtues of Innocence: Humility, Patience, Repentance and Meekness

In classical drama, the plot progresses through the hero's actions. In Traherne's ethics, these heroic actions are voluntary acts of virtue. The plot, as outlined in *Select Meditations*, is the difficult labour to rebuild Eden: 'destroying the

---

[83] Andrewes, *Holy Devotions*, 15; cf.: 'Marke the perfect man, and behold the upright' (Ps. 37.37, KJV); Aquinas considered doing good and avoiding evil as 'Quasi-Integral Parts of Justice' (*Summa Theologica*, IIB.79.i).

[84] Wilson, *A Complete Christian Dictionary*, 336b.

[85] Cf. the Douay-Rheims translation of Gen. 20.5: 'in the simplicity of my heart, and cleanness of my hands'; Geneva translation: 'with an upright mind, and innocent hands'.

[86] Henry Ainsworth, *Annotations upon the Five Bookes of Moses, the Booke of the Psalms, and the Song of Songs* (London, 1627), 78 (Gen. 20.5).

wild Beasts and Dressing the feilds ... [to] Restore the world to the Beauty of Paradice' in a field where 'wisdom is now become profound, Happieness concealed, Felicity Buried: we must Sweat For her as for Hidden Treasures'.[87] The innocence of virtuous acts is not the limited or narrow innocence described by Seneca, which merely follows the law.[88] As described in *Kingdom of God*, it is the living motion of 'a free Agent, Glorious and Holy', not the automated movements of 'Mecanical Instruments, Dead, and Passiv'.[89] The Christian virtues are the activities of innocence. They are infused with its beauty, express its dual harmlessness and work to restore its kingdom.

The 'Christian virtues' of the third estate – humility, patience, meekness and repentance – are those that only become active after the Fall and in response to sin.[90] More's *Divine Dialogues* summarise this notion, exclaiming: 'What would become of those enravishing Vertues of Humility, Meekness, Patience and Forbearance, if there were no Injuries amongst men?'[91] Traherne styles them Christian virtues because they are 'taught ... in the Christian Religion ... founded on the Love of Christ, and the only Vertues distinguishing a *Christian* from the rest of the World'.[92] They are interlocking virtues; humility 'rooteth in *meekness*, becaus it maketh a man Despise Himselfe' and 'enduceth *Patience* as Knowing we have Deserved Greater Calamities', which acknowledgement is a sign of repentance.[93] As virtues which avoid causing harm, they could be interpreted as the passive side of Andrewes' twofold 'Quickning of the new man': the avoidance of evil that complements actively pursuing goodness.[94] Aquinas certainly classified meekness among the privative virtues, which are inferior to active righteousness.[95] In Traherne's *Christian Ethicks*, however, these virtues together express the wholeness of an innocent life in both its privative and positive aspects.

The virtue of patience has already been discussed. It is 'that Vertue by which we behave our selves constantly and prudently in the midst of Misfortunes and Troubles'. Patience reflects the invulnerable integrity of a kept innocence, as

---

[87] Traherne, *Select Meditations*, III.31.ii, III.42.

[88] Seneca, 'De Ira', II.28.ii–iii, in *Moral Essays*, trans. John W. Basore, LCL (Cambridge, Mass.: Harvard University Press, 1928), vol. 1; see Thomas P. Harrison, 'Seneca and Traherne', *Arion* 6/3 (1967), 403–5.

[89] Traherne, *Kingdom of God*, 288.

[90] Traherne, *Christian Ethicks*, 33, 128, 185, 194.

[91] More, *Divine Dialogues*, 309–10.

[92] Traherne, *Christian Ethicks*, 24-5.

[93] Traherne, *Select Meditations*, IV 68 (italics added).

[94] Andrewes, *Holy Devotions*, 215.

[95] Aquinas, 'Of Clemency and Meekness', *Summa Theologica*, IIB.157.iv.

'Nothing can quell him, or discourage, or overcome him, that is compleat in Patience'. However, it also exhibits the divine art of transforming evil to good 'by a true Courage [which will] improve our Afflictions, and turn them into the *Spoils* of Invincible Reason'. Like humility, it is a paradoxical virtue that 'raises a Man by depressing him, it elevates by overwhelming, it honours by debasing, it saves by killing him'.[96]

Humility has been discussed above as a feature of the honesty of sincerity and as the invulnerable simplicity of Adam and the atom. Humility also protects against hypocrisy by granting the regenerate 'a sence that now He is restored from an Estate worse then nothing', so that 'being Redeemed, For evry Sin committed Since, it is more Deeply Humble'.[97] Humility is linked to repentance, 'for an Humble man condescendeth to look into his Wants, to reflect upon all his Vices, and all his Beginnings, with far deeper designs than is ordinarily done'.[98]

Humility is a sincere vision of the world most 'agreeable to the Truth of our Condition'. As such it is the conduit from the shadowy world of misery to the true world of God's kingdom: the means 'by which we leave the phantastick World, with all its Shews and Gauderies; and through many Afflictions and Persecutions, come to the real and solid World of Bliss and Glory'. The truth revealed by humility is that of human identity. This is not a nadir of self-confidence but a centre of self-knowledge, which like a mirror on the ground reflects the heavens in the abyss and 'toucheth all *Extreams* together'. Humility is long-sightedness, not a contracted self-contemplation focused on sin but an extension of self-knowledge which, as a rational faculty, is able to see humanity's beginning, middle and end and its nature in all the estates of the soul.[99]

Repentance is labelled a fourth theological, or Christian, virtue because it is directed towards God.[100] It represents the conjunction of innocence and guilt which glorifies the regenerate:

> It is a Strange Kind of off-spring, which flows from Parents so infinitely different, and has a mixture in its Nature, answerable to either an *Evil* which it derives from *Sin*, and a *Goodness* which flows from *Mercy*. Its Evil is that of Sorrow, Indignation and Shame, Its Goodness is the usefulness, and necessity of the thing, considering the Condition we are now in.[101]

---

[96] Traherne, *Christian Ethicks*, 187, 198, 188.
[97] Traherne, *Select Meditations*, IV 66.
[98] Traherne, *Christian Ethicks*, 212.
[99] Ibid. 206, 210, 209.
[100] Ibid. 23.
[101] Ibid. 125.

'Innocency of Life'   145

This admirable mixture, 'that Sin and Mercy should be united ... for the production of a Child so Black and so Beautiful, is the Greatest Wonder which the Soul can contemplate on this side [of] Heaven'.[102] Repentance evokes the freshness of newly regenerate innocence, as 'the *Conception* of Felicity, and the *New Birth* of the *Inward Man*'.[103] Through repentance the '*indelible Stain and Guilt of Sin*' in the believer is not destroyed but beautified.[104] It therefore surpasses an innocence that is ignorant of sin: '[for] tho Repentance be not in it selfe a desirable Vertue ... yet upon the Account of our Saviours Merits, and GODS Love to Sinners, it is preferred above the Greatest Innocency and Purity whatsoever'.[105] Repentance represents the mixedness of quotidian existence, but also the loveliness of humanity's state through grace. Like humility and patience, it not only expresses the qualities of an innocent life but is a tool for remaking innocence in despite of evil.

Meekness: Christian Harmlessness

As the virtue of harmlessness, meekness exemplifies Christian innocence. According to the Aristotelian/Thomist ethics adopted by Allestree, meekness was merely a form of temperance, the moderation of anger.[106] In scripture and Christian literature, meekness has also been married to humility, suffering and eschatological victory.[107] Traherne echoes John Chrysostom and Calvin in his view that this victory is at least partly manifest in the present age:

> If all his other Vertues are beautified by Meekness, such a man will be like an Angel ... So that Meekness is his real exaltation. And this made our Saviour to call

---

[102] Ibid.

[103] Ibid. 129.

[104] Ibid. 99.

[105] Ibid. 127.

[106] See Aquinas, *Summa Theologica*, II.2.157.i, iii; Aristotle, *Nicomachean Ethics*, IV.5.i–ii, trans. D. Ross (rev. edn, Oxford: Clarendon, 1998); Allestree, *The Practice of Christian Graces*, 150–51.

[107] Traherne couples meekness with humility in *Inducements to Retirednes*, 14 (along with courage); *A Sober View*, 129; *Church's Year-Book*, 88, 112, 159, 168, 186; see also John Chrysostom, *Homilies on the Gospel of Saint Matthew*, XII 3 (Matt. 3.13); XXIII 12 (Matt. 7.1), trans. George Prevost, NPNF[1] 10 (Grand Rapids, Mich: Eerdmans, 1983), 74, 163; Pss 10.17, 29.19, 37(36).11, 76.9(75.10), 147(146).6, 149.4; 'What is meant by *meekness*? ... because the Martyrs suffered, and neither "fell away," nor yet offered resistance; confessing everything, concealing nothing; prepared for everything, shrinking from nothing. Marvellous *meekness!*' (Augustine, *Expositions on the Book of Psalms*, Ps. 45.3 ¶xv).

146   *Boundless Innocence in Thomas Traherne's Poetic Theology*

out that Blessing for the Meek, *The Meek shall inherit the Earth*. Even here upon Earth the Meek are they that are most blessed.[108]

Primarily, however, Traherne describes meekness as the quality of the suffering innocent, as 'The Injuries that we receive from others are its proper Objects'.[109] Benjamin Whichcote's aphorisms similarly took their model of meekness from Christ's passion: 'Christ, who was Innocent, was dealt withal, *as if* he were Faulty; that we, who *are* Faulty, might be dealt withal, as if we were Innocent.'[110] *A Sober View* applies this redemptive principle to the Christian life, as God teaches us to 'seek the Love of our Greatest Enemies; yea tho we are Innocent, and they Guilty'.[111] This section focuses on *Christian Ethicks'* presentation of meekness as a quality of the innocent life that refuses to return evil for evil. This is an active virtue characterised by supernatural grace, the application of strength in weakness and the unity of inward and outward integrity, enacted in the drama of spiritual life.[112]

Traherne's depiction of meekness responds to the humane critique that it 'encourageth all People to trample us under feet'. He does not deny that meekness may lead to persecution, but, since 'Love is the Life and Soul of every Vertue', naturally without it, meekness is merely 'a sheepish Tameness'.[113] By contrast, a godly meekness 'springs from Love, and tends to its Continuance and Preservation', with none of the weakness of its mundane counterpart.[114] This contradicts Charron's argument that doing good to the wicked exhibits the deficiencies of innocence:

---

[108] Traherne, *Christian Ethicks*, 201; see Chrysostom, *Homilies on the Gospel of Saint Matthew*, XV 5 (Matt. 5.1–2), 90–91; 'Though exposed to all the slings of fortune ... they live securely under God's protection, and even now enjoy this grace of God' (John Calvin, *A Harmony of the Gospels of Matthew, Mark, Luke*, trans. A.W. Morrison, ed. D.W. and T. Torrance [Edinburgh: Saint Andrew Press, 1972], vol. 1, 171 [Matt. 5.5]); cf. 'your innocence will be sufficient to confound' your enemies (id., *The Epistle of Paul the Apostle to the Hebrews and The First and Second Epistles of St Peter*, trans. William B. Johnston [Edinburgh: Oliver & Boyd, 1963], 290 [1 Peter 3.16]).

[109] Traherne, *Christian Ethicks*, 194; cf. Gregory the Great, *Morals on the Book of Job*, I.I.16.xii.

[110] Whichcote, *Moral and Religious Aphorisms*, #401.

[111] Traherne, *A Sober View*, 158.

[112] Traherne, *Christian Ethicks*, 194–205.

[113] Ibid. 154, 152.

[114] Ibid. 194.

> How should he be good, since he is not evill, to those that are evill? We should
> rather call this kind of goodnesse innocencie, as men call little children sheepe,
> and the like, innocent creatures. But an active, valiant, manly, and effectuall
> goodnesse is that I require, which is a readie, easie, and constant affection unto
> that which is good, right, just, according to reason and nature.[115]

Traherne accepts the dictates of human reason, but asserts the pre-eminence of grace: '[to] do good to an innocent Person is Humane, but to be kind and bountiful to a man, after he has been Injurious, is Divine'.[116] This is a principle that runs throughout Traherne's works.[117] He accepts that meekness contradicts the laws of nature according to which 'we are to be Just and Good towards all that are Innocent ... but it is not by Nature either just or rational that we should love any Creature that is Evil'. Nevertheless, meekness 'carries us above all the Rules of Nature, above all the Principles of Reason, and in that is Supernatural'.[118] This defence disassociates meekness from natural existence and mundane ethics, identifying it instead with regenerate nature and the divine order of grace.

Divine meekness applies the principle of 2 Corinthians 12.9, of strength made perfect in weakness: 'though it be as soft as *Wool*, [it] is able with more success to repel the violence of a Cannon-Bullet, than the rough temper of a *Stone-Wall*.'[119] Meekness is an aspect of temperance, but not as a mean between two extremes. Rather it represents the 'most weak and naked' virtues which through their 'full composition and use' can achieve the highest ends. Temperance does not limit the virtues but uses them to the full, so it 'takes off the stupidity and sluggishness of our Meekness; puts activity and vigour into it, that it may not be a Sleepish, but Heroick Vertue'.[120] An innocent life may be mundanely associated with

---

[115] Charron, *Of Wisdom*, 263; see also Charron's diatribe against a 'cowardly and idle innocencie, *quae nisi metu non placet!* Thou keepest thy selfe from wickednesse, because thou darest not be wicked' (ibid. 288); see also Aristotle, *Nicomachean Ethics*, V.5.iv.

[116] Traherne, *Christian Ethicks*, 201.

[117] See the inserted passage: 'To do infinit Good to an Innocent Creature is nothing to that of doing Good for an evil creature, nay of suffering all Evil for a guilty one (Traherne, *Kingdom of God*, 303); 'For tho Angels are bound to lov ... Men as themselvs, while they are innocent ... yet they are not bound by vertu of this Law to die for men being Wicked and Deformed' (id., *Centuries of Meditations*, II 32); Christ 'was infinitly great towards Innocent Persons in his Goodness before. Now he is infinitly Great towards Sinners in the Riches of his free Grace and Lov unto them' (id., 'Assumption', *Commentaries of Heaven, Part 2*, 287).

[118] Traherne, *Christian Ethicks*, 195.

[119] Ibid. 197.

[120] Ibid. 175; see also Plotinus, *Enneads*, I.2.vii.

sheep-like cowardice, weakness and folly, but its divine sense is more akin to Charron's 'active, valiant, manly, and effectuall goodnesse'.

Meekness is harmlessness in both the inward affections and outward actions. To refuse to take revenge is to repudiate the evil inflicted, so meekness preserves both 'outward *Security*, and inward *Contentment*'. Outwardly, it prevents the cycle of harm caused by vengeance by preserving friendship through forgiveness.[121] Inwardly, meekness enables one to 'maintain the quiet of his own Soul in the midst of [others'] distempers', unlike 'He that permits the Tumult of the World to enter into his Soul, and suffers the Temple of the Holy Ghost to be defiled with Rage and Anger'.[122] So, meekness is a kind of integrity, having 'something peculiar in its nature, because it gives Immutability to Goodness, and makes our Worth not to depend on other Mens Deservings, but our own Resolutions'.[123] This is akin to Sterry's opinion of 'the incorruptibleness of a meek spirit, [which] preserveth in it self a Divine Beauty and Sweetness, which is ever perfect, which never passeth away, in the midst of all changes of Life, in Death, to Eternity'.[124] It adapts Aquinas' characterisation of meekness as the virtue of self-possession, as that which 'makes Goodness invincible and unalterable' and preserves inner peace.[125] The immutable integrity of meekness is the security of a soul that owns itself and in so doing owns all things.

Meekness encapsulates the plot of the drama of innocence through the language of spiritual warfare and paradisal restoration. 'This glorious mystery of Patience and Meekness' is that

> by which in despite of all the Corruptions and Violences in the World, the holy Soul of a quiet Man is armed and prepared for all Assaults, and so invironed with its own repose, that in the midst of Provocations it is undisturbed, and dwells as it were in a Sanctuary of Peace within it self, in a Paradice of Bliss, while it is surrounded with the howlings of a terrible Wilderness. Nothing else can make us live happily in this World, for among so many Causes of Anger and Distaste, no man can live well, but he that carries about him perpetual *Antidotes* and *Victories*.[126]

---

[121] Traherne, *Christian Ethicks*, 197, 199.

[122] Ibid. 198, 197.

[123] Ibid. 194.

[124] Sterry, *A Discourse of the Freedom of the Will*, xv.

[125] Aquinas, *Summa Theologica*, IIB.157.iv; Traherne, *Christian Ethicks*, 199.

[126] Traherne, *Christian Ethicks*, 197.

'Innocency of Life'   149

As a weapon of spiritual warfare, meekness is a partner to courage, a theme that finds scriptural roots in Joel 3.19 and Daniel 3. The two virtues are cited together in *Inducements to Retirednes*, and *Church's Year-Book* charts the unity of 'Meekness Humility Courage Self Denial Truth zeal and Lov' in John the Baptist.[127] As part of the warfare of innocence, meekness is the '*Bulwark*' of security and 'the retreat of Goodness', cultivating Edenic peace and felicity through retirement from the world.[128] It can be an indirect revenge for wrongs, 'For our Repose is their punishment and torment that hate us'. However, it wins victory primarily by transforming evil into good and hell into heaven: 'Our Goodness is made by their Evil ... we improve their Injuries and turn them into Benefits, we make a Vertue of Necessity, and turn their Vices into Graces.'[129] In the same way, Christ 'Triumphed over the sins of other Men, Grew great by Injuries ... Even sins themselvs, the sins of others, being turned into Advantages'.[130]

The meekness of Christ is the epitome of 'Innocency of the Act'. As seen in Chapter 4, Christ is the dramatic character who models innocency of life in trial. Meekness is essential to the sacrificial innocence of trial, as in *The Ceremonial Law*: 'one thats meek in Mind, / The only proper Sacrifice we find.'[131] As discussed above, Christ is the author of the Christian virtues. His blood is the 'ground' of meekness because it makes possible the restoration of sinners.[132] Christ is also the divine exemplar of meekness, which in *A Serious and Pathetical Contemplation of the Mercies of GOD* is described as an 'Immortal, / Sovereign, / Divine, / Invincible' love of one's enemies' and 'The Master point of Art / In Christian Religion, / Which my Saviour taught on the Cross.'[133] Meekness transfigured by love into an active element of the life of faith expresses the drama of innocent activity at war with sin, through the imitation of Christ-like virtue. It exemplifies harmlessness through the principle that evil unreturned is evil unreceived and manifests the paradoxical weakness and strength of integrity as a kind of deponent virtue: passive in form, active in intent.

---

[127] Traherne, *Inducements to Retirednes*, 12; id., *Church's Year-Book*, 172.
[128] Traherne, *Christian Ethicks*, 384, 388.
[129] Ibid. 197, 199.
[130] Traherne, 'Second Adam', *Commentaries of Heaven, Part 1*, 231.
[131] Traherne, *Ceremonial Law*, 199; see Matt. 11.29.
[132] Traherne, *Christian Ethicks*, 195.
[133] Traherne, *A Serious and Pathetical Contemplation of the Mercies of GOD*, 369–70.

Innocency of the Act

'Innocency of the Act' is found in the battle against the evils of persecution and the false innocence of hypocrisy. It appears out of the unity of sincere affections and righteous actions: the protection and pursuit of innocence. It is therefore active both in the motion of the soul and in the life of heroic virtue. A mature innocent life is possible through the practice of the Christian virtues. These harmless virtues present an active innocence belonging to the state of grace as 'drama in the form of "living holiness".[134] This is the innocence for which Andrewes prays, 'a pure, mild, peaceable, and humble *heart*, which may think harm to no man, nor recompense evil for evil, but good for injuries'.[135]

Innocency of the act encapsulates several important features of Trahernian innocence. The deponent quality of innocent virtues, which appear passive but are weapons against sin, expresses the paradox of weakness and strength inherent in innocence. Its dual harmlessness and invulnerability demonstrates its roots in the Latin etymology of innocence but also its interpretation through the imagination of Eden. This broad innocence, encompassing internal affections and the outward manifestations of innocent action, confirms Augustine's assertion that 'The whole of righteousness, therefore, is reduced to the one word, innocence'.[136]

'Innocency of Life': The Priestly Vocation

The ethics of innocence discussed above comes out of Traherne's priestly vocation to exhort the reader to an innocent life. The preservation of innocence was also a subject of clerical self-examination. In some prayers of the *Select Meditations*, Traherne's concern is more general, that as a temple of the Holy Spirit he must 'keep my vessel all ways Pure, and Take Heed that I Send Him not a way Greived'.[137] However, innocency of life was also a specifically clerical requirement. The Book of Common Prayer's ordination service includes the collect: 'so replenish them with the truth of thy Doctrine, and adorn them with innocency of life, that, both by word and good example, they may faithfully serve thee in this Office'.[138] The preservation of innocence and the pursuit of an innocent life were clearly

---

[134] Quash, *Theology and the Drama of History*, 64.

[135] Andrewes, *Holy Devotions*, 106–7.

[136] Augustine, *Expositions on the Book of Psalms*, Ps. 101.2, ¶iv.

[137] Traherne, *Select Meditations*, IV 42.

[138] Book of Common Prayer, 'The Form and Manner of Ordering of Priests'.

of concern to Traherne, not only for personal purity but also for an effective ministry. Praying for ministers to be like the 'Sacred Preacher' John the Baptist, *Church's Year-Book* writes of the dependence of priestly authority upon holiness: 'one Blemish so fatal and Destructiv therto, keep me Pure and Spotless, that I may win and save thy People'.[139] The priestly pursuit of innocence was played out through spiritual retirement and the sacrifice of praise.

Retirement and Virgin Purity

Inducements to Retirednes discusses the virtues of retirement, responding to contemporary debates over the possibility of innocence in urban and rural living. George Mackenzie thought that only in country retirement 'old age crowns, with innocence's livery, these who have innocently improven their youth'.[140] John Evelyn critiqued his parochialism, arguing instead that 'to be so innocent *there* [in town], where there is so much *temptation*, is so much the greater merit'.[141] From the previous discussion one might assume that Traherne would incline to the latter view, and yet this treatise exhorts the reader to retirement. However, Traherne is not concerned with physical retirement from city to country but with an 'Introversion of Spirit' manifest in contemplation and chastity.[142] Virgin retirement was, for Traherne, an aspect of his priestly vocation to an innocent life.

Traherne's defence of virginity must be read in the context of contemporary mistrust of a celibate priesthood. Virginity's association with innocence is rooted in patristic ascetical writings.[143] Post-Reformation England demonstrated ambivalence towards this long heritage through anti-Catholic sentiment on the one hand and libertine love poetry on the other.[144] Nevertheless, the Virgin Mary remained an object of admiration in devotions inspired by contemporary

---

[139] Traherne, *Church's Year-Book*, 170–71.

[140] George Mackenzie, *A Moral Essay, Preferring Solitude to Publick Employment* (Edinburgh, 1665), 106.

[141] John Evelyn, *Employment and an Active Life Prefer'd to Solitude* (London, 1667), 40.

[142] Traherne, *Inducements to Retirednes*, 5.

[143] For example, Mary's virginity came to be associated with ascetical purity through the *Protevangelium of James* (Mary Foskett, *A Virgin Conceived: Mary and Classical Representations of Virginity* [Bloomington: Indiana University Press, 2002]; see also Gregory of Nyssa, 'On Virginity', 20, in *Ascetical Works*, trans. Victoria Woods Callahan [Washington, DC: Catholic University of America Press, 1967]).

[144] See e.g. John Donne's encomium on the marriage bed, 'Epithalamion made at Lincolnes Inne', in *The Complete Poems of John Donne*, ed. Robin Robbins (revd edn, London: Longman/Pearson, 2010); Andrew Marvell, 'Upon Appleton House', stanzas 11–34, in *The Poems of Andrew Marvell*, ed. Nigel Smith (London: Longman/Pearson, 2003).

152   *Boundless Innocence in Thomas Traherne's Poetic Theology*

Catholic works and medieval tradition.[145] In addition, the Platonic ideal of chaste love presented an alternative model of spiritual virginity.[146]

Traherne's praise of virginity sits in this complex hinterland. He treats the 'Innocency of a Virgin' as an aphoristic statement and defends chastity through Marian reverence.[147] His distinctively Anglican attitude accommodates anti-Catholic sentiment while preserving aspects of traditional Marian devotion.[148] *Church's Year-Book* commends virgin saints for their 'Beauty Innocency Virtue and Chastity', but the section on Mary owes more to the Anglican theology of Herbert's 'To All Angels and Saints' than to Luis de la Puente's Catholic *Meditations*.[149] *Commentaries of Heaven*'s devotion to Mary is marked by respect for virginal qualities but is opposed to excessive veneration and belief in the Assumption, following John Rainolds.[150] Although *Inducements to Retirednes* recommends clerical celibacy, Traherne draws on Augustine's arguments against the Manicheans to condemn its papal enforcement in 'Antichrist'.[151]

Virginity is a social as well as a spiritual virtue. Traherne attacks the libertines who declared that 'virginity kept is virginity lost'.[152] He argues that 'if thou

---

[145] See e.g. Luis de la Puente, *Meditations on the Mystery of Our Holie Faith*, trans. J. Weigham (2 vols, St Omers, 1619), which influenced Traherne's *Meditations on the Six Days of Creation* (although the attribution to Traherne is doubtful), *Church's Year-Book* and *A Serious and Pathetical Contemplation of the Mercies of GOD* (Day, *Thomas Traherne*, 54–60, 63–5, 70–1); on medieval influences, see John Bugge, *Virginitas: An Essay in the History of a Medieval Ideal* (The Hague: Martinus Nijhoff, 1975).

[146] For a source of seventeenth-century ideas of Platonic love, see Marsilio Ficino, *Commentary on Plato's Symposium on Love*, II.1, 5; IV.5–6, trans Sears Reynolds Jayne (revd edn, Dallas: Spring Publications, 1985); see also Trimpey, 'An Analysis of Traherne's "Thoughts I"', 91; Sarah Hutton, 'Introduction to the Renaissance and Seventeenth Century', in Baldwin and Hutton (eds), *Platonism and the English Imagination*, 72.

[147] Traherne, *Church's Year-Book*, 172.

[148] Allchin corrects Marks' assumption that Traherne's devotion to Mary must have a Roman Catholic source (Allchin, 'Sacrifice of Praise and Thanksgiving', 32; Carol L. Marks, 'Traherne's Church's Year-Book', *PBSA* 60 [1966], 31–72 [64]).

[149] Traherne, *Church's Year-Book*, 250, 260; cf. Luis de la Puente, *Meditations upon the Mysteries of our Faith Corresponding to the Three Wayes, Purgative, Illuminative, and Unitive* (Saint Omer, 1624), 53–6, 80–82.

[150] Traherne, 'Assumption', *Commentaries of Heaven*, Part 2, 291; John Rainolds, *The Summe of the Conference Betweene John Rainoldes and John Hart* (London: George Bishop, 1588), 413.

[151] Traherne, *Inducements to Retirednes*, 15; id. 'Antichrist', *Commentaries of Heaven*, Part 2, 110.

[152] Francis Quarles gives this argument to the serpent tempting Eve (*Emblemes Divine and Moral* [London: George Miller, 1635], 5; cf. Marvell, 'To his Coy Mistress', esp. lines 25–32).

contain; Thou reservest that flower Pure, Thou Addest the Beauty of thy Self Denial, Thou makest thy self a more pleasing Spectacle, and Inheritest all in a more perfect maner'.[153] Sexual ethics are not unimportant to Traherne, although only treated explicitly in *Commentaries of Heaven*'s entries for 'Adulterie' and 'Bastard'.[154] He sees adultery as a worse crime than the Fall: 'If the Eating of the forbidden fruit brought destruction upon the World how much more this Heinous Sin!'[155] The *Early Notebook* adopts a social defence of chastity through a misreading of Bacon's 'Of Marriage and Single Life', that changes wives from 'companions for middle age' to 'burdens of middle age'.[156]

However, for Traherne, virginity is primarily a spiritual virtue, following the Platonic ideal of chaste love.[157] He uses the language of virgin integrity primarily with reference to moral righteousness, without explicit allusion to female physical intactness.[158] Virgin purity is not abstention from physical pleasure but 'To give one Self wholy and Singly to God'.[159] Nor is virginity a distinctively feminine virtue, since Traherne's virgin-figures are often androgynous or explicitly male, including Joseph and John the Baptist.[160] The virtue of clerical chastity lies in its imitation of Christ's 'Solitary and Virgin State', which enables him to love all people infinitely and not to confine his love to one person.[161] Virginity for Traherne is thus not Donne's feminine 'mild innocence' but an expansive virtue which enables the soul to encompass all things in love.[162] Clerical chastity is a masculine and active state of the will.[163] For Traherne, virginity is not in itself an ideal of spiritual innocence but an aid to the clerical vocation to love all.

---

[153] Traherne, 'Abstinence', *Commentaries of Heaven, Part 1*, 52; see also the deleted section on 'the Hidden use of thy unused Treasures' (id., *Church's Year-Book*, 310).

[154] Traherne, *Commentaries of Heaven, Part 1*, 255–60; id., *Commentaries of Heaven, Part 2*, 466–8.

[155] Traherne, 'Adulterie', *Commentaries of Heaven, Part 1, 259*.

[156] Bacon, *Essays, Civil and Moral*, #8; Traherne, 'Of Single Life', *Early Notebook*, 113; see Marks, 'Thomas Traherne's Early Studies', 525.

[157] On the classification of virginity into sexual, social and spiritual meanings, see Mary Ludlow, *Gregory of Nyssa: Ancient and (Post)modern* (Oxford: Oxford University Press, 2007), 185–6.

[158] Traherne, *Inducements to Retirednes*, 10.

[159] Ibid. 15.

[160] See Traherne, *Church's Year-Book*, 144, 165.

[161] Traherne, *Inducements to Retirednes*, 16.

[162] Donne, 'To the Countesse of Huntingdon', line 9, in *The Complete Poems*.

[163] See J.H. Arnold, 'The Labour of Continence: Masculinity and Clerical Virginity', in Anke Bernau, Ruth Evans and Sarah Salih (eds), *Medieval Virginities* (Cardiff: University of Wales Press, 2003), 102–19.

154   *Boundless Innocence in Thomas Traherne's Poetic Theology*

The 'sweet Singer of Israel!' Restoring Liberty through Praise

David is the priestly voice of praise in Traherne's theology of the innocent life. He functions as a multi-vocal 'second self' in Traherne's meditations and prayers, an everyman of the life of faith.[164] In *Centuries of Meditations*, he is a 'Man after Gods own Heart', a guide for action, 'teaching us what we ought to do, that we might becom Divine and Heavenly'.[165] David teaches, through example, the regenerate innocence restored through repentance of a 'Soul [that] recovered its Pristine Liberty and saw thorow the Mud Walls of flesh and Blood'.[166] As the sin of adultery 'blotted out those Sweet and Innocent Apprehensions he had of GOD', so the recovery of freedom through penitence grants a vision of salvation that David saw 'only in the Light of faith' but which through Christ has been accomplished.[167]

Traherne's 'emulation of David' has been connected with a literary tradition that adopted David as exemplary poet. Michael Ponsford likened Traherne's use of David to the satirical imitation genre's adoption of the persona of a classical poet. Given Traherne's sparse references to classical satire, it seems more likely that he relied upon devotional tradition and scriptural interpretation than classical literary theory.[168] Traherne's psalmic passages rest on a Reformed devotional culture that highly valued the Psalms and whose origins lie in Basil of Caesarea and Athanasius.[169]

---

[164] On David as a 'second self' and part of a fluid 'cosmic personality' in *Centuries of Meditations*, see Joan Webber, '"I" and "Thou" in the Prose of Thomas Traherne', *Papers on Language and Literature* 2 (1966), 260; Stewart sees David as 'a comprehensive figure, the ultimate man' (*The Expanded Voice*, 141; cf. Traherne, *Centuries of Meditations*, III 69).

[165] Traherne, *Centuries of Meditations*, III 70, 92.

[166] Ibid. III 95.

[167] Traherne, *A Sober View*, 105–6; id., *Centuries of Meditations*, III 96.

[168] Michael Ponsford, 'Men After God's Own Heart: The Context of Thomas Traherne's Emulation of David', *Studia Mystica* 9/4 (1986), 3–11.

[169] See Edward A. Gosselin's seminal study on the Protestant rehabilitation of David (*The King's Progress to Jerusalem: Some Interpretations of David during the Reformation Period and Their Patristic and Medieval Background* [Malibu, Calif.: Undena Publications, 1976]); Barbara Pitkin follows Gosselin in rooting Protestant identification with David as a model of regenerate living in Nicholas of Lyra's historical-literal exegesis and Lefèvre d'Étaples' 'prophetic sense' ('Imitation of David: David As a Paradigm for Faith in Calvin's Exegesis of the Psalms', *Sixteenth Century Journal* 24/4 [1993], 843–63). For a study that marries the devotional and literary use of the Psalms in the early modern period, see Hannibal Hamlin, *Psalm Culture and Early Modern English Literature* (Cambridge: Cambridge University Press, 2004).

Traherne's immersion in this tradition is reflected in his choice of scriptural references, which can privilege the commonly defined 'poetic' passages of the Bible. Philip Sidney's *Apology for Poetry* (1595) followed Franciscus Junius and Emanuel Tremellius in listing the Old Testament poetic passages as David's psalms, Solomon's books, Moses and Deborah's hymns and Job.[170] Old Testament quotations throughout Traherne's *Kingdom of God* draw particularly on the Psalms, Proverbs and Song of Songs, as well as poetic passages from Ecclesiastes, Daniel, Isaiah, Jeremiah, Deuteronomy and Genesis.[171]

The Psalms were arguably the most important of the Old Testament poetic passages in seventeenth-century devotion, through daily recitation and the popularity of psalm paraphrases.[172] The devotional tradition on which Traherne drew saw the Psalms as an epitome of Old Testament wisdom and a portrayal of the affections of the heart, whose power lies not in teaching but in demonstrating the way to salvation through experience.[173] As his first entry into the Bible, Traherne saw the Psalms not only as a summary of the scriptures but the centre from which the divine light emanates and is 'spread abroad over the whole Bible'.[174] Their affective and experiential tone is echoed in Traherne's didactic use of personal experience.

The voice of the 'sweet Singer of *Israel*!' sounds the praise that is intrinsic to Traherne's theology.[175] Raymond-Jean Frontain has described praise in Traherne's

---

[170] Philip Sidney, *An Apology for Poetry (or The Defence of Poesy)*, ed. Geoffrey Shepherd and R.W. Maslen (rev. edn, Manchester: Manchester University Press, 2002), 86.

[171] For a section drawing extensively on poetic passages, see Traherne, *Kingdom of God*, 446–7.

[172] Popular poetic paraphrases of the Psalms include Matthew Parker, *The Whole Psalter Translated into English Metre* (London: John Daye, 1567); Edwin Sandys, *Sacred Hymns Consisting of Fifty Select Psalms of David and Others* (London: Thomas Snodham, 1615); George Wither, *The Psalmes of David Translated into Lyrick Verse* (Amsterdam: Cornelis Gerritis van Breughel, 1632); Henry King, *The Psalmes of David, from the New Translation of the Bible Turned into Meter* (London: Ed. Griffin, 1651); compilations of poetic paraphrases include John Saltmarsh, *Poemata Sacra* (Cambridge: Thomas Buck and Roger Daniel, 1636).

[173] See Anne Lake Prescott, 'King David as a "Right Poet": Sidney and the Psalmist', *ELR* 19/2 (1989), 134–46; Gosselin, *The King's Progress to Jerusalem*, 72–3; the Psalms epitomised the Old Testament not only in content but generic styles (see Lewalski, *Protestant Poetics*, 39–53, 131–8); Mary Ann Radzinowicz sees the various Psalmic genres as embodied in the different perspectives in Milton's *Paradise Lost* and *Paradise Regained* (*Milton's Epics and the Book of Psalms* [Princeton: Princeton University Press, 1989]).

[174] Traherne, *Centuries of Meditations*, III 66.

[175] Traherne, *A Serious and Pathetical Contemplation of the Mercies of GOD*, 329; on psalmic praise in Traherne's works, see Margaret Bottrall, *Thomas Traherne and the Bible: A Book from Heaven* (Paris: Group de Recherche 'Litterature et Réligion', Université Paris-

works as an 'act of self-creation', which spiritualises the world, reforming public worship through the private voice and applying the lyric of interior meditation to communal living.[176] However, Traherne's Davidic paraphrase goes deeper than the unity of public and private devotion because his theology is fundamentally oriented towards gratitude.[177] As *Centuries of Meditations* explains, mere sight of the world is a 'fuel to foment and increase your Praises'. Praise is the result of the natural cycle of gift and receipt. As many benefits as we receive we return in praise 'for Praises are Transformed and returning Benefits'. The Christian-Platonist roots of this theme are evident in Traherne's description of praise as a primordial and direct emanation of God, 'the Reflexion of His Beams'. Later, the same sentiment is expressed in the terms of mystical union, as 'our Praises enter into the very secret of His Eternal Bosom, and mingle with Him who Dwelleth in that Light which is inaccessible'.[178] Praise is thus bound up with the philosophical and theological underpinnings of Traherne's thought.

Praise is a form of dialogic action. The series of 30 meditations on David, the Psalms and praise in Century III begins with the realisation that worshipful contemplation is communication: 'Little did I imagine that, while I was thinking these Things, I was Conversing with GOD.'[179] This new understanding draws private lyrical meditation into dialogue with metaphysical speculation. The conversation of praise is a particular feature of the estate of glory. *Select Meditations* describes how in heaven 'Shall we Sing His Praises all the Day Long. ... There it is the Joy of all to be Communicativ and He most Happy that is Infinitly So.'[180]

In the Latin tradition illustrated by Lactantius, innocence is the condition for and content of this dialogue of true worship. Humanity was created 'that we might with pure and uncorrupted mind worship Him who made the sun and the heaven', for which 'nothing more than innocence alone' is sufficient.[181] The connection between innocence and worship was taken up in seventeenth-

---

Nord, 1988); on psalmic language in *A Serious and Pathetical Contemplation of the Mercies of GOD*, see Stewart, *The Expanded Voice*, 95–101.

[176] Raymond-Jean Frontain, 'Tuning the World: Traherne, Psalms, and Praise', in Blevins (ed.), *Re-Reading Thomas Traherne*, 105–6, 108–9.

[177] On 'gratitude' as Traherne's 'first and final virtue', see Inge, *Wanting Like a God*, 261; on Traherne 'accomplishing the truth through praise ... thinking by thanking', see McIntosh, *Discernment and Truth*, 247.

[178] Traherne, *Centuries of Meditations*, II 94, III 82.

[179] Ibid. III 66–96.

[180] Traherne, *Select Meditations*, III 65.

[181] Lactantius, 'Of the Worship of the True God, and of Innocency, and of the Worship of False Gods', *Divine Institutes*, VI 1; see Ps. 51.17; James 1.27.

'Innocency of Life' 157

century devotion by the Cambridge Platonists, including Whichcote, for whom true worship of God in spirit was the 'Religion of the State of Innocency' which is perfected in the 'State of Glory'.[182] Traherne's use of David's voice similarly expresses an innocence enacted in praise which responds to the creative act through dialogue with God.

The dialogue of praise is the primary work of innocence. *Centuries of Meditations* adopts an Augustinian theology of humanity's principal relationship to God as a relationship of praise. Where Augustine prays, 'You stir man to take pleasure in praising you, because you have made us for yourself, and our heart is restless until it rests in you', Traherne asks, 'Are not Praises the very End for which the World was created?' [183] 'Silence' describes praise as Adam's primary role:

> The first and only Work he had to do,
> Was in himself to feel his Bliss, to view
> His Sacred Treasures, to admire, rejoyce
> Sing Praises with a Sweet and Heavnly voice.[184]

The recovery of Adamic innocence is therefore appropriately articulated through the language of praise. Davidic praise is a recapitulation and completion of Adam's work, through which the eschatological and protological, the estates of glory and innocence, are united.

Praise restores paradise by cultivating an apprehension of the world in its glory as created by God. The link between Adam and David is drawn explicitly early in *Centuries of Meditations*, where Traherne begins with the perfect conditional sense of longing for past innocence: 'Had I been alive in Adams steed, how should I hav Admired the Glory of the world!' He then moves into the present interrogative of Psalm 8.4–6, 'What is Man that Thou art Mindfull of Him?'[185] Through this transition, Traherne does not rest in lament for lost innocence but resumes Adam's work through David's voice. According to Whichcote, 'Conversation with God, Innocency, and Righteousness, is *Heav'n* begun here'.[186] In this way, Traherne's dialogical recovery of paradise through

---

[182] Whichcote, *Moral and Religious Aphorisms*, #762.

[183] Augustine, *Confessions*, I.1; Traherne, *Centuries of Meditations*, III 82.

[184] Traherne, 'Silence', *Dobell Folio*, 24–5; see also id., 'Adam', *Commentaries of Heaven, Part 1*, 217; 'Second Adam', *Commentaries of Heaven, Part 2*, 227.

[185] Traherne, *Centuries of Meditations*, I 65.

[186] Whichcote, *Moral and Religious Aphorisms*, #818.

praise unites primordial innocence with eschatological felicity. This is the priestly sacrifice of the soul and the fulfilment of his vocation.[187]

'I must Becom a Child Again' and 'I will wash my hands in innocence': Innocence in the Imperative and Intentional Moods

The ethical compulsion towards innocency of life is expressed through the imperative mood of 'I must' and the intentional mood of 'I will'. These tones protect Traherne's ethics from deconstructionist critiques of innocence as a false or hypocritical claim to purity, since they express innocency of life only as an object of desire and the will and not as an achieved goal. The imperative and intentional tones have already been encountered in Traherne's longing for Adamic innocence, the command to fulfil the baptismal promises and the exhortation to preserve innocence. The implications of these moods are here explored through the two important phrases, 'I must Becom a Child Again' and 'I will wash my hands in Innocency'.

The first phrase appears in several forms. In *Centuries of Meditation* III 3 it is in the present tense of the process that the soul is now undergoing in obedience to Christ's injunction, to 'becom as it were a little Child again, that I may enter into the Kingdom of GOD'.[188] *Centuries of Meditation* III 5 meditates on the meaning of this command to 'be Born again and becom a little Child', as something 'Deeper far then is generaly believed'.[189] Traherne believes that it rests not only in a childlike dependence on God or in the child's limited capacity for evil outlined in Augustine's *Confessions* 'but in the Peace and Purity of all our Soul. Which Purity also is a Deeper Thing then is commonly apprehended'.[190] It thus models childlike innocence on the purity of the soul. Chapter 4 began with the Book of Common Prayer's exhortation to follow children's innocence. Traherne's repetition of Christ's injunction may also be read through this liturgical lens, as a call to baptismal regeneration and a reminder of the innocent life that is available through Christ's grace and love.

---

[187] On the priestly sacrifice of the soul to God, see Traherne, *Kingdom of God*, 276.

[188] On the innocent child in the synoptic tradition and its hellenistic roots, see S. Légasse, *Jésus et l'enfant: "Enfants", "petits" et "simples" dans la tradition synoptique* (Paris: J. Gabalda, 1969), 276–9.

[189] Traherne, *Centuries of Meditations*, III 5

[190] Augustine, *Confessions*, I.18.

The imperative to become a child concerns the preservation and pursuit of purity.[191] It is a pursuit because it is a process of becoming, and it concerns preservation because it implies the attainment of a state which must then be retained. The urgency of this imperative is expressed in the conclusion to the poem, 'Innocence': 'Within, without me, all was pure. / I must becom a Child again.'[192] The appropriation of the divine command into the first person indicates the soul's participation in the drama of salvation and the investment of the will and the affections in the pursuit of purity. The imperative to become a child again is a theme that unites the estates. The notion of 'becoming again' is an existential process in misery and grace that both recovers protological innocence and progresses into glory.

The scriptural reference for Wilson's secondary definition of innocence is 'Psalm 26.6,11. *I will wash my hands in innocency*. This is innocency of a person restored.'[193] Through this reference, regenerate innocence is framed in the intentional mood of the will to an innocent life. Andrewes' *Sermons* uses this reference as a sign of the righteous will to act innocently, the washing of hands in innocency manifesting 'a steadfast purpose of keeping our selves cleane'.[194] The symbolism of 'innocent hands' has been discussed above as concerning both inner activity and outward action.

This variety and depth of meaning underlies Traherne's use of the phrase in *Inducements to Retiredness* and *A Serious and Pathetical Contemplation of the Mercies of GOD*, in his own paraphrases of Psalm 26: 'I will wash my hands in Innocency: so will I compass thine Altar, O LORD.'[195] The first reference appears in the context of an exhortation to meditate on glory and so to think like God; the second is a prayer of repentance. The first expresses a desire to become united with God; the second is an intention to act innocently. The washing of hands in these two references thus encompasses innocency of the act: the dynamic integrity of an unblemished soul and the affective sincerity of a pure heart, which combine the activity of the inner person with the public actions of the life of faith. The imagery of washing also carries connotations of baptism, ritual purification and Pilate washing his hands of the blood of Christ.[196] The

---

[191] See also 'An Infant-Ey', *Poems of Felicity*, 98.

[192] Traherne, 'Innocence', *Dobell Poems*, 10.

[193] Wilson, *A Complete Christian Dictionary*, 336b.

[194] Andrewes, *XCVI Sermons*, 744.

[195] Traherne, *Inducements to Retirdness*, 8; id., *A Serious and Pathetical Contemplation of the Mercies of GOD*, 332.

[196] On the cultic connotations of ritual washing, see Mary Douglas, *Purity and Danger: An Analysis of Concepts of Pollution and Taboo* (London: Ark, 1966), 44.

intention to wash one's hands in innocence therefore concerns innocent hands – the organs of innocent action – and the innocent blood of Christ in which they are cleansed. This Christological frame of reference for the intentional mood of innocence combines the virtuous innocence of sanctification with the imputed innocence of justification.

The estates of misery–grace are a theatre of trial: not that of the divine law court but the hero's battlefield. The battle is fought through harmless and holy innocence, which is an active affection and an aspect of righteousness. Innocence in this sphere is not an abstract ideal, since it is enacted within the existential drama of experience. Within this battle there are miseries and difficulties but also graces which point towards the final victory. These graces include the innocent affections of sincerity, integrity and purity and the Christian virtues of humility, patience, meekness and repentance. The drama's plot is oriented towards glory through the human vocation to an innocent life, which is articulated through exclamations of praise and intention, and through a willing response to the divine command. Whether expressed in the personal tone of prayer and praise or in the more didactic voice of moral theology, these enact the priestly vocation both to live and to exhort others to live an innocent life.

Chapter 6

'A Light So Endless unto me': The Glory of Innocence

'A Sight of Innocence': The Soul in Glory

An Innocent 'I'

This chapter explores the poetic imagery that addresses the 'who' question of human identity through visions, emblems and metaphorical conceits of the soul's glory. Lyrical poetic conceits express the glory of innocence by transcending the boundaries of conceptual terminology and encapsulating complex philosophical notions in sensory imagery.[1] As Ricoeur says of metaphor, they rule 'in the field of sensory, emotional, aesthetic, and axiological values', their meaning is encapsulated in the senses they evoke and they teach by guiding the affections.[2] From the perspective of theological anthropology, the lyric mode addresses the 'who' question of human existence by asking, 'who am *I*?[3] In his study of evil through Job, Philippe Nemo argues that lyric is the voice of innocence. He associates the nominative 'I' of the internal lyric monologue with the child's certain self-knowledge: 'The nominative is the case of innocence.' Nemo searches for a Christian concept of innocence by tracing, through grace, the transition from an accusative or accused sinful 'me' to a nominative, 'named and hence innocent "I"'.[4]

The lyric 'I' of Traherne's poems and meditations similarly declares the soul's innocence in the estate of glory. The first-person confessional voice of his lyrical conceits views the world through the mirror of the self. *Select Meditations* mentions criticism of his apparently solipsistic trait of 'Speaking in the Singular number, and Saying I'. Traherne sees this critique as symptomatic of humanity's

---

[1] See S.T. Kimbrough, 'Lyrical Theology: Theology in Hymns', *TT* 63/1 (2006), 22–37.

[2] Ricoeur, *Time and Narrative*, vol. 1, xi; see also Janet Soskice, *Metaphor and Religious Language* (Oxford: Clarendon, 1985).

[3] For a definition of lyric as soliloquy, see Quash, *Theology and the Drama of History*, 43.

[4] Philippe Nemo, *Job and the Excess of Evil*, trans. Michael Kigel (Pittsburgh, Pa.: Duquesne University Press, 1998), 242, 234.

earthly tendency to turn virtue into vice and felicity into misery, whereas in glory 'it shall be our Glory and the Joy of all to Acknowledge, I'. Traherne defends the first person as due recognition of the individual's glory, created by God to inherit the world: 'Can the Freind of GOD, and the Heir of all Things in Heaven and Earth Forbear to say, I.'[5] Each time Traherne declares 'I', he affirms humanity's glory and induces the reader to participate in it by reading their own 'I' into the divine image being represented.

The innocence of the lyric 'I' is illustrated by the pun that links self with vision, 'I' with 'eye'.[6] The poem, 'An Infant-Ey', imagines the soul's unsullied view of the world: 'A Beam that's purely Spiritual, an Ey / That's altogether Virgin.'[7] It sees the world in the clear light of heaven and sees all things as its possession, which is to see its glory. Using Galen's classical physiology of the eye which sheds light on the world, rather than Kepler's experimentalist theory of the eye as a receptive organ, the 'Sight of Innocence' is a product of the active emanations of the innocent soul.[8] This imagery presents the glory of innocence as the soul's innate, or innated, purity disseminated upon the world, an act of self-giving which resonates with the kenotic movement of the drama of innocence.

The Mystery of the Soul

Traherne looks for a 'sight of innocence' through meditation on the soul: the central theme of *Seeds of Eternity*. This is not a systematic work but a meditation on the soul's glory. Against patristic and classical treatises and unmentioned contemporaries such as Kenelm Digby, Traherne proposes to 'enter into these unknown Regions of the Immortal Soul, in such a Sort as will display its Glory, before we meddle with its Criticismes and Niceties'.[9] He was frustrated by his

---

5   Traherne, *Select Meditations*, III 65.

6   On the link between 'eye' and 'I', see Marie-Dominique Garnier, 'Thomas Traherne, poète de l'infini' (PhD thesis: Université de Paris, Nanterre, 1987), 347; A. Leigh DeNeef traces Traherne's mental development through a Lacanian 'mirror stage', a desirous interplay between eye and 'I' or self and other (*Traherne in Dialogue*, 115–38).

7   Traherne, 'An Infant-Ey', *Poems of Felicity*, 96; See Ridlon, 'The Function of the "Infant-Ey" in Traherne's Poetry'.

8   Traherne, 'Innocence', *Dobell Folio*, 10.

9   Traherne, *Seeds of Eternity*, 239. Treatises by Augustine, Dionysius the Areopagite, Jerome, Gregory of Nyssa, Tertullian, Hermes Trismegistus, Plato, Theophrastus, Plotinus, Chalcidius, Proclus, Iamblichus and Tullius are mentioned (ibid. 238-9). Traherne asserts humanity's glory using Ovid's *Metamorphoses*: 'God gave to man a lofty countenance / That he to heaven might his face advance' (ibid 241; Ovid, *Metamorphoses*, I 76, trans. E.J. Kenney [Oxford: Oxford University Press, 1986]); cf. Kenelm Digby's in-depth exposition of the

university studies of Aristotle's *De anima*, which failed to address 'the Pith of [that] perfection and glory I expected', the soul's final cause in God.[10] Aristotle's partial image of the soul is 'like a broken Monument, whose fragments are seen, but lying in the Rubbish. For the Glory and Beauty of the object Springeth from the Union of all the Parts.'[11]

Sight of a pure soul 'not defiled with guilt' is next to the awe and joy of contemplating God, but the soul that Traherne glorifies is that which he has defiled.[12] This is a source of shame, but also of repentance and praise for the creator God.[13] Knowledge of its true glory, he believes, will lead people to care for their soul 'and fear to sin, and desire Glory'.[14] The main concern of this treatise is thus to draw the reader into a virtuous life through contemplation of the soul's perfection.

The Capacity of Perfection

The soul's perfection lies in its capacity for God. Capacity is represented by the intromissive eye, which 'letteth in the Beauty of all the Univers, informing the Soul with the Glory of Heaven and Earth'.[15] Capacity is also illustrated by the Platonic language of ascent by which the human mind 'goeth easily from it self to the Divine Nature from whence it came. Whatsoever perfection it hath, finding it in God the Fountain of all Perfections'.[16] While refusing to outline a precise concept of the soul, Traherne's closest notion is expressed in *Commentaries of Heaven*'s account of 'Assimilation':

> The Soul is [Nothing but] an Abilitie of becoming All Things. It is an Empty Chaos of Faculties and Powers, that can no where be imagined or conceived to exist, till it does actualy contemplat som Object ... The Soul being so meer a Capacitie of resembling, that till it think on its Power to contain all, it is not like it self: but when it does the Image of infinite Space may be seen within it.[17]

'niceties' of the soul (*Of Bodies and of Mans Soul to Discover the Immortality of Reasonable Souls* [London, 1669]).

[10] Traherne, *Seeds of Eternity*, 236.
[11] Ibid. 237.
[12] Ibid. 234.
[13] Ibid. 235.
[14] Ibid. 236.
[15] Ibid. 242.
[16] Ibid. 238 [.
[17] Traherne, 'Assimilation', *Commentaries of Heaven, Part 2*, 261, [] indicates deletion.

The soul's infinite capacity is akin to the primordial void because it has no substance of itself but through contemplation can image the infinite God. This image of perfection echoes the semantic connotations of innocence as the privation of evil which lets in the light of the good. It intimates that the soul's spiritual innocence is simply the reflection of God.

The capacious soul which reflects God, also communicates God. As Traherne explains in *Kingdom of God*, the soul's glory is marked by God: 'As evry Being hath a Spark of Excellency which it deriveth from the Nature and Power of GOD, So hath it the Stamp of his Omnipresence, and the Character of his Goodness impressed upon it; And is So far Communicativ after his Similitude, as it is Excellent in Nature'.[18] This language veers perilously close to Platonic notions of the soul as a seed of divinity.[19] However, Traherne is clear that the soul is not itself divine but contains God as light is contained in the world:

> When the Light of God is in the Intelligible Sphere of the understanding, it is So Incorporated with it, as Light in the Air: A Man would take them to be one. All that Glory being indeed Dependent, though it Seemeth inherent, it seemeth to be our own while it is derived, and borrowed. When all the Light and Glory of Eternity shineth in the Soul, God is in the Beam and the Beam in the Beatifick Vision.[20]

While this statement clearly asserts the derivative nature of the soul's glory, greater ambiguity elsewhere in his works appears as an attempt to preserve the mystery of the soul. *Centuries of Meditations* equivocates, 'Whether it be the Soul it self, or God in the Soul, that shines by Lov, or both it is difficult to tell'.[21] Traherne is deliberately obscure as to the precise nature of the soul, but its innocence is clearly both divine and derivative: analogous to God's perfection but arising from its privative capacity.

Mirroring Divine Simplicity

If perfection is the capacity to reflect God, then the innocent soul mirrors God's attributes, as Jackson asserted: 'the soule thus recovering her native-splendor, becomes a true glasse for right representation of Gods image or his

---

[18]   Traherne, *Kingdom of God*, 381.

[19]   Cf.: 'there is in us the principle of all excellence, all virtue and wisdom, and every higher thing that we conceive' (Gregory of Nyssa, 'On the Making of Man', XVI 11, *Dogmatic Treatises*, trans. H.A. Wilson, NPNF² 5 [Buffalo, NY: Christian Literature, 1893]).

[20]   Traherne, *Kingdom of God*, 354.

[21]   Traherne, *Centuries of Meditations*, IV 83.

attributes'.[22] Traherne preserves an ontological distinction between God and humanity, so the mirror-image cannot equal God. In *Commentaries of Heaven's* description of 'Almighty' God the soul is like 'those things which are infinit *in som respect* ... [but] weak and naked and little in comparison of the Deitie, ever depending on, and Subject to him'.[23] As *Kingdom of God* explains, it is unlike God in finitude, dependence, mutability, potential to fall back into nothing and in being compounded of power and act, essence and existence, substance and accidents.[24] It follows that there should be a distinction between simple divine innocence and that of humanity: as Gregory of Nazianzus asserted, 'to be utterly sinless belongs to God, and to the first and uncompounded nature ... but to sin is human and belongs to the Compound on earth (for composition is the beginning of separation)'.[25] So Traherne's poem 'My Spirit' defines the infinite unity of the soul in likeness to God, while preserving an ontological distinction between the two by describing it through a simile as 'Simple *like the Deitie*'.[26]

Simplicity thus takes it primary significance from the classical diving attribute, intimating absolute sinlessness through a picture of unity and integrity. However, in seventeenth-century devotion, simplicity was also a Christian virtue. Jeremy Taylor described Christian simplicity as guileless ignorance or honesty, Quarles attributed the humility and purity of 'simple innocence' to Job, while Andrewes praised the purity of 'simplicity of heart'.[27] These characterisations drew an implicit connection between the Christian quality and the divine attribute of simplicity.

How can a compound soul mirror divine simplicity? *Kingdom of God* draws a correlation between God's essential and the soul's derivative simplicities, similar to that of Bernard of Clairvaux's. Bernard saw Christian simplicity as a gift of grace: the soul is made 'simple in its Nature, by Him Who is simple in His Essence'; Traherne states: 'His Essence being most Simple is a fair Inducement to believ, that his Image is as Simple, as it is possible for any Created Existence

---

[22]   Jackson, *A Treatise containing the Originall of Unbeliefe*, 445; see also id., *A Treatise of the Divine Essence and Attributes*, 21.

[23]   Traherne, 'Almighty', *Commentaries of Heaven, Part 1*, 404.

[24]   Traherne, *Kingdom of God*, 461.

[25]   Gregory of Nazianzus, 'On Holy Baptism', *Select Orations*, XL 7, trans. Charles Gordon Browne and James Edward Swallow, NPNF[2] 7 (Buffalo, NY: Christian Literature, 1894).

[26]   Traherne, 'My Spirit', *Dobell Folio*, 27 (italics added).

[27]   Taylor, 'Of Christian Simplicity', in *The Whole Works*; Quarles, *Job Militant*, 36; Andrewes, *Holy Devotions*, 4, 198.

166   *Boundless Innocence in Thomas Traherne's Poetic Theology*

to be made.'[28] Humanity in the image of God is as simple as material existence can be, and as innocent as it is simple.

Imaging the Innocent God

The soul is not a static mirror of divine innocence, but a living and active *imago Dei*. In *Seeds of Eternity*, it is an altar of praise that will '*communicat* it self in the Image of the Deitie'.[29] *Kingdom of God* expresses Traherne's theology of the image through Aristotelian metaphysics: 'the Soul was made the Image of God in power, that it might hav the Pleasure of becoming So in Act'.[30] The potentiality of power intimates the subjunctive nature of the soul's innocence, as a gift of grace that must be actualised through an act of the will.

The distinction between power and act underlies Traherne's elevation of embodied existence above pure spirit: 'the Image of God in a Body, is yet Somthing higher then one purely Spiritual, or Incorporeal'.[31] This theology of the *imago Dei* highlights his non-dualist valuing of the material world and the human body in particular. The Hermeticist notion of the soul as 'the Golden Link uniting Intelligible and Corporeal Nature' identifies humanity's glory in its unification of body and soul.[32] Human perfection is not therefore purely spiritual. The final section of *Seeds of Eternity* begins with an aside on the body and its relationship to the soul. Traherne rejects the anti-materialism expressed in Plato's allegory of the cave and the 'vulgar Error, that maketh [the body] the impediment and prison of the mind'. He asserts instead the body's glory as an 'Instrument and Companion of the soul'.[33] Its beauty, symmetry and perfection is evidence of its divine origin: 'the order is so curious clean and perfect that … there is not an Atom defective or redundant … which sheweth the whole microcosm to be the product of intire and perfect Reason, and if so then of infinit and Eternall'.[34] Traherne sees human perfection in the unity of soul and body not in spirit alone. The relationship between spirit and matter in Traherne's

---

[28]   Bernard of Clairvaux, *The Song of Songs*, sermon 81; Traherne, *Kingdom of God*, 461.

[29]   Traherne, *Seeds of Eternity*, 239.

[30]   Traherne, *Kingdom of God*, 457.

[31]   Ibid. 481–7.

[32]   Traherne, *Seeds of Eternity*, 237, see also 238; *Hermes Mercurious Trismegistus, His Divine Pymander*, X. 60–64, 71–3, 99–101.

[33]   Traherne, *Seeds of Eternity*, 240; see Plato, *Republic*, 514a–520a, trans. G.M.A. Grube, in *Complete Works*.

[34]   Traherne, *Seeds of Eternity*, 240.

visions of human perfection is illustrated further by his images of the angel and the atom.

Angels: Spiritual Innocence

Angels are a conventional but potent symbol of spiritual innocence.[35] In the context of Traherne's Renaissance humanist theological anthropology, which placed incarnate humanity above the angels, angels do not image perfection as such but the perfection of the spiritual capacities.[36] In *Church's Year-Book*, angels epitomise spiritual qualities of incorporeality, intelligibility, immortality and perfection, being 'Spirits Immaterial and Intellectual' made of 'Powers Inclinations and Principles'.[37] In human beings, they symbolise pure affections: 'My Affections are Angels, if Divine and Heavenly: if unmanaged and Disorderd, Infernal Divels'.[38] In *Commentaries of Heaven*, 'Angelical' or 'Divine' affections are 'Motions of the Mind caused and compleated by Eternal Principles', such as joy instigated by 'the Intuition or Contemplation of eternal Love'.[39] Angels emblematise the inner innocence of the affections.

Angelic innocence is retirement into spirit. Adapting Gregory of Nazianzus' encomium on virginity, the 'Angell' in *Commentaries of Heaven* mirrors virgin retirement from the world, as they 'have no Wives no Cares no Sadning Griefs'.[40] The grace of retirement grants them impassibility, incorruptibility and immortality, making them 'immovable towards Evil'.[41] Angelic retirement also intimates the pure sight of infinity. *Commentaries of Heaven* earlier instructs:

---

[35] Robert Ellrodt concludes that Traherne's angels are 'types of Adamic innocence' ('Angels and the Poetic Imagination from Donne to Traherne', in John Careu and Helen Peters (eds), *English Renaissance Studies: Presented to Dame Helen Gardner in Honour of Her Seventieth Birthday* [Oxford: Clarendon, 1980], 179).

[36] See Traherne, *Select Meditations*, IV 37; Poole claims Traherne's source is Irenaeus, *Apostolic Preaching*, 12 ('Frail Originals', 281); see also B. Gordon, 'The Renaissance Angel', in Peter Marshall and Alexandra Walsham (eds), *Angels in the Early Modern World* (Cambridge: Cambridge University Press, 2006), 42–3.

[37] Traherne, *Church's Year-Book*, 207–9.

[38] Ibid. 220.

[39] Traherne, 'Affection', *Commentaries of Heaven, Part 1*, 276–7.

[40] Traherne, 'Angell', *Commentaries of Heaven, Part 2*, 80–81, citing Gregory of Nazianzus, 'In Laudem Virginitatis', 1.2.1, *On God and Man: The Theological Poetry of St Gregory of Nazianzus*, trans. Peter Gilbert (Crestwood, NY: St Vladimir's Seminary, 2001); on Gregory's influence, see also Traherne, 'Angell', *Commentaries of Heaven, Part 2*, 66; id., *Centuries of Meditations*, III 65, drawing on Gregory of Nazianzus, 'On the Theophany, or Birthday of Christ', *Select Orations* XXXVIII 9.

[41] Traherne, 'Angell', *Commentaries of Heaven, Part 2*, 67.

'Disentangle thy self from Worldly Cares, that Thou mayst see like an Angel, the Accurat Exactness and Glory of his Doings.'[42] Similarly, in *Inducements to Retirednes*, a retired man sees all things, being 'accompanied with Angels, and present with the Ages'.[43] This is the innocence of the apprehensions.

In addition, Traherne's critical appropriation of standard sources on angelology presents the protective power of innocence, the infinite unity of spirit and the communicative nature of perfection. His most straightforward embracement of tradition draws on reception of Daniel 3, in which angels aided the three 'children' in the fire.[44] Thus in *Church's Year-Book*, following Jerome, Traherne describes angels as the protectors of innocence, assigned to each child to 'withhold us from Sinning'.[45] *Church's Year-Book*'s devotions to St Michael more critically adopt Dionysius' celestial hierarchy.[46] Against Andrewes' interpretation of Dionysius, Traherne distinguishes the angelic orders not according to their species but their office. He therefore defines angels as all alike created in God's image, symbolising the perfect unity of human spirit: 'all most Pure and Glorious Spirits ... of one Nature, Will and Beauty'.[47]

Commentaries of Heaven cites Gregory the Great to defend this definition of angels through their heraldic office.[48] Just as the soul both reflects and communicates God, so Traherne's depiction of people as 'Incarnate Angels' may perhaps indicate humanity's apostolic role as well as its spiritual nature, as in *Select Meditations*, which parallels angelic sight with the declaration of God's glory: 'He onely Blessed is that praises Sings. / That sees with Angels Eys, Soares on the wings.'[49] Similarly, naming people as 'incarnate Cherubim' may have less

---

[42] Traherne, 'Accuratness', *Commentaries of Heaven, Part 1*, 137.

[43] Traherne, *Inducements to Retirednes*, 22.

[44] Traherne calls them children while Puente calls them young men (Traherne, 'Angell', *Commentaries of Heaven, Part 2*, 79; Puente, *Meditations Upon the Mysteries of our Holie Faith*, 55).

[45] Traherne, *Church's Year-Book*, 210, 211; see also id., 'Angell', *Commentaries of Heaven, Part 2*, 79; id., 'Ambassadors', *Commentaries of Heaven, Part 2*, 23; Jerome, *Commentary on Matthew*, Matt. 18.10; Jerome, *Commentary on Matthew*, Fathers of the Church 117, trans. Thomas P. Scheck (Washington, DC: Catholic University of America Press), Matt. 18.10.

[46] Dionysius the Areopagite, *De coelesti hierarchia, De ecclesiastica hierarchia, De mystica theologia, Epistulae*, ed. Günter Heil and Adolf Martin Ritter (Berlin: De Gruyter, 1991); see Denys Rutledge, *Cosmic Theology: The Ecclesiastical Hierarchy of Pseudo-Denys: An Introduction* (London: Routledge & Kegan Paul, 1964), 47–59.

[47] Traherne, *Church's Year-Book*, 217.

[48] Traherne, 'Angell', *Commentaries of Heaven, Part 2*, 61, 62; Gregory the Great, 'Homily 34', *Forty Gospel Homilies*, trans. Dom David Hurst (Kalamazoo, Mich.: Cistercian Publications, 1990), 280–300.

[49] Traherne, *Select Meditations*, I 100; see id., *Centuries of Meditations*, IV 29; id., *Christian Ethicks*, 146; id., *Ceremonial Law*, 234.

to do with childlikeness than with pure affections and apprehensions, since in the celestial hierarchy their office is to 'see and Know'.[50] Angels thus intimate the offices of innocent affections and apprehension, which provide the spiritual protection of purity, but do not merely fly from the world, also having a duty to declare God's glory within it.

The Atom: The Innocence of 'Material Spirits'

The atom is a broad conceit which indicates the unity of matter and spirit and the parallels between innocence and glory. Chapter 2 discussed the atom as the materiality of original innocence, whose smallness and simplicity mirrored Adam's humble yet divine beginnings, echoing the glory of humanity created *ex nihilo*. Its recapitulation here indicates the ubiquity of innocence across the estates. The atom also illustrates divine innocence, the soul's spiritual glory. Its qualities express the soul's primordial and eschatological nature and are a mirror into essential innocence: 'the clear Sight of them is like the Knowledge of first Principles'.[51]

Traherne's extended treatments of atoms in *Commentaries of Heaven* and *Kingdom of God* address both matter and spirit in a manner which undoes atomism's contemporary atheistical associations.[52] While both treatises ostensibly address the material atom, Traherne's theological concerns are clear in *Kingdom of God*, which prioritises the spiritual 'Matter of Gods Kingdom' over the 'Matter of the World'.[53] The *Kingdom of God* entry appears to have been written later, as it responds to the question posed at the end of the *Commentaries of Heaven* entry. It confirms that the resurrected body would contain the same atoms as its original, implicitly acknowledging the eternal glory of material existence.[54] Atoms are a metaphor for the soul, based upon a Democritean principle which designates them the principles of matter when at rest and the principles of spirit when in motion: 'Atoms united in quiet make the Solid ones: Atoms dispersed and Scattered in Motion makes its Volatile Spirits.'[55] Following

---

[50] Traherne, 'Angell', *Commentaries of Heaven, Part 2*, 62; see also id., *Select Meditations*, II 17 vi.

[51] Traherne, 'Atom', *Commentaries of Heaven, Part 2*, 333.

[52] On seventeenth-century atomism, see Antonio Clericuzio, *Elements, Principles, and Corpuscles: A Study of Atomism and Chemistry in the Seventeenth Century* (Dordrecht: Kluwer, 2000); Christopher Meinel, 'Early Seventeenth-Century Atomism: Theory, Epistemology, and the Insufficiency of Experiment', *Isis* 79/1 (1988), 68–103.

[53] Traherne, 'Atom', *Commentaries of Heaven, Part 2*, 333; id., *Kingdom of God*, 341.

[54] Traherne, 'Atom', *Commentaries of Heaven, Part 2*, 363; id., *Kingdom of God*, 345.

[55] Traherne, *Kingdom of God*, 345–6.

Gale they are the 'Material Spirits' which bridge the gap between material and spiritual worlds, like the soul in hermetic philosophy.[56]

As the atom is 'a Mirror of his Essence', so atomic qualities are those of a soul in right relation to God.[57] Its smallness, mentioned above as primal purity, is also the soul's capacity; the source of its simplicity, indivisibility and volatility.[58] Its simplicity signifies both fragility and divinity:

> For an Atom is most Simple and uncompounded, Immutable and Incorruptible
> ... This therfore being altogether Simple and Indivisible is utterly divested of all
> these, and so Weak of it self an Atom is that it cannot be the Object of any Sence.
> Yet as its Existence So Divine and Glorious, that all the Angels in heaven are not
> able to Creat a Simple Atom out of Nothing, Its Essence being as Great a Miracle
> in nature as its Smallness.[59]

This definition connects the weakness of human simplicity with the glory of divine simplicity. It is the naked purity of the soul whose 'Simplicity is such, that it is wholy divested of all First, Second and Third Qualities'.[60]

The atom's indivisibility intimates the transfigurative power of regeneration. The indivisible atom images the pure heart that 'cannot hav a mixt Inclination' but is wholly directed to one object. Because of its wholeness, 'an Atom being moved, its Nature is changed'.[61] This signifies the soul's transfiguration into the image of God, transformed into the object of its affection. It is expressed in the metamorphic imagery of the phoenix, which intimates the infinitely transformative nature of the atomic soul, 'ever Dying, Expiring and Reviving every moment'.[62] Indivisibility, therefore, does not entail a static wholeness but

---

[56] Traherne, 'Atom', *Commentaries of Heaven, Part 2*, 351; id., *Kingdom of God*, 349; on atoms as the 'materiall Principles of all bodyes, yea of the human Soul', see id., 'Atoms', *Commonplace Book*, 18v 2:10–11, 217, citing Gale, *Court of the Gentiles*, vol. 2, 205–8.

[57] Traherne, *Kingdom of God*, 348.

[58] Traherne, 'Atom', *Commentaries of Heaven, Part 2*, 342–8.

[59] Traherne, *Kingdom of God*, 343.

[60] Ibid.

[61] Traherne, 'Atom', *Commentaries of Heaven, Part 2*, 347; see id., *Kingdom of God*, 345; Plotinus, *Enneads*, IV.1.

[62] Traherne, *Select Meditations*, II 77; see: 'As Earthly Vapours' (id., 'Atom', *Commentaries of Heaven, Part 2*, 352–3; see also *Centuries of Meditations*, IV 29); on the phoenix as emblem of Christ resurrected, see Colie, *Paradoxia Epidemica*, 130–32; Inge, *Wanting Like a God*, 236; on the 'fair phoenix bride', which restores nature through transfigurative affections, see Donne, 'An Epithalamion on the Lady Elizabeth and Frederick, Count Palatine', lines 29, 97–100, in *The Complete Poems*.

the volatility of a unified soul in obedience to the motion of love.[63] This is not a holiness of retirement from the world, but the Christological activity of one who descends into the 'Mire', to illuminate, 'to purifie, to Quicken, to preserv'.[64]

The volatile atom illuminates the apparent paradox of privative and positive innocence. In essence it is a 'meer privative' which will remain motionless with no imposition of force. However, this privative nature is also its capacity, which entails the possibility of infinite propulsion with every action upon it.[65] At rest it represents the static state of ease, which would have continued indefinitely without opposition; but the soul impressed by sin is transformed into an active subject whose innocence is pursued rather than kept, as in 'Ease':

> How easily doth Nature teach the Soul,
> How irresistible is her Infusion!
> There's Nothing found that can her force controll,
> But Sin. How weak and feeble's all Delusion![66]

The atom is an image of the complex innocence of the soul in its material and spiritual, privative and positive nature.

'Hierogliphicks': Sacramental Emblems of Innocence

Traherne's poetic conceits function not only as images, but as *'Hierogliphicks and Emblemes'* of innocence, which subvert traditional associations and sacramentalise conventional imagery to reveal hidden truth.[67] Emblem books were a popular genre in early modern literature.[68] They combined a variety of media, including pictures, poetry, epigrams and scriptural quotations. Michael Bath has defined them as 'an assemblage or *bricolage* of elements of varying authority, none of which speaks with the same voice'.[69] Lewalski has argued that,

---

[63] On the motion of atoms, see Digby, *Of Bodies and of Mans Soul*, 94–123; Gale, *Court of the Gentiles*, vol. 2, 443.

[64] Traherne, 'Atom', *Commentaries of Heaven, Part 2*, 353.

[65] Traherne, *Kingdom of God*, 345.

[66] Traherne, 'Ease', *Dobell Folio*, 34.

[67] Francis Quarles, 'To the Reader', *Emblemes Divine and Moral*, A3; on the law as a celestial hieroglyph, see Traherne, *Ceremonial Law*, 197.

[68] See e.g. George Wither, *A Collection of Emblemes, Ancient and Moderne* (London: Augustine Mathewes, 1635).

[69] Michael Bath, *Speaking Pictures: English Emblem Books and Renaissance Culture* (London; Longman, 1993), 212–13; see also Rosemary Freeman, *English Emblem Books*

172   *Boundless Innocence in Thomas Traherne's Poetic Theology*

of all the seventeenth-century religious lyric poets, Traherne is the least rooted in the Petrarchan traditions of emblematic poetry.[70] Nevertheless, his poetic conceits function emblematically, as they construct meaning analogically by combining sometimes incongruent elements into a composite whole.

The emblem tradition illuminates the sacramental function of Traherne's images of innocence, both as mysteries and as material signs of spiritual truths. Colie has explained how the seventeenth-century devotional lyric appropriated conventional emblematics, noting in particular how the poetry of Herbert and Marvell 'sacramentalizes' popular emblematic images.[71] Emblems are not straightforward symbols, but work by allusion and association: the term 'hieroglyphics' indicates the occult opacity of their language, which echoes the sacramental *mysterion*. Bacon defined emblems as tropes that 'reduce conceits intellectual to images sensible'.[72] The 'sensible' or material aspect of the emblem is essential to its sacramental function, as seen in Traherne's theology of creation as a sacrament or visible sign of God's presence.[73]

The Sacramental Child[74]

As outlined in the Introduction, Traherne's child is not a straightforward symbol of innocence. The sacramental regeneration discussed in Chapter 4 and the injunction to become a child addressed in Chapter 5 do not fully cover the strikingly paradoxical poetic function of the child. Traherne's 'Babe' is an object of both contemplation and participation and is to be both admired and

---

(London: Chatto & Windus, 1948), 238–9.

[70]   Lewalski, *Protestant Poetics*, 208.

[71]   Rosalie L. Colie, *The Resources of Kind: Genre-Theory in the Renaissance*, ed. Barbara Lewalski (London: University of California Press, 1973), 37, 38, 57, cited in Alastair Fowler, *Kinds of Literature: An Introduction to the Theory of Genres and Modes* (Oxford: Clarendon, 1982), 109; see also T.M. DiPasquale, *Literature and Sacrament: The Sacred and the Secular in John Donne* (Pittsburgh, Pa.: Duquesne University Press, 1999), 16–18; R.M. Schwartz, *Sacramental Poetics at the Dawn of Secularism: When God Left the World* (Stanford, Calif.: Stanford University Press, 2008), 3–17; R. Whalen, *The Poetry of Immanence: Sacrament in Donne and Herbert* (Toronto: University of Toronto Press, 2002).

[72]   Bacon, *The Advancement of Learning*, II.15.iii.

[73]   See Gavin Kuchar, *Divine Subjection: The Rhetoric of Sacramental Devotion in Early Modern England* (Pittsburgh, Pa: Duquesne University Press, 2005), 184; Kershaw, 'The Poetic of the Cosmic Christ', 285; Sawday, *The Body Emblazoned*, 257–9.

[74]   For a fuller version of this argument, see Elizabeth Dodd, 'The Sacramental Image of the Child in the Thought of Thomas Traherne, and its Theological Significance', K.E. Lawson (ed.), *Understanding Children's Spirituality: Theology, Research, and Practice* (Eugene, Oreg.: Cascade, 2012), 84–105 (material reproduced with permission).

imitated: 'a surprizing Wonder great enough to astonish even Men of yeers'.[75] It possesses the power that Augustine attributed to emblems, which 'move and kindle our affection much more than if they were set forth in bald statements, not clothed with sacramental symbols'.[76] Traherne's sacramental model of regenerate innocence lies not in baptism alone but also in the sacramental function of the child emblem, which moves the affections, is rooted in experience and draws material existence into eternity.

Whether Traherne's depictions of childhood are interpreted as literal autobiography, metaphor of spiritual progress or symbolic imagery, they seem full of inconsistencies.[77] The divine child of the poems and *Centuries of Meditations* is unrecognisable to the unregenerate candidate for baptism in *A Sober View*.[78] Innocence is only one aspect of the child image and arguably a minor one. The Babe in *Commentaries of Heaven* is a metaphor for three different sorts of spiritual childishness: aged and supposedly wise 'Old Babes, that will never be men', 'Weak and unskillfull men' who are set to rule over 'Sinfull Nations' and 'Raw Christians' who are not yet ready for the meat of acquaintance 'with the Mysteries of all Ages'.[79] Traherne's *Commonplace Book* quotes several sources which associate the child with perverseness and indiscretion and *Select Meditations* describes 'Foolish Childishness' as selfishness, greed and ingratitude.[80]

Childlike innocence is expressed in the subjunctive mood of the lyric poems. 'The Preparative' presents the possibility of a life lived '*As if* there were nor Sin, nor Miserie.'[81] The subjunctive tone is embedded in uncertainty, as Traherne equivocates in 'Innocence':

---

[75]   Traherne, 'Babe', *Commentaries of Heaven, Part 2*, 438.

[76]   Augustine, *Letters*, LV.11.xxi, trans. J.G. Cunningham, NPNF[1] 1 (Edinburgh: T.&T. Clark, 1886).

[77]   See Wade, *Thomas Traherne*, 27–37; Salter, *Thomas Traherne*, 22–38; Clements, *The Mystical Poetry of Thomas Traherne*, 16, 18, 31; Stewart, *The Expanded Voice*, 212; Sherrington, *Mystical Symbolism in the Poetry of Thomas Traherne*, 70–82; on the conflicting attitudes to the child which are embedded in Christian tradition, see Hugh Pyper, 'Children', in Hastings, Mason and Pyper (eds), *The Oxford Companion to Christian Thought*, 110.

[78]   See Traherne, 'The Salutation', 'Wonder', 'Eden', 'Innocence', 'The Preparative', *Dobell Folio*, 3–13; id., *Centuries of Meditations*, III 1–4; id., *A Sober View*, 81, 85.

[79]   Traherne, 'Babe', *Commentaries of Heaven, Part 2*, 438–9; cf. Wilson, who cites the aphorism *temperantia in senecture non est temperantia sed impotentia*, on old age's impotence as an inferior form of innocence (*A Complete Christian Dictionary*, 336b).

[80]   Traherne, 'Corruption', *Commonplace Book*, 30v 1–2 (source unknown); id. 'Retirement', *Commonplace Book*, 83r 1, citing Jackson, *A Treatise containing the Originall of Unbeliefe*, 200–203; id., *Select Meditations*, I 84.

[81]   Traherne, 'The Preparative', *Dobell Folio*, 12 (italics added).

> Whether it be that Nature is so pure,
> And Custom only vicious; or that sure
> God did by Miracle the Guilt remov
>
> .　　.　　.　　.
>
> What ere it is, it is a Light
> So Endless unto me
> That I a World of true Delight
> Did then and to this Day do see.[82]

Whether this infant vision is possible or impossible, remembered or imagined, natural or resulting from grace, it provides the knowledge of and desire for the good that inspires the search for felicity. In the memory or imagination of infancy, the light of nature becomes the light of grace through which we see and love the world. Grace being an object not of lament but of hope, this permits Traherne to seek infancy without nostalgic regression. However, this ideal image, as an object of admiration and desire but not necessarily of imitation, does not encompass the whole of Traherne's sacramental poetics of childlike innocence.

An emblematic reading acknowledges the ambiguities of experience alongside the symbolic ideal child. Understanding Traherne's child not as a purely visual 'icon' but a multi-sensory emblem, elucidates the combination of the material and spiritual which is found in the figure of a Babe. This child is 'wrapt up' literally and figuratively 'in the Swaddling clothes of his own infirmities'. He is compound of a glorious soul and a finite body, 'as Great in his Hopes and Possibilities, as he is Small in the Appearance of his present Attainments'. He is a symbol of beginnings, potentiality and hope, both in body and spirit: 'If we consult either his Body, or his Soul, he is but a Seed of his future Perfection.'[83] In his fusion of bodily infirmity and spiritual expansiveness, Traherne's Babe is a sacramental emblem of human perfection.

According to Williams, sacramental language evokes particularity: 'to think "this, not that; here, not there; now, not then"'.[84] Traherne's non-specific style evinces particularity not through detailed description but through personal experience and emotion. So, *Centuries of Meditations* describes how in infancy 'the Green Trees when I saw them first through one of the Gates Transported and Ravished me; their sweetnes and unusual Beauty made my Heart to leap'.[85]

---

[82]　Traherne, 'Innocence', *Dobell Folio*, 10.

[83]　Traherne, 'Babe', *Commentaries of Heaven, Part 2*, 437.

[84]　Rowan Williams, 'Between Politics and Metaphysics: Reflections in the Wake of Gillian Rose', *MT* 11/1 (1995), 116.

[85]　Traherne, *Centuries of Meditations*, III 3.

The materiality of the sacramental is reflected in Traherne's interest in the infant body in 'The Salutation':

> These little Limmes,
> These Eys and Hands which here I find,
> These rosie Cheeks wherwith my Life begins.[86]

Sacramental experience is expressed through the language of the spiritual senses, the 'State of Innocence' in 'Wonder' being a world which 'did fill my Sence'.[87] This affective language and sensory imagery intimates the incarnational nature of Traherne's child emblem, which is rooted in the body while being drawn into spirit.

The sacramental child presents a fragmentary and ambiguous infant innocence that reflects human finitude. Infant innocence is juxtaposed with guilt and defined through sin. In 'Innocence', Traherne combines a long list of the qualities of innocence (bliss, purity, brightness, light, joy, summer, admiration, prizing, praise, love, humility, contentment and delight) with an equally long list of terms associated with sin (stain, spot, darkness, guilt, night, avarice, pride, lust, strife, pollution, fraud, anger, malice, jealousy and spite).[88] Infant innocence appears like the fragments of paradise amidst, and in contrast to, an overshadowing guilt. Within compound fallen nature, innocence's strengths and weaknesses are inseparable. The Babe has a double nature, expressed as a 'feeble Spark of immortal fire, that can never be extinguished', its helplessness, nakedness, littleness and exposure to injuries are intertwined with enduring strength.[89] 'My Spirit' demonstrates the infant's complex innocence in exclamations such as 'My Naked Simple Life was I'.[90] Nakedness suggests an ambiguous innocence that is simultaneously unmediated relationship to God and vulnerability to the world. Simplicity reflects the divine attribute but is also associated with ignorance. The supreme 'I' denotes the individual's glory in relation to God and world but attracts accusations of solipsism.

The incarnational, partial and complex innocence manifest in the sacramental child presents the mystery of human glory alongside the experience of guilt and finitude, revealing a less optimistic theological anthropology than that often attributed to Traherne. It draws a line, however fine, between perfect

---

86   Traherne, 'The Salutation', *Dobell Folio*, 3; cf. id., 'The Preparative', *Dobell Folio*, 11.
87   Traherne, 'Wonder', *Dobell Folio*, 5.
88   Traherne, 'Innocence', *Dobell Folio*, 8–10.
89   Traherne, 'Babe', *Commentaries of Heaven, Part 2*, 437.
90   Traherne, 'My Spirit', *Dobell Folio*, 26.

Edenic innocence and the partial innocence of misery–grace. Adam and Eve's innocence – without blemish, glorious, powerful and protected though capable of falling – metamorphoses into the child's innocence – inseparable from guilt and weakness. Despite its ambiguities, the child remains a sacrament of innocence in the subjunctive mood, where it encompasses all the estates of eternity, nature, misery and redemption in possibility, as celebrated in *Ceremonial Law*: 'Who would expect that ... All things to one new born should so relate, / And all the Ages be his own Estate?'[91]

The Celestial Stranger

The child is not Traherne's only sacramental emblem of innocence. The Celestial Stranger bears striking similarities to the innocent infant. This curious theme in *Kingdom of God* has been described as an alien visitor but is also akin to an angel.[92] Traherne muses that a man who had 'been allwayes in one of the Stars, or Confined to the Body of the Flaming Sun, or surrounded with nothing but pure AEther' could not imagine the earth's 'World of Mysteries'. On encountering it, this person would react with awe and delight: 'Thus would a Celestial Stranger be Entertained in the World.'[93] This echoes Sterry's paraphrase of Plato, who

> somewhere saith, something like this, that if we stood in the Sun, all things, even this dark mass of Elements, and elementary composition to us, beholding them from that center of Light, would appear in a *Sun-like* Glory. Be thou this *Angel,* or in *this* an *Angel-like* Spirit, stand in this *Sun,* the glorious circle of *divine Love*.[94]

Sterry may be referring to Plato's *Republic*, which defines truth as the soul's apprehension of the region of light and ignorance its decline into earthly darkness.[95] The light of the Celestial Stranger is thus the light of love and truth, expressing the innocence of apprehensions unacquainted with the world.

---

[91] Traherne, *Ceremonial Law*, 203; see also id., 'Babe', *Commentaries of Heaven, Part 2,* 437.

[92] Traherne, *Kingdom of God*, 388–90; cf.: 'What if the Stars should be all Inhabited', then 'Creatures in those remoter Orbes should be very Strange; and more Wonderfull' (ibid. 372–3); on the stranger as alien, see King, 'Thomas Traherne', 370–71; on the existence of perfect beings in other worlds, see Giordano Bruno, *On the Infinite Universe and Worlds* (Venice, 1584), 'Argument of the Third Dialogue, ninethely'.

[93] Traherne, *Kingdom of God*, 390.

[94] Sterry, *A Discourse of the Freedom of the Will*, xviii.

[95] Plato, *Republic*, VI 508d.

The Celestial Stranger also echoes the devotional trope that one should be a stranger in the world.[96] This is spiritual retirement from world to spirit, as opposed to the self-alienation of misery wherein 'the Soul was changd, / And gadding outward, from it self estrangd.'[97] However, rather than feeding into a discourse on spiritual retirement, this image explores the beneficent effect of a pure, holy, spiritual stranger on the world of experience in the way that love, as a 'strang Being here upon Earth', beautifies and glorifies it.[98] This expresses the communicative nature of innocence.

The infant is a form of celestial stranger. Following the description of the Stranger, *Kingdom of God* recounts: 'I know a Stranger upon Earth in his Infancy that thought the Heavens more Sublime then Saphires.'[99] In *Commentaries of Heaven* the Babe is a 'Stranger newly come into the World'.[100] In 'The Salutation' the infant meets the world as:

> A Stranger here
> Strange Things doth meet, strange Glories See;
> Strange Treasures lodg'd in this fair World appear,
> Strange all, and New to me.[101]

A comparison between *Select Meditations*' description of the infant and *Kingdom of God*'s account of the Celestial Stranger shows that the latter surpasses the former in innocence. *Select Meditations* describes how, in Traherne's infant eyes, the chambers of the city where he lived were 'Innocent and all Misterious, Soe they appeared to the little Stranger, when I first came into the world. As sweet every thing as paradice could make it. For I saw them all in the light of Heaven.'[102] *Kingdom of God* contains a much expanded version of this vision. Where the infant saw only the city's 'Temple streets skies Houses Gates and people', the Celestial Stranger sees the whole world: from colours to prayers, to the influence of the stars, to all humanity; a list of wonders that lasts nearly six folio pages. The Celestial Stranger expresses a childlike innocence of inexperience. However, liberated from the child's association with ignorance, naïveté and limit, it presents this quality in an unbounded sense. The Celestial Stranger may be a purer emblem of innocent

---

[96]   See Ps. 119.19; Heb. 11.13.
[97]   Traherne, *Ceremonial Law*, 232.
[98]   Traherne, *Select Meditations*, II 64.
[99]   Traherne, *Kingdom of God*, 391.
[100]   Traherne, 'Babe', *Commentaries of Heaven, Part 2*, 437.
[101]   Traherne, 'The Salutation', *Dobell Folio*, 4.
[102]   Traherne, *Select Meditations*, III 29.

178   *Boundless Innocence in Thomas Traherne's Poetic Theology*

apprehensions than the child, as it seems to epitomise the delight, awe and wonder of an innocent, unmediated and un-premeditated encounter with the world.

'A-biding, for ever': The Glory of Innocence across the Estates

Traherne's poetic conceits express the glory of innocence in eternity, where the estates are 'at once in God changeable in them selves and Succeeding each other, but Standing there and A-biding, for ever'.[103] Extended metaphors draw connections between innocence across the estates: the garden, shield and diamond symbolise innocence's protective power, while nakedness, white robes and the pearl are its glory. The dragon and the dove link earth and heaven, signifying the transformative power of regenerate innocence, while the virgin and Amazon Queen draw experience into infinity, imaging the innocent desire which yearns for glory.

The Garden, Shield and Diamond: The Protective Power of Innocence

The protective power of innocence had an ambiguous status in seventeenth-century literature. This was evident in contradictory aphorisms such as 'No innocence is safe, when power contests' and 'Innocencie beareth her defence with her'.[104] The debates were rehearsed in the brothers' discussion of the strength of chastity in Milton's *Comus*.[105] Traherne asserts the protective power of harmless innocence in the conceits of the garden and shield. The garden typology was mentioned in Chapter 2 as an expression of the organic growth of innocence. It also carries connotations of a garden enclosed, in conformity to contemporary interpretations of the Song of Songs.[106] Milton's *Paradise Lost* drew on this tradition in its depiction of Eden, which

> crowns with her enclosure green,
> As with a rural mound the champain head

---

[103] Ibid. I 94.

[104] Cited in Ben Jonson, *Sejanus* (1605), IV.i.40; J. Florio, *Florio his Firste Fruites* (London, 1578) (*The Oxford Dictionary of English Proverbs*, ed. F.P. Wilson [3rd edn, Oxford: Oxford University Press, 1970], 4).

[105] Milton, *Comus*, lines 331–480, in *The Major Works*.

[106] See Song 4.12; on contemporary usage of this imagery, see Stanley Stewart, *The Enclosed Garden: The Tradition and the Image in Seventeenth-Century Poetry* (London: University of Wisconsin Press, 1966), 31–45.

Of a steep wilderness, whose hairie sides
With thicket overgrown, grottesque and wilde,
Access deni'd.[107]

Select Meditations adopts a similar tone, depicting Israel as 'fenced with hedges, that non might pluck her', while in *Church's Year-Book* the Christ-tended church is 'a fenced Garden'.[108] Although it is an expansive organic theme, the imagery of enclosure ties the garden to the original innocence of the state of ease.

A different model of protective innocence is required for the active soul battling sin in a world of trial. In *Kingdom of God* and *Commentaries of Heaven*, the garden emblem of protection and security is transfigured into a shield. *Kingdom of God* describes the estate of innocence's walled garden 'Keeping evil out', but later this becomes Christ the 'shield to save us, by receiving the Wounds himself, that are Inflicted on his People'.[109] The proximity of evil and the danger of trial are emphasised through Christ's defensive wounds. This theme is echoed in *Commentaries of Heaven*, where humanity's glorious estate is such 'that God himself may becom his Shield, his Battle Axe, and his Castle'.[110] It is not only Christ's imputed innocence which protects the righteous, but also the shield of faith 'wherewith ye shall be able to quench all the fiery darts of the wicked'. This image of innocent purity explicitly alludes to Edmund Spenser's *Faerie Queene*: 'Spencers Shield of Diamond ... Unvaild and Naked ... Defaceth all our Weaker Enemies'. The naked diamond shield is the glory and power of protective purity, which 'is Impenetrable, yet all Light!' and 'All-One, All-Bright, / All Fair, all Dreadfull, Terrible, Divine.'[111]

The garden is the protective enclosure of retirement from the world, while the shield is martial innocence at war. The garden is akin to the all-encompassing protection of the womb, while the shield is a heroic image. The metamorphosis from one emblem to another expresses innocence's changing character through

---

[107] Milton, *Paradise Lost*, IV 133–7.

[108] Traherne, *Select Meditations*, III 25; id., *Church's Year-Book*, 19.

[109] Traherne, *Kingdom of God*, 290, 302.

[110] Traherne, 'Armour', *Commentaries of Heaven, Part 2*, 216; on the virtue of solitude and retirement which 'secureth more then a Castle', see id., *Inducements to Retirednes*, 10.

[111] Traherne, 'Armour', *Commentaries of Heaven, Part 2*, 217; see Edmund Spenser, *The Faerie Queene*, ed. A.C. Hamilton (London: Longman, 1977), I.7, II.8.xxxv, III.8.xlii, V.11. xxvii, VI.6.xxvi; for modern critical interpretations of Spenser's shield as the shield of faith of Eph. 6.16 or St George's silver shield against the dragon, see W.J.B. Pienaar, 'Arthur's Shield in the "Faerie Queene"', *MP* 26/1 (1928), 63–8; D.C. Allen, 'Arthur's Diamond Shield in the Faerie Queene', *JEGP* 36 (1937), 234–43; H. Edward Cain, 'Spenser's "Shield of Faith"', *Shakespeare Association Bulletin* 10 (1935), 163–6.

the estates of innocence and trial. The diamond represents the otherworldly innocence of glory, fleetingly interposing into worldly battles. It is full of light, beauty and strength but also a cold and stony weapon. The three images of garden, shield and diamond express the protective power of innocence in the different estates. They are the quality of the Christian in spiritual retirement, 'endued with Power so Great, that neither Wilde Beasts nor Thievs nor Death can injure him'.[112]

Nakedness, White Robes and Pearls: The Glory of Innocence

Nakedness, white robes and pearls signify the glory of innocence in the estates of innocence, glory and misery. Adam's nakedness and the white robes of Revelation are mirror-images of purity. Nakedness denotes freedom from shame; white robes, the glory and joy of restored purity; pearls, the treasure of repentance.

Nakedness carries several connotations in Traherne's works, including vulnerability and weakness as well as openness and freedom. Chapter 2 mentioned nakedness as a signal of barbarism, weakness and dependence on God. Natural nakedness is the vacuity of the soul which is allied to purity but not identical with it: in *Christian Ethicks*, humanity is 'Naked by Nature, though Pure and clean'.[113] In *Inducements to Retirednes*, nakedness is unqualified openness to the other, so that 'a man may talk face to face with God, even while He is as Naked as Adam', while the love of God 'desire[s] nothing but Naked Lov'.[114] More negatively, nakedness denotes the vulnerability of solitude, 'for what is more naked then a Man that is alone'.[115]

Nakedness is also a symbol of original innocence and its eschatological recapitulation. *Select Meditations* writes of the 'Naked Grandure of [Adam's] High Estate'.[116] In *Christian Ethicks*, Adam and Eve's naked innocence is the glory of being unclothed yet unashamed: 'the Splendor and Ornament of Men, as it will be in Heaven'.[117] The recovery of nakedness without shame signifies the eschatological hope of innocence. Gervase Babington's notes on Genesis similarly described how 'the innocency that then was in them is now lost by sinne, yet regayned in measure by Christ, and shall perfitly be inioyed in the life

---

[112] Traherne, *Inducements to Retirednes*, 22.
[113] Traherne, *Christian Ethicks*, 31.
[114] Traherne, *Inducements to Retirednes*, 11.
[115] Ibid. 22.
[116] Traherne, *Select Meditations*, III 10.
[117] Traherne, *Christian Ethicks*, 33.

'A Light So Endless unto me'

to come, when nakednesse shall shame us no more then it did at the first'.[118] For Willett, also, unashamed nakedness is the hope of innocence:

> Some thinke, that there remaineth yet in children that are not ashamed of their nakednesse, some shadow of our first estate: but children are therein unshamefast for want of reason, as the like is to be seene in bruit beasts. But in the kingdome of heaven, we shall be all naked, and without shame as *Adam* was: and without feare or danger of sinne which *Adam* was not.[119]

Nakedness is a paradoxical type of glory and shame. 'Apparel' in *Commentaries of Heaven* gives Adam's nakedness a twofold typological significance, absence of shame and lack of possessions: 'It was the Happiness of Adam in Innocence that like a Jewel his own Nativ Lustre and Beauty was his best Attire' until 'Shame the Daughter of Guilt made Apparel necessary'.[120] Since the Fall, humanity 'found out Poverty as well as Sin' and turned to costly clothes to cover up nakedness' lowliness and shame.[121] This corruption is redressed in a double manner: 'Spiritual Apparel' adorns the naked soul with precious virtues, while Christ's imputed righteousness covers the elect 'that the Shame of thy Nakedness do not appear'.[122] The shame of post-lapsarian nakedness may only be undone with spiritual clothing.

White robes signify the treasure and glory of recovered shamelessness. They are a type of the 'Righteousness of the Saints', the acquired righteousness of sanctification and the imputed righteousness of Christ.[123] This symbol originates in Genesis and Revelation and has both protological and eschatological connotations. Ainsworth interpreted Jacob wearing Esau's robes as 'those *robes* of innocency and righteousnesse, wherewith the saints are clothed', while Donne's

---

[118] Gervase Babington, *Certaine Plaine, Briefe, and Comfortable Notes upon Everie Chapter of Genesis* (London: for Thomas Clarke, 1592), 18.

[119] Andrew Willet, *Hexapla in Genesin & Exodum: That is, a Sixfold Commentary Upon the First Bookes of Moses* (London: John Haviland, 1633), 32.

[120] Traherne, 'Apparel', *Commentaries of Heaven, Part 2*, 133; on nakedness and clothes as 'types', see ibid. 135; on nakedness as freedom from possessions without poverty, see id., *Centuries of Meditations*, IV 36.

[121] Traherne, 'Apparel', *Commentaries of Heaven, Part 2*, 136; Traherne follows Isaac Barrow's view that nakedness in misery signifies poverty ('Death I', *Commonplace Book*, 32v, citing *The Duty and Reward of Bounty to the Poor* [London, 1671], 160).

[122] Traherne, 'Apparel', *Commentaries of Heaven, Part 2*, 134–5; see also id., 'Antichrist', *Commentaries of Heaven, Part 2*, 99; id., *A Sober View*, 81, which interprets Rev. 3.17–18 in the light of James 1.5.

[123] See Traherne, *Kingdom of God*, 362.

'Second Anniversary' sees death's white shroud as both eschatological progression and return to nakedness, where 'They reinvest thee in white innocence'.[124]

White robes depict the eschatological restoration of innocence as proleptically present through the sacraments, spiritual virtues and, most importantly, the resurrection. In *Church's Year-Book* and *Commentaries of Heaven*, Traherne translates Revelation's eschatological white robes into the 'purity and Joy of their Souls ... received in Baptism' and the internal 'clean white Linnen which is the Righteousness of the Saints'.[125] *Kingdom of God* cites Chrysostom, exhorting the reader 'to be prepared with a Diviner Philosophie; not Washing the Attires of our Bodie, but Cloathing our Soules with the long white Robes of Truth and Righteousness'.[126] In *Church's Year-Book*, the angel of Christ's resurrection images eschatological innocence's proleptic presence: 'He was Clothed in White, becaus White is the Color of Gladness and Innocency. To shew us the Estate of the Resurrection is a Joyfull Estate, as full of Joy, as it is of Verdure Strength and Rest; and as full of Honor as it is of Innocency.'[127] This eschatological vision links innocence with the joy, glory, fertility, strength and retirement of the resurrection life.

The irreversible progression from Edenic nakedness to the white robes of Revelation implies a transition from original to eschatological unashamedness. However, the symbolic parallels between these mirror-images of innocence transcend the boundaries of the estates. This is seen in *Ceremonial Law*'s confusion of present and past tense:

> GOD *sees* the Nakedness that Man *was* in,
> Covers His Shame, & clothes him with the Skin
>
> .   .   .   .
>
> From Him the Robes of Righteousness we take,
> Which only Clothes, and doth us Glorious make.[128]

As, in eternity, humanity is both naked and robed, so Christ is naked in his birth and crucifixion, and clothed in white in his resurrection. In this duality Christ

---

[124] Ainsworth, *Annotations upon the Five Bookes of Moses* (Gen. 27.15); Donne, 'The Second Anniversary: Of the Progress of the Soule', line 114, in *The Complete Poems*.

[125] Traherne, *Church's Year-Book*, 146; id., 'Apparel', *Commentaries of Heaven, Part 2*, 135; see Rev. 3.4, 5; 4.4; 6.11; 7.13; 19.14.

[126] Traherne, *Kingdom of God*, 266, citing Chrysostom, *Homilies on the Gospel of Saint Matthew*, II.1 (Matt 1.1).

[127] Traherne, *Church's Year-Book*, 17.

[128] Traherne, *Ceremonial Law*, 198–9 (italics added).

'A Light So Endless unto me'   183

becomes humanity's unashamedness, as Gregory of Nazianzus described him: 'a Lamb was chosen for its innocence, and its clothing of the original nakedness. For such is the Victim, That was offered for us, Who is both in Name and fact the Garment of incorruption.'[129]

Between nakedness and white robes lies the pearl, an emblem of repentance. Its rich history of associations with purity, virginity and primordial origins was enhanced through the legacy of Elizabethan literature's devotion to the virgin queen.[130] In general, Traherne's pearl denotes worldly or spiritual treasure.[131] A more lively image emerges from a combination of theories of liquefaction with classical myths of the living origins of jewels. Traherne describes water in *Kingdom of God* thus: 'Evry drop of these Fresh and pure streams is a Living pearl, melted by Lov, that it might be serviceable'.[132] Water as a liquid living pearl identifies value with usefulness, and combines the connotations of treasure with the fluidity of life and the heat of desire.

Applied to tears of penitence, this imagery intimates the passion of pure desire. Penitent tears are an eternal treasure. Drawing on Psalm 6.6, *Select Meditations* says that 'Sinners Tears are Dissolved pearl that Shine forever'.[133] *Centuries of Meditations* reverses this process, crystallising the purgative experience so that God 'turneth our true Penitent Tears into Solid Pearl'.[134] Tears are a spiritual treasure which mortify the soul and prepare it for regeneration. Love is the life of these living pearls which would otherwise be dead and cold. Traherne's pearl is thus more than conventional treasure or purity, it is the glory of penitence.

---

[129] Gregory of Nazianzus, 'The Second Oration on Easter', *Select Orations*, XLV 13.

[130] See Helen Hackett, *Virgin Mother, Maiden Queen: Elizabeth I and the Cult of the Virgin Mary* (Basingstoke: Macmillan, 1996); for a medieval example, see 'The Pearl', in *Sir Gawain and the Green Knight: Pearl; and Sir Orfeo*, ed. J.R.R. Tolkien (London: Unwin, 1979), 89–122; on ancient usage of the term and its protological connotations, see N. Ibrahim Fredrikson, 'The Pearl, Between the Ocean and the Sky: Origins and Evolution of a Christian Symbol', *Revue de l'histoire des religions*, 220/3 (2003), 283–317.

[131] The pearl indicates conventional treasure in Traherne, *Centuries of Meditations*, IV 85; id., 'The Salutation', *Dobell Folio*, 3; id., 'Wonder', *Dobell Folio*, 6; id., 'The Estate', *Dobell Folio*, 43; id., 'Hosanna', *Poems of Felicity*, 191; see also George Herbert, 'The Pearl. Matth. 13' in *The English Poems*.

[132] Traherne, *Kingdom of God*, 396; see also id., 'Speed', *Dobell Folio*, 35; on Traherne's water typology, see Donald Dickson, *The Fountain of Living Waters: The Typology of the Waters of Life in Herbert, Vaughan, and Traherne* (Columbia: University of Missouri Press, 1987), 168–77.

[133] Traherne, *Select Meditations*, I 93.

[134] Traherne, *Centuries of Meditations*, III 48.

184   *Boundless Innocence in Thomas Traherne's Poetic Theology*

The Dragon and the Dove: The Transformation of Regenerate Innocence

The conceits of the dragon and the dove intimate the soul's transformation into regenerate innocence. Dragons are an emblem of false or inverted innocence.[135] In *A Sober View*, they represent delusions and idolatry, and, in *Commentaries of Heaven*, 'Antichrist' is a 'counterfeit Lamb, and a real Dragon'.[136] In *Select Meditations*, the dragon parodies the dove. Its skin is 'clad with Golden Ore' yet 'Overcast with Greenish Gore', compared to Psalm 68.13's 'wings of a dove covered with silver, and her feathers with yellow gold'.[137] This is not simply a representation of evil but the 'poysond Splendor' of the corrupted soul.[138] Traherne laments the lost image of God, buried like the pearl of great price or the jewel in a dragon's brain:

> His Image in themselves laid in a Grave,
> Is Dead and Buried! The Treasure
> Which they lik Dragons in them have
> Unknown's unknown![139]

The dragon signifies the Fall's corruption, through which 'Thy Turtle Doves O Lord to Dragons turn!' A devastating alteration, it turns the whole world into a 'Salvage Wilderness'.[140] In *Kingdom of God*, it appears in a ghoulish parody of the atonement, wherein Adam and Eve's 'Crime was as The Blood of Dragons'

---

[135] On dragons in Christian tradition, see T.H. Gaster, 'Dragon', in G.A. Buttrick et al. (eds), *Interpreter's Dictionary of the Bible: An Illustrated Encyclopedia*, vol. 1: *A–D* (New York: Abingdon, 1962), 868a.

[136] Traherne, *A Sober View*, 190; see Isa. 35.7; Traherne, 'Antichrist', *Commentaries of Heaven, Part 2*, 97; see also 100, 103; cf.: 'Lamb which had the Dragons voice' (Henry Vaughan, 'Constellation', *Silex Scintillans, or Sacred Poems and Private Ejaculations* [London: T.W., 1650], 96:43).

[137] Traherne, *Select Meditations*, II 17. Tertullian contrasts the dove, which symbolises Christ, and the serpent, his tempter, in his interpretation of Matt. 10.16 and compares the simplicity of dovelike Christians to the mystery-loving serpentine Gnostics, including a graphic description of the serpent who skulks underground (*Against the Valentinians*, 2–3, cited in Kittel and Friedrich [eds], *Theological Dictionary of the New Testament*, vol. 6, 71).

[138] Traherne, *Select Meditations*, II 17.

[139] Ibid.; see Matt. 13.44; on the tradition of the jewel in the dragon's brain, see Smith, note on Traherne, *Select Meditations*, II 17.

[140] Traherne, *Select Meditations*, II 17; see: 'IT is impossible to conceive, how great a change a slight Action may produce. It is but pressing the Wick a little with ones Finger, and a Lamp is extinguished, and Darkness immediately made to overspread the Room' (id., *Christian Ethicks*, 38).

to God, replacing Christ's regenerative pure blood with poison.[141] The intensity of this imagery emphasises the wonder of regeneration, wherein the dragon becomes an angelic virgin bride:

> Then Shall thy Turtle Dove a gaine return
> A filthy Dragon No More be
> Her face Shall Like an Angel burn,
> And She a cherub in Her Lov to Thee
>
> .   .   .   .   .
>
> Angelique Life
> Throughout her Skin
> Shall clad thy wife and mak her Shine within.[142]

As an emblem of the regenerate soul, doves express more than innocence alone.[143] In *Commentaries of Heaven*, they symbolise the affection of love through their supposed natural ability to 'love and take pleasure in one another'.[144] They both love and are loved; expressing in *Select Meditations* the beloved yet imperilled nation and Church of England.[145] Primarily, doves symbolise spirit, presenting innocence as a flight from the world to God.[146] *Church's Year-Book*'s prayers on the Ascension adapt Psalm 55.6, seeking purgation so that the soul may, through prayer, 'Ascend easily like a clean Bird, and fall no more from Grace'.[147] This flight

---

[141] Traherne, *Kingdom of God*, 290, misquoting Deut. 32.33; 'Their *wine* is the *poison* of dragons' (italics added); cf. 'their poison is like the poison of a serpent' (Ps. 58.4); see also: if we do not praise God 'we give Him Dragons Blood to Drink' (Traherne, *Select Meditations*, III 49); sin's poison made treasure by God (id., *A Sober View*, 148–9); 'IF Sin had been like *Circe's* Cup, and changed the shape of Mans Body, to that of a *Swine* or *Dragon*, the Depravation of his Nature had been plain and visible' (id., *Christian Ethicks*, 37).

[142] Traherne, *Select Meditations*, II 17; see: 'A Toad transformed to the Whitest Dove/ Unjust and loathsom Hatred turnd to Love' (id., 'Amendment', *Commentaries of Heaven, Part 2*, 53–4).

[143] On the 'almost inexhaustible symbolical power' of the dove in Christian tradition, see Kittel and Friedrich (eds), *Theological Dictionary of the New Testament*, vol. 6, 63.

[144] Traherne, 'Affection', *Commentaries of Heaven, Part 1*, 286.

[145] Smith, note on Traherne, *Select Meditations*, II 17; see Ps. 74.19; Song 2.14; 5.2. Herbert describes Christ's spouse the Church as as 'chaste as the dove' ('The Church Militant', 15).

[146] Cf. Sterry, who seeks to be like 'those beautiful and lovely Birds, sacred to love, in a whiteness of unspotted Candor, [so his essay] may be a birth of Love, though weak, and flying low, sent forth to allure and guide thee into those ever lasting Heavens of Divine Truth and Goodness' (*A Discourse of the Freedom of the Will*, xix).

[147] Traherne, *Church's Year-Book*, 88, 94.

186   *Boundless Innocence in Thomas Traherne's Poetic Theology*

of spiritual ascent echoes Gregory of Nyssa's description of the soul's progress from glory to glory or 'From Dove to Dove'.[148]

The dove is an emblem of spiritual ascent but also of God's descending Holy Spirit, based on Genesis 8.9 and Christ's baptism. *Church's Year-Book*'s devotions on the descent of the Holy Spirit insert innocence into a paraphrase of Daniel Featley's prayer, which states:

> O Eternall and infinite *Holy Ghost*, the love of the Father and the Sonne, who diddest *descend* upon our Saviour in the *likenesses of a Dove*, without gall, purge out of my conscience all *gall* of malice and *bitternesse*, and grant that with *meekenesse I may receive the ingraffed Word which is able to save my soul.*[149]

Traherne's adaptation prays: 'Giv me the Properties of a Dov; Mildness, Meekness, Innocence, Purity, Chastity, Constancy, yea Diligence and Swiftness.'[150] The dove's innocence is not only divine perfection but an object for emulation, since the descent of the Spirit signifies 'the Innocence and fecundity of Good works, in those whom He Inspireth; as well as His own Meek and Excellent Nature'.[151] Dovelike innocence is both a creaturely quality

---

[148] This is the title given by Jean Daniélou to an extract from Gregory of Nyssa's *Commentary on the Song of Songs*, which likens the call to 'arise' and 'come' (Song. 2:10) to 2 Corinthians 3:18, as an expression of the soul's infinite ascent into the infinite goodness of God (Gregory of Nyssa, *Commentary on the Song of Songs*, sermon 5, 873C–876C, in *From Glory to Glory: Texts from Gregory of Nyssa's Mystical Writings*, ed. Jean Daniélou, trans. Herbert Musurillo [Crestwood, NY: St Vladimir's Seminary, 1995], 189–91; cf. Plato, *Phaedrus*, 246c–d).

[149] Daniel Featley, 'Prayer for Whitsunday', in *Ancilla Pietatis: or, The Hand-Maid to Private Devotion* (London: James Young, 1647), 476–8, paraphrased in Traherne, *Church's Year-Book*, 148–9; see Ross, notes, ibid. 288–9 (Ross only mentions pp. 477–8); see also Featley, 'Prayer for Ascension Day', in *Ancilla Pietatis*, 461–6, paraphrased in Traherne, *Church's Year-Book*, 104–6; see Ross, notes, ibid. 279 (Ross only mentions pp. 461–3).

[150] For other potential sources, see: 'The *Dove* is a creature sociable, innocent, chaste, mournfull, quiet, fearfull, given to meditation' (Ainsworth on Lev. 1.14, *Annotations upon the Five Bookes of Moses*, 8); 'a Payre of Turtle Doves; Simplicity, and Sweetnesse; or, an Innocent Integrity with an Humble Meekenesse' (Peter Sterry, 'To The Honorable House of Commons', *The Clouds in which Christ Comes Opened in a Sermon before the Honourable House of Commons* [London, 1648]), 10; 'Lord, give my soul the milk-white innocence / Of Doves, and I shall have their pineons too' (Quarles, *Emblemes Divine and Moral*, 294); 'Give me, O Lord, the innocence of Doves; and fill my soul with thy mild spirit: / Then shal I need none of their wings; since heav'n it self wil dwel in my hart' (Birchley, *Devotions in the Ancient Way of Offices*, 47).

[151] Traherne, *Church's Year-Book*, 129; earlier, Traherne appropriates Christ's ascension into human ascent by misquoting Featley, changing 'This Day Thou didst Transport *thy* Body

'A Light So Endless unto me'

and a divine attribute: it connects the ascending spiritual innocence of the regenerate soul with the descent of the dovelike Holy Spirit, linking earth with heaven.

Virgin Purity and the Amazon Queen: Desiring Innocence

Chapter 5 discussed Traherne's priestly vocation to retirement through chastity. Virginity also functions in his work as a metaphor of innocent purity, although sex was not necessarily absent from innocent Eden.[152] Traherne's use of 'virgin' as an adjective echoes Irenaeus' reference to the protological purity of Eden's 'virgin soil', a usage also found in Donne's and Vaughan's poetry.[153] Vaughan in particular exploited garden imagery to signify the purity of creation, its 'virgin-flowers' and 'Virgin-soile'.[154] Traherne sometimes applies this imagery to the 'Virgin Piety' of the church but more often to the individual soul.[155] In his poems, it expresses the affections of 'Virgin Love' and the clear apprehension of 'Virgin-Eys'.[156] It is the pure faculties in their 'virgin' states, such as 'Admiration', 'a yong Virgin Newly Married to Wonderfull Objects' and 'Ambition', 'a pure Virgin destined to wear the Crown of Eternal Glory.'[157] The purity of 'Virgin Youth' is that of unadulterated origins.[158] 'The World' declares:

---

into Heaven' to 'This Day Thou didst Transport *my* Body into Heaven (Featley, 'Prayer for Ascension Day', 466; Traherne, *Church's Year-Book*, 106 [italics added]).

[152] See Traherne, *Christian Ethicks*, 145; cf. Milton, *Paradise Lost*, IV.506; see James Grantham Turner, *One Flesh: Paradisal Marriage and Sexual Relations in the Age of Milton* (Oxford: Clarendon, 1987), 232–65.

[153] Irenaeus of Lyons, *Against the Heresies*, III.18.vii; see Benjamin H. Dunning, 'Virgin Earth, Virgin Birth: Creation, Sexual Difference, and Recapitulation in Irenaeus of Lyons', *JR* 89/1 (2009), 57–88; on virginity as recapitulation of innocent origins, see Matthew Craig Steenberg, 'The Role of Mary as Co-recapitulator in St Irenaeus of Lyons', *VC* 58 (2004), 117–37; see Donne, 'A Funeral Elegy', 75.

[154] Vaughan, 'The Search', *Silex Scintillans*, 18:70; id., 'Regeneration', *Silex Scintillans*, 8:29.

[155] On the church as virgin child, see Traherne, *Church's Year-Book*, 45; id., 'Images', *Commonplace Book*, 55v 1:31–4, citing Jackson, *A Treatise containing the Originall of Unbeliefe*, 301.

[156] Traherne, 'The Designe' ('The Choice'), *Dobell Folio*, 37; id., 'Christendom', *Poems of Felicity*, 126; see also id., 'An Infant-Ey', *Poems of Felicity*, 96.

[157] Traherne, 'Admiration', *Commentaries of Heaven, Part 1*, 238; id., 'Ambition', *Commentaries of Heaven, Part 2*, 34.

[158] Traherne, 'Nature', *Dobell Folio*, 31.

188   *Boundless Innocence in Thomas Traherne's Poetic Theology*

> My virgin-thoughts in Childhood were
> Full of Content,
> And innocent,
> Without disturbance, free and clear.[159]

Virginity thus expresses innocent faculties through the associations of primitive purity, their 'Native Truth, and Virgin-Purity ... [and] uncorrupt Simplicity'.[160]

Virginity is not only a symbol of purity but also of anticipation and desire. Traherne's 'virgin Infant Flame' is desire for God.[161] Christ's long engagement to the church, described in 'Affinity', associates virginity with the anticipation, desire and peril of pre-conjugal affection. Without passionate desire, the virgin-bride would not sustain faithful purity until the consummation of eternal bliss.[162] This aspect of virginity is central to the 'Amazon Queen': the extended metaphor of the final section of *Kingdom of God*, who also appears in *Commentaries of Heaven*.[163] She is a virgin-bride who signifies spiritual love for God, but this conceit is more reminiscent of erotic medieval mysticism informed by courtly love traditions and the Song of Songs than the impassive Platonic love of Origenist allegory.[164] In *Kingdom of God*, God is the king who woos not the church in general but each individual, as 'the peculiar Bride, not of Heaven, But of GOD'.[165] 'Allurement' in *Commentaries of Heaven* reverses this allegory so that God is the 'Proud, but tamd, enflamd, heart-wounded Queen / Subdud by Love.'[166] The reciprocal passion of pure desire is thus central to the virgin-emblem.

---

[159]   Traherne, 'The World', *Poems of Felicity*, 109.

[160]   Traherne, 'Adam's Fall', *Poems of Felicity*, 107. Virginity had Mariological as well as protological connotations, as in: 'Make me a *pure* and a chast soule, that as thy *Sonne* was borne of a Virgins wombe, and lay *buried* in a Virgin tombe: so he may abide in my Virgin and undefiled soule' (Featley, 'The Prayer for Saturday Evening', in *Ancilla Pietatis*, 375–6).

[161]   Traherne, 'Desire', *Dobell Folio*, 71.

[162]   Traherne, 'Affinity', *Commentaries of Heaven, Part 1*, 301–3; see Frances Rous, *The Mysticall Marriage, Experimentall Discoveries of the Heavenly Marriage betweene a Soule and her Saviour* (London: William Jones, 1631), 14.

[163]   Maule coined this title in 'Five New Traherne Works'.

[164]   See Ann W. Astell, *The Song of Songs in the Middle Ages* (London: Cornell University Press, 1990), 6–10; Noam Flinker, *The Song of Songs in English Renaissance Literature: Kisses of Their Mouths* (Cambridge: D.S. Brewer, 2000), 20–28; Denys Turner, *Eros and Allegory: Medieval Exegesis of the Song of Songs* (Kalamazoo, Mass.: Cistercian Publications, 1995); Amy Hollywood, *The Soul as Virgin Wife: Mechthild of Magdeburg, Marguerite Porete, and Meister Eckhart* (London: University of Notre Dame Press, 1995).

[165]   Traherne, *Kingdom of God*, 392–3.

[166]   Traherne, 'Allurement', *Commentaries of Heaven, Part 1*, 369.

The Amazon Queen is a virgin but is not a model of mildness or feminine passivity.[167] In *Kingdom of God*, this soul-bride is first described as the feminine partner, 'more weak, and Tender, and delicat', adopting receptive roles of enjoyment, inheritance, dependence on God and subordinate rule under God.[168] However, half way through, the doctrine of free will forms a pivot on which these characteristics are reversed, to establish the queen's strength and glory: 'but She may forbear to Lov him, neither befits it the Estate of a Queen to be Compeld'. The virgin state is instituted for the exercise of free will, to accept or reject love, but is also intended for the experience of desire: 'that She might Experience all the Approaches of So Beautifull a Suitor'. Trial as a period of anticipation before nuptial consummation expresses the soul's danger but also its possibility of glory through hazard: 'The Virgin is an Amazon, a Beautifull Soldier that hath many Enemies to Conquer.'[169] The Amazon Queen is a pure and innocent virgin but resists the privative connotations of chastity. It is a model of the power and glory of the soul's desire for God, which draws it into glory.

'Had Adam continued innocent': Innocence in the Subjunctive Mood

The visions of innocence discussed above all subsist in the subjunctive mood of imagination and hope.[170] They present the interposition of glory into the world of experience and create a sensory vision which draws the reader into the divine. Ricoeur described the imagined myth of innocence as not only 'a state realized "elsewhere" and "formerly"' but also 'an indispensable mode of the investigation of the possible'.[171] For him, theological expressions of innocence are inherently subjunctive. Subjunctive innocence is seen in Traherne's imagination of humanity's state had Adam not fallen. In *Select Meditations*, he explains that, because of sin, it is natural that 'we should see only the Future Emergencies

---

[167]   Traherne, *Kingdom of God*, 502–3.

[168]   Cf. Bernard of Clairvaux, *The Song of Songs*, sermon 31.

[169]   Traherne, *Kingdom of God*, 503.

[170]   On Traherne and imagination, see Ronald W. Hepburn, 'Thomas Traherne: The Nature and Dignity of Imagination', *Cambridge Journal* 6 (1953), 725–34.

[171]   Paul Ricoeur, *Fallible Man*, trans. Charles A. Kelbley (revd edn, New York: Fordham University Press, 1986), 144–5; on the theological subjunctive mood, see David Ford, 'Dante as Inspiration for Twenty-First-Century Theology', in Vittorio Montemaggi and Matthew Treherne (eds), *Dante's Commedia: Theology as Poetry* (Notre Dame, Ind.: Notre Dame University Press, 2010), 322.

190   *Boundless Innocence in Thomas Traherne's Poetic Theology*

of the Ages in Eden, (which would have followed mans Abiding Innocence) in their Possibilitie', and not in actuality.[172]

The possibility of innocence appears in recurring projections of the state of the world 'had Adam continued innocent'. In *Commentaries of Heaven*, subjunctive innocence is the possibility of sincerity: 'had men continued Innocent all had been Friends to Veritie'.[173] In *A Sober View*, the subjunctive laments the loss of blessings and the grace of right reason: 'What an infinit Blessing had Adam been to all Mankind had he stood in Innocency!' and, following Romans 3, 'had all men been Innocent No man should have been born an Ideot'. The subjunctive also, however, highlights the grace of humanity's present estate: 'had [Man] continued Innocent, and been saved being pure by his own Care, might have had some thing to glory of' but being saved by grace owes glory to God.[174]

These subjunctive conjectures are not mere scholastic hypotheses but address important questions of human identity. The subjunctive of innocence is the imagination of humanity as it might progress from innocence to grace to glory without sin. *Commentaries of Heaven* describes the maturation of innocent 'Ability' thus: 'In the Estate of Glory, had it continued Innocent, it had by reason of Experience and frequent Exercise, been without interruption confirmed as it were in perfect Manhood'.[175] Ultimately, this is a vision of God's kingdom, as *Commentaries of Heaven* declares: 'What a Wonderfull Benefit had Adam been to Mankind had he stood. All Kingdoms by his Act being filled with Innocence Peace and Glory.'[176] When expressed in the present tense, these imaginations take on a hortatory tone which judges current existence against the heavenly standard of eternity, as in *A Sober View*'s citation of Deuteronomy 32.29: 'O that they were Wise that they understood this, that they would consider their later End!'[177]

Subjunctive innocence plays on the literary themes of light and shadow, reality and the dream. The poem 'Dreams' asserts the reality of childlike thoughts while, in a more conventional turn, 'Awake' describes dreaming as the 'Lethargie Sleep and Darkness' of spiritual death.[178] Traherne's defence

---

[172]   Traherne, *Select Meditations*, III 52.

[173]   Traherne, 'Acknowledgement', *Commentaries of Heaven, Part 1*, 157.

[174]   Traherne, *A Sober View*, 85, 86, 161

[175]   Traherne, 'Human Abilitie', *Commentaries of Heaven, Part 1*, 28.

[176]   Traherne, 'Adam', *Commentaries of Heaven, Part 1*, 222; see also id., *Kingdom of God*, 290.

[177]   Traherne, *A Sober View*, 70; see also 'where all virtue and Innocency is there is little need of Government and Subjection' (id., 'Angell', *Commentaries of Heaven, Part 2*, 62).

[178]   Traherne, 'Dreams', *Poems of Felicity*, 180; id., 'Awake', *Commentaries of Heaven, Part 2*, 433.

of the reality of the spiritual, internal and divine over the material, external and fallen is a Platonic defence of thoughts over things or the reality of divine ideas, wherein to be truly awake is to 'measure Spiritual Things with Spiritual'.[179] Similarly, for Jackson, the subjunctive of creaturely goodness in its 'Logical Possibility' is not defined according to the subjective goodness of current existence but in 'consonancy to infinite and eternal goodness'.[180] Traherne is sympathetic to the rabbinic notion of material things as the type (or sacrament) of spiritual things, so that 'Bodies are but Shadows of Souls, and things Visible of him that is invisible'.[181] The divine subjunctive reality of innocence is not therefore the 'dreaming innocence' of immature utopianism.[182] Instead, the actuality of the subjunctive is called into being by its invocation. It is a potentiality that is as real as actuality and is closer to the divine mind than quotidian existence.

The subjunctive of post-lapsarian innocence is a feature of Traherne's hopeful theology, defined as eschatologically oriented rather than simply reliant upon psychological optimism. Hope is found in recurrent references to Ephesians 3.20, which praises 'him who is able to do far more abundantly than all that we ask or think'. Although the KJV translates Ephesians 3.20 as 'exceeding abundantly', the phrase 'far more' occurs frequently throughout Traherne's works as a sign of the infinity of hope.[183] It refers to the 'more excellent' things of God, spirit and human nature and the 'far more' wonderful things that are possible for the innocent, wise, holy and righteous person.[184] Traherne's explicit allusions to Ephesians 3.20 intimate the infinite blessings yet to be revealed, as they praise God's revelation of the kingdom of God, God's exaltation of

---

[179] Traherne, 'Awake', *Commentaries of Heaven, Part 2*, 434; see Plato, *Timaeus*, 52c, trans. Donald J. Zeyl, in *Complete Works*.

[180] Jackson, 'Of the Primæval Estate of the First Man', 3178.

[181] Traherne, 'Assimilation', *Commentaries of Heaven, Part 2*, 260; see id., *Kingdom of God*, 262; Jackson, *A Treatise of the Divine Essence and Attributes*, 83.

[182] See Peter Slater, 'Tillich on the Fall and the Temptation of Goodness', *JR* 65/2 (1985), 196–207; Paul Tillich, *Systematic Theology* (London: James Nisbet, 1957), vol. 2, 38–41.

[183] Cf. Fynn Fordham's interpretation of Traherne's editing style as evidence of the *epektasis* of the search for perfection ('Motions of Writing in the *Commentaries*: the "Volatilitie" of "Atoms" and "Aetyms"', in Blevins [ed.], *Re-Reading Thomas Traherne*, 115–34); on Traherne's expansive joy, see Jean-Louis Chrétien, *La Joie spacieuse: Essai sur la dilatation* (Paris: Éditions de Minuit, 2007), 173–205.

[184] See e.g. Traherne, *Inducements to Retirednes*, 13 (line 327), 32 (lines 1105–6); *A Sober View*, 75 (line 176), 106 (line 159), 147 (line 136), 148 (line 40), 158 (line 50–51); *Seeds*, 241 (line 394), 244 (lines 528–9); id., *Kingdom*, 284 (line 129), 266 (line 8), 411 (line 88), 442 (line 147).

humanity, the height of God's love, knowledge of God's goodness and God's redemptive grace.[185] As a conclusion to prayers, they draw the reader into infinitely extended contemplation of God's immeasurable abundance and power.[186] They express the infinite blessings of humanity's estate, praising the trinity for making humanity the end of all things and praising God for giving Adam all things.[187] In *Christian Ethicks*, this verse defends hope itself, asserting the certain hope of the consummation of infinite desire, as promised by God: 'HOPE is for its Extent and Dimensions vast and wonderful. All ... that is concievable in Time or Eternity, may be hoped, for ... all that Fancy can imagine Possible and Delightful; Nay *more then we are able to ask or think*.'[188]

Traherne's subjunctive emblems present an eschatological vision of innocence. They express a hopeful affection for perfection that, in the words of *Select Meditations*, will 'breath after Eternal Life in another place, where all the purity of every Excellence shall Eternaly remain'.[189] In More's *Divine Dialogues*, Philotheus the 'sincere Lover of God' similarly describes the hope of innocence as a faith in eternal bliss which is the source of present happiness: 'The firm belief of this in an innocent Soul is so high a prelibation of those eternal Joys, that it equalizes such an one's Happiness.'[190] This disposition also echoes Augustine's Pauline sentiment that, although we are saved, 'Nevertheless we still act on faith, not yet by sight, "For by hope we have been saved"'.[191] In subjunctive innocence the translucence of imagination, absent in the realm of possibility, is joined by the present virtue of hope, whose infinite 'far more' draws the soul ever further into a joyful vision of glory.

---

[185] Traherne, *Kingdom of God*, 258, 283, 495; id., 'Angell', *Commentaries of Heaven, Part 2*, 74; id., 'Article', *Commentaries of Heaven, Part 2*, 230.

[186] Traherne, 'Abundance', *Commentaries of Heaven, Part 2*, 63; id., 'Almighty', *Commentaries of Heaven, Part 2*, 383.

[187] Traherne, *Centuries of Meditations*, I 69, II 52.

[188] Traherne, *Christian Ethicks*, 122.

[189] Traherne, *Select Meditations*, II 97.

[190] More, *Divine Dialogues*, 2–3.

[191] Augustine, *Confessions*, XIII.13.

Chapter 7

'Were all men Wise And Innocent …':
Innocence in the Optative Mood

Wisdom and Innocence

The previous chapters have discussed the boundlessness of Traherne's innocence, aspects of which permeate each estate of the soul from before creation to the final end in glory. Not a narrow ideal of perfection based only on paradisal archetypes, innocence in Traherne's works is also a quality of the regenerate Christian life which is an object of celebration and lament, duty and desire, memory and imagination. Boundless innocence is also evident in the desire embodied in the optative phrase 'Were all Men Innocent'.[1] This expresses the impulse behind the Nyssan progress of *epektasis* or excess, leading further into God.

Wisdom and Innocence in Seventeenth-Century Devotion

Christ's injunction in Matthew 10.16 to be as wise as serpents and innocent as doves and Paul's exhortation in Romans 16.19 to be wise to the good and simple concerning evil, have been important texts for interpretations of Christian innocence and the Christian life in general. The Matthew passage in particular has been significant in discussions of an innocent Christian response to persecution. Chrysostom interpreted serpentine wisdom as that of saints under persecution who, snakelike, relinquish their body to save their head (their soul), and whose dovelike harmlessness refuses to revenge wrongs.[2] The 'innocence' of both passages is the Greek ἀκέραιος. Together they provide a rich but also potentially contradictory source for reflection on Christian innocence. For

---

[1]   David Ford associates Traherne particularly with the optative mood (*Self and Salvation: Being Transformed* [Cambridge: Cambridge University Press, 2007], 275–80).

[2]   Chrysostom, *Homilies on the Gospel of Saint Matthew*, XXXIII.3 (Matt. 10.16); for a seventeenth-century equivalent, see: '[in persecution] ye must most strictly preserve your innocence, use no forcible, or unlawful means to preserve your selves' (Henry Hammond, *A Paraphrase, and Annotations Upon all the Books of the New Testament* [London, 1653], 56 [Matt. 10.16])

194 *Boundless Innocence in Thomas Traherne's Poetic Theology*

example, Gregory the Great's *Morals on the Book of Job* spoke of Job's innocence as wise to goodness and ignorant respecting evil, following the Romans passage.[3] By contrast, Gregory of Nazianzus drew on both Matthew and Romans when he wrote that his father united 'the wisdom of the serpent, in regard to evil, with the harmlessness of the dove, in regard to good, neither allowing the wisdom to degenerate into knavery, nor the simplicity into silliness'.[4] Is the Christian character to know good and be ignorant of evil, or are they wise to evil but innocent in their harmlessness? These contradictory statements reflect the complex history of interpretation of Christian innocence built on New Testament interpretation.

In seventeenth-century devotion, the phrase 'wise and innocent' had taken on a rich variety of connotations. For Taylor, it was axiomatic for Christian life: to behave 'as becomes persons wise and innocent' was to be 'like Christians'.[5] The phrase was so deeply embedded as to be used as a generic term for a good person, as in Walter Charleton's translation of Epicurus: 'a Wise and Innocent person may be wounded by his malicious Enemies'.[6] The various scriptural translations available at the time provided sources for a range of interpretations. The Tyndale, Coverdale and Geneva versions all translated ἀκέραιοι from Matthew 10.16 as 'innocent'. The KJV opted for comprehensiveness over clarity, following the Bishops' Bible and the Greek *textus receptus* to translate it as 'harmless', with the Wycliffite and Vulgate 'simple' as a marginal alternative. The reference to ἀκέραιος in Romans 16.19 was translated as 'simple' rather than 'innocent' in all major post-Reformation English translations except that of Tyndale and the Great Bible of 1540. These translations of ἀκέραιος as 'harmlessness' and 'simplicity' may have encouraged the association of innocence with the moral qualities discussed in Chapters 5 and 6.

Despite the important influence of the KJV, which translated Matthew 10.16 as 'wise and harmless', seventeenth-century devotional literature continued to use the phrase 'wise and innocent' in continuity with Tyndale or Geneva.[7] The oxymoronic implications of the phrase 'wise and innocent' as opposed to 'wise

---

[3] Gregory the Great, *Morals on the Book of Job*, I.I.1.ii.

[4] Gregory of Nazianzus, 'On the Death of his Father', *Select Orations*, XVIII 27.

[5] Jeremy Taylor, *Antiquitates Christianae, or, The History of the Life and Death of the Holy Jesus* (London, 1675), 354.

[6] Epicurus, *Morals*, trans. Walter Charleton (London: W. Wilson, 1656), 129.

[7] Clement Cotton translates Matt. 10.16 as 'innocent' in *The Christians Concordance Containing the most Materiall Words in the New Testament* (London, 1622), s.v. 'Innocent', but his *Complete Concordance of the Bible of the Last Translation by Helpe Whereof any Passage of Holy Scripture may bee Readily Turned Unto* (London, 1631) uses the 'last translation' or KJV; for uses of the phrase 'wise and innocent', despite quoting the KJV of Matt. 10.16, see William

'and harmless' may have appealed to the early modern love of paradox.[8] It was used in a variety of senses but generally expressed a unification of the opposing emblems of the dove and serpent, of the opposite qualities of meekness, innocence or harmlessness with intelligence, discretion or policy. Bacon, for example, credited Machiavelli with reporting the truth of human evil: 'For it is not possible to join serpentine wisdom with the columbine innocency, except men know exactly all the conditions of the serpent. ... For without this, virtue lieth open and unfenced.'[9]

The paradoxical combination of wisdom and innocence sometimes indicated the merits of a moderate middle way. Aristotle conceived virtue as the golden mean or intermediary between excess and deficiency.[10] Based on this principle, 'wise and innocent' was often interpreted as a prudent *via media* between the excesses of wisdom and innocence, a *prudente simplicitate*, as George Wither put it: 'Man's life, no Temper, more doth blesse / Then Simple-prudent-harmelessenesse.'[11] For Thomas Watson, who described the dove as both 'innocent' and 'harmless', this meant the 'Qualification' of one virtue by the other or 'a Wisdom mixt with Innocency'.[12] Similarly, for Taylor, wisdom and innocence combined was 'a wary and cautious innocence, a harmless prudence and provision'.[13] Such a mixed virtue is alien to the virtuous excess of pure prudence outlined in Traherne's *Christian Ethicks*.[14] For him, to be

---

Denny, *Pelecanicidium or the Christian Adviser against Self-Murder* (London, 1653), 215; Thomas Powell, *A Sanctuary for the Tempted* (London, 1679), sermon 4, 409–10.

[8] On the seventeenth-century predilection for discourses of 'Contrariety' and 'Inversion', see Stewart Clark, *Thinking with Demons: the Idea of Witchcraft in Early Modern Europe* (Oxford: Oxford University Press, 1999), 43–79.

[9] Bacon, *The Advancement of Learning*, II.21.ix.

[10] Aristotle, *Nicomachean Ethics*, 1106a (II 6), summarised in Eustachius a Sancto Paulo, *Ethica, sive, Summa Moralis Discipline* (Cambridge, 1654), 105–6; cited in Traherne, *Early Notebook*, 16; see id., *Christian Ethicks*, 172 (lines 15–16n, 354).

[11] Wither, *A Collection of Emblemes*, 151; see also Richard Baxter, *Now or Never the Holy, Serious, Diligent Believer Justified, Encouraged, Excited and Directed* (London, 1662), 22; Calvin, *Commentaries*, Matthew 10.16.

[12] Thomas Watson, *A Body of Practical Divinity* (London: Thomas Parkurst, 1692), 966.

[13] Taylor, 'Of Christian Simplicity', in *The Whole Works*, 166.

[14] On various early modern interpretations of excess, see Joshua Scodel, *Excess and the Mean in Early Modern English Literature* (Princeton, NJ: Princeton University Press, 2002). In his discussion of Bacon, Scodel uses Traherne as an example of the scholastic principle that 'presumption' and 'despair' of salvation are the extremes of which hope is the golden mean (ibid. 66, 309 n. 67). In fact Traherne is dissatisfied with this circumscribed binary framework which does not account for the various 'Kinds and Degrees of Hope' (*Christian*

196   *Boundless Innocence in Thomas Traherne's Poetic Theology*

'Wise as Serpents, Innocent as Doves', signifies not a middle way but the fullness of virtue, based on an interpretation of prudence as the ability 'to joyn many Vertues together'.[15]

Traherne's Wisdom and Innocence

For Traherne, the conjunction of wisdom and innocence is neither paradoxical nor oxymoronic, but a creative amalgamation of complementary properties. This interpretation was found elsewhere in contemporary devotion. Birchley, for example, described the descent of the Holy Spirit on the disciples as 'Mingling thus together into one blest compound those cheif ingredients of excellent vertue ... Innocence to adorn the light of knowledg; and knowledg to direct the simplicity of innocence'.[16] Throughout Traherne's works, wisdom is accompanied not only by innocence but also appears in equivalent pairings with holiness, happiness, righteousness, goodness, glory, grace, love and justice.[17] Based on this one cannot automatically assume that wisdom and innocence should be opposites, just as wisdom is not the opposite of holiness, happiness or righteousness.

The appeal to wisdom and innocence expresses a yearning for the paradise of ease found in innocence and glory, which is now achieved through effort. In *Christian Ethicks* this desire is expressed thus:

> Were all men Wise, Divine, and Innocent
>
> .   .   .   .   .
>
> 'Twere easie then to live
> In all Delight and Glory, full of Love,
> Blest as the Angels are above.[18]

This triune relation of wisdom, divinity and innocence supersedes the binary dialectic between wisdom and innocence. The quality of divinity not only

---

Ethicks, 122–3). Scodel cites Traherne more accurately as an example of the exhortation to excessive or infinite love of God (*Excess and the Mean in Early Modern English Literature*, 152, 325 n. 24).

   [15]   Traherne, *Christian Ethicks*, 157.

   [16]   Birchley, *Devotions in the Ancient Way of Offices*, 392.

   [17]   Traherne, *Kingdom*, 287 (line 28); *Sober View*, 146 (lines 93–4); 'Acceptance', *Commentaries*, 79 (lines 104–5); 'Appearance', *Commentaries*, 140 (line 124); *Select Meditations*, I.92; *Yearbook*, 72 (lines 2–3), 49 (lines 16–17); *Ethicks*, 158, 201; *Inducements*, 12 (line 300); *Ceremonial Law*, 229.

   [18]   Traherne, *Christian Ethicks*, 196.

'Were all men Wise And Innocent ...' 197

disrupts the dualistic juxtaposition but also provides a connecting line between wisdom and innocence that draws them into corresponding aspects of holiness. A similar device is employed in the poem 'Eden', which begins:

> A Learned and a Happy Ignorance
> Divided me,
> From all the Vanitie
>
> .   .   .   .
>
> The madness and the Miserie
> Of Men.[19]

Traherne here adapts the commonplace phrase, 'learned ignorance', from Nicholas of Cusa's treatise of that name.[20] Through it, he unites the apparent opposites of education and ignorance through felicity, just as in *Christian Ethicks*, wisdom and innocence are joined through spirit. Wisdom and innocence as divergent, but not contradictory, aspects of human experience are united through the themes of love and felicity, which draw them into a vision of glory.

In *Inducements to Retirednes*, wisdom and innocence are complementary properties of Christian life in misery–grace. They are the subject of two related sections on the benefits of retirement. 'Were all men wise', then retirement would be attractive because people would 'know the Glory which might there be Enjoyed'. 'Were all men innocent', the retired life would be easier to pursue because temptations would be easier to resist: 'Exposures would be far more safe and Happy then they are. there would be less in them either of Danger or Temptation.'[21] This treatise does not seek a mean between wisdom and innocence but both in their wholeness.

The optative of yearning lament in the phrase 'Were all men Wise and Innocent' expresses the pursuit of an innocent life in spite of evil. In *Centuries of Meditations*, Traherne's wise man 'always thought, that to be Happy in the midst of a Generation of Vipers was becom his Duty'. He continues, 'Were all men Wise and Innocent, it were easy to be Happy. for no man would injure and molest another'.[22] Here, wisdom combined with innocence is a harmlessness that leads to felicity. This decisive phrase unites the estates in the pursuit of innocence. It refers to the easiness of innocency, the felicity of glory and the harmlessness of misery–grace. It laments innocence's loss, desires regeneration

---

[19]   Traherne, 'Eden', *Dobell Folio*, 7.
[20]   Nicholas of Cusa, *On Learned Ignorance*.
[21]   Traherne, *Inducements to Retirednes*, 10, 13.
[22]   Traherne, *Centuries of Meditations*, IV 20.

198   *Boundless Innocence in Thomas Traherne's Poetic Theology*

and sees it as a promise for the soul in glory. It thereby intimates the harmony of innocence across the estates.

The combination of wisdom and innocence is the pursuit of the wise man or the poet. For Sterry, it was a sign of self-knowledge: 'the *Innocency* and *Wisdome* which maketh them *blessed*, who aspire to it' was the recognition of one's failings and the candour to admit them.[23] For Traherne, knowledge of humanity's humility and glory instigates a desire for the perfection of the image of God. The wise, good and holy man knows his soul enough to seek its glory and to pursue divine innocence: to bring 'His Heart to that Estate, that he might be / As Spotless Even as the Deitie.'[24] The phrase, 'were all men wise and innocent' thus encapsulates the place of innocence in the Christian life: an aspect of holiness allied to wisdom, the glory of the individual and an object of both lament and desire.

The Harmony of Innocence

Traherne's poetic theology of innocence is not a straightforward progression from the estate of innocence through misery and grace to glory. Nor is it the linear spiral of Ricoeur's hermeneutics of naïveté. Rather, this study has demonstrated how innocence is a seed of grace and glory which permeates Traherne's 'Pomgranat' world.[25] It appears within, crosses borders between and transcends each estate of the soul, as all things are united in the light of eternity.

The various aspects of innocence have been seen in the different tenses, genres and moods of Traherne's poetic theology. These form part of an affective poetics which draws the reader into loving good and abhoring evil. Traherne celebrates innocence through the anamnesis of origins. This is not an absolute but a creaturely perfection hinted at through the interplay of perfect past and imperfect past tenses. The loss of innocence is lamented through the negative tense of 'no man is innocent', which also evokes the apostolic testimony that points to grace and the possibility of innocence restored. The kenotic plot of the drama of living innocently in a sinful and suffering world is an object of admiration which draws the reader into praise. The imperative and intentional moods of moral theology exhort the reader to both protect and pursue innocence. The experience of the sacramental combined with the lyrical subjunctive of

---

[23]   Sterry, 'To the Reader', *A Discourse of the Freedom of the Will*, xxviii–xxix.

[24]   Traherne, *Kingdom of God*, 404.

[25]   Traherne, *Centuries of Meditations*, II 96.

imagination creates a sensory vision of innocence which is a source of hope. The optative of yearning combines wonder, lament, intention and hope in its desire for innocence. Together, these distinct tones form a multi-layered harmony of innocence, akin to the compound comprehensiveness of the Renaissance epic.

Traherne's various aspects of innocence may not be completely reconcilable. Tenses and persons can be jumbled and confused, doctrine and experience may appear to conflict with one another, various philosophical schools and metaphysical frameworks are juxtaposed with little thought for their contradictions. This combination of voices reflects the partial vision of misery–grace. The wise man's ideal of Edenic paradise in *Centuries of Meditations* manifests the 'Principles of Upright Nature', but these are seen in misery as 'Muddied and Blended and Confounded'. Only the angelic eye can 'see the Intire Piece'.[26] Traherne's contrapuntal representation of innocence exposes the composite ambiguity of misery–grace, expressed in disparate voices on the stage of the divine drama.

Innocence remains an elusive concept in Traherne's works. This is evident in the interplay of its positive and privative qualities, of light and shade, reality and the dream; in the absent presence of memory and imagination; in its negation through guilt and hypocrisy; in the ephemeral affections of will, love, hope and desire. As it straddles the estates, innocence sits uncomfortably between the vision of pure spirit and the experience of physical existence. However, like the human *hymanaeus*, it also mediates between the spiritual and material worlds, drawing them together.

Innocence also remains a potent image of human perfection. The kenotic implications of its privative semantics are the creative void out of which springs a world of bliss. This infinite ascent further into excess gives innocence its optative nature. More than a mere sin-less or harm-less negation of evil, innocence is an aspect of the pursuit of righteousness. More than merely an enclosed wholeness, it is the path of integrity and the white hands which impart a radiance to upright action. More than mere avoidance of blame, it is an unblameable status before God. More than following the law, it reflects the volatility of life swayed by the motion of love. It is not a perfection of nature alone but of creation and grace, subsisting in relationship to God.

In misery–grace, innocence is active in conflict with guilt and sin. Its apparently fragile virtues are bulwarks against the trials of the world: patience against affliction, humility against self-sufficiency, repentance against guilt, meekness against persecution. They manifest innocence's protective power not

---

[26] Ibid. IV 54.

as the walled garden of ease but the diamond shield which overpowers the enemy with brilliance. The centre of this activity is the self-love which is the foundation of the sacrificial impulse and the divine lodestone that is the gravitational centre of all things.[27] This is the divine–human innocence exemplified by Christ the 'Prince of Peace and Innocence', no nostalgic retreat into the womb but a mature spiritual innocence integral to the life of faith.[28]

Traherne's theology of innocence is poetic, in Sidney's sense of a medium 'full of virtue-breeding delightfulness'.[29] The various tenses, moods and genres of innocence all tend towards this goal. His poetics of innocence fuses beauty and joy in an attempt to uncover a vision of the soul's perfection and nurture the human vocation to peace and purity, which is 'a Deeper Thing then is commonly apprehended'.[30]

Boundless Innocence and Modern Theology

Traherne has been discussed against the background of issues and trends in modern theology, some of which illuminate, others obscure, innocence's history of interpretation. Correspondingly, this study of seventeenth-century theology raises questions about innocence in modern theology. This final section indulges in a few tentative suggestions on this subject.

The Introduction presented Kelsey's 'what', 'how' and 'who' questions as a way of categorising innocence's function in theological anthropology. As described by Henderson and Kelsey, 'classic' models of innocence as absolute perfection only answer the 'what' question of human essence as originally created. Innocence in Traherne's theological anthropology is also key to discussions of 'what' humanity has fallen to, 'who' humanity is in relation to God and in response to sin and suffering, 'how' humanity is to behave in right relation to self, world and God, and 'who' humanity is to be in God's glorious image. If innocence in Traherne's theological anthropology is not an aspect of perfectionism or a source of shallow optimism but a key category for human existence, then perhaps it may also have wider applications for modern theological anthropology.

---

[27] See ibid. I 56–7, 59; J.J. Balakier, 'A Pre-Newtonian Gravitational Trope in Thomas Traherne's *"Centuries of Meditations"'*, *English Language Notes* 39/1 (2001), 32–41.

[28] Birchley, *Devotions in the Ancient Way of Offices*, 230.

[29] Sidney, *An Apology for Poetry*, 116.

[30] Traherne, *Centuries of Meditations*, III 5.

Henderson and Kelsey's critiques of Edenic innocence as a model of human perfection emerge out of the loss of the historical Eden in modern thought.[31] Hence, Kelsey believes that modern theological anthropology should be 'formulated in ways logically independent of the historicity of Adam, Eve and the fall'.[32] Having rejected Eden, Kelsey has sought a Wisdom-centred theological anthropology in Job, whose finite perfection better reflects humanity's existential quotidian than Adam's innocence.[33] Standing on the cusp of modernity, Traherne's creaturely perfection evokes an internal Edenic paradise that nevertheless remains tied to material existence. He moves well beyond the *imitatio Adami* to various exemplary characters of innocence, including Job, David, the lamb, the child, the Celestial Stranger and the Amazon Queen, which culminate in Christ the epitome of human and divine innocence. If innocence is not exemplified by Adam alone then, one might suggest, the displacement of Eden as a primary model of human perfection need not necessarily entail the neglect of innocence.

The dialectical progress of Ricoeur's hermeneutics of naïveté – from first naïveté through deconstruction to a second naïveté in and through criticism – echoes broader movements of enchantment, disenchanmtent and re-enchantment in modern theology.[34] In studies of Romantic literature, deconstructionist critiques of the ideal child are increasingly supplemented by nuanced counter-narratives of Romantic innocence as a mature and complex theme.[35] This reassessment of Traherne's boundless innocence may be considered a similar move towards re-enchantment but one of expansion as well as recapitulation, as it moves beyond the child to explore other aspects of innocence. As a potential source for critical re-enchantment, Traherne's is not an innocence of bare nature but of created nature infused by grace. It is not a fixed ideal of perfection, but is present in quotidian existence through the translucence of poetic language. It is not a purely regressive nostalgia or an abstract utopianism, but a theology built upon the *anamnesis* of remembrance and the *epektasis* of hope.

---

[31]   On the development of interpretation, see Gregory Allen Robbins (ed.), *Genesis 1–3 in the History of Exegesis: Intrigue in the Garden* (New York: Edwin Mellen, 1988); for a response to the decline of Eden, see Raymund Schwager, *Banished from Eden: Original Sin and Evolutionary Theory in the Drama of Salvation*, trans. James Williams (London: Gracewing, 2006).

[32]   Kelsey, *Eccentric Existence*, 41.

[33]   Ibid. 176–89, 242–308, 321–8.

[34]   See e.g. Patrick Sherry, 'Disenchantment, Reenchantment, and Enchantment', *MT* 25/3 (2009), 369–86; Charles Taylor, 'Disenchantment–Reenchantment', in *Dilemmas and Contradictions: Selected Essays* (Cambridge, Mass.: Harvard University Press, 2011), 287–303.

[35]   See e.g. Reena Sastri, *James Merrill: Knowing Innocence* (London: Routledge, 2007).

References

Works of Thomas Traherne

Manuscripts

Beinecke Rare Book and Manuscript Library, Yale University, New Haven, Connecticut
        James Marshall and Marie-Louise Osborn Collection, Osborn b308: 'Select Meditations', 'Love' [frag.].
Bodleian Library, Oxford
        MS.Eng.Poet.c.42: 'Dobell Poems', 'Commonplace Book'.
        MS.Eng.th.e.51: 'Church's Year-Book'.
        MS.Lat.misc.f.45: 'Early Notebook'.
        MS.th.e.50: 'Centuries of Meditations'.
British Library, London
        Add.MS.63054: 'Commentaries of Heaven'.
        MS. Burney 126: 'Ficino Notebook'.
        MS. Burney 392: 'Poems of Felicity'.
Folger Shakespeare Library, Washington DC
        MS.V.a.70: 'The Ceremonial Law'.
Lambeth Palace Library, London
        MS.1360: 'Inducements to Retirednes', 'A Sober View of Dr Twisses his Considerations', 'Seeds of Eternity', 'The Kingdom of God'.

Published Works

Centuries, Poems, and Thanksgivings, vol. 1: *Centuries*; vol. 2: *Poems and Thanksgivings*, ed. H.M. Margoliouth (Oxford: Oxford University Press, 1958).

Christian Ethicks, or, Divine Morality Opening the Way to Blessedness (London: printed for Jonathan Edwin, 1675); *Christian Ethicks*, ed. George Robert Guffey and Carol L. Marks (New York: Cornell University Press, 1968).

The Poetical Works of Thomas Traherne, B.D., 1636?–1674: Now First Published from the Original Manuscripts, ed. Bertram Dobell (London, The Editor, 1903; 2nd edn, 1906).

Roman Forgeries, or a True Account of False Records (London: S.&B. Griffin for Jonathan Edwin, 1673).

Select Meditations, ed. Julia Smith (Manchester: Carcanet, 1997).

A Serious and Pathetical Contemplation of the Mercies of GOD, in Several Most Devout and Sublime Thanksgivings for the Same (London: George Hickes, 1699).

The Works of Thomas Traherne, vol. 1: *Inducements to Retirednes, A Sober View of Dr Twisses his Considerations, Seeds of Eternity or the Nature of the Soul, The Kingdom of God*; vol. 2: *Commentaries of Heaven, Part 1: Abhorrence to Alone*; vol. 3: *Commentaries of Heaven, Part 2: Al-Sufficient to Bastard*; vol. 4: *Church's Year-Book, A Serious and Pathetical Contemplation of the Mercies of GOD, [Meditations on the Six Days of the Creation]*; vol. 5: *Centuries of Meditations and Select Meditations*; vol. 6: *Poems from the Dobell Folio, Poems of Felicity, The Ceremonial Law, Poems from the Early Notebook*, ed. Jan Ross (Cambridge: D.S. Brewer, 2005–).

[Attrib.], *Meditations on the Six Days of Creation* (London, 1717).

Secondary Sources

Acosta, Ana M., *Reading Genesis in the Long Eighteenth Century: From Milton to Mary Shelley* (Aldershot: Ashgate, 2006).

Ainsworth, Henry, *Annotations upon the Five Bookes of Moses, the Booke of the Psalms, and the Song of Songs* (London, 1627).

Allchin, A.M., *Participation in God: A Forgotten Strand in Anglican Tradition* (London: Darton, Longman and Todd, 1988).

—— 'Sacrifice of Praise and Thanksgiving', in A.M. Allchin, Anne Ridler and Julia Smith (eds), *Profitable Wonders: Aspects of Thomas Traherne* (Oxford: Amate, 1989), 22–37

—— 'The Whole Assembly Sings: Thomas Traherne', in *The Joy of All Creation* (London: Darton, Longman & Todd, 1984), 78–89.

Allen, D.C., 'Arthur's Diamond Shield in the Faerie Queene', *Journal of English and Germanic Philology* 36 (1937), 234–43.

Allestree, Richard, *The Practice of Christian Graces, or, The Whole Duty of Man* (London, 1658).

Allik, Tiina, 'Narrative Approaches to Human Personhood: Agency, Grace, and Innocent Suffering', *Philosophy and Theology* 1/1 (1987), 305–33.

Allitt, John Stewart, *Thomas Traherne: Il poeta-teologo della meraviglia e della felicità* (Milan: Edizioni Villadiseriane, 2007).

Almond, Philip C., *Adam and Eve in Seventeenth-Century Thought* (Cambridge: Cambridge University Press, 1999).

Ames, Kenneth John, *The Religious Language of Thomas Traherne's* Centuries (New York: Revisionist, 1978).

Ames, William, *The Marrow of Sacred Divinity* (London: Edward Griffin, 1642).

Andrewes, Lancelot, *XCVI Sermons by the Right Honourable and Reverend Father in God, Lancelot Andrewes, Late Lord Bishop of Winchester* (London: George Miller, 1629).

—— *Holy Devotions with Directions to Pray* (5th edn, London, 1663).

Aquinas, Thomas, *The Literal Exposition on Job: A Scriptural Commentary Concerning Providence*, trans. Anthony Damico (Atlanta, Ga.: Scholars, 1989).

—— *Summa Theologica*, trans. Thomas Gilby (Cambridge: Blackfriars, 1964–81).

Ariès, Philippe, *Centuries of Childhood*, trans. Robert Baldick (London: Jonathan Cape, 1962).

Aristotle, *Nicomachean Ethics*, trans. D. Ross (revd edn, Oxford: Clarendon, 1998).

—— *On the Soul*, trans. W.S. Hett, LCL (revd edn, Cambridge, Mass.: Harvard University Press, 1986).

—— *The Poetics*, trans. W. Hamilton Fyfe, LCL (revd edn, Cambridge, Mass.: Harvard University Press, 1982).

Arnold, J.H., 'The Labour of Continence: Masculinity and Clerical Virginity', in Anke Bernau, Ruth Evans and Sarah Salih, *Medieval Virginities* (Cardiff: University of Wales Press, 2003), 102–19.

Astell, Ann W., *The Song of Songs in the Middle Ages* (London: Cornell University Press, 1990).

Augustine, *The City of God against the Pagans*, trans. R.W. Dyson (Cambridge: Cambridge University Press, 1998).

—— *Confessions*, trans. Henry Chadwick (Oxford: Oxford University Press, 1991).

—— *Expositions on the Book of Psalms* (6 vols, Oxford: J.H. Parker, 1847–57).

—— *Letters*, trans. J.G. Cunningham, NPNF[1] 1 (Edinburgh: T.&T. Clark, 1886).

Austin, William, *Devotionis Augustinianae flamma* (London, 1635).

Babington, Gervase, *Certaine Plaine, Briefe, and Comfortable Notes upon Everie Chapter of Genesis* (London: for Thomas Clarke, 1592).

Bacon, Francis, *The Advancement of Learning; and, New Atlantis*, ed. Arthur Johnston (Oxford: Clarendon, 1974 [1605]).

—— *Essays, Civil and Moral*, Harvard Classics 3/1 (New York: P.F. Collier and Son, 1909–14).

Bakhtin, Mikhail, *Problems of Dostoyevsky's Poetics*, trans. R.W. Rotsel (Ann Arbor, Mich.: Ardis, 1973).

Balakier, J.J., 'Felicitous Perceptions as the Organizing Form in Thomas Traherne's Dobell Poems and *Centuries of Meditations*', *Bulletin de la Société d'études Anglo-Américaines des XVIIe et XVIIIe siècles* 26 (1988), 53–68.

—— 'A Pre-Newtonian Gravitational Trope in Thomas Traherne's "Centuries of Meditations"', *English Language Notes* 39/1 (2001), 32–41.

—— 'Thomas Traherne's Dobell Series and the Baconian Model of Experience', *English Studies* 70 (1989), 233–47.

Balthasar, Hans Urs von, 'Jesus as Child and His Praise of the Child', trans. Adrian Walker, *Communio* 22/4 (1995), 625–34.

Barber, Benjamin J., 'Syncretism and Idiosyncrasy: The Notion of Act in Thomas Traherne's Contemplative Practice', *LT* 28/1 (2014), 16–28.

Barrow, Isaac, *The Duty and Reward of Bounty to the Poor* (London, 1671).

Bartlett, Alan, *A Passionate Balance: The Anglican Tradition* (London: Darton, Longman & Todd, 2007).

Bates, Catherine (ed.), *The Cambridge Companion to the Epic* (Cambridge: Cambridge University Press, 2010).

Bath, Michael, *Speaking Pictures: English Emblem Books and Renaissance Culture* (London: Longman, 1993).

Baxter, Richard, *Now or Never the Holy, Serious, Diligent Believer Justified, Encouraged, Excited and Directed* (London, 1662).

Beachcroft, Thomas O., 'Traherne and the Cambridge Platonists', *Dublin Review* 186 (1930), 278–90.

—— 'Traherne and the Doctrine of Felicity', *Criterion* 9 (1930), 291–307.

Beal, Peter, 'Thomas Traherne', *Catalogue of English Literary Manuscripts* <http://www.celm-ms.org.uk/introductions/TraherneThomas.html#> (accessed 1 Oct. 2014).

Bentley Hart, David, 'Impassibility as Transcendence: On the Infinite Innocence of God', in James J. Keating and Thomas Joseph White (eds), *Divine Impassibility and the Mystery of Human Suffering* (Grand Rapids, Mich.: Eerdmans, 2009), 1–26, 299–323.

Bergren, Theodore A., and Alfred Schmoller, *A Latin–Greek Index of the Vulgate New Testament: Based on Alfred Schmoller's Handkonkordanz Zum Griechishen Neuen Testament*, Resources for Biblical Study 26 (Atlanta, Ga.: Scholars Press, 1991).

Bernard of Clairvaux, *The Song of Songs: Selections from the Sermons of S. Bernard*, ed. B. Blaxland (London: Methuen, 1901).

Berryman, Jerome, 'Children and Christian Theology: A New/Old Genre', *Religious Studies Review* 33/2 (2007), 103–11.

Birchley, William, *Devotions in the Ancient Way of Offices* (London, 1668).

Blake, William, *Songs of Innocence and of Experience: Shewing the Two Contrary States of the Human Soul*, ed. Geoffrey Keynes (Oxford: Oxford University Press, 1967).

Blevins, Jacob (ed.), *Re-Reading Thomas Traherne: A Collection of New Critical Essays* (Tempe: Arizona Center for Medieval and Renaissance Studies, 2007).

Boas, George, *The Cult of Childhood* (London: Spring Publications, 1990).

Boesak, Allan Aubrey, *Farewell to Innocence: A Socio-Ethical Study on Black Theology and Black Power* (Maryknoll, NY: Orbis, 1974).

Boehme, Jacob, *Mysterium Magnum, or An Exposition of the First Book of Moses called Genesis* (London: Lodowick Lloyd, 1656).

Boston, Thomas, *Human Nature in its Fourfold State: Of Primitive Integrity, Entire Depravity, Begun Recovery and Consummate Happiness or Misery* (Edinburgh, 1720).

Bottrall, Margaret, *Thomas Traherne and the Bible: A Book from Heaven* (Paris: Group de Recherche 'Litterature et Réligion', Université Paris-Nord, 1988).

—— 'Traherne's Praise of the Creation', *Critical Quarterly* 1/2 (1959), 126–33.

Bouchard, Larry D., *Theater and Integrity: Emptying Selves in Drama, Ethics, and Religion* (Evanston, Ill.: Northwestern University Press, 2011).

—— *Tragic Method and Tragic Theology: Evil in Contemporary Drama and Religious Thought* (University Park: Pennsylvania State University Press, 1989).

Brock, Rita Nakashima, 'Losing Your Innocence but not Your Hope', in Maryanne Stevens (ed.), *Reconstructing the Christ Symbol: Essays in Feminist Christology* (New York: Paulist Press, 1993), 30–53.

Bromiley, Geoffrey W., *Baptism and the Anglican Reformers* (London: Lutterworth, 1953).

Brundt, I., 'Cognitive Development', in S.J. Ulijaszek, F.E. Johnston and M.A. Preece (eds), *The Cambridge Encyclopedia of Human Growth and Development* (Cambridge: Cambridge University Press, 1998), 245–6.

Bruno, Giordano, *On the Infinite Universe and Worlds* (Venice, 1584).

Bugge, John, *Virginitas: An Essay in the History of a Medieval Ideal* (The Hague: Martinus Nijhoff, 1975).

Bullinger, Heinrich, *A Brief and Compendiouse Table, in a Maner of a Concordaunce* (London: S. Mierdman, 1550).

Bunge, Marcia J. (ed.), *The Child in Christian Thought* (Grand Rapids, Mich.: Eerdmans, 2001).

—— 'The Child, Religion, and the Academy: Developing Robust Theological and Religious Understandings of Children and Childhood', *JR* 86/4 (2006), 549–79.

Burckhardt, Jacob, *The Civilization of the Renaissance in Italy* (London: Phaidon, 1990 [1860]).

Burrow, Colin (ed.), *Metaphysical Poetry* (London: Penguin, 2006).

Bush, Douglas, *English Literature in the Earlier Seventeenth Century* (Oxford: Clarendon, 1962).

Brown, Russell M., 'Knowledge and the Fall of Man in Traherne's *Centuries* and Milton's *Paradise Lost*', *Lakehead University Review* 4/1 (1971), 41–9.

Cain, H. Edward, 'Spenser's "Shield of Faith"', *Shakespeare Association Bulletin* 10 (1935), 163–6.

Calvin, John, *The Epistles of Paul the Apostle to the Galatians, Ephesians, Philippians and Colossians*, trans. T.H.L. Parker (Edinburgh: Oliver & Boyd, 1965).

—— *The Epistle of Paul the Apostle to the Hebrews and The First and Second Epistles of St Peter*, trans. William B. Johnston (Edinburgh: Oliver & Boyd, 1963).

—— *A Harmony of the Gospels of Matthew, Mark, Luke*, trans. A.W. Morrison, ed. D.W. Torrance (3 vols, Edinburgh: Saint Andrew Press, 1972).

—— *Institutes of the Christian Religion*, trans. Henry Beveridge (London, 1953).

Cassirer, Ernst, *The Platonic Renaissance in England*, trans. James P. Pettegrove (Edinburgh: Nelson, 1953).

Cefalu, Paul, *English Renaissance Literature and Contemporary Theory: Sublime Objects of Theology* (New York: Palgrave Macmillan, 2007).

—— *Moral Identity in Early Modern English Literature* (Cambridge: Cambridge University Press, 2004).

—— 'Thomistic Metaphysics and Ethics in the Poetry and Prose of Thomas Traherne', *LT* 16/3 (2002), 248–69.

Certaine Sermons or Homilies Appointed to be Read in Churches in the Time of Queen Elizabeth I, ed. Mary Ellen Rickey and Thomas B. Stroup (2 vols, Gainesville, Fla.: Scholars' Facsimiles and Reprints, 1968).

Chambers, A.B., *Transfigured Rites in Seventeenth-Century English Poetry* (Columbia: University of Missouri Press, 1992).

Charleton, James, *Non-Dualism in Eckhart, Julian of Norwich and Traherne* (London: Bloomsbury, 2012).

Charron, Pierre, *Of Wisdom Three Bookes*, trans. Samson Lennard (London: William Hole, 1608).

Chartres, Richard, 'From the Miserable Gulph to a Second Innocence – A Travel Guide', *Church Times* 7727 (21 Apr. 2011).

Chrétien, Jean-Louis, *La Joie spacieuse: Essai sur la dilatation* (Paris: Éditions de Minuit, 2007).

Christ, Ernst, *Studien zu Thomas Traherne* (Tübingen: Eugen Göbel, 1932).

Clark, Ira, *Christ Revealed: The History of the Neotypological Lyric in the English Renaissance* (Gainesville: University Presses of Florida, 1982).

Clark, Stewart, *Thinking with Demons: the Idea of Witchcraft in Early Modern Europe* (Oxford: Oxford University Press, 1999),

Clément, Olivier, *The Roots of Christian Mysticism* (London: New City, 1993).

Clements, Arthur L., *The Mystical Poetry of Thomas Traherne* (Cambridge, Mass.: Harvard University Press, 1969).

Clericuzio, Antonio, *Elements, Principles and Corpuscules: A Study of Atomism and Chemistry in the Seventeenth Century* (London: Kluwer, 2000).

Clines, David J.A., *Job 1–20*, Word Biblical Commentary 27 (Dallas: Thomas Nelson, 1989).

Clucas, Stephen, 'Poetic Atomism in Seventeenth-Century England: Henry More, Thomas Traherne and "Scientific Imagination"', *Renaissance Studies* 5 (1991), 327–40.

Colby, Frances L., 'Thomas Traherne and Henry More', *MLN* 62 (1947), 490–92.

—— 'Thomas Traherne and the Cambridge Platonists: An Analytical Comparison' (PhD thesis: Johns Hopkins University, 1947).

Colie, Rosalie Littell, *Paradoxia Epidemica: The Renaissance Tradition of Paradox* (Princeton, NJ: Princeton University Press, 1966).

—— *The Resources of Kind: Genre-Theory in the Renaissance*, ed. Barbara K. Lewalski (London: University of California Press, 1973).

—— 'Thomas Traherne and the Infinite: The Ethical Compromise', *HLQ* 21/1 (1957), 69–82.

Connolly, Brian W., 'Knowledge and Love: Steps Toward Felicity in Thomas Traherne' (PhD thesis, University of Pittsburgh, 1966).

Cotton, Clement, *The Christians Concordance Containing the most Materiall Words in the New Testament* (London, 1622).

—— *A Complete Concordance of the Bible of the Last Translation by Helpe Whereof any Passage of Holy Scripture may bee Readily Turned Unto* (London, 1631).

Countryman, L. William, *The Poetic Imagination: An Anglican Spiritual Tradition* (London: Darton, Longman & Todd, 2000).

Cox, Gerard Hutchinson, 'Thomas Traherne's *Centuries*, a Platonic Devotion of "Divine Philosophy"', *MP* 69/1 (1971), 10–24.

Cragg, Gerald R. (ed.), *The Cambridge Platonists* (Oxford: Oxford University Press, 1968).

Cudworth, Ralph, *A Sermon Preached before the Honourable House of Commons at Westminster, March 31, 1647* (Cambridge: Roger Daniel, 1647).

—— *The True Intellectual System of the Universe. Wherein all the Reason and Philosophy of Atheism is Confuted and its Impossibility Demonstrated* (London: for Richard Royston, 1678).

Culverwel, Nathaniel, *An Elegant and Learned Discourse of the Light of Nature* (London, 1652).

Cummings, Brian, and Freya Sierhuis (eds), *Passions and Subjectivity in Early Modern Culture* (Farnham: Ashgate, 2013),

Cunningham, Hugh, *The Children of the Poor: Representatives of Childhood since the Seventeenth Century* (Oxford: Blackwell, 1991).

Curtin, Kathleen, 'Jacobean Congregations and Controversies in Thomas Wilson's *Christian Dictionary* (1612)', *Seventeenth Century* 25/2 (2010), 197–214.

Dante Alighieri, *The Divine Comedy*, trans. Allen Mandelbaum (Berkeley: University of California Press, 1980).

Davidson, Anne, 'Innocence Regained: Seventeenth Century Reinterpretations of the Fall of Man' (PhD thesis: Columbia University, 1956).

Davis, Robert A., 'Brilliance of a Fire: Innocence, Experience and the Theory of Childhood', *Journal of Philosophy of Education* 45/2 (2011), 379–97.

Day, Malcolm M., '"Naked Truth" and the Language of Thomas Traherne', *SP* 68 (1971), 305–25.

—— *Thomas Traherne* (Boston: Twayne, 1982).

—— 'Traherne and the Doctrine of Pre-Existence', *SP* 65 (1968), 81–97.

Deigh, John, 'Innocence', in Lawrence C. Becker and Charlotte B. Becker (eds), *Encyclopaedia of Ethics* (2nd edn, New York: Routledge, 2001), vol. 2, 856b–858b.

Delumeau, Jean, *History of Paradise: The Garden of Eden in Myth and Tradition* (New York: Continuum, 1995).

DeNeef, A. Leigh, *Traherne in Dialogue: Heidegger, Lacan and Derrida* (Durham, NC: Duke University Press, 1988).

Denny, William, *Pelecanicidium or the Christian Adviser against Self-Murder* (London, 1653).

Denonain, Jean-Jacques, *Thèmes et formes de la poésie 'métaphysique'* (Paris: Presses Universitaires de France, 1956).

De Waal, Esther, *Lost in Wonder: Rediscovering the Spiritual Art of Attentiveness* (Norwich: Canterbury Press, 2003).

Dickson, Donald, *The Fountain of Living Waters: The Typology of the Waters of Life in Herbert, Vaughan, and Traherne* (Columbia: University of Missouri Press, 1987).

Dickson, Gary, *The Children's Crusade: Medieval History, Modern Mythistory* (Basingstoke: Palgrave Macmillan, 2008).

Digby, Kenelm, *Of Bodies and of Mans Soul to Discover the Immortality of Reasonable Souls* (London, 1669).

Dionysius the Areopagite, *De coelesti hierarchia, De ecclesiastica hierarchia, De mystica theologia, Epistulae*, ed. Günter Heil and Adolf Martin Ritter (Berlin: De Gruyter, 1991).

DiPasquale, T.M., *Literature and Sacrament: The Sacred and the Secular in John Donne* (Pittsburgh, Pa.: Duquesne University Press, 1999).

Dixon, Leif, 'Calvinist Theology and Pastoral Reality in the Reign of King James I: The Perspective of Thomas Wilson', *Seventeenth Century* 23/2 (2008), 173–97.

Dockrill, D.W., 'The Heritage of Patristic Platonism in Seventeenth-Century Philosophical Theology', in G.A.J. Rogers, J.M. Vienne and Y.C. Zarka (eds), *The Cambridge Platonists in Philosophical Context: Politics, Metaphysics and Religion* (Dordrecht: Kluwer, 1997), 55–77.

Dodd, Elizabeth S., 'Joanna Picciotto, *Labors of Innocence in Early Modern England* (Cambridge, Mass.: Harvard University Press, 2010)', *Seventeenth Century* 27/2 (2012), 235–7.

—— '"Perfect Innocency By Creation" in the Writings of Thomas Traherne', *Literature and Theology* 29/2 (2015), 216–36.

—— 'The Sacramental Image of the Child in the Thought of Thomas Traherne, and Its Theological Significance', in Kevin E. Lawson (ed.), *Understanding Children's Spirituality: Theology, Research, and Practice* (Eugene, Oreg.: Cascade, 2012), 84–105.

Donne, John, *The Complete Poems of John Donne*, ed. Robin Robbins (revd edn, London: Longman/Pearson, 2010).

—— *Devotions Upon Emergent Occasions* (Ann Arbor: University of Michigan Press, 1959).

—— *Two Sermons Preached before King Charles, Upon the XXVI Verse of the First Chapter of Genesis* (Cambridge, 1634).

Doughty, William L., *Studies in Religious Poetry of the Seventeenth Century* (London: Epworth Press, 1946).

Douglas, Mary, *Purity and Danger: An Analysis of Concepts of Pollution and Taboo* (London: Ark, 1966).

Drake, Ben, 'Thomas Traherne's Songs of Innocence', *Modern Language Quarterly* 31 (1970), 492–503.

Dreher, Diane Elizabeth, *The Fourfold Pilgrimage: The Estates of Innocence, Misery, Grace, and Glory in Seventeenth-Century Literature* (Washington DC: University Presses of America, 1982).

Dryden, John, *Of Dramatic Poesy and other Critical Essays*, ed. George Watson (2 vols, London: Dent, 1962).

Dudley, M.R., '*Natalis Innocentum*: The Holy Innocents in Liturgy and Drama', in David Wood (ed.), *The Church and Childhood* (Oxford: Oxford University Press, 1994), 233–42.

Duffy, Jeannie DeBrun, 'Henry Vaughan and Thomas Traherne and the Protestant Tradition of Meditation upon the Book of Creatures' (PhD thesis: Brown University, 1973).

Duncan, Joseph Ellis, *Milton's Earthly Paradise: A Historical Study of Eden* (Minneapolis: University of Minnesota Press, 1972).

Dunning, Benjamin H., 'Virgin Earth, Virgin Birth: Creation, Sexual Difference, and Recapitulation in Irenaeus of Lyons', *JR* 89/1 (2009), 57–88.

Duport, John, *Thenothriambos, sive, Liber Job Graeco carmine redditus* (Cambridge: Thomas Buck and Roger Daniel, 1637).

The Earlier Version of the Wycliffite Bible, ed. Conrad Lindberg (Stockholm: Almquist and Wiksell, 1959–97).

Eliot, T.S., 'Mystic and Politician as Poet: Vaughan, Traherne, Marvell, Milton', *Listener* 3 (2 Apr. 1930), 590–91.

Ellis, Marc H., *Beyond Innocence and Redemption: Confronting the Holocaust and Israeli Power: Creating a Moral Future for the Jewish People* (San Francisco: Harper & Row, 1990).

Ellrodt, Robert, 'Angels and the Poetic Imagination from Donne to Traherne', *English Renaissance Studies: Presented to Dame Helen Gardner in Honour of Her Seventieth Birthday*, ed. John Careu and Helen Peters (Oxford: Clarendon, 1980), 164–79.

—— 'Scientific Curiosity and Metaphysical Poetry in the Seventeenth Century', *MP* 61/3 (1964), 180–97.

—— *Seven Metaphysical Poets: A Structural Study of the Unchanging Self* (Oxford: Oxford University Press, 2000).

Epicurus, *Morals: Collected Partly out of his Owne Greek Text, in Diogenes Laertius, and partly out of the rhapsodies of Marcus Antonius, Plutarch, Cicero, & Seneca. And faithfully Englished*, trans Walter Charleton (London: W. Wilson, 1656).

Eustachius a Sancto Paulo, *Ethica, sive, Summa Moralis Discipline* (Cambridge, 1654).

Evans, J. Martin, *Paradise Lost and the Genesis Tradition* (Oxford: Clarendon, 1968).

Evelyn, John, *Employment and an Active Life Prefer'd to Solitude* (London, 1667).

Fantino, J., 'Le Passage du premier Adam au second Adam comme expression du salut chez Irénée de Lyon', *VC* 52 (1998), 418–29.

Featley, Daniel, *Ancilla Pietatis: or, The Hand-Maid to Private Devotion* (London: James Young, 1647).

Ficino, Marsilio, *Commentary on Plato's Symposium on Love*, trans. Sears Reynolds Jayne (revd edn, Dallas: Spring Publications, 1985).

Findley, Carl E., III, 'Perfecting Adam: The Perils of Innocence in the Modern Novel' (PhD thesis: University of Chicago, 2011).

Fisch, Harlod, 'Creation in Reverse: The Book of Job and *Paradise Lost*', in James H. Sims and Leland Ryken (eds), *Milton and Scriptural Tradition: The Bible into Poetry* (Columbia: University of Missouri Press, 1984), 104–16.

Fish, Stanley, *Surprised by Sin: The Reader in Paradise Lost* (London: Macmillan, 1967).

Flinker, Noam, *The Song of Songs in English Renaissance Literature: Kisses of Their Mouths* (Cambridge: D.S. Brewer, 2000).

Ford, David F., *Christian Wisdom: Desiring God and Learning in Love* (Cambridge: Cambridge University Press, 2007).

—— 'Dante as Inspiration for Twenty-First-Century Theology', in Vittorio Montemaggi and Matthew Treherne (ed.), *Dante's Commedia: Theology as Poetry* (Notre Dame, Ind.: Notre Dame University Press, 2010), 318–28.

—— *Self and Salvation: Being Transformed,* Cambridge Studies in Christian Theology (Cambridge: Cambridge University Press, 1999).

Fordham, Fynn, 'Motions of Writing in the *Commentaries*: the "Volatilitie" of "Atoms" and "Aetyms"', in Jacob Blevins (ed.), *Re-Reading Thomas Traherne:*

A Collection of New Critical Essays (Tempe: Arizona Center for Medieval and Renaissance Studies, 2007), 115–34.

Foskett, Mary, *A Virgin Conceived: Mary and Classical Representations of Virginity* (Bloomington: Indiana University Press, 2002).

Fowler, Alastair, *Kinds of Literature: An Introduction to the Theory of Genres and Modes* (Oxford: Clarendon, 1982).

Fredrikson, N. Ibrahim, 'The Pearl, Between the Ocean and the Sky: Origins and Evolution of a Christian Symbol', *Revue de l'histoire des religions* 220/3 (2003), 283–317.

Freeman, Rosemary, *English Emblem Books* (London: Chatto & Windus, 1948).

Freud, Sigmund, *On Sexuality: Three Essays on the Theory of Sexuality and Other Works*, ed. Angela Richards (London: Penguin, 1977).

Frontain, Raymond-Jean, 'Tuning the World: Traherne, Psalms, and Praise', in Jacob Blevins (ed.), *Re-Reading Thomas Traherne: A Collection of New Critical Essays* (Tempe: Arizona Center for Medieval and Renaissance Studies, 2007), 93–114.

Gale, Theophilus, *The Court of the Gentiles* (4 vols, Oxford and London, 1660–78).

Garnier, Marie-Dominique, 'The Mythematics of Infinity in the *Poems* and *Centuries* of T. Traherne: A Study of its Thematic Archetypes', *Cahiers Élisabéthains* 28 (1985), 61–71.

—— 'Thomas Traherne, poète de l'infini' (PhD thesis: Université de Paris, Nanterre, 1987).

Gaster, T.H., 'Dragon', in G.A. Buttrick et al. (eds), *The Interpreter's Dictionary of the Bible: An Illustrated Encyclopedia*, vol. 1: *A–D* (New York: Abingdon, 1962), 868a.

Givens, Terry L., *When Souls Had Wings: Pre-Mortal Existence in Western Thought* (Oxford: Oxford University Press, 2010).

Gordon, B., 'The Renaissance Angel', in Peter Marshall and Alexandra Walsham (eds), *Angels in the Early Modern World* (Cambridge: Cambridge University Press, 2006), 41–63.

Gosselin, Edward A., *The King's Progress to Jerusalem: Some Interpretations of David during the Reformation Period and Their Patristic and Medieval Background* (Malibu, Calif.: Undena Publications, 1976).

Gouldman, Francis, *A Copious Dictionary in Three Parts* (London: John Field, 1664).

Grandvoinet, Renée, 'Thomas Traherne and the Doctrine of Felicity', *Études de lettres* 13 (1939), 164–77.

Grant, Patrick, 'Original Sin and the Fall of Man in Thomas Traherne', *ELH* 38/1 (Mar. 1971), 40–61.

—— *The Transformation of Sin: Studies in Donne, Herbert, Vaughan, and Traherne* (Amherst: University of Massachusetts Press, 1974).

Gray, F. Elizabeth, *Christian and Lyric Tradition in Victorian Women's Poetry* (Abingdon: Routledge, 2010).

Green, Ian M., *The Christian's ABC: Catechism and Catechizing in England* (Oxford: Oxford University Press, 1996).

—— *The Re-establishment of the Church of England, 1660–1663* (Oxford: Oxford University Press, 1978).

Greene, Robert A., 'Whichcote, the Candle of the Lord, and Synderesis', *JHI* 52/4 (1991), 617–44.

Gregory of Nazianzus, *On God and Man: The Theological Poetry of St Gregory of Nazianzus*, trans. Peter Gilbert (Crestwood, NY: St Vladimir's Seminary, 2001).

—— *Select Orations*, trans. Charles Gordon Browne and James Edward Swallow, NPNF^2 7 (Buffalo, NY: Christian Literature, 1894).

Gregory of Nyssa, *From Glory to Glory: Texts from Gregory of Nyssa's Mystical Writings*, ed. Jean Daniélou, trans. Herbert Musurrillo (Crestwood, NY: St Vladimir's Seminary, 1995).

—— *Dogmatic Treatises*, trans. H.A. Wilson, NPNF^2 5 (Buffalo, NY: Christian Literature, 1893).

—— *Ascetical Works*, trans. Victoria Woods Callahan (Washington, DC: Catholic University of America Press, 1967).

Gregory the Great, *Forty Gospel Homilies*, trans. Dom David Hurst (Kalamazoo, Mich.: Cistercian Publications, 1990).

—— *Morals on the Book of Job*, trans. C. Marriot, Library of the Fathers of the Holy Catholic Church (Oxford: John Henry Parker, 1844–47).

Guffey, George Robert, *A Concordance to the Poetry of Thomas Traherne* (Berkeley: University of California Press, 1974).

—— 'Thomas Traherne on Original Sin', *N&Q* 14 (1967), 98–100.

—— *Traherne and the Seventeenth-Century English Platonists, 1900–1966*, Elizabethan Bibliographies Supplements 11 (London: Nether Press, 1969).

Guilhamet, Leon, *The Sincere Ideal: Studies on Sincerity in Eighteenth-Century English Literature* (Montreal: McGill-Queen's University Press, 1974).

Haakonssen, Knud, 'Divine/Natural Law Theories in Ethics', in Daniel Garber and Michael Ayers (eds), *Cambridge History of Seventeenth-Century Philosophy* (Cambridge: Cambridge University Press, 1998), 1317–57.

Hackett, Helen, *Virgin Mother, Maiden Queen: Elizabeth I and the Cult of the Virgin Mary* (Basingstoke: Macmillan, 1996).

Hamlin, Hannibal, *Psalm Culture and Early Modern English Literature* (Cambridge: Cambridge University Press, 2004).

Hammond, Henry, *A Paraphrase, and Annotations Upon all the Books of the New Testament* (London, 1653).

—— Χάρις και Ἐιρήνη, *or, a Pacifick Discourse of Gods Grace and Decrees in a Letter ... to ... R. Sanderson* (London, 1660).

Harrison, Peter, *The Bible, Protestantism, and the Rise of Natural Science* (Cambridge: Cambridge University Press, 1998).

Harrison, Thomas P., 'Seneca and Traherne', *Arion* 6/3 (1967), 403–5.

Hart, Trevor A., and Steven R. Guthrie (eds), *Faithful Performances: Enacting Christian Tradition* (Aldershot: Ashgate, 2007).

Hawkes, David, 'Thomas Traherne: A Critique of Political Economy', in *Idols of the Marketplace: Idolatry and Commodity Fetishism in English Literature, 1580–1680* (New York: Palgrave, 2001), 191–212.

Hayward, A., 'Suffering and Innocence in Latin Sermons for the Feast of the Holy Innocents, *c*.400–800', in David Wood (ed.), *The Church and Childhood* (Oxford: Oxford University Press, 1994), 67–80.

Hedley, Douglas, and Sarah Hutton (eds), *Platonism at the Origins of Modernity: Studies on Platonism and Early Modern Philosophy* (Dordrecht: Springer, 2008).

Hegel, George William Friedrich, *The Phenomenology of Spirit*, trans. A.V. Miller (Oxford: Oxford University Press, 1977).

Henderson, Ian, 'Innocence', in James F. Childress and John Macquarrie (eds), *A New Dictionary of Christian Ethics* (London: SCM, 1986), 302b–303a.

Hepburn, Ronald W., 'Thomas Traherne: The Nature and Dignity of Imagination', *Cambridge Journal* 6 (1953), 725–34.

Herbert, George, *The English Poems of George Herbert*, ed. Helen Cox (Cambridge: Cambridge University Press, 2007).

Herdt, Jennifer A., 'The Rise of Sympathy and the Question of Divine Suffering', *Journal of Religious Ethics* 29/3 (2001), 367–99.

Hermes Mercurious Trismegistus, His Divine Pymander, In Seventeen Books, trans. John Everard (London, 1657).

Herrick, Marvin Theodore, *The Poetics of Aristotle in England* (New Haven, Conn.: Yale University Press, 1930).

Hick, John, *Evil and the God of Love* (London: Macmillan, 1966).

Hill, Christopher, *The English Bible and the Seventeenth-Century Revolution* (London: Penguin, 1993).

Hill, John Spencer, *Infinity, Faith and Time: Christian Humanism and Renaissance Literature* (Montreal: McGill-Queens University Press, 1997).

Hinsdale, Mary Ann, '"Infinite Openness to the Infinite": Karl Rahner's Contribution to Modern Catholic Thought on the Child', in Marcia J. Bunge (ed.), *The Child in Christian Thought* (Grand Rapids, Mich.: Eerdmans, 2001), 406–45.

Hoard, Samuel, *God's Love to Mankind Manifested by Disproving his Absolute Decree for their Damnation* (London, 1633).

Hobbes, Thomas, *Leviathan*, ed. Richard Tuck (revd edn, Cambridge: Cambridge University Press, 2008).

Hollywood, Amy, *The Soul as Virgin Wife: Mechthild of Magdeburg, Marguerite Porete, and Meister Eckhart* (London: University of Notre Dame Press, 1995).

Hooker, Richard, *Of the Lawes of Ecclesiasticall Politie Eight Bookes* (London, 1604).

Hopkins, Kenneth, *English Poetry: A Short History* (London: Phoenix House, 1962).

Horwich, Richard, 'Integrity in Macbeth: The Search for the "Single State of Man"', *Shakespeare Quarterly* 29/3 (1978), 365–73.

Hulme, T.E., 'Romanticism and Classicism', in Herbert Read (ed.), *Speculations: Essays on Humanism and the Philosophy of Art* (London: K. Paul, Trench, Trubner & Co., 1936), 111–40.

Husain, Itrat, *The Mystical Element in the Metaphysical Poets of the Seventeenth Century* (Edinburgh: Oliver & Boyd, 1948).

Hutton, Sarah, 'Introduction', in Anna Baldwin and Sarah Hutton (eds), *Platonism and the English Imagination* (Cambridge: Cambridge University Press, 1994), 1–8.

—— 'Platonism in Some Metaphysical Poets: Marvell, Vaughan and Traherne', in Anna Baldwin and Sarah Hutton (eds), *Platonism and the English Imagination* (Cambridge: Cambridge University Press, 1994), 163–77.

—— 'Thomas Jackson, Oxford Platonist, and William Twisse, Aristotelian', *JHI* 39/4 (1978), 635–52.

Inge, Denise, *Happiness and Holiness: Thomas Traherne and His Writings* (Norwich: Canterbury Press, 2008).

—— 'Thomas Traherne and the Socinian Heresy in *Commentaries of Heaven*', *N&Q* 54 (2007), 412–16.

—— *Wanting Like a God: Desire and Freedom in the Thought of Thomas Traherne* (London: SCM, 2009).

—— and Calum Donald MacFarlane, 'Seeds of Eternity: A New Traherne Manuscript', *TLS* (2 June 2000), 14.

Illingworth, John R., *University and Catholic Sermons* (London: Macmillan, 1893).

Irenaeus of Lyons, *Against the Heresies*, in *The Apostolic Fathers with Justin Martyr and Irenaeus*, ed. and trans. Alexander Roberts and James Donaldson, Ante-Nicene Christian Library 1 (Edinburgh: T.&T. Clark, 1869).

Jackson, Thomas, *An Exact Collection of the Works of Doctor Jackson* (London, 1654).

—— *A Treatise containing the Originall of Unbeliefe* (London: John Clarke, 1625).

—— *A Treatise of the Divine Essence and Attributes*, Part I (London, 1628).

James, Susan, *Passion and Action: The Emotions in Seventeenth-Century Philosophy* (Oxford: Oxford University Press, 1999).

Jensen, David Hadley, *Graced Vulnerability: A Theology of Childhood* (Cleveland, O.: Pilgrim Press, 2005).

Jennings, Elizabeth, 'The Accessible Art: A Study of Thomas Traherne's *Centuries of Meditations*', *Twentieth Century* 167 (1960), 140–51.

Jerome, *Commentary on Matthew*, Fathers of the Church 117, trans. Thomas P. Scheck (Washington, DC: Catholic University of America Press, 2008).

John Chrysostom, *Homilies on the Gospel of Saint Matthew*, trans. George Prevost, NPNF[1] 10 (Grand Rapids, Mich.: Eerdmans, 1983).

Johnston, Carol Ann, 'Heavenly Perspectives, Mirrors of Eternity: Thomas Traherne's Yearning Subject', *Criticism* 43/4 (2001), 377–405.

Johnson, Peter, *Politics, Innocence, and the Limits of Goodness* (London: Routledge, 1988).

Jordan, Richard Douglas, *The Temple of Eternity: Thomas Traherne's Philosophy of Time* (New York: Kennikat, 1972).

Jung, Carl J. 'The Psychology of the Child Archetype', in *Archetypes and the Collective Unconscious*, trans. R.F.C. Hull, Collected Works of C.G. Jung 9/1 (2nd edn, London: Routledge, 1968), 151–81.

Kelsey, David H., *Eccentric Existence: A Theological Anthropology* (2 vols, Louisville, Ky: Westminster John Knox Press, 2009).

Kershaw, Alison, 'The Poetic of the Cosmic Christ in Thomas Traherne's *The Kingdom of God*' (PhD thesis: University of Western Australia, 2005).

Kierkegaard, Søren, *The Concept of Anxiety*, ed. Reidar Thomte and Albert Anderson (Princeton, NJ: Princeton University Press, 1980).

Kimbrough, S.T., 'Lyrical Theology: Theology in Hymns', *TT* 63/1 (2006), 22–37.

King, Francis, 'Thomas Traherne: Intellect and Felicity', in Harold Love (ed.), *Restoration Literature: Critical Approaches* (London: Methuen, 1972), 121–45.

King, Henry, *The Psalmes of David, from the New Translation of the Bible Turned into Meter* (London: Ed. Griffin, 1651).

Kingdon, D.P., 'Innocence', in David J. Atkinson and David H. Field (eds), *New Dictionary of Christian Ethics and Pastoral Theology* (Leicester: Inter-Varsity Press, 1995), 490a–491a.

Kittel, G., and G. Friedrich (eds), *Theological Dictionary of the New Testament*, trans. G.W. Bromily (10 vols, Grand Rapids, Mich.: Eerdmans, 1964–71).

Knott, John R., 'Milton's Wild Garden', *SP* 102 (2005), 66–82.

Kohi, Tomohiko, 'The Rhetoric of Instruction and Manuscript and Print Culture in the Devotional Works of Thomas Traherne' (PhD thesis: University of Reading, 2004).

Koslowski, Peter, 'Baader: The Centrality of Original Sin and the Difference of Immediacy and Innocence', in Jon Stewart (ed.), *Kierkegaard and His German Contemporaries*, vol. 1: *Philosophy* (Aldershot: Ashgate, 2007), 1–14.

Koyré, Alexander, *From a Closed World to the Infinite Universe* (Baltimore, Mass.: Johns Hopkins University Press, 1957).

Kuchar, Gavin, *Divine Subjection: The Rhetoric of Sacramental Devotion in Early Modern England* (Pittsburgh, Pa: Duquesne University Press, 2005).

—— '"Organs of thy Praise": The Function and Rhetoric of the Body in Thomas Traherne', *Religion in the Age of Reason: A Transatlantic Study of the Long Eighteenth Century*, ed. Kathryn Duncan (New York: AMS, 2009), 59–81.

Laam, Kevin, 'Thomas Traherne, Richard Allestree, and the Ethics of Appropriation', in Jacob Blevins (ed.), *Re-Reading Thomas Traherne: A Collection of New Critical Essays* (Tempe: Arizona Center for Medieval and Renaissance Studies, 2007), 37–64.

Lactantius, *The Divine Institutes*, trans. William Fletcher, ANF 7 (Buffalo, NY: T.&T. Clark, 1886).

Lane, Belden C., 'Thomas Traherne and the Awakening of Want', *ATR* 81/4 (1999), 651–64.

Légasse, S., *Jésus et l'enfant: "Enfants", "petits" et "simples" dans la tradition synoptique* (Paris: J. Gabalda, 1969).

Lehrs, Ernst, *Der Rosenkreuzerische Impuls im Leben und Werk von Joachim Jundius und Thomas Traherne* (Stuttgart: Freies Geistesleben, 1962).

Leishman, J.B., *The Metaphysical Poets: Donne, Herbert, Vaughan, Traherne* (Oxford: Clarendon, 1934).

Lewalski, Barbara, *Milton's Brief Epic* (London: Methuen, 1966).

—— *Protestant Poetics and the Seventeenth-Century Religious Lyric* (Princeton, NJ: Princeton University Press, 1979).

—— 'Typological Symbolism and the "Progress of the Soul" in Seventeenth-Century Literature', in Earl Miner (ed.), *Literary Uses of Typology: From the Late Middle Ages to the Present* (Princeton, NJ: Princeton University Press, 1977), 79–114.

Lobsien, Verena Olejniczak, 'The Space of the Human and the Place of the Poet: Excursions into English Topographical Poetry', in Andreas Höfele and Stephan Laqué (eds), *Humankinds: The Renaissance and Its Anthropologies* (Berlin: De Gruyter, 2011), 41–70.

—— *Transparency and Dissimulation: Configurations of Neoplatonism in Early Modern English Literature* (Berlin: De Gruyter, 2010).

Loewenstein, David, 'The Seventeenth-Century Protestant English Epic', in Catherine Bates (ed.), *Cambridge Companion to the Epic* (Cambridge: Cambridge University Press, 2010), 146–66.

Ludlow, Mary, *Gregory of Nyssa: Ancient and (Post)modern* (Oxford: Oxford University Press, 2007).

Luther, Martin, *Luther's Works*, ed. E. Theodore Bachmann and Helmut T. Lehmann (55 vols, Philadelphia, Pa.: Muhlenberg Press, 1960).

Luttikhuizen, Gerard P. (ed.), *Paradise Interpreted: Representations of Biblical Paradise in Judaism and Christianity* (Leiden: Brill, 1999).

McAdoo, Henry R., *The Spirit of Anglicanism: A Survey of Anglican Theological Method in the Seventeenth Century* (London: A.&C. Black, 1965).

Macaulay, Rose, *Some Religious Elements in English Literature* (London: Hogarth, 1931).

McColley, Diane Kelsey, *Poetry and Ecology in the Age of Milton and Marvell* (Aldershot: Ashgate, 2007).

McFadyen, Alistair I., *Bound to Sin: Abuse, Holocaust, and the Christian Doctrine of Sin* (Cambridge: Cambridge University Press, 2000).

McFarland, Ronald E., 'Thomas Traherne's *Thanksgivings* and the Theology of Optimism', *Enlightenment Essays* 4/1 (1973), 3–14.

MacFarlane, Calum Donald, 'Transfiguration as the Heart of Christian Life: The Theology of Thomas Traherne (1637?–1674) with Special Reference to "the Kingdom of God" and other Recently Discovered Manuscripts' (PhD thesis, University of Southampton, 2005).

McIntosh, Mark Allen, *Discernment and Truth: The Spirituality and Theology of Knowledge* (Edinburgh: Alban, 2004).

Mackenzie, George, *A Moral Essay, Preferring Solitude to Publick Employment* (Edinburgh, 1665).

MacKinnon, Donald M., *The Problem of Metaphysics* (Cambridge: Cambridge University Press, 1974).

—— *Themes in Theology: The Three-Fold Cord: Essays in Philosophy, Politics and Theology* (Edinburgh: T.&T. Clark, 1987).

Maitland, Peter Kennedy, 'Thomas Traherne's Path to Felicity: The Missing Christ' (MA thesis: Carleton University, Canada, 1994).

Manuel, Frank E., and Fritzie P. Manuel (eds), *Utopian Thought in the Western World* (Oxford: Basil Blackwell, 1979).

Marcus, Leah S., *Childhood and Cultural Despair: A Theme and Variations in Seventeenth-Century Literature* (Pittsburgh, Pa.: University of Pittsburgh Press, 1978).

Marks, Carol L., 'Thomas Traherne and Cambridge Platonism', *PMLA* 81/7 (1966), 521–34.

—— 'Thomas Traherne and Hermes Trismegistus', *Renaissance News* 19/2 (1966), 118–31.

—— 'Thomas Traherne's Early Studies', *PBSA* 62 (1968), 511–36.

—— 'Traherne's Church's Year-Book', *PBSA* 60 (1966), 31–72.

Marshall, William H., 'Thomas Traherne and the Doctrine of Original Sin', *MLN* 73 (1958), 161–5.

Martin, John Jeffries, 'Inventing Sincerity, Refashioning Prudence: The Discovery of the Individual in the Renaissance', *American Historical Review* 102/5 (1997), 1309–42.

Martz, Louis Lohr, *The Paradise Within: Studies in Vaughan, Traherne, and Milton* (New Haven, Conn.: Yale University Press, 1964).

Marvell, Andrew, *The Poems of Andrew Marvell*, ed. Nigel Smith (London: Longman/Pearson, 2003).

Masciandaro, Franco, *Dante as Dramatist: The Myth of the Earthly Paradise and Tragic Vision in the Divine Comedy* (Philadelphia: University of Pennsylvania Press, 1991).

Matar, Nabil I., 'The Anglican Eschatology of Thomas Traherne', *ATR* 74/3 (1992), 289–303.

—— 'Aristotelian Tragedy in the Theology of Peter Sterry', *LT* 6/4 (1992), 310–19.

—— 'A Note on Thomas Traherne and the Quakers', *N&Q* 28 (1981), 46–7.

—— 'The Political Views of Thomas Traherne', *HLQ* 57/3 (1994), 241–53.

—— 'Thomas Traherne and St Bernard of Clairvaux', *N&Q* 32 (1985), 182–4.

Maule, Jeremy, 'Five New Traherne Works: An Overview of London, Lambeth Palace Library MS 1360' (transcript of notes from a talk presented to the Thomas Traherne Conference, Brasenose College, Oxford, 30 July 1997).

May, Rollo, *Power and Innocence: A Search for the Sources of Violence* (New York: Norton, 1972).

Meinel, Christopher, 'Early Seventeenth-Century Atomism: Theory, Epistemology, and the Insufficiency of Experiment', *Isis* 79/1 (1988), 68–103.

Merton, Thomas, *Mystics and Zen Masters* (New York: Farrar, Straus and Giroux, 1967).

Miller, Justin, 'Thomas Traherne: Love and Pain in the Poet of Felicity', *Historical Magazine of the Protestant Episcopal Church* 49 (1980), 209–20.

Miller, Perry *The New England Mind: The Seventeenth Century* (New York: Macmillan, 1939).

Milton, John, *The Major Works*, ed. Stephen Orgel and Jonathan Goldberg (Oxford: Oxford University Press, 1991).

Mintz, Samuel I., *The Hunting of Leviathan: Seventeenth-Century Reactions to the Materialism and Moral Philosophy of Thomas Hobbes* (Cambridge: Cambridge University Press, 1962).

Moberly, Elizabeth W., *Suffering, Innocent and Guilty* (London: SPCK, 1978).

Molnar, Thomas, *Utopia: The Perennial Heresy* (London: Tom Stacey, 1972).

Moltmann, Jürgen, 'Child and Childhood as Metaphors of Hope', *TT* 56/4 (2000), 592–603.

—— *The Crucified God*, trans. R.A. Wilson and John Bowden (2nd edn, New York: Harper & Row, 1974).

More, Henry, *An Account of Virtue: Or Dr. Henry More's Abridgement of Morals, Put into English* (London, 1690).

—— *Divine Dialogues, Containing sundry Disquisitions & Instructions Concerning the Attributes and Providence of GOD* (London, 1668).

—— *Philosophical Poems* (Cambridge, 1647).

Mozley, J.K., *The Impassibility of God: A Survey of Christian Thought* (Cambridge: Cambridge University Press, 1926).

Murphy, Francesca Aran, '"Whence Comes this Love as Strong as Death?": Rosenzweig's "Philosophy as Narrative" in Hans Urs von Balthasar's Theo-Drama', *LT* 7/3 (1993), 227–47.

Murphy, Katherine, '"Aves quaedam macedonicae": Misreading Aristotle in Francis Bacon, Robert Burton, Thomas Browne and Thomas Traherne' (PhD thesis: University of Oxford, 2009).

Needler, Benjamin, *Expository Notes, with Practical Observations; Towards the Opening of the Five First chapters of the First Book of Moses called Genesis* (London: T.R. and E.M., 1644).

Nemo, Philippe, *Job and the Excess of Evil*, trans. Michael Kigel (Pittsburgh, Pa.: Duquesne University Press, 1998).

Nethercot, Arthur H., 'The Reputation of the "Metaphysical Poets" during the Age of Johnson and the "Romantic Revival"', *SP* 22 (1925), 81–132.

Newey, Edmund, *Children of God: The Child as Source of Theological Anthropology* (Farnham: Ashgate, 2012).

—— '"God Made Man Greater When He Made Him Less": Traherne's Iconic Child', *LT* 24/3 (2010), 227–41.

Newman, John H., *Parochial and Plain Sermons* (8 vols, London: Rivintons, 1868).

Nicholas of Cusa, *On Learned Ignorance: A Translation and an Appraisal of De Docta Ignorantia*, trans. Jasper Hopkins (Minneapolis, Minn.: Arthur J. Banning, 1981).

Nicolson, Marjorie Hope, *The Breaking of the Circle: Studies in the Effect of the 'New Science' Upon Seventeenth Century Poetry* (Evanston, Ill.: Northwestern University Press, 1950).

Nietzsche, Friedrich, *On the Genealogy of Morals: A Polemic*, trans. D. Smith (Oxford: Oxford University Press, 1996).

O'Day, Daniel, 'Quest for Childhood: A Critical Study of Henry Vaughan and Thomas Traherne' (PhD thesis: Columbia University, 1972).

O'Loughlin, Michael, 'The Curious Subject of the Child', in Michael O'Loughlin and Richard T. Johnson (eds), *Imagining Children Otherwise: Theoretical and Critical Perspectives on Childhood Subjectivity* (New York: Peter Lang, 2010), 207–28.

Onions, C.T., et al. (eds), *The Oxford Dictionary of English Etymology* (revd edn, Oxford: Oxford University Press, 1969).

Origen, *De Principiis*, trans. Frederick Crombie, ANF 4 (Edinburgh: T.&T. Clark, 1885).

Osborn, James M., 'A New Traherne Manuscript', *TLS* (8 Oct. 1964), 928.

Ottley, Robert L., 'Innocence', in James Hastings et al. (eds), *The Encyclopaedia of Religion and Ethics* (Edinburgh: T.&T. Clark, 1914), vol. 7, 329a–330a.

Ovid, *Metamorphoses*, trans. E.J. Kenney (Oxford: Oxford University Press, 1986).

Owen, John, *Of Temptation* (Oxford, 1658).

Oxinden, Henry, *Jobus Triumphans* (London, 1651).

Parker, Matthew, *The Whole Psalter Translated into English Metre* (London: John Daye, 1567).

Parker, Samuel, *A Free and Impartial Censure of the Platonick Philosophie* (Oxford: W. Hall, 1666).

Patrides, Charles A., *The Cambridge Platonists* (London: Arnold, 1969).

—— 'Milton and the Protestant Theory of the Atonement', *PMLA* 74/1 (1959), 7–13.

Perkins, David, *Wordsworth and the Poetry of Sincerity* (Cambridge, Mass.: Harvard University Press, 1964).

Petrus Ravanellus, *Petri Ravanellie Uticensis Occitani Bibliotheca Sacra* (Geneva, 1650).

Peyre, Henri, *Literature and Sincerity* (New Haven, Conn.: Yale University Press, 1963).

Piaget, Jean, *The Moral Judgement of the Child*, trans. Marjorie Gabain (New York: Free Press, 1965).

Picciotto, Joanna, *Labors of Innocence in Early Modern England* (Cambridge, Mass.: Harvard University Press, 2010).

Pico della Mirandola, Giovanni, *Oration on the Dignity of Man*, trans. A. Robert Caponigri (Chicago: Regnery Gateway, 1956).

Pienaar, W.J.B., 'Arthur's Shield in the "Faerie Queene"', *MP* 26/1 (1928), 63–8.

Pinsent, Patrick, 'The Image of Christ in the Writings of Two Seventeenth-Century English Country Parsons: George Herbert and Thomas Traherne', in Stanley E. Porter, David Tombs and Michael A. Chaplain Hayes (eds), *Images of Christ: Ancient and Modern* (Sheffield: Sheffield Academic Press, 1997), 227–38.

Pitkin, Barbara, 'Imitation of David: David as a Paradigm for Faith in Calvin's Exegesis of the Psalms', *Sixteenth Century Journal* 24/4 (1993), 843–63.

Plato, *Complete Works*, ed. John M. Cooper (Indianapolis: Hackett, 1997).

Plotinus, *The Enneads*, trans. S. MacKenna (revd edn, London: Faber & Faber, 1969).

Plotz, Judith, *Romanticism and the Vocation of Childhood* (New York: Palgrave, 2001).

Ponsford, Michael, 'Men after God's own Heart: The Context of Thomas Traherne's Emulation of David', *Studia Mystica* 9/4 (1986), 3–11.

—— 'Traherne's Apostasy', *Durham University Journal* 76 (1984), 177–85.

Poole, William, 'Frail Originals: Theories of the Fall in the Age of Milton' (PhD thesis, University of Oxford, 2000).

Powell, Thomas, *A Sanctuary for the Tempted: Being a Discourse on Christ's Friendly Admonition to Peter Wherein the Fall and Rising of Peter, is at Large Considered* (London: T.M., 1679).

Powell, Vavasor, *A New and Useful Concordance to the Holy Bible* (London, 1671).

Prescott, Anne Lake, 'David as a "Right Poet": Sidney and the Psalmist', *ELR* 19 (1989), 131–51.

Puente, Luis de la, *Meditations upon the Mysteries of our Faith Corresponding to the Three Wayes, Purgative, Illuminative, and Unitive* (Saint Omer, 1624).

Pyper, Hugh, 'Children', in Adrian Hastings, Alistair Mason and Hugh Pyper (eds), *The Oxford Companion to Christian Thought* (Oxford: Oxford University Press, 2000), 110.

Quarles, Francis, *Emblemes Divine and Moral* (London: George Miller, 1635).

—— *Job Militant: With Meditations Divine and Morall* (London: Felix Kyngston, 1624).

Quash, Ben, *Theology and the Drama of History*, Cambridge Studies in Christian Doctrine (Cambridge: Cambridge University Press, 2005).

Radzinowicz, Mary Ann, *Milton's Epics and the Book of Psalms* (Princeton: Princeton University Press, 1989).

Rahner, Karl, 'Ideas for a Theology of Childhood', *Theological Investigations* (London: Darton, Longman & Todd, 1971), vol. 8, 33–50.

Rainolds, John, *The Summe of the Conference Betweene John Rainoldes and John Hart: Touching the Head and the Faith of the Church* (London: George Bishop, 1588).

Rainy, Robert, *Sojourning with God and Other Sermons* (London: Hodder & Stoughton, 1902).

Read, Herbert, *The Cult of Sincerity* (London: Faber & Faber, 1968).

Reid, David, *The Metaphysical Poets* (Essex: Pearson Education, 2000).

—— 'Traherne and Lucretius', *N&Q* 45 (1998), 440–41.

Richardson, Alan, *Literature, Education and Romanticism* (Cambridge: Cambridge University Press, 1994).

Ricoeur, Paul, *Fallible Man*, trans. Charles A. Kelbley (revd edn, New York: Fordham University Press, 1986).

—— *Freud and Philosophy: An Essay on Interpretation* (New Haven, Conn.: Yale University Press, 1970).

—— *The Symbolism of Evil*, trans. Emerson Buchanan, Religious Perspectives 17 (New York: Harper & Row, 1967).

—— *Time and Narrative*, trans. Kathleen McLaughlin and David Pellauer (3 vols, Chicago: University of Chicago Press, 1984–8).

—— 'Toward a Hermeneutic of the Idea of Revelation', *Harvard Theological Review* 70/1–2 (1977), 1–37.

Ridler, Anne, 'The Essential Thomas Traherne', in A.M. Allchin, Anne Ridler and Julia Smith (eds), *Profitable Wonders: Aspects of Thomas Traherne* (Oxford: Amate, 1989), 9–21.

Ridlon, Harold G., 'The Function of the "Infant-Ey" in Traherne's Poetry', *SP* 61 (1964), 627–39.

Robbins, Gregory Allen (ed.), *Genesis 1–3 in the History of Exegesis: Intrigue in the Garden* (New York: Edwin Mellen, 1988).

Rolle, Richard, *The Psalter or Psalms of David, and Certain Canticles*, ed. and trans. H.R. Bramley (Oxford: Clarendon, 1884).

Rose, Elliott, 'A New Traherne Manuscript', *TLS* (19 Mar. 1982), 324.

Rous, Francis, *The Mysticall Marriage, Experimentall Discoveries of the Heavenly Marriage betweene a Soule and her Saviour* (London: William Jones, 1631).

Rousseau, Jean-Jacques, *Discourse on the Origins of Inequality (Second Discourse); Polemics; and, Political Economy*, ed. Roger D. Masters and Christopher Kelly, trans. Judith R. Bush (Hanover, NH: University Press of New England, 1992).

Russell, Angela, 'The Life of Thomas Traherne', *Review of English Studies* 6/21 (1955), 34–43.

Rutledge, Denys, *Cosmic Theology: The Ecclesiastical Hierarchy of Pseudo-Denys: An Introduction* (London: Routledge & Kegan Paul, 1964).

Salter, Keith William, 'Thomas Traherne and a Romantic Heresy', *N&Q* 200 (1955), 153–6.

—— *Thomas Traherne: Mystic and Poet* (London: Edward Arnold, 1964).

Saltmarsh, John, *Poemata Sacra* (Cambridge: Thomas Buck and Roger Daniel, 1636).

Sandbank, S., 'Thomas Traherne on the Place of Man in the Universe', *Scripta Hierosolymitana* 17 (1966), 121–36.

Sandys, Edwin, *Sacred Hymns Consisting of Fifty Select Psalms of David and Others* (London: Thomas Snodham, 1615).

Sastri, Reena, *James Merrill: Knowing Innocence* (London: Routledge, 2007).

Sauls, Richard Lynn, 'Traherne's Hand in the Credenhill Records', *The Library* 24 (1969), 50.

Saward, John, *The Way of the Lamb: The Spirit of Childhood and the End of the Age* (Edinburgh: T.&T. Clark, 1999).

Sawday, Jonathan, *The Body Emblazoned: Dissection and the Human Body in Renaissance Culture* (London: Routledge, 1995).

Sayers, Dorothy L., 'The Beatrician Vision in Dante and Other Poets', *Nottingham Medieval Studies* 2 (1958), 3–23.

Schreiner, Susan E., *Where Shall Wisdom be Found? Calvin's Exegesis of Job from Medieval and Modern Perspectives* (Chicago: University of Chicago Press, 1994).

Schwager, Raymund, *Banished from Eden: Original Sin and Evolutionary Theory in the Drama of Salvation*, trans. James Williams (London: Gracewing, 2006).

Schwartz, R.M., *Sacramental Poetics at the Dawn of Secularism: When God Left the World* (Stanford, Calif.: Stanford University Press, 2008).

Scodel, Joshua, *Excess and the Mean in Early Modern English Literature* (Princeton: Princeton University Press, 2002).

Seelig, Sharon Cadman, *The Shadow of Eternity: Belief and Structure in Herbert, Vaughan and Traherne* (Lexington: University Press of Kentucky, 1981).

—— 'Origins of Ecstasy, Select Meditations', *ELR* 9 (1979), 419–31.

Seetaraman, M.V., 'The Way of Felicity in Thomas Traherne's "Centuries" and "The Poems"', in V.S. Seturaman (ed.), *Critical Essays on English Literature: Presented to M.S. Duraiswami on the Occasion of his Sixty-First Birthday* (Bombay: Orient Longmans, 1965), 81–104.

Selkin, Carl Matthew, 'The Language of Vision: Traherne's Cataloguing Style', *ELR* 6 (1976), 92–104.

Seneca, *Moral Essays*, trans. John W. Basore, LCL (Cambridge, Mass.: Harvard University Press, 1928).

Shanks, Andrew, *Against Innocence: Gillian Rose's Reception and Gift of Faith* (London: SCM, 2008).

Sherer, Gertrude Roberts, 'More and Traherne', *MLN* 34 (1919), 49–50.

Sherrington, Alison J., *Mystical Symbolism in the Poetry of Thomas Traherne* (St Lucia: University of Queensland Press, 1970).

Sherry, Beverley, 'A "Paradise Within" Can Never Be "Happier Farr": Reconsidering the Archangel Michael's Consolation in *Paradise Lost*', *Milton Quarterly* 37 (2003), 77–91.

Sherry, Patrick, 'Disenchantment, Reenchantment, and Enchantment', *MT* 25/3 (2009), 369–86.

Shuger, Deborah Kuller, *The Renaissance Bible: Scholarship, Sacrifice, and Subjectivity* (Berkeley: University of California Press, 1994).

Sidney, Philip, *An Apology for Poetry (or The Defence of Poesy)*, ed. Geoffrey Shepherd and R.W. Maslen (revd edn, Manchester: Manchester University Press, 2002).

Sir Gawain and the Green Knight: Pearl; and Sir Orfeo, ed. J.R.R. Tolkien (London: Unwin, 1979).

Skeen, James, 'Discovering Human Happiness: Choice Theory Psychology, Aristotelian Contemplation, and Traherne's Felicity', *Quodlibet Journal* 5/2–3 (2003), <http://www.quodlibet.net/articles/skeen-choice.html> (accessed 1 Jan. 2012).

Slater, Peter, 'Tillich on the Fall and the Temptation of Goodness', *JR* 65/2 (1985), 196–207.

Sluberski, Thomas Richard, *A Mind in Frame: The Theological Thought of Thomas Traherne, a Seventeenth Century Poet and Theologian* (Cleveland, O.: Lincoln Library Press, 2008).

Small, Robin, 'Nietzsche and a Platonist Tradition of the Cosmos: Center Everywhere and Circumference Nowhere', *JHI* 44/1 (1983), 89–104.

Smith, Abraham, 'Innocence', in Katherine Doob Sakenfeld (ed.), *The New Interpreter's Dictionary of the Bible* (Nashville: Abingdon, 2009), vol. 3, 45b–46a.

Smith, Christopher R., 'Chiliasm and Recapitulation in the Theology of Irenaeus', *VC* 48 (1994), 313–31.

Smith, John, *Select Discourses* (London: J. Flesher, 1660).

Smith, Julia J., 'Attitudes towards Conformity and Nonconformity in Thomas Traherne', *Bunyan Studies* 1/1 (1988), 26–35.

—— 'Thomas Traherne and the Restoration', *Seventeenth Century* 3/2 (1988), 203–22.

—— 'Tombes, John (1602–1676)', *ODNB*.

—— 'Traherne, Thomas (*c*.1637–1674)', *ODNB*.

—— and Laetitia Yeandle, '"Felicity Disguised in Fiery Words": Genesis and Exodus in a Newly Discovered Poem by Thomas Traherne', *TLS* (7 Nov. 1997), 17.

Smith, Nigel, *Perfection Proclaimed: Language and Literature in English Radical Religion, 1640–1660* (Oxford: Clarendon, 1989).

Sommerville, Charles John, *The Rise and Fall of Childhood* (London: Sage, 1982).

Soskice, Janet, *Metaphor and Religious Language* (Oxford: Clarendon, 1985).

Sparke, Edward, *Scintilla-Altaris* (London: W.G. and R.W., 1660).

Spenser, Edmund, *The Faerie Queene*, ed. Albert Charles Hamilton (London: Longman, 1977).

Spinks, Brian D., *Reformation and Modern Rituals and Theologies of Baptism: From Luther to Contemporary Practices* (Aldershot: Ashgate, 2006).

Sprat, Thomas, *Observations on M. De Sorbier's Voyage into England* (London, 1665).

Spurr, Barry, 'Felicity Incarnate: Rediscovering Thomas Traherne', in Eugene R. Cunnar and Jeffrey Johnson (eds), *Discovering and (Re)covering the Seventeenth Century Religious Lyric* (Pittsburgh, Pa.: Duquesne University Press, 2001), 273–89.

Steenberg, Matthew Craig, *Irenaeus on Creation: The Cosmic Christ and the Saga of Redemption* (Leiden: Brill, 2008).

—— 'The Role of Mary as Co-recapitulator in St Irenaeus of Lyons', *VC* 58 (2004), 117–37.

Stein, Arnold, 'The Paradise Within and the Paradise Without', *Milton Quarterly* 26 (1965), 586–600.

Sterry, Peter, *The Clouds in which Christ Comes Opened in a Sermon before the Honourable House of Commons* (London, 1648).

—— *A Discourse of the Freedom of the Will* (London, 1675).

—— *Free Grace Exalted, and Thence Deduced Evangelical Rules for Evangeical Sufferings* (London, 1670).

Stewart, Stanley S., *The Enclosed Garden: The Tradition and the Image in Seventeenth-Century Poetry* (London: University of Wisconsin Press, 1966).

—— *The Expanded Voice: The Art of Thomas Traherne* (San Marino, Calif.: Huntingdon Library, 1970).

Stillingfleet, Edward, *Origines Sacræ, or a Rational Account of the Grounds of Christian Faith* (London: R.W., 1662).

Stone, Michael E., *A History of the Literature of Adam and Eve* (Atlanta, Ga.: Scholars Press, 1992).

Stortz, Martha E., '"Where or When Was Your Servant Innocent?" Augustine on Childhood', in Marcia J. Bunge (ed.), *The Child in Christian Thought* (Grand Rapids, Mich.: Eerdmans, 2001), 78–102.

Stump, Eleonore, 'Aquinas on the Suffering of Job', in ead. (ed.), *Reasoned Faith* (Ithaca, NY: Cornell University Press, 1993), 328–57.

Suarez, Michael F., 'Against Satan, Sin, and Death: Thomas Traherne and the "Inward Work" of Conversion', in J.C. Hawley (ed.), *Reform and Counterreform: Dialectics of the Word in Western Christianity since Luther* (Berlin: Mouton de Gruyter, 1994), 77–103.

Symson, Andrew, *Lexicon Anglo-Graeco-Latinum Novi Testamenti, or, A Complete Alphabetical Concordance of All the Words Contained in the New Testament* (London: W. Godbid, 1658).

Taylor, Charles, 'Disenchantment–Reenchanmtent', in *Dilemmas and Contradictions: Selected Essays* (Cambridge, Mass.: Harvard University Press, 2011), 287–303.

Taylor, Jeremy, *Antiquitates Christianae, or, The History of the Life and Death of the Holy Jesus* (London, 1675).

—— *The Rule and Exercises of Holy Living* (London, 1650).

—— *Unum Necessarium, or, The Doctrine and Practice of Repentance* (London: James Flesher, 1655).

—— *The Whole Works of the Right Rev. Jeremy Taylor*, ed. Reginald Heber (15 vols, London: Ogle, Duncan and Co., 1822).

Tennant, F.R. *The Concept of Sin* (Cambridge: Cambridge University Press, 1912).

Tertullian, *Apology and De Spectaculis; with Octavius*, trans. T.R. Glover, LCL (Cambridge, Mass.: Harvard University Press, 1931).

Thiel, John E., *God, Evil, and Innocent Suffering: A Theological Reflection* (New York: Crossroad, 2002).

Thomas à Kempis, *Imitation of Christ*, trans. Aloyisus Croft and Harold Bolton (Nashville, Tenn.: Thomas Nelson, 1999).

Thornton, Helen, *State of Nature or Eden? Thomas Hobbes and His Contemporaries on the Natural Condition of Human Beings* (Rochester, NY: University of Rochester Press, 2005).

Tillich, Paul, *Systematic Theology* (3 vols, London: James Nisbet, 1957).

Tillotson, John, *Of Sincerity and Constancy in the Faith and Profession of the True Religion* (London, 1695).

Tombes, John, *Anti-Pædobaptism* (3 vols, London, 1652–57).

Towers, Francis, 'Thomas Traherne: His Outlook on Life', *Nineteenth Century* 87 (1920), 1024–30.

Trench, Robert C., *Synonyms of the New Testament: The Two Parts in One* (revd edn, London and Cambridge: Macmillan, 1865).

Trilling, Lionel, *Sincerity and Authority* (Cambridge, Mass.: Harvard University Press, 1971).

Trimpey, John E., 'An Analysis of Traherne's "Thoughts I"', *SP* 68 (1971), 88–105.

Trinkaus, Charles E., *In Our Image and Likeness: Humanity and Divinity in Italian Humanist Thought* (Notre Dame, Ind.: University of Notre Dame Press, 1995).

Turner, Denys, *Eros and Allegory: Medieval Exegesis of the Song of Songs* (Kalamazoo, Mass.: Cistercian Publications, 1995).

Turner, James Grantham, *One Flesh: Paradisal Marriage and Sexual Relations in the Age of Milton* (Oxford: Clarendon, 1987).

Twisse, William, *The Riches of God's Love unto the Vessells of Mercy, Consistent with his Absolute Hatred or Reprobation of the Vessells of Wrath. Or, An Answer unto a Book, Entituled: God's Love unto Mankind, Manifested by Disproving His Absolute Decree for their Damnation* (Oxford: L.L. and H.H., 1653).

Ulijaszek, S.J., 'Neurological Development', in S.J. Ulijaszek, F.E. Johnston and M.A. Preece (eds), *The Cambridge Encyclopedia of Human Growth and Development* (Cambridge: Cambridge University Press, 1998), 164–5.

—— F.E. Johnston and M.A. Preece (eds), *The Cambridge Encyclopedia of Human Growth and Development* (Cambridge: Cambridge University Press, 1998).

VanGemeren, Willem A. (ed.), *New International Dictionary of Old Testament Theology and Exegesis* (5 vols, Carlisle: Paternoster, 1996).

Vaughan, Henry, *Silex Scintillans, or Sacred Poems and Private Ejaculations* (London: T.W., 1650).

Vienne, J.M., 'Introduction', in G.A.J. Rogers, J.M. Vienne and Y.C. Zarka (eds), *The Cambridge Platonists in Philosophical Context: Politics, Metaphysics and Religion* (Dordrecht: Kluwer, 1997).

Wacior, Slawomir, *Strategies of Literary Communication in the Poetry of Thomas Traherne* (Lublin: Redakcja Wydawnictw Kul, 1990).

Wade, Gladys Irene, *Thomas Traherne: A Critical Biography. With a Selected Bibliography of Criticism, by Robert Allerton Parker* (Princeton, NJ: Princeton University Press, 1944).

Walker, Daniel Pickering, *The Ancient Theology: Studies in Christian Platonism from the Fifteenth to the Eighteenth Century* (London: Duckworth, 1972).

Wall, John, 'Fallen Angels: A Contemporary Christian Ethical Ontology of Childhood', *International Journal of Practical Theology* 8/2 (2004), 160–84.

Wallace, Dewey D., *Shapers of English Calvinism, 1660–1714: Variety, Persistence, and Transformation*, Oxford Studies in Historical Theology (Oxford: Oxford University Press, 2011).

Wallace, John Malcolm, 'Thomas Traherne and the Structure of Meditation', *ELH* 25/2 (June 1958), 79–89.

Wallace, Mark I., *The Second Naiveté: Barth, Ricoeur, and the New Yale Theology*, Studies in American Biblical Hermeneutics (Macon, Ga.: Mercer, 1990).

Warner, Marina, *Managing Monsters: Six Myths of our Time* (London: Vintage, 1994).

Warren, Edward, *No Præexistence; Or, A Brief Dissertation against the Hypothesis of Humane Souls* (London: T.R., 1667).

Watson, Robert N., *Back to Nature: The Green and the Real in the Late Renaissance* (Philadelphia: University of Pennsylvania Press, 2006).

Watson, Thomas, *A Body of Practical Divinity* (London: Thomas Parkurst, 1692).

Webber, Joan M., *The Eloquent 'I': Style and Self in Seventeenth Century Prose* (Madison: University of Wisconsin Press, 1968).

—— "'I" and "Thou" in the Prose of Thomas Traherne', *Papers on Language and Literature* 2 (1966), 258-4.

—— *Milton and His Epic Tradition* (Seattle: University of Washington Press, 1979).

Weil, Simone, *Gravity and Grace* (London: Routledge, 1952).

Wells, Samuel, *Improvisation: The Drama of Christian Ethics* (London: SPCK, 2004).

West, Angela, *Deadly Innocence: Feminist Theology and the Mythology of Sin* (London: Mowbray, 1995).

Westermann, Claus, *Blessing in the Bible and the Life of the Church*, trans. K. Crim (Philadelphia, Pa.: Fortress, 1978).

Whalen, R., *The Poetry of Immanence: Sacrament in Donne and Herbert* (Toronto: University of Toronto Press, 2002).

Whately, William, *Prototypes, or, The Primarie Precedent Presidents out of the Booke of Genesis* (London: G. Miller, 1640).

Whichcote, Benjamin, *Moral and Religious Aphorisms*, ed. W.R. Inge (London: E. Mathews & Marot, 1930)

White, Helen C., *The Metaphysical Poets: A Study in Religious Experience* (New York: Macmillan, 1956).

White, John, *A Commentary upon the Three First Chapters of the First Book of Moses Called Genesis* (London, 1643).

White, Keith D., *John Keats and the Loss of Romantic Innocence*, Costerus NS 107 (Amsterdam: Rodopi, 1996).

White, R.S., *Natural Law in English Renaissance Literature* (Cambridge: Cambridge University Press, 1996).

Willcox, Louise Collier, 'A Joyous Mystic', *North American Review* 193/667 (1911), 893–904.

Willet, Andrew, *Hexapla in Genesin & Exodum: That is, a Sixfold Commentary Upon the First Bookes of Moses* (London: John Haviland, 1633).

Willett, Gladys E., *Traherne (An Essay)* (Cambridge: W. Heffer & Sons, 1919).

Willey, Basil, *The Seventeenth Century Background* (New York: Columbia University Press, 1967).

Williams, Rowan, *Anglican Identities* (London: Darton, Longman & Todd, 2004).

—— 'Between Politics and Metaphysics: Reflections in the Wake of Gillian Rose', *MT* 11/1 (1995), 116.

—— '*Poetic and Religious Imagination*', *Theology* 80 (May 1977), 178–87.

—— 'Trinity and Ontology', in K. Surin (ed.), *Christ, Ethics and Tragedy: Essays in Honour of Donald MacKinnon* (Cambridge: Cambridge University Press, 1989), 71–92.

—— *The Truce of God* (London: Collins, 1983).

Willy, Margaret, *Three Metaphysical Poets* (London: Longmans, 1961).

Wilson, F.P. (ed.), *The Oxford Dictionary of English Proverbs* (3rd edn, Oxford: Oxford University Press, 1970).

Wilson, Thomas, *A Complete Christian Dictionary: Wherein the Significations and several Acceptations of All the Words mentioned in the Holy Scriptures of the Old and New Testament, are fully Opened, Expressed, Explained*, ed. J. Bagwell and A. Simson (7th edn, London: E. Cotes, 1661).

Wither, George, *A Collection of Emblemes, Ancient and Moderne* (London: Augustine Mathewes, 1635).

—— *The Psalmes of David Translated into Lyrick Verse* (Amsterdam: Cornelis Gerritis van Breughel, 1632).

Wöhrer, Franz K., 'The Doctrine of Original Sin and the Idea of Man's Perinatal Intimations of the Divine in the Work of Thomas Traherne', *Wiener Beiträge zur Englischen Philologie* 79 (1984), 89–106.

—— *Thomas Traherne: The Growth of a Mystic's Mind. A Study of the Evolution and the Phenomenology of Traherne's Mystical Consciousness* (Salzburg: Salzburg University, 1982).

Wolf, William J., 'The Spirituality of Thomas Traherne', in id. (ed), *Anglican Spirituality* (Wilton, Conn.: Morehouse, 1982), 49–68.

Wood, Anthony, *Alumni Oxonienses 1500–1714*, ed. Joseph Foster (Oxford: Parker & Co., 1892).

Wood, David Houston, *Time, Narrative and Emotion in Early Modern England*, Literary and Scientific Cultures of Modernity (Farnham: Ashgate, 2009).

Woodhouse, A.S.P., *The Poet and his Faith: Religion and Poetry in England from Spenser to Eliot to Auden* (Chicago: University of Chicago Press, 1965).

Wordsworth, William, *The Collected Poems of William Wordsworth*, ed. Antonia Till (Ware, Herts.: Wordsworth Editions, 1994).

Wright, Stephen, 'Wilson, Thomas (1562/3–1622)', *ODNB*.

Young, Frances W., 'Suffering', in Adrian Hastings, Alistair Mason and Hugh Pyper (eds), *The Oxford Companion to Christian Thought: Intellectual,*

Spiritual, and Moral Horizons of Christianity (Oxford: Oxford University Press, 2000), 687b–689a.

Young, Robert, *Analytical Concordance to the Holy Bible* (8th edn, London: Lutterworth, 1961).

Zhelezcheva, Tanya, 'The Poetics of the Incomplete in the Works of Thomas Traherne (ca. 1638–1674)' (PhD thesis, Northeastern University, 2011).

General Index

Abyss (*see* Void) 71, 79–80, 83–4, 88, 123, 144

Accident 8, 23, 43, 84–6, 89, 108, 110, 111, 165

Act, Activity, Action 14, 16–17, 20, 22, 23, 24, 35, 38, 39, 41, 43, 48, 51, 53–4, 57, 58, 62, 66, 68, 74, 93, 94, 102–4, 109–10, 111, 115, 120, 122, 131–7, 137–43, 147–50, 153, 156, 159–60, 162, 165, 166, 171, 184, 190, 199

Adam 3, 14, 19, 20, 22, 23, 26–8, 38, 39, 47–51, 55–60, 62, 68–9, 71, 76–8, 83, 100, 102, 105, 113, 115, 130, 135, 140, 144, 157–8, 167, 169, 176, 180–81, 185, 189–90, 192, 201

Affections 11–12, 21, 31, 39, 64, 71, 73, 76–7, 81–3, 103–4, 111, 118, 122, 130–34, 137–9, 142, 147–8, 150, 155, 159–60, 161, 167–70, 173, 185, 187–8, 192, 199

Ainsworth, Henry 142, 181, 186

Alighieri, Dante 4, 18, 53, 189, 190

Allestree, Richard 137–8, 145

Amazon Queen 24, 178, 187–9

Andrewes, Lancelot 88, 89, 95, 141–3, 150, 159, 165, 168

Angel 3, 30, 48, 49, 52, 60, 78, 101, 102, 115, 126, 145, 147, 152, 167–9, 170, 176, 182, 185, 190, 192, 196, 199

Apophatic 23, 45, 88, 90
Via Negativa 11

Apprehension 12, 31, 76–7, 80, 81, 129, 138, 140–41, 154, 157, 16–19, 176–8, 187

Aquinas, Thomas 8, 31, 64, 107, 116–7, 142–3, 145, 148

Aristotle 8–9, 17, 26, 41, 42, 93, 94, 104, 107, 115, 125, 133, 145, 147, 163, 195
Aristotelian 7, 23, 41–2, 64, 74, 85, 131, 166

Atom/Atomism 8, 9, 24, 45–6, 48, 51–3, 63, 66, 144, 166–7, 169–71

Augustine 17, 26, 33, 39, 47, 49, 50–51, 53, 66, 71–3, 100, 102, 107, 119, 134, 145, 150, 152, 157–8, 162, 171, 173, 192

Bacon, Francis 8, 62–3, 126, 130, 136, 153, 172, 195

Bakhtin, Mikhail 93–4

Baptism 23, 38, 44, 73, 93, 95–7, 100, 116, 158–9, 165, 173, 182, 186

Barrow, Isaac 181

Bernard of Clairvaux 26, 61, 165–6, 189

Blake, William 2–5, 129, 131

Boehme, Jacob 102

Book of Common Prayer 12, 73, 75, 95–7, 112, 150, 158

Calvin, John 62, 95, 102, 119, 145–6, 154, 195

Cambridge Platonism 5–7, 46, 59, 66, 81, 157

Capacity 21, 26, 39, 48, 104, 110, 120, 133, 141, 158, 163–4, 167, 170–71

Cataphatic 11, 88

Celestial Stranger 24, 176–8, 201

Character 6, 22–3, 55, 94, 114–21, 124, 133, 138, 149, 164, 194, 201

236 *Boundless Innocence in Thomas Traherne's Poetic Theology*

Charron, Pierre 60, 107, 130, 135, 137, 146–8
Chastity (*see* Virginity) 24, 115, 151–3, 178, 185–9
Child (*see* Infant) 1–5, 13–16, 23–4, 25–31, 38–9, 42, 49, 56, 60, 68–9, 71–2, 95–6, 116, 129, 139, 145, 147, 158–9, 161, 168, 172–6, 181, 188, 190, 201
Christ
    Apostasy Against 77
    Ascension of 187
    Baptism of 186
    As Bridegroom 188
    Chastity of 153
    Cosmic 57, 120
    Crucifixion of 17, 20, 80, 105, 122–4
    As Gardener 52
    Meekness of 143, 147, 149
    As modelling the character of innocence 22, 23, 34, 59, 68, 91, 115, 120–22, 183, 200–201
    Perfection/Sinlessness of 28–9, 33, 38, 97, 135, 138
    Resurrection of 170, 182
    As second Adam 49, 55–9, 115
    As source of regeneration, salvation and sanctification 73–4, 95, 149, 154, 158, 160, 171, 179, 180–81
    Suffering innocence of 109, 111–13, 146, 159, 179
Courage 103, 109, 115, 118, 134–5, 144, 145, 149
Cross, the 105, 120, 122–4, 149
Cudworth, Ralph 9, 44, 66, 110
Culverwel, Nathaniel 59–60, 140

David 22, 55, 114–5, 118–9, 154–8, 201
Desire 11–12, 16, 19, 20, 24, 39, 43–4, 62, 66, 74, 77, 79–82, 86, 91, 93, 99, 103, 105–6, 111, 123, 132, 140, 158–9, 163, 174, 178, 180, 183, 188–9, 192, 193, 196–9
Dialogue 3, 11, 86–7, 93, 114–5, 118–9, 156–7

Diamond 179–80, 199
Donne, John 3, 104, 107, 151, 153, 170, 182, 187
Dove 24, 39, 113, 170, 178, 184–7, 193–5
Dragon 101, 126, 178–9, 184–7
Dream 18, 27, 82, 86–7, 93, 133, 136–7, 190–91, 199
Dryden, John 93, 104

Eden 1–3, 14, 18–20, 22, 25–8, 31, 38, 41, 44, 47–9, 52–4, 58, 60, 62, 64–5, 67–9, 71–2, 77, 86, 101–2, 123, 130, 135, 140, 142, 149–50, 175–6, 178–9, 182, 187, 190, 197, 199–201
Emanation/ Emanationism 130, 156, 162
Emblem 21, 24, 113, 161, 167, 170, 171–6, 178, 179–80, 183–6, 189, 192, 195
Enchantment (including Disenchantment, Reenchantment) 28, 201
Epektasis 10, 24, 193, 201
Estates of the soul 17–20, 22–4, 45–6, 57, 61, 67, 83, 110, 144, 169, 176, 178–80, 198–200
    Glory 49, 53, 69, 79, 97, 99, 123, 156–7, 161–2, 190, 198
    Innocence 15, 16, 17, 20, 23, 38, 41, 44–50, 53, 62, 66–8, 123, 179, 198
    Misery-Grace 57, 79, 93, 101, 124, 143–4, 160
    Trial 19–20, 23, 50, 73, 79, 93, 101–4, 115, 123, 125–6, 160, 179–80, 189
Experience 4, 8, 13, 18, 24, 27, 60, 63, 68–9, 71–2, 75, 78, 83, 86–8, 94, 104, 116, 120, 126, 129–31, 139, 155, 160, 173–5, 177, 178, 183, 189–90, 197–9
Experiment/Experimentalism 8–9, 54, 66, 129–31, 162, 169

Featley, Daniel 186–8
Felicity 5, 8, 9, 15, 16, 36, 43–4, 54, 86, 98–100, 105–6, 118, 122, 125, 141, 143, 145, 149, 158, 162, 174, 197
Ficino, Marsilio 7, 152

General Index

Findley, Carl E. III 31–2, 38, 134
Ford, David F. 10, 20, 189, 193
Fragments 23, 62, 124, 163, 175
Freud, Sigmund 14, 19, 28, 29

Gale, Theophilus 7, 9, 131, 170, 171
Garden 24, 48, 52–3, 76, 178–9, 180, 187, 199–200
Genre 10, 20, 35, 42, 93, 154, 155, 171–2, 198, 200
  Drama 20, 24, 55, 80, 88, 93–4, 100, 102–4, 107, 111, 114–6, 118, 121, 124, 125–7, 129–31, 132–3, 142, 146, 148–50, 159–62, 198–9
  Epic 10, 19, 41–3, 94, 116, 133, 199
  Lyric 3–4, 24, 82, 94, 118, 119, 124, 156, 161–2, 172, 13, 198
Grammar 2, 10, 20, 31, 35
  Moods
    Imperative 24, 61, 69, 97, 158–60, 198
    Indicative 42
    Intentional / Hortative 24, 31, 39, 108, 132, 133, 137, 138, 149, 158–60, 198
    Optative 12, 24, 97, 193–8, 199
    Subjunctive 11, 24, 166, 173, 176, 189–92
  Tenses
    Future 18, 28, 68, 69, 96, 101, 108, 174, 190
    Negative 23, 24, 45, 47, 50, 60, 68, 71, 77, 87, 88–91, 109, 110, 141–2, 198, 199
    Past and Present 19, 23, 26, 67–9, 182, 198
    Pluperfect 27
Grant, Patrick 49, 56, 71–2
Gregory the Great 107, 115–7, 146, 168, 194

Hammond, Henry 74, 77, 193
Harmlessness 1, 19, 24, 32–7, 39, 112, 125–6, 133–6, 143, 145, 148–50, 160, 178, 193–5, 197

Hegel, G.W.F. 68, 115
Henderson, Ian 26–8, 48, 200
Hoard, Samuel 74
Herbert, George 3, 107, 152, 183, 185
Hobbes, Thomas 8–9, 23, 61, 77
Holy Innocents 112
Hooker, Richard 65
Hope 14–15, 20, 22, 24, 28, 29, 54, 58, 63, 69, 80, 90, 91, 97, 100, 111, 115, 117, 126, 134, 174, 180–81, 189, 191–2, 195, 198–9, 201
Humanism 14, 15, 71, 167
Humility 16, 36, 49, 51–2, 58, 88, 105, 135–6, 142–5, 149, 150, 160, 165, 169, 175, 186, 198, 199
Hypocrisy 136–7, 138, 142, 144, 150, 158, 199

Ignorance 26–9, 31–3, 39, 60–62, 71, 76–7, 96, 120, 130, 142, 145, 165, 175–7, 194, 197
Illingworth, John 26, 28
Image of God/ *imago Dei* 59, 85, 137, 139, 166, 170, 184, 198
Impassibility 110–12, 167, 188
Infant/Infancy (*see* Child) 3–4, 13–14, 18, 39, 41, 46, 49, 95, 97, 129, 139, 174–5, 176, 177, 188
Infant-Ey 64, 159, 162, 187
Infinite Sphere 44, 123, 143, 146
Infinity 23, 43, 43–4, 48–51, 78–81, 83–4, 88, 98, 99, 101, 110, 111, 112, 118, 124, 125, 127, 131, 133, 144, 147, 153, 156, 163–8, 170–71, 176, 178, 186, 190, 191, 192, 196, 199
Inge, Denise 6, 10, 15–16, 46, 56, 66, 102, 113, 120, 131, 156, 170
Innate 7, 64, 130, 162
Innocence
  Blood of 34, 113, 121–4, 149, 159–60, 185
  Dialectic of 100–101, 129, 196, 201
  Glory of 180–84

Inward and Outward 22, 39, 54, 63, 66,
73, 117, 131–4, 136–9, 142, 145–6,
148, 150, 159, 167
Of Life 24, 38, 121, 131, 138, 149,
150–51, 158
Power of 36, 39, 50, 51, 58, 81, 166, 168,
170, 176, 178–80
Preservation of 11, 24, 31, 63, 67, 88,
105, 137–8, 140–42, 146, 148, 150,
158, 159, 171, 193
Privative and Positive 23, 24, 33, 35, 45,
48, 67, 87, 110, 136, 142, 143, 164,
171, 189, 199
Pursuit of 24, 56, 58, 78, 124, 126, 130,
138, 139, 140–42, 143, 159, 171,
197–9
Suffering of 23, 30, 34–6, 63, 106–14
Trial of 23, 50, 97–106, 112, 116–9,
124, 125–6, 129, 149, 199
Integrity 24, 32–4, 36, 90, 119, 135, 137,
138, 140–43, 146, 148–9, 153, 159,
160, 165, 186, 199–200
Irenaeus of Lyons 56–9, 7–3, 76–7, 79, 96,
123, 167, 187

Jackson, Thomas 7, 47, 64, 85, 89, 136,
140, 164, 165, 173, 187, 191
Job 22, 23, 27, 55, 90, 107, 115, 116–19,
126, 146, 155, 161, 165, 194, 201
John Chrysostom 145, 146, 182, 193
Jung, Carl 14,

Kelsey, David 21–2, 27, 35, 42, 114, 131,
200–201
Kenotic 23, 80, 110, 114, 120, 122–4, 127,
140, 162, 198–9
Kershaw, Alison 21, 56, 86, 102–4, 120,
123, 131, 172
Kierkegaard, Søren 26–7, 68,

Lactantius 22, 26, 31, 36, 156
Lamb 23, 63, 112–3, 122, 183, 184, 201
Light 3, 9, 23, 54, 59, 62, 63–5, 69, 84,
86–8, 100, 124, 125, 129, 130, 134,
154, 155, 156, 161, 162, 164, 174,

175, 176, 177, 179, 180, 190, 196,
198, 199
Shade 48, 50, 78, 86–8, 99, 107, 1924,
136–7, 144, 175, 181, 190, 191
Love 3, 9, 20 43, 44, 51, 52, 64, 126, 175,
176, 177, 183, 196, 197
As Affection 99, 111, 132, 171, 185–6,
199
Attraction of 24,
of Christ 124, 143, 158
for Enemies 146–9
And the Fall 23, 58, 73–84
for God 28, 140, 192, 196
of God 50, 66–7, 117–8, 131, 138, 145,
167, 176, 180, 192
for the Good 65, 89, 103, 133
And the Law of Nature 59, 61–2, 65–6
Sacrificial 109, 114
Of Self 61–2, 87, 134, 199
And Sex 151–3, 187–9
For the World 174
Luther, Martin 65, 87, 95, 110-, 117

Mackinnon, Donald 94, 107, 120, 135
Meekness 32, 39, 113, 115, 142–9, 160,
186–7, 195, 199
Milton, John 52–4, 72, 74, 86, 103–4, 116,
155, 178, 187
Misapprehension 76–7, 80
More, Henry 7, 44, 46, 51, 66, 139, 143,
192

naïveté 1, 4, 10, 12, 18–19, 24, 31, 82, 177,
198, 201
Nakedness 24, 59–60, 62–3, 66, 124, 147,
165, 170, 175, 178, 179–83
Nature 16
Human 14, 51, 59–60, 62, 64, 77, 85–7,
120, 191
Innocent 49, 61–3, 171, 174, 175, 180,
199
Law of 65–6, 89–90, 147
Light of 9, 63–5
Mysticism of 5, 59, 121
Praise of 13

General Index

State of 1, 13, 23, 60–62
Nazianzus, Gregory of 165, 167, 183, 194
Newey, Edmund 15–16, 51,
Newman, John Henry 26, 28
Nicholas of Cusa 7, 44, 197
Nietzsche, Friedrich 29, 44
Nostalgia 1, 4, 14, 15, 23, 54, 174, 200, 201
Nyssa, Gregory of 151, 153, 162, 164, 186, 193

Optimism 4, 10, 12, 14–15, 34, 35, 71, 82, 89, 98, 175, 191, 200
Origen 53, 56, 84, 89, 107, 188
Original Sin 13, 23, 48, 56, 68, 71, 95,
Ottley, Robert 25–8, 31, 34
Ovid 162, 163
Owen, John 105

Paradise (*see* Eden)
Paradox 36, 50, 58, 85–6, 88, 90, 117, 119, 121–2, 135, 144, 149–50, 171, 172, 181, 195, 196
Patience 11, 31, 95, 108–12, 115, 116, 119, 142–4, 148, 160, 199
Pearl 24, 137, 178, 180, 183–4
Perfection 1, 10, 24, 26–9, 32, 34, 35, 46, 48–9, 50, 53, 55–8, 65, 68, 102–3, 116, 124, 138, 163–7, 174, 191, 193, 198–201
Piaget, Jean 13
Picciotto, Joanna 54, 56, 130
Pico della Mirandola 7, 9
Poole, William 60, 71–3, 167
Plato 47, 62, 130, 162, 166, 176, 186, 191
  Christian Neo-Platonism 7–9, 15, 23, 46, 54, 64, 74, 152–3, 156, 163, 164, 188, 191
Plotinus 43, 50, 98, 110, 130, 147, 162, 170
Possibility 18, 24, 27, 33, 72, 86, 104, 119, 165, 173, 174, 176, 189–92
Praise 10–13, 24, 36, 45, 49, 62, 75, 77, 82, 104, 114, 117, 119, 130, 151, 154–8, 160, 163, 166, 168, 175, 185, 191–2, 198

Pre-existence 7, 46–7
Primitivism 3, 59–63, 83, 129, 188,
Prudence 137, 141, 143, 195–6
Puente, Louis de la 152, 168
puritanism 5, 6, 9, 132
Purity 24, 26, 32–3, 35, 36, 39, 48, 51, 59, 61, 62, 63, 64, 66, 69, 73, 88–90, 95, 98, 103, 105, 113, 115, 116, 124–5, 129, 136, 137–41, 145, 150, 151, 153, 156, 158–60, 162, 163, 165, 166, 168, 171, 174, 175

Quarles, Francis 90, 115, 117, 152, 165, 171, 186
Quash, Ben 42, 93–4, 115, 119, 121, 129, 150, 161

Reason 43, 59, 63, 64, 75–7, 81, 111, 117, 129, 144, 147, 166, 181, 190
Recapitulation 18, 28, 42, 52, 55–9, 157, 169, 180, 187, 201
Regeneration 23, 33, 38, 39, 44, 87, 88, 94–7, 144–5, 147, 154, 158, 159, 170, 172, 173, 178, 183, 184–7, 193, 197
Repentance 17, 73, 90–91, 98, 100, 143–5, 154, 159, 160, 163, 180, 183, 199
Retirement 141, 149, 151, 167, 171, 177, 179, 180-, 182, 187, 197
Ricoeur, Paul 18–21, 93, 107, 109, 119, 133, 161, 189, 198, 201
Righteous 20, 21, 32–5, 37, 38, 39, 58, 60, 85, 88, 110, 118, 126, 132, 135, 136, 138, 141–2, 150, 153, 157, 159, 179, 181–2, 191, 196, 199
Roman Catholic 6, 28, 152
Romanticism 1–5, 13, 15–16, 27–8, 31, 72, 134, 139, 201
Rousseau, Jean-Jacques 60, 62–6, 171–6, 182, 191, 198

Sacrament 11, 21, 23, 24, 28, 88, 94
Sacrifice 34–6, 57, 61, 106, 109, 112–14, 120–23, 127, 149, 151, 158, 200
Seneca 143

Shame 34, 63, 79, 144, 163, 180–83
Simplicity 1, 8, 18, 24, 26–8, 32–6, 39,
    49, 51–2, 54, 60, 63, 64, 67, 84,
    85, 87, 112, 113, 116–7, 126, 130,
    138–9, 142, 144, 158, 164–6,
    169–70, 175, 184, 186, 188, 191,
    193–6
Simul Justus et Peccator 84, 87, 117
Sincerity 1, 24, 61, 90, 95, 100, 113, 115,
    117, 136–40, 142, 144, 150, 159,
    160, 190, 192
Smith, John 9, 20, 134
Sparke, Edward 112,
Spenser, Edmund 179, 186
Sterry, Peter 107, 113, 118, 148, 176, 185,
    198
Stillingfleet, Edward 88, 121

Taylor, Jeremy 95, 132, 133, 138, 141, 165,
    194, 195
Temptation 20, 23, 26, 59, 97, 100, 104–5,
    119, 151, 152, 184, 197
Tennant, F.R. 26, 28–9
Tertullian 22, 26, 35, 36, 162, 184
Theological Anthropology 21–2, 56,
    114, 131, 239, 161, 167, 175,
    200–201
Thomas à Kempis 101, 104, 105
Tillich, Paul 27, 191
Tillotson, John 138
Tombes, John 96
Traherne, Thomas
    As Anglican Divine 6, 9–13, 49, 65,
        71, 73, 95, 152
    Biography 5–9
    As Mystic 2, 5, 6, 13–15, 21, 24, 59, 67,
        71, 72, 84, 121, 156, 188
    As Poet 1–4, 9–12, 20–22, 30, 36,
        41–2, 46, 55, 59, 62, 72, 75, 81–3,
        86, 94, 105, 114, 115, 126, 139,
        154–5, 161, 171–2, 198, 200, 201

Trismegistus, Hermes 7, 44, 45, 134, 135,
    162, 166
    Hermeticism 7, 45, 49, 53, 69, 166, 170
Twisse, William 74

Unblameable 58, 74, 141, 142, 199
Upright 32–4, 36, 38–9, 62, 116–7, 126,
    140, 142
Utopianism 1, 4, 14, 18, 24, 60, 139, 191,
    201

Vaughan, Henry 3, 30, 184, 187
Via Media 11, 49, 73, 195
Virginity (*see* Chastity) 1, 24, 29, 31, 62,
    113, 151–3, 162, 167, 170, 178,
    183, 185, 187–9
Virtue 20, 23–4, 31, 39, 51–3, 77, 81, 84,
    86–8, 94, 95, 98–9, 101, 103–4,
    106, 108–9, 112, 118–9, 123, 125,
    130, 132, 134–5, 137–9, 142–51,
    152, 153, 156, 160, 162, 164, 165,
    179, 181, 182, 190, 192, 195–6,
    199–200
Void 23, 24, 45, 47–8, 52, 67, 84, 101, 114,
    133, 164, 199

War with sin 88, 94, 100–101, 133–6,
    148–9, 179
Weil, Simone 67
Whichcote, Benjamin 64, 138, 146, 157
Whiteness 24, 32, 103, 113, 124, 178,
    180–83, 185, 186, 199
Williams, Rowan 11, 20, 21, 29, 107, 120,
    174
Wilson, Thomas 22, 24, 37–9, 44, 45, 47,
    48, 67, 96, 110, 131–2, 135, 136,
    139, 140, 142, 159, 173
Wisdom 36, 43, 54, 58, 79, 85, 90, 109,
    116, 119, 123, 124, 125, 143, 155,
    164, 193–8, 201
Wordsworth, William 2–4, 15, 139

Index of Biblical References

Genesis 10, 27, 60 , 71, 155, 180, 181
  1.2 45
  1.26–7 38
  2.6 52
  8.9 186
  20.5 32, 35, 142
  27.15 182
Deuteronomy 155
  21.8 34
  21.9 35
  27.25 34
  32.5 125
  32.29 190
  32.33 185
1 Samuel
  26.9 33
2 Kings
  2.31 34
Job
  1.1 108, 115, 116–17
  1.9 119
  1.12 116
  1.18 32
  2.3 34
  7.17–18 117
  8.20 116
  9.23 35, 118–9
  12 119
  14.4 116
  22.19 32
  27.5 34
  28 119
  33.9 35
  36 119
Psalms 12, 118, 154–6
  6.6 183
  7.8 38
  8.4–6 117, 157

8.9 34
11.4–5 105
14 88
14.5 35
17.28 33
19.20 35
23.4 33
26.6, 11 38, 159
26.11 141
37.37 34, 142
45.3 145
51.17 156
55.6 186
56.13 119
57.8 119
58.4 185
68.13 184
74.19 185
77.4 102
84.11 34
93.21 34
101.2 34, 51, 150
105.38 34
119.19 177
143.2 89
Proverbs
  13.6 36
  22.3 33
Ecclesiastes 155
  4.1 34, 35
  7.20 88
Song of Songs 74, 80, 136, 155, 166, 188–9
  2.2 126
  2.10 186
  2.14 185
  4.12 178
Isaiah 155
  35.7 184

53.3 77
53.7 113
59.7 34
Jeremiah
2.34 34
2.35 35
7.6 34
19.3 34
22.3 34
22.17 34
25.29 35
26.15 34
31.11 52
46.28 35
Daniel 155
3 149, 168
11.35 105
Joel
3.19 34, 149
Jonah
1.14 34
Zechariah
13.9 105
1 Maccabees
1.8 34
2 Maccabees
1.39 34
Matthew
1.1 182
2.16–18 112
3.13 145
5.1–2, 5 146
7.1 145
10.16 39, 125, 184, 193–5
11.29 149
12.7 33, 35
13 183
13.24–30 86
13.44 184
17.17 125
18.3 27
18.10 168
27.24 34, 35
Mark
1.7 91
10.15 27

Luke
9.41 125
10.3 125
18.7 27
Acts
8.32 113
Romans
3.10 88
5.12–21 57
8.19 83
8.28 125
9.13 74
16.19 33, 193–4
1 Corinthians
15.22 57
2 Corinthians
3.18 186
5.12 137
9.7 138
12.9 147
Galatians
2.20 91
Ephesians
1.4–5 74
3.17 75
3.18 84
3.20 191
4.18–19 77
6.11–17 134
6.16 179
Philippians
2.15 125
4.8 98
1 Timothy
4.2 136
Hebrews
2.10 109
7.26 33
James
1.5 181
1.27 156
1 Peter
3.10–13 141
3.16 146